TWENTY COUNTRIES, FOUR CONTINENTS AND THREE WEDDING RINGS

A Year of Travels Around the World

TWENTY COUNTRIES, FOUR CONTINENTS AND THREE WEDDING RINGS

A Year of Travels Around the World

Ian Barnes

ATHENA PRESS
LONDON

TWENTY COUNTRIES, FOUR CONTINENTS
AND THREE WEDDING RINGS
A Year of Travels Around the World
Copyright © Ian Barnes 2008

All rights reserved

No part of this book may be reproduced in any form
by photocopying or by any electronic or mechanical means
including information storage or retrieval systems
without permission in writing from both the copyright
owner and the publisher of this book.

ISBN 10-digit: 1 84748 193 0
ISBN 13-digit: 978 1 84748 193 1

First published 2008
ATHENA PRESS
Queen's House, 2 Holly Road
Twickenham TW1 4EG
United Kingdom

Printed for Athena Press

*For Claudia
whose company
brings joy
to life's journey*

Contents

Maps
Americas   11
Eastern Asia and Oceana   12

Prologue   13

Part One
The United States of America
1. New York   19
2. Boston   23
3. Cape Cod and Mount Washington   28
4. Los Angeles and San Diego   35
5. Route 1 – the Californian Coast   39
6. National Parks – Yosemite, Death Valley and Zion   44
7. The Grand Canyon and Las Vegas   50

Part Two
Mexico, Guatemala and Belize
8. Mexico City   59
9. Tenochtitlan and Teotihuacan   64
10. Oaxaca and San Cristobal de las Casas   69
11. Into Guatemala   76
12. Panajachel and Lake Atitlan   82
13. Antigua   87
14. Tikal   94
15. Belize City and Cay Caulker   98

Part Three
Peru, Bolivia, Chile and Brazil

16	Lima to Cuzco	107
17	Machu Picchu	114
18	Lake Titicaca	121
19	La Paz and the Bolivian Highlands	125
20	Northern Chile	132
21	Santiago and Patagonia	137
22	Rio de Janeiro	145
23	Ilha Grande and Paraty	152
24	Easter Island	156

Part Four
Fiji, New Zealand and Australia

25	Fiji	165
26	New Zealand's North Island	171
27	New Zealand's South Island	178
28	Sydney	185
29	Blue Mountains	188
30	New England	193
31	Uluru	196

Part Five
Singapore, Malaysia and Thailand

32	Singapore	205
33	Kuala Lumpur and Penang	209
34	The Cameron Highlands	215
35	South Thailand	219
36	Thailand Beaches	225
37	Bangkok	231
38	Chiang Mai	240

Part Six
Cambodia, Vietnam and Laos

39	Angkor	251
40	River Journey	260
41	Battambang and Phnom Penh	264
42	The Mekong Delta	271
43	Ho Chi Minh City	276
44	Mui Ne	281
45	Nha Trang and Hoi An	285
46	Savannakhet and Vientiane	291
47	Vang Vieng	297
48	Luang Prabang	302
49	Luang Nam Tha	307

Part Seven
China

50	Jinghong	317
51	Dali	323
52	Lijiang and the Tiger Leaping Gorge	329
53	Nanning and Guilin	336
54	Yangshuo	341
55	Pingan	346
56	Hong Kong	352
57	Beijing	357

Part Eight
India and Nepal

58	Delhi	367
59	Varanasi	373
60	Pokhara	380
61	Annapurna Trek	384
62	Kathmandu	391

63	Everest	399
64	Agra	401
65	Palaces and Forts – Jaipur, Jodhpur and Udaipur	406
66	Rajasthan Journeys	411
67	Temples – Pushkar, Ranakpur and Bikaneer	416
68	Jaisalmer	420

Bibliography	423
Index	425

Our route through the Americas

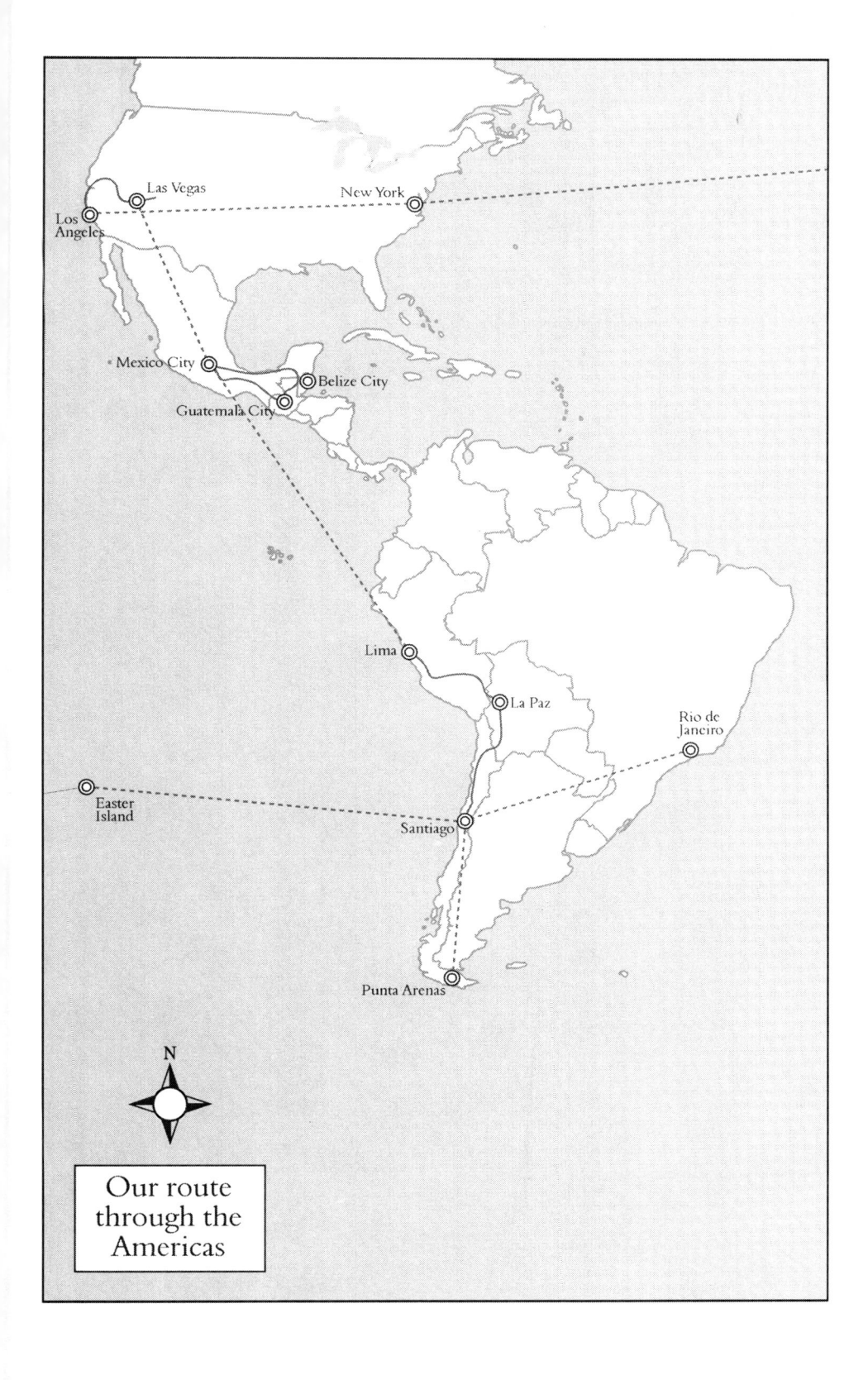

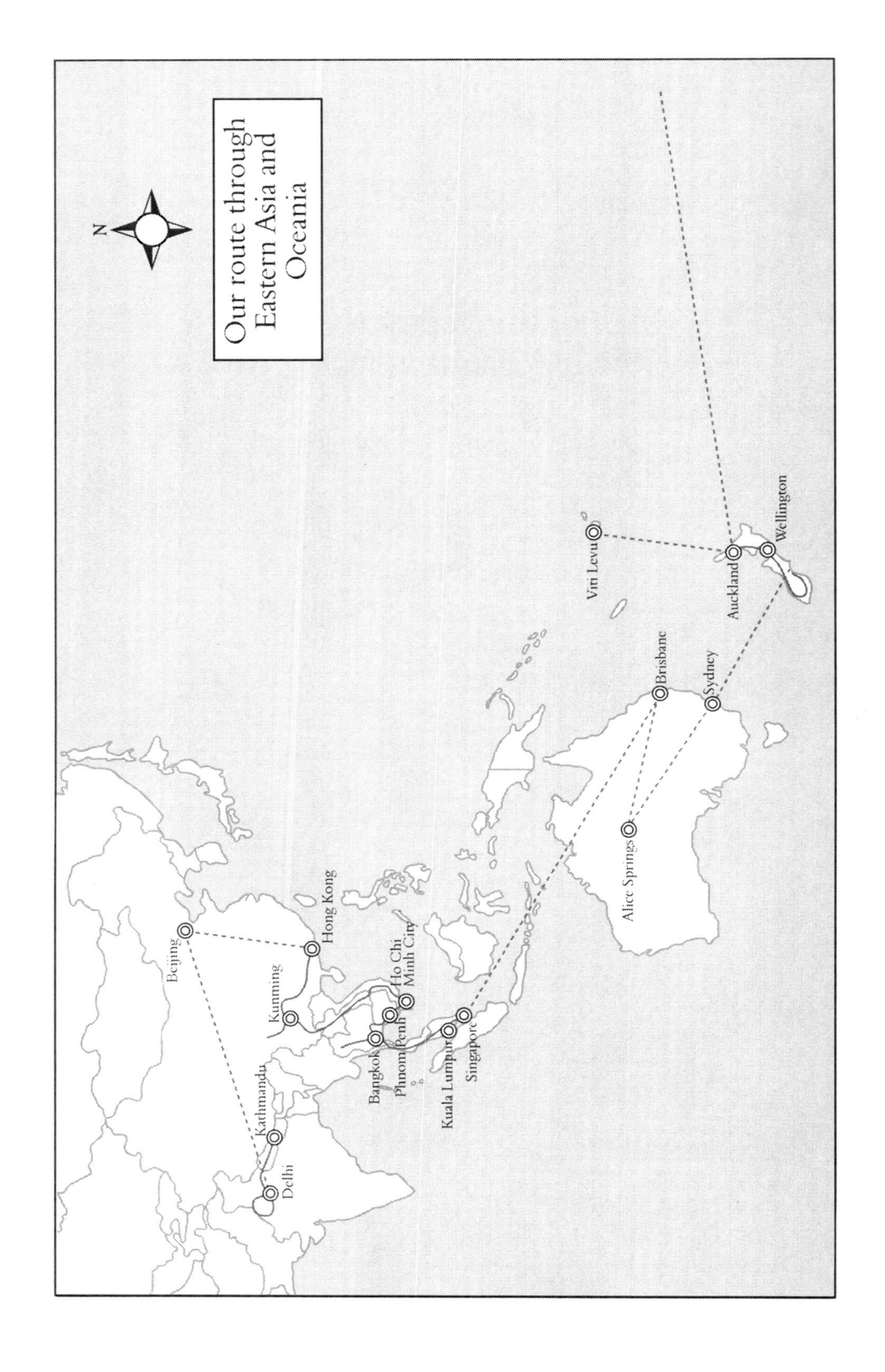

Prologue

Claudia and I met whilst we were teaching in secondary schools in Cambridgeshire, England. We decided to take a year off to travel the world together, and to get married along the way. People have often asked us whether our trip was difficult to organise, how much planning was involved, what we took with us. So, before the story of our journey begins, here is how we did it.

When we committed to the idea by handing in our resignations, we only had vague ideas about places or countries we wanted to see, such as the Grand Canyon, Machu Picchu and China, but nothing much more than that. It was only the evening before we went to see a travel agent that we sat down with a scrap of paper to start our planning. It took a couple of glasses of wine to sketch out a route around the world, which started in North America and headed south all the way to Patagonia. From there we wanted to cross the Pacific Ocean to New Zealand and Australia. Then we would turn north again, on the backpacker trail through South East Asia, before visiting China, Japan and India. We thought that would probably do us. To finish our work, we scribbled an approximate length of time for each region, off the top of our heads, and juggled the numbers until they fitted into a year. That was the way we planned our trip around the world.

For three hours in the travel agent's, with a world map and a calendar, we studied flight paths and possible airport destinations, eventually booking a package of twenty flights. We had to leave out Japan, but had the unexpected bonus of squeezing in both Fiji and Easter Island. Serendipity always was a major part of final outcomes and we were quite happy for it to be so, determining that we would savour the moments as we travelled rather than chase after destinations. As we progressed, the locations of the airports and the dates of the flights would be our only fixed points for a whole year. To get all the way around the world we had to keep fairly closely to our flight itinerary; as long as we reached each airport on time, we were fine. Often we only began to think about the next stage on the plane before we landed there. Most days, the significant decisions were where to eat or sleep, or which sight to visit.

After booking the flights, there were two areas that needed some advanced planning. One was the visas that we would need. One day, we collected application forms, passport photographs and cash together and set off for London, to India House first. We queued in their crowded hall for over an hour, finally getting the chance to present our applications. All was going well until I noticed that they were intending to give us a visa for 2005, rather than 2006. We were then told that we couldn't have a visa beyond six months in advance, which seemed reasonable enough – if only we had thought about it earlier. As it was, we would collect visas as we went around the world, namely in Sydney and Bangkok.

The second area was vaccinations. Some of these required several boosts some weeks apart, and potentially boosters after that. We had expected multiple jabs, but the cost of them, malaria tablets, insect repellent, sterile medical kits and so on put us back several hundred pounds. Ouch. And that was before travel insurance, which just had to be the most expensive, because we were including high altitude trekking as well as the USA on our itinerary.

With those minor details out of the way, we eventually gave some thought to packing. I was determined that we shouldn't both carry a large rucksack, as they are so inconvenient to manhandle around buses, trains and shops. Finally I ended up with a large one while Claudia took a smaller one, although what hers lacked in size it usually made up for in weight. Starting with a smaller volume had its advantages and disadvantages. As the amount packed always tends to fill the space available, it was a good thing that we were forced to restrict what we carried. Unfortunately, because our bags were full, the souvenirs we bought – like a rolled up carpet and a couple of hammocks – had to be lugged around in a third bundle through Central America. We even carried a four-foot long pole around for a while, before losing it off the top of a Land Rover somewhere on the Bolivian altiplano.

There were several items that we grew to be thankful for having packed. A small daypack for essential items was invaluable, with a padlock for security. I wouldn't go without the footwear of: a pair of flip flops, for use inside dirty bathrooms; travelling sandals, which we wore to exhaustion in hot, sweaty climes; and robust trekking shoes for when more protection is needed. A thin sleeping bag turned out to be ideal for the occasions that bed linen in hostels was unsavoury, and could also be used as a travelling blanket for overnight trains and air-conditioned buses. We each took a set of 'smart' clothes to dress up in now and again, which tended to restore some sense of humanity and self-respect after wearing – literally – the same three T-shirts month after month. My 'smart' set also came in handy on our wedding day.

One of the best of the few purchases we made for the trip was a travel chess set, with pieces that would remain safely in their positions if the game was interrupted. Many, many hours were passed sitting on park benches, in bus stations, airports and on trains, most of which were spent playing chess. Unfortunately I taught Claudia so well that by the end of the year she was regularly beating me, which had never been the idea at all.

Another useful piece of accidental preparation was to open an account with an online photograph processing website. This was intended to be an insurance against losing photo-CDs that we would post home – which turned out to be unnecessary as all of them made it back – but it became a precious link for friends and family through the sharing of images as we progressed around the world. On the subject of photographs, we found that having a camera each was essential. One of the very few things that could irritate both of us was having to stand and watch the other person taking ages constructing their perfect photograph, usually just as something far more interesting was happening behind their back. And we learnt to our cost that it was better to end up with duplicate photographs – we took some 10,000 between us during the year – than to have all our eggs in one basket and end up losing the lot, as happened when our pictures of Cambodia were stolen.

Of course, these snippets of idiosyncratic wisdom come from hindsight – the only way to discover them is to go out and do it. We set off into the unknown one September morning, nearly failing to make it to Heathrow on time on account of the traffic jams. As we dashed into the airport with barely a 'goodbye' to my family, I somehow lost my wristwatch. This was not too surprising in itself, as I am forever losing watches, but as we boarded the plane to New York we hoped that this first morning wasn't an omen of what was in store. Perhaps it was – as well as shedding my mobile phone and laptop, now I had no alarm clock either. We were free at last, with the world ahead of us. It was a liberating feeling.

Part One
The United States of America

Chapter 1: New York

After being welcomed into the USA by having our fingerprints scanned and our faces photographed, we joined a minibus into the city which dropped its passengers off in turn at various classy hotel entrances. We waited for our call but after a tour of upmarket New York we eventually found ourselves sitting alone and wondering if we had been forgotten. That slightly unnerving feeling of being adrift in the unknown was one we would become familiar with as we back-packed our way around the world over the next twelve months.

New York City is the original and smallest of the five city districts, but whatever it lacks in area it makes up for in height. The land is crowded with a multitude of individual tower blocks, all different in shape and style. The city is a showcase of high-rise urban buildings where the dominant dimension is not horizontal but vertical. The tower blocks seemed to be striving for space, pushing each other aside to get their share of the limelight. Their sheer density and scale was quite awesome at times, particularly from the bottom, at street level. It felt a bit like being in a narrow gorge, with the walls rising like sheer cliffs on either side – too high to be comfortable, almost creating a sense of claustrophobia. New York was skyscraper city, the most oppressive that we encountered anywhere around the world, with the possible exception of Hong Kong. It did not do small, apart from one building. Right on the waterfront a little church nestled at the feet of the brash modern giants that towered above it, the unlikely juxtaposition only serving to enhance the church's humble dignity.

Some eleven months after first arriving in New York, we were sitting in a lodge in the mountains of Nepal. On the walls were posters of sights around the world, such as the Sydney Opera House or London's Tower Bridge. One was a panorama of the New York skyline. Right in the centre, dominant over everything else, were the Twin Towers. I hadn't appreciated just how colossal these buildings had been until I saw that poster; they appeared twice as tall as any of the surrounding skyscrapers – some feat in New York! And only then did I appreciate how the loss of their presence must have affected New Yorkers. When we visited Ground Zero for ourselves, it was the *absence* of any building that was haunting. In the midst of such a dense concrete forest, here was nothing but a hole, an emptiness that created a toothless gap in the skyline.

We had expected we would find New York glitzy and glamorous, as befitting the city showcased by *Friends* or *Sex in the City*, but we were to be disappointed. In West Village, where our minibus driver finally dropped us, the streets were grey and grimy, strewn with litter. The buildings were often dilapidated, with dirty old air-conditioning units hanging out of the endless apartment windows. It was our luck to find ourselves staying on the fourth floor of one of these apartment blocks, in a poky budget hotel that had more in common with a grotty student hall of residence. A few streets nearby did manage a bit more charm; behind rows of trimmed trees, large Georgianesque buildings fronted with broad steps and shiny black railings had an almost Parisian elegance. We were surprised to find many small shops eking out their independent existences in these suburban districts, just a stone's throw from the Financial District. The little stores reminded me of old English corner shops, with two rows of shelves inside holding a limited range of papers and sweets, a few tins of food, maybe a carton of milk or two. It was not the image of New York that I had expected to see. Nor was the sight of men pulling collections of rubbish along in supermarket trolleys – sometimes it was hard to believe that we were in New York, USA, rather than on the streets of a developing world city.

Wandering around Manhattan, between the Financial District and Central Park, was an intense experience. In the narrow confines of these busy streets, we found everything hemmed in like a pressure cooker. New York, along with most cities in the USA, has a very regular, systematic road layout. The streets all follow a grid pattern, numbered from south to north in rows and then east or west outwards from a central axis. It made navigation relatively easy, but driving must have been a nightmare of stopping and starting, with crossroads between each square 'block' of buildings. To confuse matters, city planners had tackled congestion by designating some of the 'rows' as one-way streets, so that along one street everything was going east and then along the next, only westwards.

When the lights went green, traffic surged forward, hundreds of shiny custard-yellow taxis weaving across the lanes, beeping their horns as they jostled for position, before braking to a standstill at the next red light twenty yards further on, where they would wait until the next chaotic release of their pent-up energy. It was all a bit much – fast and furious, an urban maelstrom where it was hard to take everything in. Claudia summed it up in a typically succinct way: 'It gives me a headache.' Amidst the traffic were unexpected sights like a young man on rollerblades with black knee- and elbow-pads travelling smoothly between the lanes of cars. At the same time, someone hailed a taxi in the middle of a junction, ignoring the horns of the drivers queued behind.

To escape from the intensity of the streets, we dived into a coffee shop, looking for a warm and friendly refuge. 'Yes? Whaddyawant?' was the reception that met us. We asked for a coffee, please. Our Austrian and English accents frequently took people in New York by surprise, but this time it took us a few seconds' thought to work out what the cashier's response was: 'Whaddyasay?' There was great capacity for a really confused conversation here, but this clearly wasn't the place for humorous repartee. There were no friendly remarks about our being visitors, no enquiry about how we were enjoying New York. Just a barked 'Eight seventy,' followed by 'Next!' before we had even picked up our mugs and murmured a polite English 'thank you' for the excellent service.

Watching the world go by out of the window, it seemed that diversity was the single most striking feature of the citizens of New York. The only other place in the world where we would come across such a variety of people would be Hong Kong. I amused myself by trying to spot any similarity between the fashions that were modelled by passers-by. It was an exercise in failure. From flip-flops to high heels, pinstripe suits to summer dresses, Rastafarian hair to baseball caps worn at every conceivable angle, everyone and everything was different. There was a defiant individuality and independence about the citizens of New York, which might well have been liberating, but which had its unwelcome side too. As we walked around, it was notable that no one made eye contact and no one returned our smiles. We began to feel stifled by the atmosphere on the streets and to wish our way to somewhere with space to relax in and clean, fresh air.

There was one place in the city that managed to provide a respite from the immediate intensity of the city: Central Park. This was something like the parks of London in its location and size, where it was possible to walk or cycle along the broad, carefully landscaped walkways that swept their way beneath shady canopies of trees. The paths meandered between outcrops of rock, leading to expanses of green grass that were dotted with New Yorkers taking time out. It truly was a haven, calm and peaceful. Yet even here we couldn't escape the constant rumble of traffic in the background, or the buildings always visible over the treetops. This was just an oasis, and it could not fully shut out the overwhelming presence of New York.

We took a boat cruise out around the harbour, in the company of a tour guide whose resonant bass voice thundered out the history of the various sights. The most famous of these was the Statue of Liberty, which had been built in Paris in the late nineteenth century. She stands quite a long way out into the harbour, far enough to at first look much smaller than expected. I also had in mind beforehand that she would be standing in untouchable isolation on the water, but that wasn't the case. She is mounted on a giant square plinth of grey-brown bricks, which itself sits on a twelve-acre island. Grass, bushes and trees surround the plinth, and a pedestrian walkway circles in front, with dozens of tourists ambling past, cameras slung around their necks as if they were going for a stroll in a park. When we were directly underneath the statue, however, the figure had a striking visual impact. This is, after all, one of the most iconic images in the world, quite apart from the fact that it stands over 305 feet high. What caught my eye about her was not the symbolic flaming torch, the stone tablet or her crown, but her overall posture. She has a determined step, as if going forwards in defiance of all who might challenge her. With an attitude like that, I thought, she would fit right into the streets of Manhattan.

The Statue of Liberty was erected in 1886 as a symbol of welcome to the United States of America. At that time, hundreds of thousands of people were arriving into the USA on steamships from across the Atlantic. Their first port of call was the Ellis Island Immigration Centre. Between 1892 and 1954 this centre processed 12 million immigrants, including no less than 11,747 during a single day in 1907. Today, it is estimated that 40 per cent of Americans can trace their ancestry directly back to Ellis Island. We would later come across some of those 100 million people. We always had to smile when we heard, in a strong American accent, the proclamation, 'I'm Irish,' or, 'I'm from Scotland.' Ancestry appeared much more immediate and relevant to Americans – and indeed Australians – than it had ever felt to us in Europe. We quickly fell into the routine of telling people that we were both from England, as the concept of Austria seemed too remote to comprehend.

The scale of the migrations was staggering, in particular from Ireland. From Ulster alone, around 500,000 people arrived from 1720 onwards, escaping the hardships of taxes and land reform. In 1821 the potato famine hit Ireland, and by 1825 there were 50,000 applicants for the 2,000 places on a government scheme of transportation to North America – and that was even before the severe winters of the late 1820s. Eventually a whole third of the Irish population would move to America.

To visit the site of the very first European settlement on the continent we took a bus northwards to Boston. With relief, we found that not every city in the USA is like New York. Boston was an intellectual city, rich in heritage, with an altogether different pace and quality of life from Manhattan.

Chapter 2: Boston

'Hey, d'ya need any help, guys?' It took both of us a couple of seconds to register what had just happened. We were being stopped on the street by a stranger who was asking if we needed help! And this had come immediately after having been welcomed and assisted in a very friendly way by a lady in the National Park Information Center, where we had gone to track down the last affordable bed in Boston, using a public phone that wasted a precious quarter with every fruitless call. Perhaps 'affordable' is not quite accurate: the motel cost us US $95 per night – before tax, that is. I kept the receipt as a reminder of how the advertised 'rack rate' was increased by a state tax, a local tax and also a convention tax, which together added US $12 to the nightly bill. To make up for this expense, we crammed our pockets full of their free muffins, bagels and bananas each morning – and spent our last night in Boston sleeping in the airport. But that is a digression. We had called the motel from the Information Center and now were on our way to a distant metro station, where we hoped a car from the hotel would collect us.

The amiable stranger had stopped us perhaps fifteen metres away from the entrance to the metro station. With our backpacks on, we thought it was fairly obvious where we were headed, so we gestured towards it. 'Oh, sure! Where d'ya want to get to?' Well, Alewife, actually. 'Right, well, in that case you want... Oh no, c'mon, let me show you.'

Claudia and I turned to each other and grinned. This was not New York, then. We followed our new friend into the station entrance and were shown the very obvious route map, which clearly indicated that we should take the orange line for one stop and then change for the red line. This was carefully explained to us, after which we said our thanks and goodbye, still pleased at the novelty of such kindness. Little did we know that it is possible to have too much of a good thing.

A hundred yards further we paused where the tunnel split and instantly were accosted by another Bostonian. 'Where do you want to go?' Alewife. 'Well...' All three of us together looked at the large signs right above our heads and read that it was the right-hand tunnel. 'That's where you need to go!' Thanks for the help, again. Somehow, we managed to navigate the metro system on our own all the way to Alewife, and even found a row of public telephone booths there. Not that they did us any good, for none would connect us to our motel. Payphones in the USA are – to put it politely – not the most reliable. Perhaps this is because mobile phones are so ubiquitous. If so, the same kind of logic could have applied to the Internet; the USA was to be the hardest country in the world for us to find public Internet cafés.

But for now we were stuck and had to ask directions. The cheerful young policeman whom we found outside was new to this beat and couldn't really advise us, but that didn't matter because within seconds we heard a 'Perhaps we can help? We live round here.' How lovely, just what we needed, we thought, as we turned gratefully to the two middle-aged ladies. They gave us directions to a motel, not entirely sure either whether it was the right place or whether it was possible to get there on foot. Sitting at a service station an hour later, after having risked life and limb along the verge of Route 6, not to mention scrambling twice up overgrown embankments in the dark, the only things we were clear about was that this was not the right place, and it hadn't been a good way to get here, wherever 'here' was.

Still, the service station attendant, Simon, was very friendly. He offered us the use of his mobile phone to call our hotel and ask their car to pick us up. Unfortunately, his phone cut out just before the guy at the other end could hear that the 'station' concerned was a petrol – or 'gas' – station. We waited as the motel car went to the metro station instead, and to pass the time we watched Simon serve customers. Pretty much everyone prepaid at the pump with cards for their petrol, so Simon's job seemed to consist of giving directions to passing members of the general public. One man called in to ask where a liquor store could be found.

'About a quarter of a mile away,' Simon told him, 'so best go back and get your car.'

This was a typical attitude: walking just was not done in the USA, unless it was for sport. Meanwhile, our evening was turning into a long night. Just before our lift finally arrived, Simon asked us whether we had a reservation. 'No? Oh, I should have asked sooner. You could have stayed at the place just across the street.'

Bostonians really were very friendly people. They caught our eyes and smiled when passing. They asked how we were and seemed to care about the answer. They said 'You're welcome' a lot. They offered unsolicited advice, they went out of their way to, well, to just be nice. I'm sure I've seen an episode of *Star Trek* where the inhabitants of some distant planet had created a society where everything is harmonious and everyone smiles all the time. It must have been modelled on Boston.

Coming from Cambridge, England, we were quite keen to see Cambridge, Massachusetts, and Harvard University. Harvard is the oldest university in the USA, founded in 1636, just sixteen years after the arrival of the first settlers. It has a statue of its first benefactor in its grounds, and the inscription reads 'John

Harvey, Founder, 1638'. The statue is called the statue of three lies, as John Harvey didn't found the university, which in any case didn't happen in 1638, and the statue couldn't be a likeness of him anyway because no image of him was ever preserved. Still, it remains as a feature, part of the tourist attraction.

Harvard was as popular for tourists as the Cambridge colleges are back at home, but here we could wander freely through the university grounds. There were a mix of old but still impressive wooden New England buildings – the oldest dating from 1720 – and some more modern stone and brick ones, often with grandiose entrances of flights of steps and neoclassical columns. The buildings stood slightly apart from one another around the edges of grassy squares that were crossed by pathways and pleasantly shaded by trees. The whole place seemed designed to ooze a blend of studious learning and serenity, much like a giant open-air public library. And it worked. It was also a charmingly normal place, unlike the cloistered atmospheres of the English colleges. We were even allowed to walk on the grass!

Just outside one entrance we had a coffee with blueberry bagels in a cafe beside a paved public square, where several tables were set out with chess games. Couples were enjoying the game in the open air and sunshine, while other individuals sat reading the high-brow *Boston Globe* newspaper or their own weighty paperback tomes. Some had papers spread on the tables, no doubt scribbling notes for future academic publications. There was an atmosphere of relaxed intelligentsia; it seemed a place where it was usual, even expected, to be continually exercising one's mind. There was no pretension and no sense of snobbery. The people we had seen in and around Harvard seemed to make a point of dressing casually as if to emphasise the naturalness of their vocation. Professors wore sneakers and there wasn't a single stuffy tie in sight. This was an environment that I hadn't encountered before and I found it quite refreshing, even stimulating. Claudia and I duly pretended to be part of the crowd and came up with some deep, profound thoughts for this book, which have been long since forgotten or abandoned.

The *Boston Globe* newspaper was a welcome publication for us, although we appreciated the quality of the *Wall Street Journal* even more. We were already getting tired of television news programmes in the USA. Eventually we would reject them altogether, finding them more a source of frustration and irritation than an authoritative source of news. Of all the countries around the world, only Australia would have worse television news. Here, we were shocked by how the broadcasters imposed their subjective and often emotive opinions onto the viewer. There seemed to be little room for unbiased, objective facts, as if viewers couldn't be trusted with forming their own opinions. Furthermore, the content was incredibly introverted; we simply couldn't find out about the rest of the world unless it was directly relevant to US concerns. For the world's most powerful country, this seemed a highly misguided state of affairs.

Back in Boston, we strolled around the city centre, underneath gleaming modernist office blocks. Everywhere in the city the streets were clean, the traffic was light, the pavements were broad and in perfect condition. There was space for people to walk around in peace. It all demonstrated how modern urbanity can still be soft on the senses, relaxed at ground level, even pleasing to the eye and mind. Boston was very easy to like, being laid-back and charming at the same time as cutting edge – an impressive achievement. The city tries to combine its commercial modernity with a preservation of history, and succeeds admirably. There were several old buildings dotted throughout the city, like the town hall and a church that has the record for the oldest Presbyterian church still in use. Coming from the European notion of history, with castles and cathedrals hundreds of years old, it was difficult to get too excited about the antiquity of Boston's heritage, but we had to respect the way that it had been preserved and included as a central component of its present character. The city sights were linked by well-marked heritage trails and the National Parks Service provided maps and offered tours from its office in the park, underneath an old clock tower that still musically chimed out the hours. It was all very nicely done.

There was an odd hut – or maybe it was a ship – sitting in the harbour beside a rickety pier. It had a label on its side which read 'Boston Tea Party' and indeed it looked as if it has not been touched or cared for since 1773. Like an abandoned bungalow standing on slowly rotting stilts, its red paintwork was peeling off the wooden planks, black painted boards were nailed over the doors and windows, and moss and grass was growing out from cracks and joints. Apparently there are plans to create a modern, renovated display of this part of Boston's – and indeed the USA's – heritage. When the three ships of the East India Company were emptied of £10,000 worth of tea in protest against English interference and taxes in the American colony, according to the historian Paul Johnson one eyewitness said at the time, 'This destruction to the tea is so bold, so daring, so firm, intrepid and inflexible, and it must have so important consequences, and so lasting, that I can't but consider it an epoch of history.' Given that it was indeed the spark that lit the fuse of open conflict between the English and the American citizens, leading to their War of Independence, he was pretty much right.

We tried to find the actual site of the original Tea Party, slightly inland of the present day shoreline and narrowed it down to a street corner, but to our disappointment the only thing on show there was roadworks.

Boston is proud of its historical role at the centre of the independence movement, but it was also a major colonial settlement in New England. It was founded in 1630, named after a town in Lincolnshire, England. The *Mayflower* had landed just ten years before to found the very first colony, touching land on the northern tip of the great curving spit that is Cape Cod. We went to Cape Cod after talking to another nice lady in the tourist information office. She had looked quite bemused at first, when we asked her what we thought was a perfectly simple, reasonable question: 'We have two weeks to spend in this area, where would you recommend visiting?'

After a couple of moments to gather her thoughts, she responded admirably and suggested two very different places. One was to the north, the White Mountains of New Hampshire and Mount Washington, the highest mountain in the eastern USA. The other was Cape Cod to the south, and we decided to go there first. Had we spent a little longer researching it, we might have realised that the easiest way to Provincetown from Boston was by boat – 1½ hours across the water. Instead, we booked a bus and spent twice that time winding all the way down to the neck of the spit and then back up again to its tip.

Chapter 3: Cape Cod and Mount Washington

The landscape of Massachusetts was a total surprise to me, both north and south of Boston. The cities were very quickly left behind for a world of trees. There was nothing but trees, for miles in every direction, an apparently unending forest of mixed oak, pine and sumac. At intervals we passed small road junctions and sometimes we caught sight of a sprinkling of wooden houses half hidden amongst the trees, in trimmed plots with white garden fences, but basically the scenery was just thick green forest. Whenever the road topped the brow of a hill I would strain to catch sight of what must lie beyond, but invariably saw only a sea of green stretching to the horizon. In its way, this blanket of leaves was quite remarkable, purely because of its scale. There are 3 million acres of forest in Massachusetts, 500,000 acres of which are owned by the state. Seeing all the forest, we began to understand how it is that in the USA, one of the most developed countries in the world, there are still large and potentially dangerous animals roaming free.

It now didn't seem so strange to read in just one local paper about plans to curb the growing population of beavers, of a car hitting a 100-pound black bear and of another fatal accident involving a moose. There are estimated to be 3,000 black bears, 500–700 moose and over 70,000 beavers in Massachusetts. Wildlife is increasing as the forests of the state regenerate, the farmers who once cleared land there having long since left their homes and villages for better prospects further west. These vast expanses of wilderness – which are not remote or inaccessible – present a very different proposition to the landscapes and wildlife of overpopulated Europe. The more we travelled in the USA, the more its undeveloped landscapes would become to us an integral part of the nature of the country.

At the end of Cape Cod, Provincetown reeked of being a seaside resort. It was in the whitewashed wooden houses, the inescapable drift of sand, and the eccentricity of the main street. The hub of the town was the waterfront, with its frankly bizarre mix of fine art shops, classy restaurants, twee arcades, more art galleries, tourist nick-nack stalls, sex shops and gay bars. Somehow the sexually liberated youngsters rubbed shoulders with refined elderly couples on coach tours, and everyone got along just fine. Climbing the Florentine-style 77-metre high Pilgrim Memorial Monument – a hollow tower made from granite blocks, looking something like a square lighthouse – gave us a great view across the sheltered bay with its boats bobbing around, the small town and the sand dunes beyond. Provincetown doesn't overdo its place in colonial history; the Pilgrim Monument and a small museum seemed to be all there were. Perhaps this was because the colonists didn't stay on the end of this long, thin stretch of sand. It was November when they arrived and a storm was brewing. They decided to look elsewhere, eventually settling in a deserted village called Patuxet that was to become known as Plymouth.

This native village had had a population of perhaps 2,000 before being totally deserted around 1616, due to an outbreak of probably either smallpox or yellow fever – European diseases to which the native people had no immunity. In 1620 the crew of the *Mayflower* moved in, but of these very first 102 settlers only fifty-two were alive by the following spring. In March or April 1621 a native American called Samoset walked into their settlement, greeting them in the English that he had learned from fishermen. He then introduced the settlers to a man who is referred to as 'Squanto', whose story has the touch of the fantastic about it. He was a native of Patuxet, who had been kidnapped by an Englishman in 1605. He worked in England for nine years, until returning home on another voyage in 1613. Only the following year he was captured again by another Englishman, who hoped to sell Squanto in Spain as a slave. He was rescued by friars, then escaped to London and visited Newfoundland twice before finally making it back to his home village in 1619, only to find it deserted, with many people having died from the introduced plague. Patuxet was to be invaluable to the settlers, helping them to fish and to grow crops of corn, beans and pumpkins.

One day we walked through regenerating beech woodland to the northern tip of Cape Cod, Race Point, to have a look out at the Atlantic Ocean from the west, but there wasn't much else there except the waves. It was a squally sea, too; we emerged from the trees just in time for a blast of cold showers to drench us. This sent all the other visitors scurrying back into their 4WD jeeps and out of the car park. We quickly had our fill of the wet beach, grey waves and rain clouds, so we headed home too. Only, we had to walk back through the rain, not to a hot bath in a cosy hotel but to a small green dome tent.

In an effort to save money, we were staying in a campsite that was tucked into a pine forest. It still cost us a steep $30 per night for the site, but there was something special about sleeping on pine needles, with their sweet scent all around and their great branches overhead stilling any breeze. The only thing we needed was for the annoyingly exuberant toddler next door to shut up, and it would have been idyllic. The campsite even offered free coffee in the mornings, but somehow we never got up in time to have any before the pot ran dry. We discovered here that we had to buy a new gas stove, as the ultra-lightweight camping stove that we had brought from England, ideal for backpacking, wasn't used by Americans. It also didn't fit their idea of camping, which required large double-burner gas stoves set on legs, that were carried in the back of their cavernous 4WDs and camper vans. That was camping, US-style. And to be fair, our new stove was to come in very handy later on, on our own road trip through California and Nevada.

Apart from being the site of the first European colony, the other thing Cape Cod is famous for is whales. The offshore Stellwagen Bank area is a rich marine environment, full of whales, dolphins, porpoise, seals, squid, tuna and sharks. Cold water currents rise upwards with their vast populations of plankton, which feed baleen whales like the finback – second only in size to the blue whale – and the famous migratory humpback. It was my birthday, and we decided to go to see the whales on a sunset cruise as a treat. It turned out to be just that. The journey out was full of anticipation as to when and where whales would be sighted. A minke whale and then two fin whales chasing through the waves were just the appetisers, although these were impressive enough. Chasing blow-spouts in the distance, our very first humpback was endearingly named 'Aswan', identifiable by its unique tail markings. Then, all of a sudden, we were amidst a pod of four or five whales.

They were feeding and so we were treated to the spectacle of each one periodically rising to the surface to blow its water spouts high into the air with a noisy hiss. This noise gave away their presence and we had just a moment or two to spot them while they took a couple of breaths. Again and again the whales surfaced, people rushed to the side of the deck and there was a chorus of camera shutters clicking furiously. We could see the tops of the whales' dark backs just visible above the water, sometimes close enough for us to get an impression of their vast bulk suspended in the water, a dark blurry mass beneath the waves. Then down they would dive again, with a slow-motion graceful arch of their backs and a final flick of their huge black and white tails. Before the novelty and sheer beauty of the experience wore off, let alone the excitement of each sighting, it was time to head back. We faced directly into a glowing red sun, sinking from the cloudless sky into the dark flat sea. Out in the bow of the boat, a couple had their *Titanic* moment silhouetted against the sunset, savouring the romance of the occasion.

When we arrived in New Hampshire a few days later, the Conway *Daily Sun* was reporting that 'a wet spring and warm, humid summer have New England bracing for one of the best fall foliage displays of colour in years'. This was just what I had wanted. The main attraction of the east coast of the USA for me had been to see the forests in their fall colours, the rich kaleidoscope of oranges, yellows, browns and reds. This was now my chance to experience the splendour of one of nature's most visual spectacles. It was the reason we were there in late September. The trouble was, the fall was forecast to start in mid-

October, by which time we would be in California. We were too early. This was one of those occasions when it occurred to us that perhaps we could have done a little more planning before booking our flights. As it was, we had only tantalising glimpses of what we were about to miss, as odd trees changed from their green summer dress to autumnal gowns of yellow and russet.

We had pitched up in the small town of Conway for two reasons. Firstly, it wasn't too far from Boston on the bus route heading towards the White Mountains, and secondly it had an international youth hostel. We couldn't have asked for a better place to spend a few days; Conway was a quiet town full of the flavour of old wooden buildings, gentle rivers, open fields, hills and woodland. The characteristic three-storey houses were made from whitewashed horizontal boards, with steep angled roofs and large windows protected by green wooden shutters. They looked like elegant stately homes, their front porches supported by white mock-Grecian columns and flights of broad steps leading down to neatly trimmed lawns that were lined with pink roses.

Quiet country roads took us past these houses and into beech and pine forest, where peaceful lakes were sheltered by the trees. Wide, smooth rivers made their gentle way beneath the branches and under covered wooden bridges. These covered bridges were a particular feature of the countryside. Only two are found in Conway, but there are over fifty in New Hampshire. They looked a bit like wooden tunnels, with dark brown walls and roofs, sometimes large enough for lorries to pass underneath, driving on thick beams like railway sleepers. It just fitted the nature of Conway that these quaint old structures, dating from the mid-nineteenth century, were being carefully preserved. There even exists a 'Covered Bridge Preservation Society', which no doubt must have a wide membership and frequent meetings. To keep in touch with the rapidly changing world of covered bridges, there is a quarterly journal of the society, and even a *World Guide to Covered Bridges*.

Outside town, the character of the large roadside properties was curious, to say the least. Many houses were not actually visible from the road, hidden from view down muddy tracks. 'Keep Out' signs were displayed prominently, though, and I had the distinct impression that trespassers would not be welcome. It was the kind of place where I felt that a shotgun might be used as a 'stay away' message. Those houses that we could see were each kept separate on isolated plots within the forest and the owners seemed to want to keep it that way. The Stars and Stripes was on show in many gardens and on rooftops. We even saw the Ten Commandments printed on large poster boards placed outside the front of one home, for all passers-by to read and presumably repent over. There was a kind of grim fanaticism about the place that suddenly brought to mind both the Protestant fervour of the early Pilgrim settlers and the later independent pride of the colonists. I wondered what legacies still live on within the woods, down the private muddy driveways.

For us, walking in and around Conway would define the character of New Hampshire. It was hard to believe that the area has changed significantly since, well, about the time of the Boston Tea Party. Life was relaxed to the point of hardly appearing to progress at all; the people were kind and welcoming; the air was clean and fresh. We were beginning to realise that despite a surprising degree of homogeneity, the different parts of the USA each have their unique characters. And, more importantly, that the image of the USA gained from abroad, through the prism of personality-focused politics – which means George W. Bush – is very far removed from the reality on the ground. Perhaps it's a bit like judging the population of Glasgow on the basis of the image of Tony Blair. We were told that in the USA, Washington is almost insignificant to people's everyday lives, especially in comparison to state and local politics. It certainly seemed that way in the fields and woods of New Hampshire.

On the way back from walking up a local mountain one day – we had been pleased to come across the path in total ignorance of the fact that it was the only such one in the local area – we were offered a ride by a friendly electrician in his red pickup, on his way home. 'If there is one thing you should do whilst you are here, you should go to Mount Washington,' he told us. So early next morning saw us driving to the foot of the mountain with a couple from the hostel who happened to have the same idea.

Claudia had known immediately that Mary was a fellow teacher: it was in the way that she fussed over Claudia, taking her to the kitchen and showing her around, in a motherly and efficient kind of way. Mary and Bill were from Los Angeles and recommended to us that we drive along Route 1 in California rather than use public transport, which turned out later to be excellent advice. They had travelled a fair bit around the world, which was quite unusual for Americans – in their words, not ours. Having received so much help from other people along the way, they felt they should pass it on whenever they could. That sounded like a good philosophy to me, and we certainly grew to appreciate the benefits of it.

If only there had been more people like them on our way back that evening. With no bus service operating, we had to hitch-hike, which everyone said would be perfectly possible. We felt just a bit self-conscious and awkward at first, sticking our thumbs out at passing cars. But as we became tired of walking and more desperate for a lift, the awkwardness soon wore off. A couple of drivers eventually took pity on us, although the first took us barely a mile down the road. The next was a strange rich lady who had a flash car and an East European toy boy. She chatted away and assured us that she would take us all the way back to Conway, right up until the point where she passed a hotel she liked the look of and immediately stopped the car. We were back on the road in the gathering dark, five miles short of our hostel. After walking a couple of miles, we gave up and went into another petrol station to call a taxi.

The oldest mountain hiking trail in the USA – the Crawford Path, which has been in continuous use since 1819 – ends at the summit of Mount Washington, which is the highest mountain in north-eastern USA at 6,288 feet (1,916 m) in altitude. I had the impression that most visitors at the top hadn't arrived there along that or any other mountain trail. They shivered briefly in their shorts and sandals beside the sign at the top for a photograph before hastening back to the shelter of their cars or the train to avoid getting hypothermia. For along with the meteorology station, café, restrooms, shop, and weather museum, there is not only a road to the top but also the world's oldest mountain-climbing railway. It began in 1869 and is the second steepest passenger railway in the world. For information, the steepest cog railway happens to be the Pilatus in Switzerland; while in the Blue Mountains of Australia is the steepest incline railway, with an angle of 52°. Back on Mount Washington, the train belched out thick black coal smoke into the otherwise pure air, looking hideous at the top of a mountain. Before too long I expect that heated, air-conditioned covered walkways will have been built between the car park and the café, so the 250,000 visitors a year don't have to be exposed to the fresh, freezing air. It was indeed bitingly cold when we were there, but could have been much worse.

At the top of Mount Washington we found a sign saying that it had 'the worst weather in the world'. This struck me as something that one would want to know before setting off. The fastest wind speed in the world was recorded here – an impressive 231 miles per hour 'in a great storm April 12, 1934'. Mount Washington is also supposed to have the second most changeable weather in the world – not that I found out how this was measured, or where the first place location is. The average temperature at the top of the mountain is -3°C and the average wind speed 35 mph. There are 100 mph winds 40 per cent of the time; in winter this happens every three days. An average of twenty-one feet of snow falls each year and it is cloudy for 300 days each year. All this weather is no joke: the mountain kills people at a rate that is not far off that of mountains like Everest. Since 1849 there have been 135 fatalities on or around the mountain, as people set out from the bottom in good conditions and are caught unprepared for the vicious weather as they climb upwards. We were fortunate enough to have neither a hurricane or a cloud in the sky, which probably explained why so many people were there with us. On a day like ours the visibility was said to be over one hundred miles. It was certainly a spectacular panorama over the White Mountains. In several places one could stand with virtually a full 180° vista over successive lines of hilltop ridges that gradually faded into the distance. It was exhilarating, but freezing cold.

That was effectively our last look at the east coast of the USA. We returned to Boston and managed a few hours' kip in between cleaners doing their rounds on the night shift in the airport. The next day saw us on the other side of the continent, in Los Angeles. That distance is equivalent to going from Ireland to Greece; but one of the incredibly special things about this massive country is that despite the scale there are enough similarities of customs and culture to know that one is always in the USA. Even if there were more muffins in Massachusetts and more Mexican food on offer in California – alongside the ubiquitous McDonald's that were literally on every street corner at times – all the states we visited were very clearly part of the same country.

Chapter 4: Los Angeles and San Diego

The image of Los Angeles that sticks most forcefully in my mind was the view out of the plane window as we flew into the city. Virtually the only thing I could see in all directions were one-or-two storey houses, arranged neatly into rows, divided into blocks by roads that formed a perfectly square gridiron pattern across the city. The blocks were countless in number; everything was ordered and regular. One of the few distinctive features was a raised motorway that stood out in a bold line, running parallel to the rows of other roads and as straight as a die. Otherwise, everything in sight was monotone urbanity, pancake flat, receding into a blanket of grey smog that smothered everything until a line of far-off blue hills. The sight was my idea of a featureless suburban nightmare.

Down at ground level, what we saw of Los Angeles was similarly characterless and uninspiring. Roads seemed to be everywhere, to the point of getting in the way of everything. The grey concrete pavements and buildings left no space anywhere for green open spaces. We found it dull and dusty, unattractive and functional. The people we came across gave much the same impression; they were doing their job, but had no inspiration to go further than that. There were no frills, no niceties, nothing to make things a bit more pleasant or simply interesting. We found a food mall one evening, consisting of several different fast-food outlets around a car park. The shops were different in that one sold Mexican food, another Indian, another burgers and chips and so on, but everything was processed, bland junk food, as repetitive and routine as everything else. Not that this stopped the mall being popular with all sorts of people who were buying their takeaway meals. Los Angeles seemed like a place where everything was ordered, regular and predictable, but plain, without much character or interest.

One thing that did give the city some character was the prevalence of the Spanish language. In the airport we noticed that the vast majority of staff spoke Spanish as their first language. Further into the city, the advertisements along the streets were also largely written in Spanish; English appeared to be the minority language. This seemed to us strange, but it was no doubt perfectly functional. Over one third of the population of California speak Spanish, largely because of immigration from Mexico and Latin America. The Hispanic population of the USA increased 58 per cent between 1990 and 2000, to over 40 million people, of whom nearly 30 million speak Spanish frequently at home – making the USA the fifth largest Spanish-speaking country in the world. The border between Mexico and the USA is the most frequently crossed international border in the world, with 350 million legal crossings and an estimated 1 million illegal crossings each year. Later on, in southern California, we would stop at a little place that could easily have been a stereotypical Mexican frontier town. It looked as if it came out of a Western movie, with its broad, dusty main street lined with wooden boarded houses and shop fronts. I half expected to see a group of stubbly men with sombreros and black leather holsters come striding around the corner. Everything was Spanish, and we got the impression at the little grocery store that to have English-speaking customers was quite unusual.

In Los Angeles we did come across one cheerful, expressive person – a lady bus driver, who laughed at our attempts at pronunciation and helped us find our way across the city. Friendly bus drivers are, in my opinion, just about the most welcome people that a traveller can encounter. Whenever we weren't sure where to go, we discovered that the best person to ask would usually be a bus driver – but not anyone behind a desk in a Greyhound bus station! We generally found these places to be dismal, staffed by unhelpful people who didn't seem to want to be there any more than unfortunate travellers did. Selling tickets was pretty much the limit of the staff's cooperation or ability.

One morning we waited in an ever more impatient queue for tickets, the customers growing increasingly exasperated as the clerk singularly failed to process them. He was apparently oblivious to the concept of speed – or the need to complete his job before passengers' buses actually departed. When we saw our bus boarding, we gave up waiting. No one minded that we by-passed the security check of our bags and loaded them ourselves onto the bus. No one seemed to care about very much. Most of the bus stations had an air of listlessly enduring the hours and days until someone ended their terminal decline. One time I asked at an information counter where we could get a local bus into the city, having already walked around the bus station twice. After being studiously ignored at first, I was told we could take a bus from 'outside'. That was it. Since our time abroad, we have been asked where we found it hardest to travel around the world. The Greyhound buses of the USA weren't the hardest as such, but they came pretty close to the top of the list of unpleasant public transport experiences, and it wasn't long before we gave up on them altogether.

From Los Angeles we headed quickly south to San Diego and then retraced our steps more slowly northwards again along the Californian coast, through Santa Barbara and culminating in the famous Route 1 scenic highway. San Diego was to us like a rich, smooth cheese after the hard, dusty chalk of Los Angeles. It was the most attractive city that we visited in the USA, above both

Boston and San Francisco. Small enough to be convenient, it was typically friendly with welcoming inhabitants, but above all was being cared for. Trouble had been taken over the visual and aesthetic appearance of flower beds, fountains, statues and even benches. Palm trees added a touch of tropical style as they graced the pavements beneath spotless blue glass office towers. The buildings were not ostentatious, but were visually engaging, from skyscrapers to more ornate and painted older houses. There was considered and tasteful colour all around. The pavements were wide and spotlessly clean. And whilst there was a sedate, almost laid-back atmosphere in the streets, the impression was of effective operation. Someone clearly was investing in making the city look good and, we assumed, function well. It was, in short, everything that New York and Los Angeles were not.

We stayed in the Gaslamp Quarter, which is named after the still functional old-fashioned street lights that give it character. It was charming, really. Classy restaurants competed next to each other for trade, with street-side tables creating a relaxed alfresco air. We decided to splash out, choosing one of the cheaper restaurants here. A glass of wine and a simple pasta meal set us back US $70. By later standards this was a horrendous amount – it was in excess of our daily budget. It turned out to be our first and last such extravagance in our year of travelling.

On the spotlessly clean seafront we enjoyed strolling around in the midday sunshine, with the choice of shopping in a large outdoor pedestrianised mall, pottering on and off the various ships of the Maritime Museum, or just sitting on a bench and watching the passers-by. There were many locals out for a jog or brisk walk, as well as tourists and ever-so-polite cycle-rickshaw drivers. Going out for some exercise was obviously one of the things to do in San Diego, often in sociable groups. As well as the more fitness-fanatic fashion-conscious individuals, we saw a forty-something businessman having fun on a weaving skateboard, a very elderly gentleman hurtling past as if competing in a sprint walking race, and a couple of suited men still with their office ties but wearing white trainers – and in one case a straw boater. It was slightly eccentric, but all very commendable and easy-going… a far cry from the stereotyped image of obese Americans, whom we didn't see anywhere.

North of rich San Diego, even more wealth visibly oozed onto the streets. From La Jolla to Del Mar and Solano Beach we went, then inland to Rancho Santa Fe and finally to Santa Barbara. We found pristine grassy parks along the coast, perched above small and often empty beaches. Rather than getting dirty and wet on the sand, people seemed to prefer promenading along wide sidewalks, in the shade of the high palm trees. Chic, sporty, and very attractive wannabe-models strutted down main streets, epitomising a *Baywatch*-style American dream. Here it was eternal summertime – 'the palm trees don't have a fall' – with around 300 days of sunshine a year. During what can't really be called the wet season, there might be an occasional rainy day about once a fortnight. If we had to choose a place to live for its climate, this would be it.

Of course, we would have to be rich enough to do so. This was the heart of affluent America, where the likes of Bill Gates have their homes. Nowhere else did we see a 'Do It Yourself Dog Wash' or a 'Dog Day Care with Webcam'. Sometimes it seemed that there was more money than sense here. In a near-perfect year-round climate, car windows were kept permanently closed so that air conditioning could artificially bring the temperature inside to a comfortable level, even if this just happened to be exactly the same temperature as the outside air. We enjoyed being able to walk outside in only shorts and a T-shirt, but we always had to carry an extra sweater because the air inside buildings was artificially chilled to the point of discomfort. We were told that it has to be like this because children grow up accustomed to air conditioning and therefore expect it all the time. The lifestyle aspiration here seemed to be to achieve maximum ease and comfort through material luxury.

The scale of the task facing campaigners for lower energy use began to dawn on me. We had arrived in the USA soon after Hurricane Katrina hit and were there during Hurricane Rita. Hurricane Katrina was the third strongest ever to hit land in the USA, with wind speeds of 175 mph. At least 1,836 people died along the coastline of the Gulf of Mexico; it was also the costliest hurricane in history, at an estimated US $81 billion. If this wasn't enough, the following month Hurricane Rita caused a further US $10 billion of damage and caused the deaths of 120 people. She was the fourth strongest Atlantic hurricane ever recorded. The combination of these two natural disasters had made climate change a very topical issue. In New Hampshire there was a fair degree of local environmentalism, but here in California the ideas of reducing air conditioning or driving in smaller cars – let alone driving *less* – seemed more like amusing jokes than practical measures. We felt that there was a good degree of social pressure to be seen to be rich here. The modern, spacious, clean double-decker Coaster train service was heavily subsidised but still underused; we were told that people simply preferred the comfort of their private cars and besides, the train was only for people who couldn't afford to drive.

Chapter 5: Route 1 – the Californian Coast

Travelling was often an exercise in frustration and bewilderment – followed all of a sudden by unexpected assistance. The best way to deal with almost any situation was with patience and a sense of humour. At one Californian railway station we arrived just in time to see our train departing the platform. We checked our timetable and went to the ticket office to purchase a ticket for the next train. At the desk the nice-but-dim clerk asked us where we were headed and when we wanted to go. 'Santa Barbara on the 13.25 departure, please,' we said. He helpfully consulted his timetable. 'You've missed that one,' he said, 'and that one has just left.' We knew that, because we had just seen it go. 'So, the next will be the 13.25.' Incidentally, to buy a ticket for this journey of twenty minutes even required us to show our passports.

As an afterthought, I asked the clerk if there was a post office nearby. 'What do you want to do?' was his response. Surprised, I replied that I wanted to post a letter. This stumped the poor man – it seemed that posting letters was not actually possible at the local post office. We were saved by someone in the queue behind who kindly gave us directions to another one. It wasn't, as it turned out, the right kind of post office either, but it was the kind that knew where the right sort actually was, so we got there in the end. Posting a letter might have been expected to be a simple enough operation, but we would learn that an integral part of travelling in cities all over the world involved spending hours on wild goose chases, trying to achieve relatively mundane tasks.

At Santa Barbara we finally gave up on public transport. We had spent 2½ days covering a net distance of 80 km, being frustrated by bus timetables and getting tired of traipsing across towns with our bags to find places to sleep and eat. After we arrived, we walked from the railway station across town to the transit centre, hoping to be able to continue our journey by bus. This was a foolish thought, for despite the many buses coming and going, there were none leaving town northwards that afternoon. We had another shot at getting local advice, asking the clerk about accommodation in town, but that was equally fruitless. So we retraced our steps back along State Street to the source of all good travel information – a bookshop. Finding a guide book, we scribbled down some notes on potential places and set off again, back the same way for the third time. But one motel was full, and the nearby cheap hostel rooms could only be reserved at a separate office next to the train station. Our rucksacks were beginning to get us down by now and we were probably fast becoming a source of amusement for the locals, who happened to include a colourful array of homeless characters. Back across Santa Barbara we went for the fourth time, and unexpectedly found a perfectly reasonably hotel just opposite the train station where we had started hours before. We gave up on buses altogether that evening and decided to look into hiring a car the following morning.

At the airport office we had another taste of the USA system of pricing. The US $540 that we had been quoted over the phone, specifically including tax and insurance, was somehow turned into US $920 after the 'extras' that hadn't been included were added on. However, the salesman was able to offer us not the smallest car possible as we had asked for, but a monstrous 4WD gas-guzzler that needed to be returned to Las Vegas. This unexpected bonus was a taste of luxury and the costs that came with it – the car proceeded to eat vast amounts of petrol, and with it our budget. However, we reckoned that overall the combined cost of hiring a car and staying in a tent was about the same as using public transport and being confined to hostels and hotels.

Thus began our USA road trip experience, which would stand out a year later as probably the most continuously enjoyable two-week period of our entire year's travelling. We grew fond of our white car and the liberty it provided us. Suddenly we were freed from timetables and could stay in out-of-the-way places. We could carry food and cook on our stove, choose our own routes and play our two music cassettes out loud. Once we stopped to visit some sand dunes, where dune buggies were racing up and down the slopes. A man in the car park there asked us how our car went 'off-road'. We had no idea and weren't about to try – but we were struck by how extravagantly absurd it was to be driving sedately along urban roads using a vehicle that was engineered with a capacity for so much more.

The drive up the Californian coast along Route 1 was a continuous show of spectacular scenery. At first the road followed the seaward edge of a rolling open ranchland landscape, with dry and rocky hillsides and sparse vegetation. Gradually we passed into the Big Sur section, named after a local river. This is the most renowned section of Route 1, perhaps about ninety miles in length. Large hillsides, decked out in white and green pampas grasses on one side of the road, were chopped off on the other side by precipitous sea cliffs. It was a dramatically wild coastline, a continuous battleground between the elemental forces of nature. Black rocky stacks and stumps jutted out starkly all along the coast, standing proud against the destructive forces that pound them. Powerful deep blue waves turned into white surf as they crashed repeatedly against the jagged stone, throwing up enough spray to form a hazy mist along the length of coast. Bright yellow flowers splashed colour into the already intense picture.

The highway itself somehow clung precariously between the steep hillsides and the cliffs, the rocks and waves. It had taken twenty years to build this road during the 1920s and '30s. The result is a tortuous but magnificent route, providing stunning views at each hairpin turn. It was exhilarating to drive, with scenery so eye-catching that we had to take turns behind the wheel, one of us focusing on the road while the other hung out of the passenger window trying to snap photographs.

The pampas vegetation slowly changed into redwood pine trees, which were small at first but grew higher all the time. We pulled off into Julia Pfeiffer Burns State Park, finding a delightfully calm grove of tall pines at the beginning of a path that ended at a waterfall plunging down onto the sands of an idyllic blue sea cove. Later we stopped again to look at a population of northern elephant seals on one particular stretch of beach. At the time we were there only young pups were ashore, their grey and white bodies lying fairly motionless on the sand. In the right season, however, the bulls can be seen fighting for their mating rights. These animals can weigh up to 2.5 tons and are taller than a fully grown man even when waddling on land. They can dive to a phenomenal depth of 1,524 m when at sea.

Other strips of coastline were inhabited by surfers and even para-surfers, creating what would have been a stereotypical Californian image of beach sports, if it were not for the thick haze of mist that obscured the sunshine. Once we came across the slightly bizarre sight of families sitting at intervals along the wide expanse of sand, each with deckchairs and parasols laid out next to the obligatory 4WD monster, all totally shrouded in a grey mist so thick that not even the sea could be seen, let alone the sun. Yet there they were, determined to have their beach experience and, presumably, to enjoy it.

Further north, the coastal drive became less spectacular. A flat terrace of land opened out between the hills and the sea, fertile enough to be intensively cultivated by farmers. Although crops such as peas and wheat were growing, in October it was pumpkins that predominated, both in the fields and stacked up by the roadside at numerous little farm shops. This is the home of pumpkin-growing competitions, the heaviest local pumpkin in 2004 year weighing some 270 kg. In Oregon, apparently, one had been grown which reached double that weight.

We stayed overnight in an unusual youth hostel, converted from a lighthouse. Or rather, we stayed in bungalow-style buildings beside the lighthouse. In the hostel a bright red poster gave advice on what to do in an earthquake, entitled 'Drop, Cover and Hold tips'. One suggestion went: 'Hold onto the desk, table or bed. If it moves, move with it.' Somehow I didn't fancy that idea. We didn't experience an earthquake here, but we would do so in Chile and New Zealand – just small shakes that made us feel unsteady and a little unnerved, but which were over almost as soon as they had started. In California there are thousands of small earthquakes a year, with large ones capable of causing serious damage occurring at an average rate of around one a year.

   Watching the sun set that night as a perfectly clear orange ball dropping into the Pacific Ocean was a real treat. Besides us, a signpost on the cliff top pointed the way to various global destinations. Wellington was 2,102 miles away, Nepal 7,649 miles and Singapore 8,442 miles – all somewhere out there beyond the Pacific Ocean. It was fun to think that in a few months we would be seeing each of those places, going right around the world; we had a real sense of travel, of gradually moving across the surface of the planet. First, however, we had the delights of Yosemite National Park, Death Valley, the Grand Canyon and Las Vegas to look forward to.

San Francisco was our next stop, again in a youth hostel, one of the biggest and best run of any we encountered. Our bunk beds were just two of perhaps thirty in a single dormitory. It was ideally located near the coast, so we could walk out of the building and along the harbour through a succession of grassy parks. The cycle paths were heavily used by joggers, but I had the impression that this was a gentle route. The joggers were almost exclusively either distinctly overweight middle-aged men puffing along trying to shed a few pounds, or sporty young mothers in tight Lycra outfits running behind the prams that they were pushing along in front of them. We pottered along at our own slow pace until we had a good view of the iconic Golden Gate Bridge.

   It was smaller and thinner than I had expected, perhaps because it was still quite a long way off. In 1937 it had been the longest suspension bridge in the world but is now merely the second longest in the USA. The bridge connects the city with brown hillsides on the other side of the 'Bay', which looked more like a wide river estuary. It reminded me of the Firth of Forth, familiar from my university days. Actually, with its two high towers and its red paintwork, the Golden Gate Bridge appeared to combine Edinburgh's Forth rail bridge with Bristol's Clifton suspension bridge, in a setting something more like Sydney's Harbour Bridge. Not a bad combination.

   From where we stood, we also had a good view out across the water to another famous landmark: Alcatraz, otherwise known as 'The Rock'. The official name derives from the Spanish for 'gannets'. This low, blocky building – or, more accurately, several separate buildings and towers – was sitting on a wider, fairly flat island that was part small rocky cliffs and part green scrubby vegetation. As well as the notorious prison, the oldest operational lighthouse along the West Coast of the USA was located on the island. The prison had no officially successful escapes, although this didn't stop prisoners trying. During fourteen unsuccessful attempts, seven men were shot and two drowned. Five are unaccounted for, including the three most notorious, who broke out in 1962 but were presumed to have drowned in the Bay.

Alcatraz was much closer to the shore than I had expected and didn't look imposing at all. Anticlimax is an almost inevitable reaction to sights that are built up beyond realism by advertising and imagination, hyped by Hollywood films that have to make everything larger than life. We would experience an 'is this it?' feeling time and again with famous sights around the world, but these were more than compensated by unexpected joys found in small, relatively anonymous locations just around the corner. So it was with San Francisco: it was not the headline sights that made the city attractive, but the atmosphere of its streets away from the water.

San Francisco was a slightly quirky place, but enjoyably so. It is named after a mission established in the late eighteenth century by Spaniards, after Saint Francis of Assisi. There are several small but steep hills in the city, so the roads went up and down a lot. One road was called the 'crookedest street in the world', although it was too new and suburban to do much for us, especially after the wild exuberance of Route 1. More appealing from the top of that particular hill was the cable car – the last permanent manually operated system in the world – that carried people up and down the road much like a tramline. I hadn't heard about this cable car before, but Claudia had, and she loved hanging out of its side as we travelled down the centre of the road.

The buildings in the city were an eccentric mixture of styles, which gave a sense of character to different locations, combining into a refreshing cocktail of modern architecture. Along the seafront were rows of four-storey terraced houses, all painted different colours like a refurbished elegant Georgian street. In the centre these gave way to towers that had very modern architectural designs, one in particular being a very peculiar pointed shape. This was the 260 m high Transamerica Pyramid, gleaming white from its surface of crushed quartz and its 3,678 windows. Everything in San Francisco was clean and well kept; it was a very pretty city, almost surprisingly relaxed as it basked in warm, bright sunshine. This would be a fun place to hang out for a few days, taking in the sights and the slightly offbeat culture. With hindsight we considered that it would compete with Rio de Janeiro and Sydney as being a top city for living in – but as ever we had to keep moving on. We had a plane to catch in Las Vegas, and there was plenty more to see in between.

Chapter 6: National Parks – Yosemite, Death Valley and Zion

Yosemite National Park is huge, in several senses. It covers 1,169 square miles, of which 95 per cent is officially wilderness. This means that most of the 3.5 million visitors per year are concentrated in a few small areas, like the beautiful Yosemite Valley. After an old lake bed had provided a flat, fertile layer of sediment in which to grow, trees such as oak, pine and cedar flourished in this sheltered valley. The park is the home of giant sequoia trees, which are the world's largest single life form, being over 90 m high and 11 m in diameter. Some are still alive after 2,500–3,000 years of growing. The oldest tree, incidentally, is the bristlecone pine, which also grows in California: one that is still alive has been dated at 4,700 years old.

We arrived in Yosemite National Park in the late afternoon, with the low sun at our backs. At first the peaceful, flat meadows and woodlands almost obscured the existence of huge granite rock faces that loomed overhead as we made our way past various car parks and campsites, but at one point we crossed a river and glanced to our right – and then immediately parked in the next available spot. Returning on foot, we looked across at a beautiful view of the Half Dome rock outcrop, standing out above the green pine trees which grew all along the banks and prettily reflected in the blue waters of the river. The Half Dome was pretty much what it sounds like: a great mound of rock rising up through the trees, like a round hill, except that half of it has been sliced off leaving an expanse of sheer rock face plunging downwards. It looked something like a giant falcon's hooked beak. Despite being the most distinctive, this was not the only extreme rock face. All around, the pleasant woodlands and meadows with their broad, shallow rivers were interrupted by the arresting sight of monstrous grey walls rising high above the treetops. One of these enormous protrusions – called El Capitan – is the world's largest granite monolith.

As well as rock climbers and botanists, geomorphologists like me could be excused for their excitement in Yosemite. From the dramatic erosional landforms to superb examples of exfoliation – rock peeling off in layers like sunburnt skin – there were features everywhere to marvel over. The landscape was predominantly glacial in origin: the sheer cliffs were carved by glaciers which filled the valley 300,000 years ago, cutting down 2,000 feet into the rocks of the Sierra Nevada uplands. In some places, the ice literally froze onto and then tore off chunks of the rock faces, while in others the glaciers acted like sandpaper, smoothing and rounding boulders. Because the valley is so deep, rivers flow out of 'hanging valleys' higher up on its sides and tumble as waterfalls over the rock faces, falling hundreds if not thousands of feet. Yosemite Falls is a staggering 739 m high, the tallest in North America and the sixth highest in the world. The dramatic sight of these waterfalls was the most impressive aspect of Yosemite for us, even though we were there during the dry season. The chasms, the huge boulders strewn around, the sheer scale of the natural features – they all made me imagine the landscape to be a giants' playground. It made mere mortals like us feel puny and insignificant, and was a humbling but at the same time enriching and uplifting experience.

At the campsite office in Yosemite Valley we were told that all the low altitude campsites were full, but we could camp at the Craneflat campground, a thousand feet higher up, which we had driven past almost an hour before. The uniformed lady behind the desk warned us that it might be quite cold up there, and then handed us information leaflets about Yosemite's black bear population.

> We call it a bear problem, but the bears are not to blame... Driven by their powerful sense of smell, black bears are drawn by the odours of human food. Once bears get this food, they continue to seek it out – from backpacks, picnic tables, ice chests and cars.[1]

The leaflet also told us that once the bears became accustomed to this unnatural source of food, they couldn't get enough of it and could become aggressive and dangerous. Every year bears cause US $650,000 of property damage and some have to be killed, as an ultimate solution to stop them coming back for more. As a result, the law here was that all food must be stored in thick metal boxes which – unlike cars – were bear-proof. And not just food, but grocery bags, garbage and all scented items such as soap, sunscreen, hairspray and toothpaste.

When we were little my dad used to tell a joke about two men who went out for a walk in the woods and met a bear. One stopped and began to change his walking boots for running shoes. 'Why are you doing that?' his friend asked. 'You will never be able to outrun the bear.'

'I don't need to outrun the bear,' came the reply, 'I just need to be able to outrun you!'

This almost seemed preferable to the actions advised in our leaflet:

> Make loud noises. Throw small stones or sticks towards the bear. If there is more than one person, stand together to look more intimidating.

---

[1] *The Bears are not to Blame...* US Department of the Interior, National Park Service, April 1999

Great. Once we had attracted the attention of the bear and annoyed it by throwing sticks at it, and failed to intimidate it by our mere presence, maybe then we would start to change our shoes! The advice didn't exactly soothe our concerns about the 'bear problem'.

Once we had pitched our tent in the gathering darkness of the pine forest, I had the joy of being able to light a blazing campfire. This is something that would be frowned upon in the UK, where the skill and pleasure of outdoor campfires is surely being lost. Thanks to a Scouting childhood, I love open fires and relished the opportunity to toast our bagels in the curling flames. Fires are also comforting, with their heat and – hopefully – ability to scare away bears. It must have worked, as we didn't see or hear any sign of bears, although the idea of meeting them made going to the toilet in the middle of the night a more nervy experience. The main feature of the night was the cold temperature; we shivered in our thin one-season sleeping bags and ended up with Claudia wrapped in both, leaving me with nothing but my cotton liner for warmth. It always seemed to happen that way... In the morning the first thing we did was to drive into Yosemite village and buy a new three-season sleeping bag, which was to come in very handy at the Grand Canyon and, several months later, in Patagonia.

From Yosemite National Park we drove on to Death Valley, through stupendous country with sweeping vistas that were mind-boggling in scale and at times achingly dramatic. The culmination was arriving at the edge of Death Valley itself, looking down into the wide, flat-bottomed, featureless valley that cut a swathe through the barren, rocky landscape. Death Valley was named by a group of 1849 pioneers who wanted to reach California from Salt Lake City before winter set in, through a new route called the Old Spanish Trail. Looking for a short cut, about twenty wagons decided to cut across the Nevada Desert. They were saved from dying of thirst by a snowstorm, and finally arrived at springs within Death Valley on Christmas Eve. The valley itself didn't cause them severe problems, but they were trapped by the steep walls on either side. The group decided to abandon their wagons and belongings, killing their oxen for meat. They walked out, and as they left they christened the place Death Valley. Afterwards they crossed the Mojave Desert Plateau, where again they struggled to stay alive by drinking from a few icy puddles. Eventually Californian cowboys rescued the eighteen survivors – from an original group of thirty – and their story passed into legend.

Our timing on arrival was once again fortunate; the sun was setting behind us and the land was given a warm ochre tinge. We wound quickly down the side of the valley, into a world of whitish rock and sand, half covered by a thin layer of low green scrub. It wasn't particularly attractive and there wasn't really all that much to see, but the vast scale of the area and the sense of desolation gave us a sense of respect for the place. So we were incredulous to see a cyclist emerging from the haze, large black panniers weighing down his bike, about to crawl up the long ascent out of the valley. His effort and endurance were admirable, but surely this was an exercise in masochism! All there was for miles around was semi-desert. This was just the first of several times in the Americas that we were to come across cyclists in the most absurd places.

We camped beside a dry river channel right in the middle of Death Valley, below sea level. Badwater, within Death Valley, is the lowest point in the USA, at 86 m below sea level. Just over seventy miles away is Mount Whitney – the highest point in the contiguous USA. During summer, Death Valley is a natural oven, trapping heat like a furnace. In July it is commonly over 50°C; the highest temperature ever recorded in the USA – 56.7°C – was recorded here. That is only one degree less than the record for maximum temperature recorded anywhere in the world, which was set in Libya in 1936. We didn't need the sleeping bag here as it was sultry well into the night.

While I played with trying to light a fire from a handful of charred remains, Claudia got on with cooking our meal. Outdoor camp cooking is another pleasure of mine – on a proper wood fire, of course – and I agree with the old adage that food always tastes better out of doors. Even if it was only a one-pot meal of rice, baked beans, sweetcorn and broccoli. We did have the luxury of peppermint tea to savour as we sat beneath a sprawling pine tree with a fabulously starry sky overhead. The next morning, incidentally, our breakfast again consisted of bagels with cream cheese. We were in the USA, after all. Lunches were usually fajita wraps – we were close to Mexico – with cream cheese and we had taken to munching our way through bags of baby carrots whilst driving through Sierra Nevada. Such are the culinary joys of budget travelling.

We drove through the desert highway in Nevada at a steady 75 mph on almost entirely empty roads, with nothing to see but hills in the distance and the occasional sign for a school or a village hall in the middle of nowhere. Then we came to a road junction and saw in front of us an opera house. It would have been fitting if that was where the cyclist had been heading, we thought to ourselves. We would drive for hours with only cacti, fences, pylons and stones for company. It was desolate, but wonderfully so: incredibly wide expanses of nothingness between lines of rocky ranges that ran parallel to our roads.

We were headed for Zion National Park, for no particular reason other than that it was there and we had the time. It is one of a series of parks that are in close proximity to each other, collectively called Canyonlands. Were I to have only a couple of weeks again to tour anywhere in the world, I would come back here. Zion itself was a truly spectacular place. Arriving at the village of Springdale in the late afternoon, we headed for a motel. After three nights in a tent, we were desperate for a hot shower and a soft bed, but we happened to have chosen the weekend of the World Senior Games and there was no accommodation for twenty miles. Just as we were turning around to leave, discussing whether to drive on or try to find somewhere nearby to camp, the owner mentioned that she had a campsite too. With showers. And a laundry. And an ice-cold swimming pool with sunloungers and a power point where we could recharge our camera batteries... These little bonuses made a huge difference to our sense of well-being.

We were allowed to pitch beside the river, in one of the few tent sites. The rest of the 'campsite' was a trailer park for the huge white campervans and trailers that are such a feature of the USA outdoor experience. They looked like a dense collection of the kind of accommodation that a movie star might have on a film set. Our campsite host told us that it was common to see 30–40 ft trailers, but even he was surprised by one – the biggest he had ever seen – which he reckoned was over 50 ft long. As we sat eating our evening meal on a park bench beside our tent, on the bank of a silvery river, the setting sun turned a line of sandstone cliffs behind us a gorgeously deep, rich red colour. Camping did have its advantages, after all.

The following morning we set out to explore Zion National Park. At its heart was a deep canyon, essentially a twisting gorge with sheer cliff walls hundreds of feet high, among the highest sandstone cliffs in the world. At the centre of the canyon was a knife-edge ridge, encircled on three sides by a meander loop of the river and its red-and-white banded vertical valley walls. It was hard to believe that the distinctly risky path to the edge of the ridge – appropriately called Angels Landing – was full of people. Just as at Mount Washington, I had the impression that the visitors didn't have a sense of the potential danger or the need for reasonable precautions. We passed toddlers being encouraged along by their parents, prim girls in high heels and middle-aged women who suddenly found themselves out of their comfort zone, scared by the drops beneath them and clinging desperately to the rock face. Once, amusingly for us, we passed a pair of plump, slightly elderly, bespectacled ladies puffing their way up the path, fully kitted out in stout shoes, gaiters and walking poles. Their guide patiently waited for them at each corner, wearing only Bermuda shorts, a T-shirt and sandals. Where the path narrowed to the width of a single person, there were queues waiting for an opportunity to get by, adding to the potential for an accident. Any serious slip here could be nothing but fatal – but no one seemed to mind. The reward at the end was a magnificent panorama along the length of the canyon. This location was as extreme as any we encountered all year, perched right out in the middle of an already impressive gorge.

Back down beside the river there was no respite from the other tourists. Zion gets nearly 3 million visitors each year. I counted heads as we walked along and found that we were always in sight of at least thirty others, all on the one single path. This was too many for us. Considering that there were no cars allowed in the canyon, achieving this number of visitors was quite a feat in its own right. It was managed by the provision of an efficient free shuttle bus service. On one of our rides we found ourselves cooped up with an annoyingly effusive overweight middle-aged Texan, who forced the unfortunate passenger beside him – and everyone else – to listen to stories about his wife, daughter, house and job. Until we were driven off the bus, we heard him start one of the anecdotes all over again, like a broken record. He probably just travelled up and down all day, telling as many people as he could about himself. It was a reminder of why we preferred to get away from the crowds. But it says something for Zion that despite all the people, the dramatic splendour of Angels Landing still lingers in my mind. It was stunning, but it was only a prelude to the main show that was just around the corner.

Chapter 7: The Grand Canyon and Las Vegas

The Grand Canyon was by a considerable margin the most dramatic natural wonder that we encountered anywhere around the world. We approached it via the quieter North Rim – nearly 5 million people a year go to the South Rim – along a delightful forest ride of dark green pines speckled with the brilliant yellows of autumnal aspen leaves. At last I was seeing my fall colours! At the rim of the Canyon I would be treated to more beautiful reds and oranges, in a setting that surely rivalled that of New Hampshire.

After pitching our tent in the campsite perched on the top of the rim, at about 2,400 m in altitude and where it literally froze at night, we drove out to the Cape Royal viewpoint. It had long been a dream of mine to watch sunset over the Grand Canyon, and Cape Royal seemed the perfect place from which to do it. It was a fair drive away from our campsite, though, and Claudia wasn't feeling very well. However, I had insisted, and even bought a bottle of wine from the campsite shop for our return, which Claudia found quite strange. Off we drove, and found a lookout spot on a promontory that gave us astounding views across the entire width and down the length of the Canyon.

In total the Canyon is 277 miles long, varying from half a mile to eighteen miles wide, and can reach 1,829 m deep. We were looking across a width of ten miles and into depths of one vertical mile. One of the distinctive aspects of the Canyon was that it dropped downwards into the earth from an almost perfectly level plateau. Most other canyons that I have experienced are accessed from the bottom, perhaps with climbs possible up to the hills above. Here, the yawning chasm opened up beneath us as a vast rift in the earth's surface, exposing layers of rock that seemed to show 'what the earth is like underground', as Claudia aptly described it.

My dream was about to be realised. We sat on a bench looking out across the vast expanse, and as the sun was turning red I took an engagement ring out of my pocket and proposed to Claudia. After she gave a beaming 'yes', we watched the scarlet sun drop down as if right into the Canyon itself. Claudia says that it would have been even more romantic if I hadn't taken so many photos, but I thought it was pretty perfect. On our way back to the car we passed an unfortunate Chinese couple who had just arrived. They asked us whether they were too late for the sunset and we had to say that yes, they were. All they could do was turn around for the long drive home.

From the North Rim we were going to walk down to the very bottom of the Grand Canyon. We actually started our hike from a side canyon, an offshoot of the main feature, although we didn't realise that at first. At the top, somewhat frustratingly, trees obscured all the views right to the very edge, but perhaps that made the sudden sight of the canyon itself right at our feet even more startling. Nothing prepared us for the nature and scale of the vertical plunge of the sheer cliffs beside the path. It was impossible to see the bottom of them, even when peering over the very edge. The drop just went down, and down, and down, a dizzying sight. We had to walk downwards for about two and a half hours before we could see the sloping floor of our side canyon below us, and still further before we could make out the Bright Angel River, which flowed along the bottom.

The descent was steady and dusty, along a well-maintained, wide pathway, the character of which was defined by the geology of the rock layers of the canyon. At first the path was carved into a great notch cut into or even through the faces of precipitous red sandstone cliffs. It was simply fabulous to walk along. Beneath the sandstone came a grey limestone layer, and with it slightly more gently angled slopes that were covered in grassy vegetation. Rivers sprang out from between the layers in noisy cascades that thundered in the narrow confines of the gorge. One of these was Ribbon Falls, 3,000 feet below the Rim, with a single sheer cliff face above spanning that drop. At the bottom of the Bright Angel Canyon, a pink gritty sandstone took over and suddenly it was as if we had entered an oasis in the desert. There were bushes and grasses, the odd tree and even cacti dotted about. The desert came alive with bees, flies and yellow flowers. Striking black, white and yellow butterflies as large as my palm glided rather than fluttered through the air. We were walking in the shade of the afternoon, but when the sun is directly overhead it glares down and the canyon becomes an oven, trapping the heat inside.

During summer the temperatures reach 40°C – in the shade – and can be dangerous for unprepared hikers. At the rim there were copious warnings about taking plenty of water and not trying to walk down and back again in a day. Apparently, most of the rescues involve young men who think they are fit enough to ignore these messages. We were lucky that it was the end of the season, and so there were camping sites available for us within the Grand Canyon itself. There were no places left for the very bottom campsite, so we had to break our hike into three sections, staying two nights at a campsite halfway down. This turned out to be an even better option. To have come to this place and not stayed as long as possible to appreciate it would have been a great shame. A friendly ranger advised us that we wouldn't need a tent or a sleeping bag – using the sensible motto that the less one carries down, the less one needs to carry back up. Despite a chill wind that made us grateful that we had decided to bring along our sleeping bags, we managed fine. We spent our nights just lying on the ground, with the dark, silent shapes of the cliffs standing guard on either side of us as we gazed up at the most brilliant display of stars, shining so brightly out of a jet black sky. It was magical and somehow quite profound to be there, within the heart of the Grand Canyon itself. It was something very special, and we didn't want our eyes to close, but of course they eventually did.

Continuing down into the depths of the Canyon the next morning, the vegetation continued to change. The grass and cacti became rocky scrub and then the Canyon opened out into a wider space thick with sage-type bushes, lush reeds and an unknown but beautiful flower that had stems at least 4 m high. We saw lizards in abundance, more butterflies, bumblebees, fat ground squirrels, even a mouse and once a snake. From here, there were the best views of the Canyon, at least from inside it. Often it was just too hard to appreciate the scale of the cliffs above, especially as the nearer faces tended to obscure or appear to merge with the more distant tops. Only in one single spot could we see the white rims of both the North and South Rims at the same time – far away, behind and above the greys, browns and reds of closer cliffs.

Leaving the wider, open section, we dropped into a box canyon – a canyon-within-a-canyon – as the geology changed once more. Intrusions of granite appeared in blotchy veins that shot through the smoother sandstone, which gave way to a mix of metamorphic dark grey gneiss and large patches of red granite. The Canyon now had a fiery lustre, perfectly complementing the idea of being deeper and deeper within the bowels of the earth. The rocks were by now 1.7 billion years old. I could easily picture the granite as superheated veins of molten rock, squeezed by massive pressures until everything became the contorted, messy indistinguishable mass that we saw in the walls. The box canyon was itself deep, with walls perhaps 150 m high. As it was only a claustrophobic 30–50 m wide, we couldn't see the wider canyon above and so lost the sense of being within the Grand Canyon. Bizarrely, we encountered a fly-fisherman here, desperately casting back and forth into a pool between the white water rapids. Finally we emerged from the box canyon to meet the Colorado River, which was something of an anticlimax. It was a wider, smoother, greener river in its own larger box canyon that still cut out most of the overhead views. We had been warned previously that not much could be seen from the very bottom of the Grand Canyon, and that is indeed true.

Just before the Colorado River was a place called Phantom Ranch. This was a collection of stone-walled, green-roofed huts, which served as toilet blocks, sleeping huts, a ranger's house, a canteen and a games room. There was a pen for mules and a stable block, even a small amphitheatre made from wooden benches. Water pipes, phone lines and street lights passed through the little village. It was all set within a patch of lush green grass and cottonwood trees, which had been planted by one of the first inhabitants of the early twentieth century. Since those pioneer days there has been quite a bit of development. The last century of tourism has had a significant impact in a short space of time. It's not quite what President Roosevelt might have had in mind in 1903 when he said:

> The Grand Canyon fills me with awe. It is beyond comparison, beyond description, absolutely unparalleled throughout the wide world… Let this great wonder of nature remain as it now is. Do nothing to mar its grandeur, sublimity and loveliness. You cannot improve on it. But what you can do is to keep it for your children, your children's children, and all who come after you, as the one great sight which every American should see.

The change in our ability to access these remote places – from the Grand Canyon to Zion and Mount Washington – and the ease with which we do so is quite profound. Bar the odd cyclist, we now cross the Sierra Nevada deserts in air-conditioned 4WDs, looking out as if through an aquarium window. Increasing numbers of visitors come to see the wild, extreme places of our planet, but few stray very far from their cars. This may be wise, for perhaps we have never been less prepared to cope with the increasingly alien environment that is the natural world around us. Everywhere we went in the USA, we saw how 'progress' has sanitised encounters with nature, to the point where people could travel in virtually the same comfort as within their own homes. Yet, in doing so, I think we lose much of the very essence of what the natural world can give to us.

As if to exemplify the extremes of human existence, we were camped one morning at the bottom of the Grand Canyon, totally absorbed by natural splendour. By that evening we had checked into a hotel and casino in the heart of Las Vegas. There could hardly be a bigger contrast of experiences. Las Vegas first appeared as a large expanse of dusty buildings squatting together on a flat plain set between hills. We approached on a six-lane highway in the midst of a sudden glut of monster trucks and jeeps which appeared from nowhere. Petrol stations, hotel billboards and junctions between multiple highways began to swamp our brains. At the centre of Las Vegas, around which everything revolved, was 'The Strip', a carnival-like procession of glitzy hotels. Ours featured palm trees beside swimming pools, two towers of hotel rooms twenty storeys high, plus another 5,000 rooms directly adjacent to the ground-floor casino. And this was not a big one. The 'New York' hotel contained a roller coaster and replicas of such landmarks as the Statue of Liberty and the Empire State Building; 'Paris' had a monstrous blue hot-air balloon, the Eiffel Tower and an Arc de Triomphe; 'Cairo' had pyramids, an obelisk and the sphinx. By night these were all illuminated by thousands of coloured lights as they competed for attention.

For all the ostentatious displays on the outside, the inside of our hotel at least was far from glamorous. The ground floor was dominated by no less than 1,400 slot machines that flashed and beeped away next to one another under bright neon lights. People milled around the floor, as welcome in shorts and sandals or jeans and T-shirts as any other dress code. This wasn't quite my image of Las Vegas gambling. Indeed, there was something quite pitiful about the way men and women put coin after coin into the machines, pressing the same button mesmerically over and over, glazed eyes fixated on the spinning dials. At 5 a.m. – when we had to leave to catch our flight to Mexico – they were still doing exactly the same thing. In our hotel restaurant, we received a bill for our not-very-nice dinner that included a 10 per cent service charge and then left a space for an additional tip – which was repeated on the credit-card receipt. We thought that being made to pay once for the bad service was quite enough.

Las Vegas came across as a place that applied lots of make-up in a superficial effort to look attractive, with the frequent result that it ended up looking cheap. All the kitsch glitz could not gloss over the core function of the city: to sell gratuitous pleasures. There was something quite seedy about the gambling and the glossy nightly shows that mixed high quality entertainers with unashamed acts of 'partial nudity'. Men and women on the street on every corner were wearing brightly coloured sweatshirts that advertised strippers, as they handed out calling cards to everyone and anyone who walked past. The name 'Sin City' is quite apt, for it was as if the activities which are normally kept hidden in other cities are here the advertised, blatant, in-your-face attractions. The city being isolated in the middle of a desert only added to the sense of a world that was distanced from normal reality. Las Vegas is somehow a self-sustaining visitor attraction, a bit like a giant theme park, that survives by prostituting itself to the tourists who flock there in their millions to watch it in action. It is the third most popular destination in the USA. The people we saw on the streets were ordinary folk, just like us perhaps, there for a day or two to 'experience' the phenomenon and see what all the fuss is about.

Las Vegas was, however, one place where we were served with genuine personal interest – away from the centre, in a quiet local mall with a laundry and post office from where we could send our souvenirs home. It had been usual in the USA to be greeted with 'Howyadoing?' or 'How are you today?' but we quickly learnt that this was just a euphemism for 'Hello,' as our polite replies ended up being spoken to turned backs. Service was, usually, just a job, to be delivered with little sincerity.

There was a lot about the USA that seemed to function at a relatively superficial level, with appearance and convenience being more important than quality. The air conditioning, the big cars and the even bigger roads, the fast food, the television news, the camper vans – so much was about convenience and comfort. We had taken advantage of these things ourselves, of course, and had enjoyed our time in the USA in part precisely because they were available even in the middle of vast landscapes.

As we left our parcels with the kindly man in the Las Vegas post office, we began to think about what we might find in Mexico and Guatemala. Not such an easy ride, certainly. We anticipated far tougher travelling challenges than the Greyhound bus services when we arrived in Mexico City. In my mind at least, our holiday was over, and the real travelling was about to begin.

Part Two
Mexico, Guatemala and Belize

Chapter 8: Mexico City

Mexico City Airport was huge. So big, in fact, that we got lost within it, wandering backwards and forwards along the giant corridors in search of a way out to public transport. Eventually we pushed through several small doors, sneaked along narrow corridors as if we were trespassing in the airport's dark recesses, and popped out of a back door beside two cleaners on a fag break. In front of us was a little road, and there we found a taxi. Before long, however, we were back in the airport, because we had forgotten to collect our tent from the luggage carousel. As we wandered around yet more corners in search of our lost property, we came across a row of modern bus ticket offices, which allowed us to purchase onward tickets with welcome ease. We eventually found our tent and even managed to navigate our way to our little back door again, to brave another taxi driver.

Mexico City – somewhat confusingly just called 'Mexico' locally – did not look like we had expected it to. We knew that it was one of the largest and fastest growing cities in the world. In fact, with a population of 18 million and an area of nearly 2,000 square miles, only the metropolises of Tokyo and New York are bigger. As I had been teaching my students only a few months earlier, its growth had been fuelled by the migration of people from rural areas into the city, so I had images in my mind of large areas of poor shanty housing receding into the distance. But there were no dusty roads with cuboid, mud brick houses; no hillsides of rock and cacti overrun by threadbare shacks; not even any Mexican sombreros or ponchos – until we saw the costumed mounted police – and Mexico hardly looked like the pictures of my imagination at all. Instead, we saw green fields of maize and marigolds, modern roads and well-built red-brick houses. There were building works going on everywhere, from individual self-improvement schemes to large-scale brand-new housing estates. It looked like a developed and prospering country, with a real sense of growth and progress. Only in odd niches, such as beside the sweeping motorway or tucked away under bridges, did I catch glimpses of squatter shacks and more severe urban poverty. There were indeed houses – shanty towns – clustered on steep hillsides towards the outskirts, but they looked older and more solid than those I had previously seen on the outskirts of Lima. So it was a surprise to learn later that fully 46 per cent of the city's population were actually living in informal settlements.

We were perhaps even more surprised by the centre of Mexico City. Our heads were full of crime rates and pollution statistics – both among the world's worst – but what we actually found were pedestrianised streets lined with alfresco sandwich bars and cafés, shaded by the green foliage of young trees. Around were upmarket restaurants, hotels and designer shops. Plenty of well-dressed young couples and families were on parade, beside businessmen in suits. This was as chic, comfortable and safe as any modern capital city. At least, this very small area, centred on just two roads, was.

Most of the city had not yet developed to that level. It was common along roadsides to see walls painted an almost garish range of colours: ochre, yellow, blue and pink. Over virtually every surface were written advertising slogans or graffiti, in bold red and black letters. The impression was of an established system that was somehow spontaneous, improvised with a splash of colourful flamboyancy. In fact, most of Mexico City seemed to manage being both ordered and chaotic at the same time.

Near to the couple of classy streets was the heart of the city, a large public square called the Zocalo. In its centre was a tall flagpole with the biggest flag we had ever seen hanging from it. The horizontal green, white and red stripes showed it to be the Mexican national flag. People were sitting on the ground or strolling across the open space of the square. It was ringed by a wide road and then by imposing public buildings, which were mainly fairly austere angular blocks, their severe exteriors only softened by many arched windows.

The notable exception was the ornate seventeenth-century baroque cathedral that dominated the fourth side of the square. This is the largest cathedral in the western hemisphere. It was perhaps the pinnacle of Spanish colonial church architecture in the Americas. A grand facade containing a mixture of stone pillars, columns and swirling decorations sat between two square belltowers rising from the corners, each 64 m high. Around and about the cathedral, virtually blocking its entrance, were a motley array of street vendors. They spread their hairbrushes and clothing out on rugs on the floor, nestled between stands of newspaper or magazine sellers. Mobile trolleys were like little canteens, cooking grilled maize cobs or other simple food. It was colourful and crowded, but in a pleasant way.

Sometimes the sights and sounds were eccentric, almost bizarre. Right outside the cathedral gates we saw a tall Batman, dressed in full black plastic costume, posing for photos with children. Beside the metal railings sat lines of men on little stools with a bag of tools at their feet and a piece of paper or cardboard that had their trade painted on. They were plumbers, painters and carpenters, unemployed and hoping that someone passing by would give them a job. On the nearby corner a man with a megaphone was loudly advertising the existence of a nearby public toilet. In the square we saw native Indians with huge feather headdresses, wearing elaborate green or red skirts. They were selling shamanistic artefacts, telling fortunes and filling the air with the smoke and smell of incense. If there were prizes for innovative ways to earn a living, the people of Mexico would quite probably take the top honours.

Around the Zocalo the streets seemed to swing from one extreme to the other. Some displayed splendidly grand colonial buildings, statues and monuments, often set beside lush green parks. These areas could compete with places in European capitals for relaxed charm and sheer architectural beauty. They were being patrolled by sombrero- and poncho-clad policemen on white horses. We trailed two of these mounted policemen along the paths for a while, hoping for a picture of them, until they caught sight of us, turned and came directly towards us. They stopped with their horses blocking our path, giving us a sense of their intimidating power. We didn't know what to do, until they indicated to us that we should take their photograph while they posed.

By contrast, the nearby side streets were filled with the crowded chaos of daily life. At times we thought that there must be impromptu festivals going on in the streets, but it was always just the vibrant noise and colour of everyday life. Lines of makeshift market stalls crowded the broken pavements with stacked piles of CDs and DVDs, watches and jewellery. Alarm clocks perpetually rang, music blared, mini-TVs showed films and traders called out, *'Cince pesos por dos!'* all day. Taxis jolted their way past semi-permanent food stalls erected in the roads. Men in pinstripe suites and ties stopped to grab a burrito or plate of tacos. Rubbish was collecting on corners between broken fences and rusting bicycles. Here it wasn't so clean or pretty, but there was plenty of character and charm to compensate.

We found Mexico City to be very appealing. It was unpretentious, easy to explore, and full of engaging attractions – at least in the centre. We did notice that the locals were often carrying their bags clutched close to their chests, as if they feared thefts. There must have been a good reason for this – we heard of a girl whose bag had been sliced open with a knife in Mexico City – but the only losses we suffered were at the hands of the taxi drivers.

The thousands of taxis were another part of Mexico City's character. The green minis and red-and-white sedans careered through the city, cheerfully getting in the way of each other and the glossy modern cars that competed for space with double-decker buses and hand-pulled carts. There was a lot of traffic on the streets – 6 million cars, actually. The taxi drivers we met were friendly, wanting to engage in conversations that inevitably returned to the same theme: 'Michael Owen' or 'Liverpool'. However friendly, though, we learned not to expect honesty or fair play from them. It took a little while before getting into the swing of the game of con tricks. The first rule was to insist on using the meter, as any randomly quoted price would be exorbitant. Even once the meter had been switched on, at the end of the trip it might suddenly – with a press of a button – 'not work' and the correct fare would be unfortunately lost, only to be replaced by a higher one. Even once the price had been determined, more or less satisfactorily, it could happen that the drivers returned incorrect change, accidentally of course. Their whole manner seemed to be designed to lull us into a false sense of security and then to attempt the various swindles so fast that we were caught on the hop and failed to challenge our new friends. Which worked quite well the first couple of times, it has to be admitted.

Learning from experience, we resorted to using the metro to get around. This had the advantages of being both first class and extremely economical. It cost two pesos (US $0.05) for each entry but there was no limit to the distance we could travel each time. The trains were frequent and fast, everything was clean and well signposted. Best of all were the stations, which used their corridors for high quality educational or graphical displays. It was like walking through a science or art museum. We saw scale models of the city and its historical sites, astronomy displays on the ceiling of a darkened tunnel, photographs of natural wonders, tips on how to save energy – it was all an excellent showcase of public information.

Slightly less professional, but with just as much character, were the hawkers who stationed themselves in every carriage, racing between train doors at each station. They would blast out music from a selection of CDs, sell boxes of chewing gum, or hand out and collect in again written requests for donations. It was all very politely done, and received in kind by the general public. I had the definite impression that people were proud that their city retained such characters with their quirky individuality.

Mexico City could also be bewildering, which of course was part of the fun. Much of our time was taken up trying to complete 'projects'. One was looking for a supermarket in the streets around the Zocalo. There were a couple, but finding them felt like being on a wild goose chase, as we wandered backwards and forwards down every street except the correct ones. We did, however, pass lots of shops selling perfumes, gold jewellery, music equipment and computers. In one of these shops we found a new digital camera, my old one having quickly succumbed to the rigours of travel. It was refreshingly typical of Mexico City that the salesmen in the shop invited us to climb a ropey wooden ladder above their counter, through a hatchway and into a little loft space in order to have a look at their computer. The camera served us well, but we didn't find a supermarket until our hostel receptionist gave us a map with a big cross marked on it.

The next day we had to look for somewhere to copy our precious photograph CDs, so that one set could be posted home. This was our routine insurance policy, not fully trusting either postal services in various countries around the world or our ability to avoid having our bags stolen. We started out at 11 a.m. and found that the one Internet café we knew about was closed. After walking around looking in vain for another, we returned to find that it had opened but its single CD-writer was broken. However, the owner told us about another tiny little computer shop, which was only too pleased to take our CDs. Fifteen minutes, he said, so we set off to find an envelope.

The one stationery shop we saw could only offer us plastic CD covers, which was not what we wanted at all. We had to walk some distance to the post office to find our envelopes; not that the post office actually sold them, of course. We asked a man in a queue who was holding a padded envelope where he had bought it from. The answer was outside, from an informal stall beside a door, where an enterprising lady was selling exactly what we – and lots of other people, presumably – needed. It appeared to us a slightly odd system but, on reflection, it was perfectly practical – once we had discovered how it worked.

Back at the computer shop again, our photographs had been copied onto a computer but not yet onto more CDs. So we took the four originals, packaged them up in the padded envelope and returned to the post office, where the lady at the counter informed us that we were only allowed to post three CDs at a time. Of course. How silly of us not to have realised that such a rule would exist! We didn't want to risk ignoring it and having our CDs end up in a bin, so we started again.

When all had eventually been posted we went back to the computer shop for the third time, only for the guy to ask us for the original CDs back again – he couldn't find our photos on his computer. We didn't know whether to laugh or cry. But the guy set to with a furrowed brow while we waited, which we should have done all along, and finally we had the precious CDs in our hands. Flushed with success, we thought we would go back to the original Internet café and post a few photographs on our photo-website for friends and family back home to look at. The Internet was working, on one computer, but unfortunately not the one that had the software to show us our photographs… Such is the way of things. We gave up: it was 6.15 p.m. and we were hungry and thirsty. It was hard to believe just how convoluted and time-consuming such 'projects' could be, but we learned to be reconciled to them, no longer assuming that anything could be quickly or easily done. In Central America particularly, everything was usually possible, but it was rarely either straight-forward or fast.

Chapter 9: Tenochtitlan and Teotihuacan

Mexico City has surely one of the most extraordinary histories of any city in the world. The modern colonial city was built exactly over the ruins of the Aztec capital, which was destroyed by Hernan Cortes in the sixteenth century. Mexico City is tropical in latitude, but high enough at over 2,000 m to have a temperate climate. It lies in a valley surrounded by 5,000 m high volcanoes, which have wonderful names like Popocatepetl and Ixtaccihuatl. In the late thirteenth century a small tribe called the Mexica – known today as the Aztecs – moved into the valley from drier northern regions. They had to settle for the poor location of swampy islands on a lake to build their home city. They were successful fighters, acting as mercenaries for – and then allies of – the dominant local force which was based in a town nearby on the lake shore. In the late 1420s the Mexica turned on their allies, with the help of a rival force, and gained a shared control of the valley. Thus began the Aztec empire, centred on their capital city of Tenochtitlan.

That city was built partly on the lake itself, with giant causeways and floating gardens full of flowers, vegetables and fruit. White stone houses were lined on the inside with coloured cotton. By the sixteenth century it is believed to have been the fourth largest city in the world, behind only Paris, Venice and Constantinople. In 1520 Hernan Cortes wrote to the Spanish Emperor that 'these people live almost like those in Spain, and in as much harmony and order as there… it is truly remarkable to see what they have achieved in all things'. Cortes also said of the Emperor's palace, 'His residence within the city was so marvellous for its beauty and vastness that it seems to me almost impossible to describe it… there it nothing like it in Spain.'

The Aztecs were expert goldsmiths; they used a pictographic system of writing; they loved dressing up with the colourful plumes of tropical bird feathers and flowers; they used a precise astronomical calendar; and they drank thick, cold *chocolatl*, flavoured with vanilla. They were also very warlike, conquering virtually all of central and southern Mexico. Their influence even extended as far south as present day Nicaragua. Neighbouring peoples were forced to submit to the authority of the Mexicas, who operated a strict tribute system in order to maintain their riches and their armies. During wars, they aimed to capture enemies alive, so that they could be used for human sacrifice.

The principal god of the Aztecs was the hummingbird, but they also worshipped the sun, which had to fight the stars every day in order to cross the sky. The sun therefore needed energy, or life in the form of human sacrifices. The Aztecs took ritual human sacrifice to probably its most extreme form in human history. For one of these ceremonies, according to Prescott's nineteenth-century account, a healthy young man would be selected a year beforehand and then spend the remainder of his life being indulged with all the luxurious living that the Aztecs had to offer. Come the day of sacrifice, however,

> ...he was stripped of his gaudy apparel and bade adieu to the fair partners of his revelries... He was received by six priests... They led him to the sacrificial stone, a huge block of jasper... On this the prisoner was stretched. Five priests secured his head and his limbs; while the sixth, clad in a scarlet mantle... dexterously opened the breast of the wretched victim... and inserting his hand into the wound, tore out the palpitating heart.[2]

After sacrifices, the warrior who had captured the victim in battle could serve the body up in a sumptuous banquet for his friends. In 1487, during the dedication of their main pyramid, prisoners who had been kept for years just for this occasion formed a procession two miles long, and over the next several days anything between 20,000 and 70,000 people were sacrificed. The skulls of victims were kept in special buildings: when the Spanish arrived in Tenochtitlan they claimed to have counted 136,000 in just one of these places.

Temples and sacrificial altars were built on the top of large pyramids, made from earth but encased in stone or brick. The main pyramid of Tenochtitlan was 60 m high. Each pyramid had four or five stepped layers, each smaller than the one below. Flights of steps would go up the side of the first layer, around a gallery to the next staircase, and so on in a circuitous fashion to the top. On the top were stone towers forty or fifty feet high, the sacrificial altar, and two fires that were kept constantly burning. Within the great temple there were 600 of these fires, brightly illuminating the night sky.

The Aztec civilisation was brought to an abrupt end in 1519 by Hernan Cortes and his band of 110 sailors, 553 soldiers, and a couple of hundred Caribbean people. There were thirty-two crossbowmen, ten heavy guns and four lighter ones, and sixteen horses. With this army he terrified and awed the natives of the Yucatan coast and founded the city of Vera Cruz. As related by Prescott, the story of the Mexican conquistadors reads like a fantastic *Boy's Own* novel, full of daring adventures in the face of overwhelming odds. In an early act that courageously committed all the Spaniards to 'do or die' – literally – Cortes destroyed his fleet of ships and then began to march inland. Somehow the conquistadors survived the full-on attacks of perhaps 50,000 Tlascalan

---

[2] Prescott, W, *History of the Conquest of Mexico*, London, George Allen & Unwin Ltd., 1925, p.37

warriors, eventually making them his crucial allies against the Aztecs.

Cortes was reluctantly welcomed as a guest into Tenochtitlan by the Aztec Emperor, Montezuma. As protection against attack, Cortes took Montezuma hostage, but even so eventually the Spaniards had to fight their way out of the city again. They regrouped, and with the help of an ever-increasing number of allies returned for a final showdown. Cortes besieged the city and then reluctantly resorted to razing it to the ground, house by house, as its trapped population suffered starvation and the ravages of smallpox. Tenochtitlan surrendered on 13 August 1521. Unfortunately, any remains of the fantastic buildings of the Aztec capital have long since disappeared underneath more modern constructions; Cortes was keen to rebuild the city in lavish style. The colonial cathedral stands exactly on the site of the original great pyramid. To one side today lie the ruins of seven more temples that were uncovered in 1978.

With the main Aztec buildings having all but completely vanished, the next best sight in present day Mexico was one which predated the Aztecs. It is the most popular visitor attraction in Mexico, still able to awe and impress the modern traveller. The city of Teotihuacan was built in around 200 BC as a planned city, reaching its height in AD 200–400. The city probably covered an area of over twenty square miles and had a population of around 200,000 people, making it one of the largest cities in the world of its time. It ruled over Central America, influencing the contemporary Mayan civilisations as far away as Honduras. The city was – and its ruins still are – centred on a giant avenue that was once four kilometres long. At the far end of this main avenue are two giant stepped pyramids, one dedicated to the Sun and the other to the Moon.

The Teotihuacan pyramids have much the same form as the Aztec pyramids described above, with tiered layers that make them look like a collapsed wedding cake. There is a third pyramid at the other end of the Avenue of the Dead, built later in AD 200, which only has four of its original seven stepped layers remaining, and of course no trace of the giant temple on its top. When work on this pyramid began, 260 men and women were sacrificed with their hands tied behind their backs. By the seventh century the city had suddenly fallen into decline, perhaps due to invasion or burning. The Aztecs knew it as a ruined site, which is probably why the Spanish left it relatively intact. The Aztecs considered Teotihuacan to be holy and named it 'place of the road of the gods', also giving the pyramids and the avenue their names.

We visited Teotihuacan on a sunny Sunday morning, along with the rest of Mexico City, their wives and their children. Thankfully, it was an extremely well-managed tourist site, able to cope with such large numbers of visitors. At first we had the impression of a large, flat grassy site that was surrounded by trees and fringed by dark green hills some way off. Rising several times higher than the treetops were the three angular stone pyramids, but from ground level it was almost impossible to get a sense of their scale. In the foreground were regular lines of low grey stone walls perfectly constructed from flush square blocks. It was hard to think that these blocks were not machine-cut, so exact were their fits. The walls lined a broad, grassy avenue that was broken up into stepped sections, making us and all the other visitors walk up and down through a series of higher and lower rectangular lawns. Everything was in order, straight and level. The avenue looked a bit like a shallow dry canal, because it appeared sunken beneath rows of stone pyramid bases that lined it, all sitting on the top of a stone wall running along its edge. The pyramid bases might have once been administrative or religious buildings. Now, though, they were topped by green grass.

We continued along the main avenue under a hot sun, getting a bit tired of the repeated ups and downs of the steep stepped walls. These must surely have tired the original inhabitants too. Today's visitors looked like a gaily coloured swarm of insects – red and white dots crawling all over the site, in thin lines going here and there, following trails just as ants do. Amongst the hordes of tourists were hawkers trying to sell statues, cloths, bows and arrows and little tortoise-shaped whistles. Very annoying little tortoise-shaped whistles. They continually shrilled with a thin but irritatingly piercing sound as the hawkers tried out various tunes to attract attention, and small children blew inanely through their new toys – until their parents bought them a new toy to shut them up. This was usually a plastic bow and arrows set, which I didn't think was an entirely sensible idea either.

The Pyramid of the Sun stands slightly to one side of the avenue. It is the third largest pyramid in the world, being 64 m high and 225 m wide at its base. Only the Great Pyramid of Giza in Egypt and the Great Pyramid of Cholula are larger. Actually, the one at Cholula – also in Mexico, dating from the second century BC – is the largest monument ever built on Earth, being 450 m wide at the base and 66 m high. The Pyramid of the Sun is colossal and yet its size was strangely hard to grasp, possibly because there was nothing around to compare it to or judge it against except the equally alien Pyramid of the Moon nearby. There was no doubt, however, that it was a long and steep climb to the top, from where the people below looked small and the city large. Only from here did we begin to get a sense of just how impressive the city was and still is, even today in its semi-ruined condition. Two thousand years ago it must have been truly awesome, when the pyramids were finished with a smooth coat of lime and red paint, and topped with richly decorated temples. Today the two lines of pyramid bases that flank the avenue in perfect formation, with their ramps facing inwards towards each other, look as if they could have been left by visitors from outer space, and behind them could be sitting the two vast brooding hulks of their mother ships. The site was immaculately clean, the pyramids were in regular order, and there was nothing between the stone monuments other than green space and tiny tourists. The view of the city spread out below our eyes from the Pyramid of the Moon is one of the great man-made sights from the ancient world. It holds its own alongside both the Egyptian pyramids at Giza and – as we would later discover – the Mayan jungle pyramids in Guatemala.

Chapter 10: Oaxaca and San Cristobal de las Casas

The southern Mexico city of Oaxaca was founded in 1521 by the Spanish, over the site of a previous indigenous settlement. The conquistadores and later colonisers built many beautiful cities, but Oaxaca is one of the best preserved, making it a UNESCO World Heritage Site. It was rated in our guide book as one of the top sights in Mexico and was conveniently en route to Guatemala, so we took a six-hour bus journey there from Mexico City. Although the present buildings of Oaxaca are colonial, in the surrounding countryside there are ruins of pre-Spanish religious and ceremonial buildings. At one of these, the uncompromising approach of the Spaniards seemed to be perfectly illustrated.

A red-domed Catholic church had been built right on top of the base of one of the native temples, using stones that had been taken from an adjacent temple. There could have been no doubting the Catholic Church's intentions; their buildings, statues and carvings all shout out an imposition of authority. Mexicans still say that they were conquered 'by the sword and the cross'. Near Oaxaca was what is claimed to be the world's widest tree, a mere 2,000 years old. It used to live in a swamp but the land dried out and now the tree has to be kept alive by being watered with hoses. Around its base it measures 42 m, with a trunk that looks like it is made of many smaller trunks all fused together. Fat branches sprout from the top of each stump, only reaching 40 m high. The tree was sacred to the native Indians, so we were not surprised to see that there was a Catholic church right alongside it, appropriating the place for that religion instead. Later on, in Peru, we would see another locally revered tree that had a picture of the Virgin Mary nailed into it. The messages of usurpation were hardly subtle.

Between Mexico City and Oaxaca the landscape was a feast for the eyes. Leaving Mexico City we looked across pleasant fields to cloud-shrouded volcanic peaks. The road wound upwards through pine trees into peculiar cacti forests. The cacti were either tall and thin, like green worms sticking out of the ground, or squat and fat with branching candelabra shapes. Then the hill slopes became steeper and the views more impressive, with Mediterranean-style rocky scrub scenery, as we climbed still higher. The road passed through cuttings that seemed to be continually collapsing, so there were road crews shovelling the landslides away at frequent intervals. At one point, in the middle of nowhere, we passed several stalls beside the road, each under a separate canopy for shade. Bizarrely, they were each selling red plastic toy trucks. Every stall had exactly the same stock displayed optimistically on the tarmac, but we didn't see any drivers stop their cars to buy.

Oaxaca itself was a pretty little town, impeccably clean, with a relaxed, laid-back atmosphere. It had many quiet, wide, cobbled streets that passed between brightly painted one- or two-storey terraced buildings. The first hostel we stumbled upon cost more than our budget allowed, but we were in need of a little comfort, the place was attractive, and we just didn't want to walk on any further. The pretty house was typical in that it was built around a square courtyard, its first-floor rooms opening out onto graceful internal balconies. The decor was a bright, modernist take on ancient designs: white stylised steps and swirls were set within bands of terracotta and yellow, all trimmed with bright blue. With trees and bushes filling the courtyard with a profusion of green, and numerous parrots in cages hanging from the branches, it was as if we had stepped into a tropical paradise.

Towards the centre of town were much larger colonial buildings. These were made from whitish blocks of stone with tall archways and gaping interiors. They were functional and graceful at the same time, both imposing and pretty. The cathedral had two square bell towers either side of a splendidly ornamented facade, just like in Mexico City. I have often wondered what English cathedrals would have looked like if the icons of their outer walls had been preserved – and here perhaps was my answer. Everything was complete, with carved statues set in alcoves that were decorated with columns and borders. All around the city were numerous other churches, all artistically sculptured. The incredible Church of Santa Domingo was decorated inside with a huge amount of gold leaf, on walls, columns, archways, domes, the ceiling – everywhere. The wealth on display was staggering. Oaxaca combined a rich mix of influences, producing a city that was undeniably pretty but also creating a slightly schizophrenic atmosphere. The conversion of Spanish houses into modern restaurants and hotels, run by Mexicans for foreigners, was all slightly incongruent.

One of the attractions of the area was the local food. Personally, I wasn't convinced by the flat oatmeal tortillas spread with a black paste and topped with stringy cheese. In the local indoor markets these were very popular items – local specialities – and the jars of black paste were sat beside other pastes, coloured green or red. They looked like a child's experimental mixing of food colouring with thick smooth mud, but actually they were cocoa-based. However unappetising, they still appealed more than the bowls of tiny red grasshoppers or maggot-like worms. Beside these temptations, the markets contained a colourful, crowded array of fruit, meats, clothing, tropical fish and fast-food stalls.

When we set out for a meal in a quiet part of town, it was difficult to communicate the idea that we wanted a meal without meat. Vegetarianism was not exactly common here. We thought we had achieved success when the owner tried to clarify our request. 'You don't want to eat meat?' he said. Exactly. 'So what about chicken?'

Whilst in Oaxaca we heard that the southern coastal route into Guatemala was closed as a result of Hurricane Stan crossing the central American isthmus, bringing with it rainstorms that caused flooding and mudslides. All bridges in the border town of Tapachula were smashed and the countless people whose homes had been destroyed by swollen rivers were facing shortages of food and water. Just over the border in Guatemala, mudslides had buried more than 130 people. We were beginning to appreciate the significance of living in areas where tropical storms can hit. These natural disasters cannot be prevented or diverted – they are forces beyond human control. The only thing that can be done is to take measures to reduce the impact and hope that they will have an effect. Just after Hurricane Stan came Hurricane Wilma, the largest for 150 years, and with record wind speeds. It was less severe by the time it hit the Mexican coast near Cancun, but nevertheless four towns declared states of emergency, and Wilma was to become the second costliest natural disaster in Mexican history.

So instead of heading to Guatemala along the Pacific Coast as we had intended, we decided to take a bus to San Cristobal de las Casas, another inland colonial town that was close to the Guatemalan border. The bus system in Mexico was superb, second only to that of Chile. Even for journeys that took twenty hours, there would be three buses travelling the route each day. At one point during a journey through the Mexican countryside, I counted the buses passing on the opposite carriageway. The road wasn't too busy, perhaps because it was morning, but after several hundred vehicles there was a consistent ratio of one bus for every four cars. That really is quite astonishing. In the capital, the bus station was a huge circular terminal next to the metro, with offices and food stalls radiating out from the hollow centre. It was large, but easy to navigate, modern and efficient – quite different to some of the bus stations in the USA. There was even a weight and security check for our baggage, which was securely tagged. In Oaxaca it got better, courtesy of our expensive first-class ticket: we had a waiting room with a security guard and a complimentary drink on the bus.

However exemplary the service, though, travelling by night on a bus was rarely very comfortable. We needed sleeping bags to keep out the chill of the air conditioning, travel cushions for seats with low backs, and eye masks to block out the dubbed films that were truly awful but irresistible to the eyes. Of course, looking at a fixed screen only made motion sickness from a rolling, swaying bus even worse. The films played until late into the night and it was hard to imagine anything more sleep-deterring than their noise and flickering light.

The journey to San Cristobal de las Casas was one of the worst bus trips we ever made. The morning dawned as we were winding along the sides of steeply incised valleys, with a cloud inversion far below. Square houses with terracotta roof tiles dotted the landscape, and small fields of maize and vineyards clung to the steep slopes. In between grew ragged clumps of trees. It may have been pretty, but all we wanted was for the ghastly journey to finish so that we could get out of the bus! Eventually we did drive into town – we had made it, just. Or so I thought. I made the mistake of packing away the sleeping bag before we reached the station, so taking my eyes off the road. This was the last straw for my poor stomach and it gave up trying to keep down its contents, a full ten seconds before parking. Wonderful.

In fact, the road just out of San Cristobal might well be the world's worst road for travel sickness. We drove along it twice more, in and out of the town, and both times we had to hang on grimly as we swung around corners that flowed smoothly from one into the next, rolling up and down as well as from side to side. Poor Claudia ate almonds in an effort to stop herself from being sick, focused on chewing each nut up to seventy times rather than thinking about the road. It was no bad thing for us that the last journey was broken up by the back wheel of our minibus coming half off. Sparks were flying and the tyre was actually alight, the flames visible outside my window as well as licking underneath the chassis, before the driver decided to stop. The sight of wrecked vehicles halfway down the steep slope below the road was at that point too close for comfort. Sometimes it seemed like we were just a hair's breadth from becoming caught up in the disasters that were all too prevalent, whether natural or man-made. Without regulated safety standards, 'normal' life often seemed to involve considerable risks – which of course made travelling more exciting, and gave us stories to tell. The thought of having to face this game of chance every day was a less pleasant one.

San Cristobal is in the Chiapas region of Mexico, which was the poorest in the country. It was home to the Zapatista movement, which called for rural reforms, for example to the pattern of land ownership. People still work the land of rich owners, who are given tributes of food in a Spanish-imported medieval system. Only once did I see a sign of the Zapatistas' existence, apart from the large army base just outside San Cristobal. On the side of a bus stop was a vivid mural of a masked man holding a gun, with a woman and child by his side. It looked very much like an IRA mural, but over the top was the slogan, *'Terreno y Libertad'* – 'Land and Liberty' – the words of the uprising. As we drove through the countryside we passed roadside villages where people lived in a mixture of small, rustic concrete or wooden buildings, usually with characteristic terracotta roof tiles. The houses opened onto rough earth yards where usually a pig or chicken pottered around, often with a young toddler for company. It was evident that life here was basic, with few home comforts.

Perhaps because it was relatively undeveloped, the area around San Cristobal retained a significant amount of indigenous culture. This was partly what made it popular with tourists. Men and women came into town from the surrounding villages in traditional – or sometimes makeshift – clothes. The women's dress was usually more attractive. They wore thick black skirts that looked like woolly rugs wrapped around their legs, tied around the waist with a thick red band of cloth. Above the skirt were blouses that were usually a glossy blue or purple colour, prettily embroidered all over with fine thread. On top, another blanket was wrapped around the head.

Old men had intensely weathered faces and were bent over at the waist, signs of a lifetime of hard country work. Their bags were carried in a traditional manner, down their back with a strap taking the weight around their foreheads. They even carried modern sports bags this way, the fashionable shoulder strap turned into a head band. They wore heavy overcoats and thick baggy trousers that half hid great black boots. Some men were draped in the thick woolly material, white or black, by means of a length of cloth with a hole cut out in the middle for the head, the rest passing over the body from front to back and tied around the middle. One costume worn by a man even looked just like a Greek toga: nothing more than a white cotton robe that came down to his knees.

San Cristobal de las Casas was named after both its patron saint and perhaps the greatest humanitarian of the Spanish conquest era. Bartolomé de las Casas was a Dominican friar who petitioned the Spanish monarchy to recognise the rightful liberty of the native Americans in the early sixteenth century. Much debate occurred amongst the Spanish as to whether the Indians of central America were 'natural slaves' who would benefit from serving the superior Spaniards; undeveloped, childlike people who were capable of being educated; or fully rational humans who should be essentially free citizens. While the Spanish argued, the indigenous population of central Mexico fell by over 85 per cent in the first one hundred years following their conquest.

San Cristobal de las Casas had a pleasantly sleepy provincial atmosphere. From various hills around the town we could look out over a pretty sprawl of terracotta rooftops, interrupted by numerous bell towers. Between the low houses painted in different colours were attractive narrow lanes. The main square was framed by colonnaded buildings and a cathedral, all less imposing here than in previous towns but making up for their smaller size with brighter colours. The cathedral was painted a lurid yellow and its statues, arches and columns were decorated red and white. To one side of it was the last church in Mexico to have an indigenous style without later architectural alterations, the inside of which looked like a plain Methodist chapel with just one display of gold behind the altar.

Outside another intensely decorated Church of Santo Domingo we found market stalls selling brightly striped traditional rugs, shawls, leather bags and other handicrafts. In the centre of town were wider streets with open air café tables and music escaping from nearby shops that discreetly occupied old buildings, without gaudy advertising. We found it easy to stroll around the streets, taking our time and soaking up the atmosphere of the various local sights. Nothing was outstanding but everything was cosy and friendly.

San Cristobal was also where we encountered real poverty for the first time on our trip. It was literally thrust into our face, as barefoot children and stooped, wrinkled old ladies tried to sell trinkets to us or simply begged on the streets. An area of shanty housing on the edge of town showed shacks made from bits of wood, corrugated metal and sheets of plastic blowing in the wind. We couldn't fail to see the suffering that accompanies real poverty. It was hard to come to terms with, particularly as we could also see well-off, smartly dressed, mobile-phone-carrying locals. The majority of people in town wore trendy clothes and modern accessories – often a wide-brimmed cowboy hat – and even drove large shiny silver cars. There was a fairly widespread level of affluence here that was surprising, mingling easily with the rural poor. One of the features of San Cristobal was how welcoming and tolerant everyone was of one another. Their inequality, however, was stark. We could be thankful that we had been born in rich countries, with no fear of hunger or thirst, but it didn't feel as if we had earned or deserved our fate any more than the children of San Cristobal had deserved theirs. There was no fairness about poverty: it was a lottery, where some children simply found themselves born in the wrong place at the wrong time.

Encouraged by our hostel owners, we took a trip to see the nearby feature of a deep canyon. We travelled with a guide in a speedboat through the first part of it, between sheer walls high enough for clouds to form halfway up, rising 450 m either side of us. Our guide claimed that further on the drop reached 1,000 m. Vultures wheeled beneath the clouds, looking like tiny black specks far above us. We glided along the muddy brown water of a river that was wide but somehow at the same time very small compared to the cliffs on either side. It was both imposing and beautiful; we wouldn't see a place like this again until we reached the Tiger Leaping Gorge in China.

We stopped to watch small vultures on the banks, cormorants perched in trees, white egrets and herons, and alligators. There were some 250 alligators in the canyon, some up to 5 m in length. The ones we saw were at most 3 m long and so not too intimidating. They lay in the shallows within reed beds, poking their noses and sometimes their jaws out of the water. Unfortunately, we didn't get to see the pumas or the jaguars, or the spider monkeys. Hurricane Wilma was giving us a day of low cloud and rain, not much good for spotting wildlife.

The previous rains from Hurricane Stan had caused so much debris – trees and rubbish – to come down the river that our way ahead was blocked by rapids. Speedboats plied back and forth, ferrying logs from the blocked area to a beach where a very large quantity was being piled up, waiting for lorries to transport the timber away. Despite the volume that had already been taken away and the intense amount of activity, our guide estimated it would take another ten days before the river was cleared. It gave a sense of scale to Stan's destruction, of which we would see more in Guatemala in a few days' time.

Mexico had been much easier to travel through than we had anticipated, largely because its infrastructure – and tourist industry – was so well developed. It was, however, proving more expensive than we could sustain. The long bus journeys in particular were eating into our budget. We had always planned to spend more than our monthly budget in the USA, which we had duly done, but we also hoped to recoup that deficit in central and southern America. Instead, we were only going deeper into the red, spending US $1800 per month between us instead of US $1500. So we decided to cut our losses and head for Guatemala, where we were looking forward to experiencing colourful, friendly indigenous cultures as yet unspoiled by tourism. Expectations can have a great effect on subsequent judgements: they allowed Mexico to provide many pleasant surprises, but they were to work in the opposite direction for our impressions of Guatemala.

Chapter 11: Into Guatemala

Before we reached the Guatemalan border we had to cross a range of forested hills, from where we could see several similarly green volcanic cones not far away. It was a world of apparently uninhabited valleys and ravines, and I felt as if we were traversing a hidden, unexplored jungle, leaving civilisation far behind. Passing through this remote landscape, moving from one country into another, gave us a sense of travel and anticipation. Vultures circled high overhead as if waiting for something unpleasant to happen – but nothing did. In fact, the border came soon after the hills, on a flat plain that was home to several settlements. But at the border we knew that we had entered another country as soon as we ducked underneath the customs barriers. The change of character between Mexico and Guatemala was very marked. Coming from a smooth, clean, open tarmac road, we found ourselves on a dusty lane that was filled with market stalls piled high with wares of anything from modern airline suitcases to Thermos flasks and Tupperware pots. It was like a bazaar, with three-wheeled scooters weaving in and out of the crowd of pedestrians. We were accosted by money changers and bus touts, all clamouring for our custom. It was noisy, confusing and distinctly rough around the edges. This would be Guatemala, then.

It took several attempts to work out which bus was going where, mainly because all the touts had a habit of instantly saying, 'Yes, yes, this one!' without apparently caring too much about where it was we actually wanted to get to. In the end we boarded a bus that we were assured went to Quetzaltenango – or Xela as it was locally known – despite all the signs indicating that it was destined for Huehuetenango – or simply Huehue. Off we raced, along the bottom of a valley for which there is no English comparison. The sides rose sharply upwards in a steep 'V' shape, carved into a continuous sequence of ever-changing slopes by small cascading tributaries plunging down incised gorges. Along the bottom of the valley wound a more significant river, and our road followed its twisting contortions. Everything was an intense green, from the plots of maize clinging to the lower slopes to the forest that continued above them. Little houses, more like hovels, perched on the hillsides too – but it seemed incredible that anyone could actually scratch a living in them. Our bus tore around the bends, overtaking anything in its way just as soon as it caught up with them, regardless of the visibility. Several times we were overtaking on the inside of blind bends, at top speed, certain to collide with anything that was oncoming. The touts laughed, heckling the driver as they hung out of the doors, shouting at anyone that we passed on the road, 'Huehue, Xela, Huehue!' If anyone decided to dice with death by indicating that they wanted to board, there was a screech as the bus came to a momentary halt, just long enough for the person to get one foot on the steps, before the gears ground and we lurched off again.

Guatemala was a poorer country than Mexico. This could be seen in the way that the roadsides were unkempt, dirty and unfinished; in the shed-like houses that had rusted corrugated iron roofs, the ramshackle fences and untidy paths outside; and in the people that we saw, many of whom were carrying back-breaking bundles of gathered wood. Guatemala was one of the poorest Latin American countries. Over half the population lived in poverty, 37 per cent lived on under US $2 per day, and more than a quarter lived in extreme poverty. This was largely the legacy of Guatemala's 36-year civil war, which ended in 1996. It had been the longest civil war in the history of Latin America, resulting in the deaths of 200,000 people.

We made it to Huehue, where we should have stopped for the night but decided to press on. It wouldn't be the last time that we did this and ended up regretting it. With hindsight, one of our maxims about travelling would be that it rarely pays to arrive somewhere after dark. But as we were still waiting for our change from the on-board tout and the bus did indeed continue straight on to Xela, we sat tight. We didn't know that it would be another three increasingly uncomfortable hours. As the bus filled up with more and more people, we began to realise our mistake.

These local buses were sometimes called 'chicken buses', which I always thought was because people could carry live chickens on board. That might be so, but after this journey I realised that they were called chicken buses because passengers were stuffed in like battery hens going to slaughter. Our bus had about twelve rows of four seats, two on each side of the aisle. When these were full, people just pushed themselves down onto the edges of seats, so there were three on each side, squashed together. When there was no more seating, people stood in the aisle, which was just a body-width wide. Eventually everyone was so crammed in that people filled the steps beside the driver, clinging to handrails even as the touts were hanging on to the outside of the open doors. There must have been a hundred people in that bus. We sat squeezed under and beside our bags, not letting them be taken onto the roof where we couldn't see them, and not realising that we would be charged extra because they took up room where a person could have fitted.

Once we were stopped at a roadblock by the police. All the men had to get out and were frisked beside the bus, in what appeared to be a routine event. The next day we read in the paper about a jailbreak, where a tunnel had been dug underneath the security fences and guard posts, as if straight from a fanciful film script. This was just the first indication that violence and criminality were closer to the surface – more real and potentially threatening – in Guatemala than in any other country we were to visit. It wouldn't take long, however, for us to find out how exposed we could be if we weren't careful.

In Xela we pulled to a halt at the edge of a main road somewhere – we had no clue as to where – and were told that this was the last stop. The tout had long since decided to keep our change as an extra charge for our bags. Before we had finished arguing about this, the bus driver simply drove off, leaving the tout to run after him. It wasn't an auspicious start. And now we were stranded in the dark. Luckily for us, two caring ladies who had been on the bus were watching us, clearly worried for our safety and their own. They asked if we were planning to travel on that night and insisted that it was too dangerous, advising us not to try to go further. We were a bit sceptical, and thought about taking a taxi, although the only ones we could see, parked on the roadside, were unlicensed. They began to start their engines and move towards us like encircling sharks. Getting into any of them would have been a very unwise idea. The ladies – a little frightened themselves – told us that they were going to try to find a hotel close by for the night; they were not about to risk the streets after dark. So we accompanied them around the corner, where, as luck would have it, there was indeed a little hotel. It was pretty shabby, with small, grotty rooms that had cardboard-thin walls, but it was a safe place for the night and therefore was a welcome sight. Only, because we hadn't changed enough money at the border, the only cash we were carrying was US dollars. This had been fine in Mexico, but the young Guatemalan clerk on duty said that he couldn't accept them. We were in a bit of a fix.

The clerk was very obliging and suggested that we walk up the hill to find a cash machine, leaving our bags in the hotel while we did so. He seemed to think that there was one close – and after all, we thought, this was the second industrial city of Guatemala. We had little choice and set off into the darkness. At the top of the hill was a small shopping square with a bakery just about to close, but there was no bank. The lady shutting up shop told us that the only cash machines were in the centre of town, down another road. But she too warned us against continuing, saying it was very dangerous. This time we took the advice more seriously and decided to turn back. Halfway down the hill we saw a bigger, more upmarket hotel and went in to see if they had rooms. They did, more expensive than our first hotel but payable with a Visa card, for an additional charge. What a stroke of luck, we thought, and set off to get our bags.

Back in our dingy place, the clerk was unhappy that we were thinking of leaving, on the principle that he had already written down in his big book that we were staying. He suggested paying in the morning, when we could go and fetch money – and we were too tired to argue much. As it turned out, we couldn't have left even if we wanted to. Xela was beginning to turn into my personal version of a nightmarish Hotel California. Our bags had been put in a room for us, but when we tried to enter it the door refused to open. We tried, the clerk tried, and then we sat and waited for twenty minutes until the hotel owner came to try. It was late, we were tired and we hadn't eaten anything for eight hours – this was all we needed.

The kind ladies came to say goodnight, no doubt hearing all the fuss, and spontaneously gave us two of their sandwiches to eat. In the midst of uncertainty and confusion, when things seemed at their worst, we nearly always encountered a touching gesture of goodwill from a stranger who had no need to do so. This was one of those moments and somehow the unwelcome experience was almost worthwhile because of it. As we sat in the semi-darkness, watching the owner and a friend of his attack the door with a screwdrivers, a pair of pliers and a candle, we could have been watching a scene from a slapstick comedy.

Eventually the lock was broken off, which made us feel bad, because we had been the source of nothing but trouble since we arrived, however accidental. With the door now unable to be locked or even shut, we thought we might get another room, but that wasn't to be. Maybe the clerk didn't want to risk any more problems. The one advantage of the mess was that the owner had said that we could pay in US dollars, allowing us to make a swift exit in the morning. For now we were safe and nothing had been stolen. Once again, we reflected, we had probably been on a knife-edge.

The next morning we walked back up the hill and into the centre of town. This was a large, unattractive square with a fenced-off park in the middle and large, drab buildings around the outside. Smaller roads fed into it and there were several banks with ATMs on their corners. After dark these alleyways were indeed favourite spots for muggings and robberies; we would have been sitting ducks had we come down here last night, two foreign tourists with cash cards. As it was, this morning we walked all around the square, fruitlessly trying one ATM after another. We weren't the only people doing this, but everyone was to be frustrated. The fact that we couldn't draw out any money in Xela seemed to say something about the condition of things in Guatemala. And with no cash, we were stuck here, unable to leave. So we went and had a breakfast coffee with the last of our small change from the bus, in – of all places – a McDonald's!

While we were there, a power cut locked us in. We wondered if anything worked in this town. When we were eventually released, we joined a queue at a cash machine which had been 'turned on' by the bank staff, in their own good time. To our relief, it now worked and we could get on our way – straight out of Xela. We hailed a passing taxicab with missing wing mirrors, one back door that hardly shut, and its whole floor about to drop right onto the tarmac. Nevertheless, the aged driver was amiable and took us to the bus station.

This was simply a road beside a large market that happened to have twenty buses parked all along it, up to three abreast. The buses were all colourfully painted in greens and reds, with their destinations written in shorthand signs that were totally indecipherable to us. We wandered along the lines, wondering which one might be ours. One burly, bearded man approached us and asked where we wanted to go. 'Panajachel,' we said, giving the name of a tourist resort further south.

'You can't go there directly, you have to get on this bus and then change,' we were told.

After our experience at the border, I wasn't inclined to take this at face value immediately, but a couple of drivers we asked said the same thing and so we climbed aboard and settled down to wait. We waited and we waited. The bus was in no hurry to set off, for the good reason that it hadn't filled up with passengers yet. To help pass the time, we were subjected to a procession of hawkers coming through the bus, presumably on sorties from the adjacent market, trying to sell us hot pizza, sweets, toothpaste, oranges, batteries, pens, books – just about anything. The culmination of these salespeople was a man smartly dressed in a dark shirt and tie. He stood at the front of the bus and addressed his audience as if from a podium in a lecture hall. With a couple of illustrated books as visual aids he talked us through several diverse bodily ailments, all of which could, he revealed, be cured or prevented by his bottles of wonder pills. And today, just for us, these were not being sold at the usual price of fifty quetzales (US $6.50). Oh no, as a special offer they were going for not thirty, not twenty, but ten quetzales! Take just two a day and we would be healthy for ever. For all his efforts, he failed to sell a single pill.

The journey to Panajachel demonstrated something of the art of extreme bus driving and restored our faith in people. The friendly bus team worked in concert to pick up or release passengers in the fastest possible time, as if they were racing against the clock. When someone wanted to get off, it was one person's job to climb out of the back of the bus while it was still moving, go up the ladder at the back to the roof, untie the baggage and have it ready to be lowered down at just the moment when the driver pulled up to let the passenger off. When it was our turn, the worker on the inside of the bus told us in good time, so we were ready for our stop, but nevertheless I still saw my rucksack moving rapidly past the door before I had descended the steps. It was being carried away on someone's head, which I didn't like until I saw it moments later halfway up the ladder of another bus. Without time for thought, we ran after our bags, jumping aboard this new bus, and within seconds of alighting from the previous one we were moving off again. It was the most efficient change of buses that we ever experienced.

All along the roadside now we could see evidence of the impact of the rainstorms associated with Hurricane Stan. Every twenty metres there was another brown scar on the hillside and a great pile of mud beside the road, which had been scraped up to clear a path for traffic. Whole tree trunks caked in mud had been moved aside too, vividly demonstrating how powerful and potentially dangerous the flows had been. At times the mudflows and landslides were even more dramatic, having gouged great chunks out of the hillside above or below the road, and sometimes the road itself. Where great bites had been taken out of the road, leaving a thin crust of tarmac overhanging a gaping hole, rings of stones had been placed about two feet from the edge as a kind of impromptu warning. Buses and lorries had to trust to their fortunes, skirting around the hole on the remaining remnants of the road.

One landslide we passed had made national news, it was so big. Our road ended abruptly halfway across a forty-metre drop, either side jutting out into open space like the ends of an incomplete bridge. The only sign of the force that had ripped away the land was a small trickle of water in a riverbed below. We bumped off-road down one muddy slope and up the other side to rejoin the road. Later we saw yet more damage. A house stood broken and half submerged in a dried river of thick mud. A village and the crops surrounding it were splattered throughout with brown wreckage from a river alongside, which had clearly been turned into a furiously raging torrent. These were sobering images that showed the reality behind media headlines and statistics. Some of the places in Guatemala that had been worst affected by Hurricane Stan were not far away.

We changed vehicles once more in order to drop down a steep hillside to the lakeside village of Panajachel. We were now put into the back of an open jeep, along with about ten other people, all of us squeezed together. We were fortunate; other jeeps were filled with some thirty people wedged against one another like sardines in a tin, with only standing room available. The jeep set off down the windy road, giving us lovely views out across the cloud-shrouded Lake Atitlan below. Several times uncleared mudslides nearly blocked the road, and finally it became impassable. A bridge that crossed a rocky river at the foot of its dramatic waterfall had been severely damaged by the water or falling boulders, or both. We piled out of the jeep and walked across the bridge, to where more jeeps waited on the other side, efficiently ferrying people backwards and forwards into the centre of Panajachel.

Chapter 12: Panajachel and Lake Atitlan

Panajachel was a gringo trap; a honeypot for both tourists and emigrants. It sat on the shore of Lake Atitlan, famous for having been called 'the most beautiful lake in the world' by Aldous Huxley. The setting was indeed idyllic, as the lake was ringed by green forested hillsides and three perfectly cone-shaped volcanic peaks that created a picturesque backdrop. The cones changed from mellow greens to soothing blues or stark black at different times of the day. Sunlight bounced off the water; white clouds rolled down the hillsides; the wind whipped up choppy waves in the afternoon. It was ever-changing and often very pretty. The lake was large enough for several villages to be spread out around its shores, each retreating up the hillsides away from the water's edge. Travel was by boat, either by little speedboats that zigzagged backwards and forwards, or by paddling narrow wooden canoes. Men were often out fishing on the lake in their precarious boats, while women and children washed at the lake's edge. In some ways the place seemed timeless, with traditional villages tucked away in a beauty spot, but in other ways it was sadly in the process of being spoiled by tourism.

There were just a handful of roads in the largest village of Panajachel, linking an old village centre with the outside world and the shoreline. The main road going to the water's edge was completely lined by a succession of hotels, cafés, restaurants, travel agents and stalls selling a myriad colourful arts and crafts to the tourist market. One of the special things about Panajachel, indeed anywhere in Guatemala, was the way that everyone in the street – in any street – would say 'Hola' or 'Buenas dias' if we caught their eye, and often even when we didn't. This was a particularly relaxed and friendly place, where time moved slowly. Market stalls were still being set up at midday. In the roadside cafés, food came quickly enough, but we could wait for ever to get a bill. There was no hurry to do anything, nothing much to rush for. When we came to leave, we weren't all that surprised that the bus was late, although exactly one hour late seemed a little extreme.

Panajachel was a gringo town, a world-within-a-world, populated by several different groups of people. The first were ageing hippie gringo types, in their forties to sixties, sporting ponytails and grunge clothing, called names such as 'New York Frank'. These expats talked English to each other, usually in American accents, as they sipped their morning tea in one of the cafés, before cycling off on green or orange mountain bikes complete with shopping baskets on the front. Some tried to fit in by wearing skirts made from the local cloth, but the combination with modern Western tops was in awful taste. There was something slightly eccentric about them, and together they created a strong flavour of 21st-century colonialism.

The next group of people were transient tourists like us, indulging in the chance to eat pizza or spaghetti and gawk at souvenir stalls. Some were clearly revelling in the carefree, almost lazy atmosphere, happy to spend time just letting the world drift by in their baggy clothes and sandals. Panajachel was, after all, the kind of place to watch a sunset by the lake shore to the sound of a traveller practising the guitar – usually badly – or to stroll past a girl quietly painting the landscape as a reminder to take home. As was invariably the case on the tourist circuit, there were more single girls than single guys, which is a credit to either the courage or the naivety of the lone female travellers.

All the tourists were prey for the third group: indigenous locals who made their living by selling handicrafts. Some would walk up and down the street for hours on end, on the lookout for bored, gullible or sympathetic targets, namely the above young travellers. There was an old man with an array of metallic objects that dangled from one arm, which he revealed to us like some shady dealer in a backstreet market. Ladies in traditional dress balanced baskets of bananas on their heads or held out a pathetic handful of key rings. Most clever and effective of all the street sellers were a pair of little girls, aged about eight to ten, who each carried an armful of material carefully folded and bundled together. They would sidle up to café tables as if they had nothing better to do with their time than spend a few minutes chatting to gringos.

After a respectable wait, they would engage. 'You want to buy? Good price. Best price for you. Want to look? Good price.' And they proceeded to gradually unpack their bundles, ignoring our requests not to do so, showing colourful piece after colourful piece. 'You want? Nice colour. Good price for you. You buy something?' They had an answer for every excuse we had not to part with our money. If we didn't like something then it became, 'A present. For your mum. She like. Good price for you.' If we said that we had already bought something, it was, 'Not like this. This special. Special memory. I make good price for you. You buy something? You like this one? Special price for you. You want?'

They were truly professional, too; we tried to draw them away into other topics of conversation, using our Spanish, and they indulged us for a bit, but they always returned to their main theme, while all the time keeping a sly look out for alternative, better prospects elsewhere. They were skilful, patient, persistent and ultimately also very cute – a winning combination that meant their tactics seemed to work as often as not. We somehow ended up with three pieces of cloth, having intended to buy just one.

There were other people who had stalls in the sleepy tourist market, where their eyes slowly closed as they sat beside their wares. Several times we heard the refrain that there was little custom at the moment, which was probably due to Hurricane Stan. Just like in the towns and villages along the coast of Thailand we would see later, which had been hit by the 2005 tsunami, the loss of income from the initial natural disaster was made worse because tourists were staying away, creating a double blow to the economy and slowing its recovery.

There was one more group of people in Panajachel. These were the locals who were simply going about their own daily business, backwards and forwards from the lake shore. Men walked past wearing traditional pyjama-style trousers that were black but embroidered with a multicoloured pattern of vertical stripes. A drab knee-length woollen 'skirt' was worn over the top of their trousers, and on their feet were often black wellington boots. Women typically wore a black wrap-around skirt held up with a belt, with a purple or blue blouse that was always finely embroidered with lines or beautiful designs. The sight of indigenous people wearing these clothes was one of the features of Lake Atitlan; each village had their own distinctive fashion.

The only exception to the laid-back rule of Panajachel came when we wanted to take a boat across the lake. Then suddenly we were accosted by hawkers, each trying to be the one to escort us to the appropriate vessel and therefore get a cut of the fare. Once a man simply walked beside us for the last twenty yards down to a boat, and was then quite aggrieved that the boatman refused to give him anything for this 'service'. The boatmen called out their destination – 'Panajachel-Pana-Pana-Panajachel!' – over and over for some fifteen to twenty minutes, drifting away from the jetty and then deciding to return again, before at last reluctantly pulling away, looking over their shoulder in the hope that yet one more customer would suddenly appear on the shore. Going across the lake meant jumping over the choppy waves out in the middle and then passing close under the shadow of the volcanoes, before reaching another set of wooden jetties beneath a collection of houses and churches. Sometimes we saw fine two-storey European-style houses around the shore, complete with private gardens. These were holiday homes for the rich, permanently tended by locals so that they were always ready in case the owners should suddenly arrive, which seemed to us again to carry a distinct whiff of modern colonialism.

The remoter lakeside villages seemed to be turning into mini-Panajachels, as the roads down to the lake were taken over by art and craft stalls for the tourist market. The centres of each village, however, were still busy, colourful local scenes – more so than at Panajachel. The traditional clothing on display was literally exquisite. In Santiago Atitlan, almost every woman wore a purple blouse with embroidered patterns of birds and flowers on the shoulders, in all shades of pink, red, yellow, green or white. The detail was fabulous; they were genuine works of art, for everyday use. The visual impact of a street crowded with women wearing these clothes was a delight. The men here hadn't missed out on dressing up, either: they wore grey pinstripe shorts down to the knee, or the same style in white but delicately embroidered with purple flower patterns. As their shorts were held up with a broad black belt, they sometimes gave the impression that they had dressed up as pirates. This was the colourful, exotic Guatemala of postcards and calendars and it was beautiful.

However, we found that the men wore European dress far more often than not, with the boys not far behind. It was incredible how globalised corporations and their fashions had reached even these tucked away corners of the world: children sported baseball caps with the Nike swoosh on and trainers that had the latest spring-loaded heels and bobble soles; there was even a mobile phone mast in the centre of Santiago Atitlan, reaching high above the churches. We wondered how long the traditional clothing would survive, or whether it would in time become just a costume for the tourist market.

With demand from tourists to see their slice of 'original' culture and with locals needing the extra income that can be earned, it must be nearly impossible to resist turning living culture into a tourist show. We were a bit surprised to be confronted with little boys and even young men who offered to take us to see the house containing the edifice of Maximom. This was an important part of local traditional culture that had somehow survived Catholicism. It was supposedly revered and respected by the villagers, but we now saw it was being exploited for the sake of a few tourist dollars. Although tourist projects are increasingly recognising the value of ecotourism as a means to protect and preserve the environment, it seems far harder to develop culturally sensitive tourism. We would come across this only rarely, where entire communities appeared to be sufficiently well managed that they could regulate both the locals' behaviour and that of tourists.

At Lake Atitlan, particularly in Panajachel, that was not the case. It had been swamped and spoiled before tourism had been brought under control. Despite the picture postcard views and the tasty food, we did not feel entirely comfortable being there. More than in most other places, it seemed to us that for all the income that tourism brings, it can also be a monster. Thailand has a reputation in South East Asia for having allowed runaway tourism to damage parts of the country, which we would experience for ourselves in several months' time. We felt here that Panajachel was a good example of unsustainable tourism in operation, and it wouldn't be the only time we felt that tourism was being allowed to develop unhealthily in Guatemala.

Meanwhile, invisible to the normal tourists, the residents of Santiago

Atitlan were still grieving the loss of nearly a hundred people who died in a mudslide that came down the flank of the adjacent volcano, surging through fields and houses. Only a couple of kilometres further away was the scene of one of the worst tragedies caused by the torrential rains. The village of Panabaj was literally turned into a graveyard by a mudflow half a mile wide and twenty feet deep. Over 150 bodies were recovered, but many others will never be found.

Chapter 13: Antigua

After Panajachel we travelled further east, to the city of Antigua. This had been the Spanish colonial capital of Guatemala between 1543 and 1776. During that time it was filled with churches, convents, a palace, a cathedral, parks and fountains, but a devastating earthquake in 1773 persuaded officials to move to Guatemala City, which remains the capital to this day. Antigua was officially abandoned, although never completely deserted. It did, however, go into serious decline until the second half of the twentieth century, when rebuilding and preservation of the ancient and historic buildings began in earnest – despite being interrupted by yet more earthquakes. All around the city were impressive colonial buildings, many of them churches and many partially ruined. Antigua had the reputation of being the finest city in Guatemala, and it was probably the main tourist centre. As in Panajachel, there was a modern colonial feel to the place, mingling with the older archetypal Spanish colonial architecture.

Antigua's setting was distinctive and special. Three coned volcanic peaks were clearly visible over the low houses and beyond the end of the straight streets, always providing an attractive backdrop to the city. In the middle of Antigua was an attractive park, which had a well laid out area of trees to give shade, benches underneath them. Beside a multi-tier fountain in the very centre of the park men would sit having their shoes cleaned, perhaps reading the paper as they waited. Around the park was a square of two-storey colonial buildings, including a splendid stark white cathedral facade, this time without bell towers for a change. Discreetly inside the buildings were banks, Internet cafés, travel agents and photography shops – there was even a Burger King and McDonald's, thankfully well hidden. A queue of perhaps fifty people lined up on one of the pavements, all hoping to be served at one of the banks.

We sat on a bench in the central park one late Sunday afternoon. The fountain was bubbling beneath the tree canopy, the outline of a volcano just rising above the tops. The sun was beginning to set and its light was losing its strength. Being a Latin American city, the plaza was still pleasantly busy with people taking time to relax and socialise. There were families strolling along, parents with their arms entwined while their children ran around together.

One young girl was learning to rollerblade beside her parents and her grandmother, who was carrying the youngest child of the family. A boy of about eight years old went past, carrying a wooden stool under one arm, his eyes searching faces in the hope of earning some money from shoe polishing. Another boy joined him, looking like an urchin out of *Oliver Twist*. His trousers were too long for him and his skin showed through the holes in them and in his unlaced shoes. The first boy approached us and insisted that my shoes needed cleaning, so I let him scrub and rub them, without any noticeable improvement in their condition. More children gathered around us. One young girl, perhaps five years old, and her slightly elder brother were trying to sell little picture cards. Their mum was elsewhere in the park, hawking traditional material, while their dad sold ice creams from a handcart. The little girl was really just a child, and amused herself by being friendly with anyone who would let her. She loved posing for photos for Claudia, who enjoyed taking them almost as much. The children didn't hang about long once they had been paid, though; they drifted away as the sky was turning a pinkish colour.

It grew too dark to see across the park and lantern lights turned on underneath the palm fronds. As we were leaving, adolescents began forming huddles in the shadows, even as toddlers still strolled past with their parents. Lads in low-cut baggy jeans loitered in corners, clutching cartons of drink and fast food in their hands as preened young ladies strutted past, all tight blue jeans and perfect white tops, flicking their hair and smiling self-consciously.

Away from the park, further out from the centre, Antiguan houses were mostly of the typical colonial one-storey terraced variety, generally painted a shade of yellow, white or an orangey-red terracotta. Thanks to efforts to preserve the colonial character, there was no outward 'glitz' or 'glamour' here, despite the high proportion of tourists and the associated gaggle of travel agents, hostels and language schools. None of the road junctions were marked, so traffic rumbled slowly down the cobbles to the next junction, where everyone stopped and looked at each other before someone took the initiative and edged forward. Bicycles and motorcycles weaved between the cars, while pedestrians hopped on and off the pavements. The pavements were often over a foot off the ground, and just walking them was a hazardous activity. They were too thin for two people to walk side by side, especially as they were full of obstacles like telegraph poles or wires, odd bits of metal sticking up from the cracked and crumbled paving, or window ledges that stuck out at head height.

We stayed our first night in Antigua in a grim cardboard cupboard of a hotel room, next door to a kitchen that threatened to cause an outbreak of food poisoning. So the next morning we toured the streets, checking out several places before deciding to stay at Don Tono's, a typically charming colonial building, with several small rooms that all faced onto an internal courtyard. The family lived in some of the rooms and let out a couple to visitors. Everyone shared the communal courtyard space, including the six tiny kittens that chased each others' tails across the floor and under the lush trees and potted plants. Don Tono told us that the kittens had fallen into the courtyard one morning, having climbed over adjacent roofs, and were now trapped until old enough to climb out again. We ate our meals at a little table and washed up our dishes in a poky sink that was used predominantly for hand-washing clothes. I don't think that the family were used to tourists living like this, but they didn't seem to mind.

At this time we were economising by eating granola – muesli – with yoghurt for breakfast, and sandwiches of cheese and tomato for lunches. To get a decent meal each night we turned to the local restaurants, of which there were many to choose from. On the first night we came across an Austrian-owned place and had to go in. The waitress was distinctly unimpressed by Claudia's being Austrian too; she was Guatemalan and didn't care. The menu did have some authentic dishes, but when they came they weren't like Claudia's home-cooked food at all – they were far too small to be a proper meal, for a start. It was disappointing, so we tried somewhere else the next day. We tracked down a vegetarian café, a typical gringo meeting point, pleasant with good music, but we again left hungry. This wasn't so good for me, or for poor Claudia, who probably suffered most when I went hungry. We turned to more central restaurants, but each time felt increasingly cheated. The epitome of the poor value in Antigua was a Greek restaurant – yes, even in Guatemala – where a main meal turned out to be nothing more than a plate of sliced tomatoes. To add insult to injury, the prices in Antigua were relatively steep. A main serving was generally about 35 quetzales (US $4.60)), a bottle of beer was 10–15 q (US $1.60) and salads were 20–30 q (US $3.30). So dinners, often with a 10 per cent service charge included, were typically 120 q, or about US $15.70 for a meal for two, that really only fed one person properly.

In many ways Antigua was a mix of modern, developed facilities and more traditional, underdeveloped ways. The tumbledown churches on every corner and the crazy pavements in between; the rabbit warren of dark market stalls; the colourful pavement fruit sellers; the women in traditional blue-green skirts and embroidered blouses balancing large bundles or baskets expertly on their heads, once even with three trays of eggs stacked up; all these intermingled with the digital camera shops, the high-speed Internet cafés, the rich cars cruising the streets, the fancy restaurants. While a little eccentric, the combination actually appeared to produce a very practical place. Life in Antigua certainly seemed to be very convenient for those who could afford it.

Another gringo expat set was in evidence here, an urban version of the types of Panajachel. These Americans spoke English when they stopped for a chat on the streets or sipped their coffee in touristy cafés and bars, which they happened to own. These places were comfortable, friendly environments designed in a quasi-European style, almost homes-from-home. In fact, on the streets around town, tourists appeared to be as prevalent as indigenous locals.

It was as if Antigua had created its own tourist bubble-world, an enclave of cheerful hostels and globalised services. It was all amenable, safe and easy, and this must be most tourists' experience of Antigua. The separation between the worlds of tourists and locals was stark, as it was across most of what we saw of Guatemala. It was possible to travel between cosy tourist centres in the relative comfort of private minibuses or first-class non-stop coaches, with the only glimpses of the 'real' world being normally on the other side of a pane of glass. But perhaps in Guatemala there was good reason for that.

From Antigua we took a trip one day to climb the nearby active volcano, Pacaya, helpfully arranged by Don Tono. There were closer volcanoes that we could have climbed independently, but the reports of hold-ups, muggings and rapes put us off. The Pacaya trips were safe, partly because the locals who might otherwise have caused problems had been given jobs within the tourist industry on the volcano. Nevertheless, we were assured that as well as a guide we would have a security guard with us. From the menacing gun that our bus driver wore, I assumed this was him.

In the weekend paper there had been an article that gave figures for the number of murders that occurred in Guatemala. On the Saturday there had been only four, all due to guns rather than knives. This was lower than normal. The daily figures that week had been: 11, 4, 10, 7, 9, 8 and now 4. Between August 2004 and March 2005 the monthly totals of murders in Guatemala had been: 156, 153, 189, 188, 166, 174 and 192. This was not an altogether quiet and peaceful country, despite the impression sometimes given within the tourist enclaves. In 2005 the murder rate was 35 for every 100,000 inhabitants – compared to 5.5 in the USA. For every ten people in the country, on average two crimes are reported each year.

'Leave at 6 a.m.,' we were told by Don Tono, so we made our lunch the night before and set the alarm. Not that we needed an alarm, of course; we woke on and off through the night and were awake at 5.45 a.m. in time to turn tour alarm off before it rang. Being half English, we politely stood in the street outside the door so that no one else would be disturbed at that time on a Sunday morning. We waited in the dark, through the lightening of the sky and the unexpectedly late sunrise colouring the clouds. Each time we heard the noise of a rumbling and clanging at the end of our road we looked up expectantly, only to see a battered car or pickup roll past. At 7 a.m., fed up with Guatemalan timekeeping and organisation, we turned around to go inside and bumped into Don Tono, who was brandishing our ticket and saying, 'Let's go.'

Suddenly something clicked in the back of my mind. Our bus had been exactly one hour late in Panajachel and now we had waited exactly one hour here. The delays were no one's fault but our own: we had omitted to put our watches back an hour at the Guatemalan border! No wonder sunrise had seemed so late… It does, perhaps, say something for Guatemalan time that we could have been an hour out all this time and not have noticed.

At the volcano, we set off in a long line of about thirty people, most young like ourselves, accompanied by a cheerful guide. He set a fast pace up the steep path, so some people dropped back, to the glee of the horseback riders who rode beside us, calling out, 'Taxi, taxi!'

After one hour we emerged from the forest onto a kind of plateau, from where away to our right we could see clearly the perfect blue cone of Antigua's closest volcano. Behind it was another, this one smoking slightly. And directly in front of us rose the black cone of Pacaya, with pure white smoke billowing from its top, blown almost horizontally sideways by the wind. We walked towards it across a lava field, which crunched beneath our feet. Through the cinders were growing patches of straggly green plants with yellow flowers; life literally rising from the ashes. Up the side of the cone we went, where the lava underfoot had been crushed to sand and dust. Wind whipped up the grit, cutting into our faces even as we were threatened with being blown off the path and down the side of the cone. Dust got into our eyes and our ears, covering our clothing in a fine light grey layer. We ploughed on, with our feet struggling for a hold and frequently sliding back. It wasn't much fun, but then climbing a volcano wasn't something that we would do every day.

Coming around a corner, we suddenly found ourselves at the bottom of a narrow gully that ran up to the very rim of the crater. White smoke rolled down it towards us like dry ice on a stage. We caught the whiff of sulphur; it was volcanic gas. Up the gully we went, into clouds of whirling smoke that made it hard to breathe. Gasping for clean air, we peered over the edge into the crater below, which was too full of white fumes to see much. But further around the edge was a rocky outcrop broken by a deep crack. Looking down into the darkness, we were astonished to see bright red-hot magma, apparently not very far away at all. It was gleaming and shimmering in its own heat, which blasted our skin as soon we were exposed to it. I was quite shocked at the proximity of this magma. I had been close to volcanism before in Iceland and would be so again in New Zealand on this trip, but here the magma had been pushed right up to the top of a volcanic peak. It was kept there and kept hot by immense pressures and heat that must have originated some way further down, and we were standing right on top of it, with nowhere else to go. We suddenly seemed very vulnerable indeed. But it was all quite safe, our guide reassured us, as the volcano was carefully monitored for any signs of eruption.

One of our main activities in Antigua turned out to be the posting of a hammock and a canvas chair that we had bought in Panajachel. We had wondered whether to carry these souvenirs through Central America until returning to Mexico City, from where postage should have been more reliable, but decided against lugging around the extra baggage. So in Antigua we tracked down the post office and asked about posting packages. No problem, we were told, but wrap it up first. So we found a *papelería* – paper shop – and bought brown paper and sticky tape. In our bedroom, we carefully wrapped everything up in a big bundle, all wound around with brown tape. Proud of our work, we returned to the post office only to be told by another lady that the parcel was too big, 120 cm long instead of the maximum 100 cm. We should have known it wasn't going to be straightforward.

    We were loath to let our good efforts go to waste, so we knocked at the window of a local parcel courier, who told us through the metal bars how to get to a DHL office. Everything was possible in Antigua, sure enough. But for a price – too much for us. So, inevitably, we went back to the beginning and started again, first to the *papelería* to buy more paper and tape, and then back to our room, where we eventually produced two separate packages. The longest was still 105 cm long, but this was accepted by a third lady at the post office. The cost of postage was going to be 690 quetzales (US $90) for one and 370 quetzales (US $48) for the other.

    The lady opened a book of stamps and tore off an entire sheet. That's a lot, I thought, but then she folded a corner and removed a few, which seemed better. She kept the few and handed me the rest of the sheet, followed by two more entire pages. These stamps each had a value of just 5 quetzales, so there were a lot of them. And we soon found that they didn't stick on to the brown tape that we had protectively wrapped all around the parcels. Actually, most of the stamps didn't stick to anything at all, which turned out to be not the problem of the lady watching our efforts from behind the counter. I ended up going back to the *papelería* to buy some glue, where I failed to remember the Spanish word and somehow managed to successfully mime 'Pritt-Stick', which seemed a triumph at the time.

    Finally we had all the stamps stuck on, in ones and two in gaps between the brown tape, and presented the parcels to the lady. I could hardly believe it when, despite having witnessed all our efforts, she started to count the stamps, just in case we had kept some behind. The first parcel she checked – with some difficulty – had two stamps less than it should have had. On a recount, she discovered where they had been hiding. The process turned from comedy into farce when she repeated the saga with the second parcel, only to state that one stamp was missing. She did eventually find it and somewhat grudgingly took the parcels from us. We spent weeks wondering if they would make it back to Europe, which they duly did without any apparent problems.

    We had to spend some time in Antigua thinking about where to go next in our journey. We had made the mistake of using Mexico City as the port for both our inward and outward flights, which meant that we had to loop all the way back again. This made the original idea of visiting Honduras no longer so appealing, as it would involve long journeys and associated travel costs. We had the option of venturing into the wilds of Guatemala, where we would undoubtedly find places that were not semi-colonial tourist traps. But after experiencing the difficulties one can get into at Xela – which itself was not even remote – and learning a little more about the condition of the country, we were not inclined to stray too far from the beaten track.

Furthermore, we were still getting into the swing of travelling for an extended period of time. We had to learn how important it was to pace our journey to prevent ourselves being travel-weary all the time. So we decided to head north towards Flores and the Mayan jungle ruins of Tikal, which was the place in Central America that I had most wanted to see before setting out. After that we planned to return slowly to Mexico City, breaking the long journey back into a series of manageable sections. But our plans never did last very long.

Chapter 14: Tikal

We arrived in Flores in the early morning, after an overnight bus journey via Guatemala City. We found a hotel and were promptly advised by the owner to make a visit to Tikal that day, as it was 1 November, the 'Day of the Dead', and people would be visiting graveyards. Tomorrow the ruins would be far busier, we were told. Going today – right now, in fact – inevitably meant doing a deal through him, and he would of course get his cut. Well, fair enough. How much of this was just a sales pitch we could never tell, although the following day we did indeed see graveyards all covered in fresh flowers. But we drew the line when he offered a bus trip back to Panajachel. We grabbed a coffee and sweetbread in a local roadside diner for breakfast, and were off again. So much for pacing ourselves.

This part of northern Guatemala was the poorest region we had seen so far. There were no maize crops and no organised agriculture. Just semi-wild scrubby bushes with a few palm and banana trees in between. The houses that stood a little way back from the roadside were small and dirty. Their walls were vertical timber planks; their roofs were simple thatch. Other more solid brick buildings did exist, some of which even advertised themselves as hotels, despite looking pretty ramshackle. But most houses looked like little huts. In front of them were dirt yards where chickens, ducks and pigs roamed freely. Women washed clothes and dishes outdoors, in cement sinks that stood under the shelter of small thatched canopies. Litter lined the dusty roadside. Dogs were everywhere, creating a hazard for drivers, and there were a surprising number of horses standing idly beside the road. The impression was of a very basic, meagre, even squalid existence. It was a sorry picture.

At the entrance to the Park of Tikal we were met by an old man who offered to be our guide. We had already decided that this time we would splash out on a guide for a change, but we had hoped for someone who spoke English. However, there was no one else around, so we had to make the best of his – or my – Spanish. He was as experienced and knowledgeable as we could have hoped for, but I suspect that his explanations lost most of their impact and quite possibly a good deal of their accuracy by the time they reached Claudia via my efforts at translating. Towards the end of the day she and our guide somehow discovered that Italian was a mutual language for them, which made things a bit easier for her – but instead left me none the wiser.

From the entrance, our guide led us off into a proper jungle. There were tall, thin tree trunks with spreading buttress roots to support them; the ground was thickly covered with huge ferns; vines and creepers were hanging down from branches laden with air plants. It was hot and humid, mosquitoes buzzed around our wrists and necks, and lines of army ants crossed the leaf litter in front of us. We couldn't see much through the dense tangle of plants, but we could hear howler monkeys calling loudly across the treetops. Twice we spied monkeys, languidly swinging their orange-brown furry bodies through the branches using all five of their long, supple limbs. We were shown trees that produced cotton, spices and even chewing gum, which our guide called 'white gold' due to its commercial value. Alligators lurked in a small lake; large turkeys with iridescent feathers stalked off through the undergrowth; brown tail-less rodents scampered along the path ahead of us; three toucans displayed their bright orange and black plumage in a nearby tree. And we hadn't even come to see the wildlife.

The Mayans developed the site of Tikal from about AD 300 until the end of the ninth century. It was built around hills which still overlook the surrounding countryside. Most of the twenty-three square miles of the ancient city is now thick forest, but then the landscape would have been cleared for fields. Not a great deal is known about the Mayans, who at one time had the most developed writing system of the Americas, and even less is known about the collapse of their civilisation and the loss of their knowledge and skills. One of the factors that led to the decline of Tikal – which had been just one of many semi-independent city states – was probably that the crops failed, owing to either infertile soil or drought, or both. By the time the Spaniards arrived in 1524 under the leadership of Pedro de Alvarado, all that was left of the Mayan empire were a series of fragmented tribes. Nevertheless, it took until 1697 for the last of these to fall to the Spanish. In fact, remnants of the Mayan population still live on to this day; many of the indigenous people around Lake Atitlan are Mayans, for example. Guatemala today has the highest proportion of indigenous Indians of any country, at around 40 per cent of the population.

The ruins of Tikal were 'discovered' in the mid-nineteenth century. Today, some of the buildings have been cleared and restored, while many others lie as they have been for hundreds of years, overgrown by trees and other plants. Walking the narrow paths was like taking a hike through a jungle, except that every so often we would come across traces of overgrown buildings. The jungle was slowly but surely taking back the land for itself, pulling down the artificial structures and replacing them with its own natural forms. We were glad we were being shown around, for we would certainly have missed some of the sights, lost as they were down small trails.

Sometimes all that could be seen of the buildings that once existed were hills of green, with slopes too regular and corners too square for them to be natural. Underneath all the vegetation there must have been large pyramids of stone waiting to be uncovered. In other places there were corners of stone walls still visible, with great tree roots pushing between the blocks and breaking apart the walls. One of the magical things about Tikal was that we could walk through the jungle on a narrow footpath, seeing nothing but trees, and then suddenly emerge into the open with a restored stone building appearing in front of us as if from nowhere, starkly bare in its forest clearing. There were houses and towers, tombs and temples, and carved stones telling of gods and of human sacrifices.

The central feature in Tikal was a plaza with a grassy square – ideal for picnics – surrounded by giant stone buildings, but most of the ruins were simply spread out across the forest. Most splendid of all were the six giant pyramids that rose steeply above the canopy, two of which dominated the central square. These dark grey stone edifices were up to 60 m high, dwarfing the surrounding trees even though their tops were crumbling away. The architecture of the square pyramids was similar to the Teotihuacan pyramids in Mexico – there was evidence of direct cultural links between the two civilisations – but the pyramids in Tikal were far narrower and steeper than the Mexican ones. Set on their tops were stone temple towers that once had been finished off with coloured carvings. We could climb up the incredibly steep flights of giant stone steps up the front of some of the pyramids, but to reach the top of others required rickety wooden scaffolding and long stepladders.

The views from the summits were both beautiful and unearthly. The undulating green jungle canopy receded into the distance, always lower than our vantage points. The tallest emergent trees stuck out slightly from the rest, like green umbrellas sheltering branches thick with moss and air plants. And out of this carpet of forest treetops protruded the grey towers, poking up like fat fingers pointing skyward. They had a certain poise about them, a grace that came from their architectural form, as if still able to hint at a previous life and vigour. Now, however, they were motionless, dead. They are dramatically stark monuments to a culture that had vanished and left them behind. Like the pyramids of Mexico, they seem alien, built long ago for a purpose that we have no connection with and that we can barely comprehend. Somehow there was a haunting sadness about that. The pyramids had been once built as tombs over dead kings, but today they were forgotten gravestones marking the passing of a civilisation.

We sat on top of one of the towers and absorbed the sight in front of us. Tikal: the forgotten, ruined city in the jungle. We would later visit Angkor Wat, which had been similarly lost within the forests of Cambodia, composed of vast, imperial complexes of well-exposed buildings. Part of the attraction of

Tikal was the number of small walls and buildings close together that were totally overgrown. It was almost impossible to tell what was jungle and what was stone; as we explored and 'discovered' new ruins we could have been on the set of an *Indiana Jones* movie, only this was for real. After all that we saw around the world, Tikal remains one of my favourite locations.

Back in Flores, we walked leisurely around the lake shore, watching wooden canoes paddle slowly across the lazy blue waters. We had time to spare, there was no rush, no hurry. Until, that is, Claudia suggested going to Belize to see the Caribbean coral reef. After all, it wasn't too far away – a poster in our hotel foyer told us that a bus could even take us straight to Belize City from Flores.

It was in the wrong direction, it would probably cost far too much, but it was a golden opportunity. Besides, the food in Flores wasn't much better than it had been in Antigua. As ever, plans changed in an instant, and we left the next morning at 5 a.m.

Chapter 15: Belize City and Cay Caulker

Belize used to be called the 'Mosquito Coast', presumably for a good reason. It was little cared about until mahogany was discovered and exploited. This industry was followed by sugar cane and coconut plantations, which still exist today. It used to be a British colony called British Honduras, becoming independent only in 1981. Guatemala didn't formally recognise its existence until 1991, due to a series of border disputes. Now tourism is the dominant industry for Belize, contributing some 25–30 per cent of its GDP.

Belize looked twee and civilised to me, like a Caribbean country with a distinct colonial heritage. Grand bungalows sat in fenced plots of land, with gravel driveways and grass lawns around them. The houses were clearly separated and carefully tended. Roads were clean, the verges even being cut with lawnmowers. The land was all tamed, managed and controlled. There were clearly ordered areas for lemon orchards, cattle pasture or coconut plantations. Children in blue school uniforms waited for their buses to take them to schools which had brightly coloured two-storey wooden chapels in front of them and large signs that proclaimed their denomination as Catholic, Anglican or Baptist. As well as churches from overseas, there were several prominent technical colleges and other progressive programmes paid for by Korea, Japan and Taiwan.

But there were other sides to the picture. We passed a sprawling roadside rubbish dump plagued by scavenging vultures. There were plenty of poky, decrepit wooden stilt houses in need of new timber and new paint. Old men sat in tatty chairs beside them, bringing to my mind stereotypical images of black townships in the southern USA, where the strains of blues coming from chairs under rotting porches would capture the heartache of decay. The connection was made stronger because of the dominance of the Afro-Caribbean population here. Between immigration control and Belize City I didn't see a single Caucasian face.

Covering the flat, low-lying land just outside the capital city were impenetrable thickets of mangroves, which sent their weird roots down into the water like the tentacles of some alien organism. We could see where the mosquitoes might have lived and bred in profusion. Areas of this land were up for sale, and some plots had been cleared, drained and raised, to be built on. The houses on the outskirts of Belize City were all wooden boxes perched high on stilts, usually painted white, with simple sloping roofs and little windows. Rickety wooden steps led up to porches and open doorways, fly-nets obscuring their interiors. Large women walked along the roadsides wearing loudly coloured wrap-around skirts, often with young children tottering along in their wake. In the small centre of the city we were shouted at by gangly young men with Rastafarian haircuts, their dark locks sprouting out from underneath their characteristic woollen hats, striped red, yellow and green. They called out to us in their Caribbean accents, 'Where you wanna go today? I take you.'

Belize City was a lively, bustling, colourful, loud town with people and cars everywhere. Street stalls selling bananas were getting in the way on the roads and pavements. Small, familiarly modern shops lined the streets. We felt a bit out of place here, standing out from the local people. It wasn't exactly a touristy place. At our friendly hostel, the hostess provided us with a map of the city and highlighted the small road where we were staying. This was safe, she said. So was the next one and she coloured that yellow, too. It was fine up until a nearby bridge, apparently. But the rest of the map she left ominously white. Having read about the crime rates in the city – murder rates are about six per month – we stayed within her limits until heading for the ferry terminal, where a group of tourists huddled together on plastic benches as if hiding from the world outside.

It was 65 million years ago that an asteroid from space 10 km in diameter smashed into what is now the Yucatan peninsula. With an impact equivalent to 6 million of the 1980 Mount St Helens eruption, the impact created a crater 150 km across, ejecting material into the atmosphere that settled in a layer all around the world. It has been suggested that the resulting clouds and dust were thick enough to block out the sun, helping to precipitate the mass extinction event that killed off most of the dinosaurs. The asteroid impact sent shock waves through the earth itself – with earthquakes of magnitude ten on the Richter scale – bending and breaking its rock layers into giant faulted ripples underneath the ocean. In the warm, shallow tropical sea where these 'ripples' reached high enough, corals began to grow. Belize now has the longest barrier reef in the western hemisphere, second only in the world to Australia's Great Barrier Reef.

Sometimes storm waves break pieces of coral off and crush them into sand that builds up on the beaches of what is now the coast of Belize. The sand even accumulates between the roots of mangrove trees that gain a toehold in shallow waters, creating islands of white sand for plants like coconut palms to colonise.

Blue skies, green sea, white sand and palm trees: the Caribbean cays. At least, that's what there should be during the dry season. We didn't plan our stay to coincide with, well, anything, so we arrived during the stormy season – just as we did a couple of months later in the South Pacific islands of Fiji.

The presence of the reef could be seen from the islands – or cays – as a continuous white line of breaking waves, a little way offshore from the cays. The reef protects the cays from the destructive power of the open sea and creates something of a calm lagoon behind. Only when hurricanes blow through do storm waves, surges and high winds wreak havoc on all the forms of life that cling precariously to their toehold existences, including the people who have built their homes on the island. Traditionally these people were fishermen or divers for sea bounty, but that traditional way of life has now all but vanished.

Cay Caulker was one of the larger islands, four miles long, although it had been cut in half by a passing hurricane that had carved out a channel in its wake. The island was part mangrove scrub, part grand Texan resorts, and part local town turned tourist colony. Tourism started early in the twentieth century with visits to the unusual manatees or sea cows that live nearby, but the industry really took off in the 1990s. Now every seafront property is a hotel-and-restaurant or an office for a tourist guide offering diving, snorkelling, kayaking or excursions to the mainland. I asked a sailboat captain if there were any restrictions on tourism and whether he thought it might spoil the area. 'There are some restrictions,' was his response, 'but it's already spoilt.'

Cay Caulker welcomed visitors with a tiled mosaic in the jetty that said, 'Go slow'. The island lived up to its own advice. With not much space to roam, people would wander up and down the few streets that were squeezed together before the land ran out at the 'Lazy Lizard' bar. There was a fairly dilapidated feel about the island, although some classy buildings had been built here and there, with price tags of US $65 per night attached. We found a couple of cheaper chalet-style huts to stay in, tucked behind what looked like a small scrapyard. They suited us because they had a barbecue grill that we could cook on, and because in a hole just beside our front door lived a monstrous iguana, who would periodically emerge to bask in the sunshine.

Transport on the island was a bit quirky. The locals and long-term tourists seemed to use oversized brakeless bicycles, weaving and wobbling around at slow speeds as if always half off balance. At that speed, they didn't need brakes. As nowhere was very far from anywhere else, I couldn't really see the need for bikes at all. More eccentric were the golf buggies, powered by electric batteries, humming quietly as they zipped past at a fast walking pace, usually driven by oversized or elderly people. The single ordinary vehicle that I saw was a jeep which served as a fire engine, complete with hoses and various equipment stashed in the back.

Strangely for an island made almost entirely out of coral sand, there wasn't actually any beach; every inch of land had been occupied to within feet of the water's edge. There was just enough room for a straggly line of palm trees and the odd palm-leaf shelter, perhaps with a ropy old hammock slung between the posts from years ago. Numerous jetties jutted out into the sea, far enough to reach beyond knee-deep water, but most were broken, either falling sideways or with great gaps in them. Next to the Lazy Lizard was a swimming place, but it was right beside the 'cut' which was used by high-speed boats, making it a rather dangerous place to splash around in. A concrete walkway did run parallel to the shore for some 25 m, creating a safe refuge of sorts, but even this was broken, sunken and only partially usable.

We couldn't really say that Cay Caulker was our idea of a tropical paradise. It was surprising to see so many features in disrepair, making parts look tatty and neglected. We asked whether all this had been caused by the recent tropical storms. Hurricane Wilma had indeed caused an unusually high wave which topped the reefs and hit the island, damaging some of the skewed wooden jetties. But the concrete walkway, the focal point for tourists – particularly with the view of the setting sun it affords – was damaged by Hurricane Mitch back in 1998. Repairs, it would seem, were going slow.

Our general impression of the island was of a fairly shabby place, if not actually dirty. It was as if no one could be bothered to make the effort to keep it looking neat or tidy. But this was the Caribbean. Chill out, relax, have a drink, be happy… Enjoy being on a tropical island with waving palm trees in front of the warm, gentle sea. As an island website described:

> Nobody wants to work hard in Cay Caulker… Mostly they want a two or three hours a day work, or 5 hours for three days a week… Life is simple if you want it, or costly if you can afford it… With fish in the sea, it is easy to eat and the weather is nice, so socialising is the preferred way of life… The laid-back atmosphere of Cay Caulker is something you must see to appreciate.[3]

The sun, when it finally arrived on our third day on Cay Caulker, was blasting hot, forcing us to retreat into the shade. The more frequent torrential tropical downpours from dark billowing clouds, heralded by rainbows and gusty winds, also forced us under shelter. All in all, sitting in a Caribbean beach bar with a cocktail, looking out across the ocean waves, seemed a fairly appropriate way to pass the time. Which might explain the three-hour-long 'happy hours' that lasted all through the afternoon until, well, dinner time. This meant that there was no need to leave the bar, especially with two-for-one cocktail offers accompanying a main meal. On the menus were, among other things, fresh fish fillets, conch snail steak, and whole grilled lobster. Probably crab too, judging by the size of the live monster that we found skulking underneath our table one evening. It had a huge claw, fully two inches long and almost as

---

[3] www.casado.net 2006–7

broad, which it waved aloft at us as if to say, 'Just try it – I dare you!' Claudia refused to put her bare toes anywhere near it until a waiter had picked it up with a stick and carried it the few yards to the shore.

When lazing in a bar wore a little thin, there was plenty to see off-shore. Diving and snorkelling on the reefs were the main attractions. Not far away was a 'blue-hole' which claimed to be the best dive site in the world. We joined a boat one day going out on a snorkelling day trip to a different marine reserve. The first stop was called 'coral garden'. It was a tame place to get used to snorkelling: we floated over delicate fan corals a foot or more in diameter, and large branching red coral with small blue fish darting in between. The headline attraction of the tour was a contrived tourist sight, called Shark Ray Alley. In an area of shallow water, about ten feet deep, our guides dropped some fresh offal overboard. Within seconds there were foot-long fish swirling around the food. Then we saw more ominous dark shadows cruising along the bottom – sharks.

Overboard we went, to have the unforgettable experience of being in the water as five-foot-long nurse sharks passed just beneath us. They were quite slim, with sleek bodies that ended in a sharply pointed nose and angular fins that jutted out from their backs. These couldn't actually bite us, as their jaws could not open wide enough to take out a chunk, but they looked the part and we were transfixed. Nurse sharks can grow up to ten foot long and then they can be dangerous; they are compared to bulldogs because they clamp their teeth in a hold that doesn't release until it has sucked the flesh away, leaving a wound behind that is very difficult to heal.

Still more dark shapes silently drifted over the sand towards us, flat and large, reminding me of giant bats. They glided smoothly along with apparently no effort or propulsion at all except the edges of their wide wings that rippled up and down. These were huge, ghostly stingrays. Drifting behind their bodies was a thin, whip-like tail with a vicious-looking arrowhead at its end. The danger from sting rays actually comes from the spine at the end of their back. The smaller spotted rays are the worst, we were told, with a sting that would make any grown man cry from the agony.

The sharks and rays tussled on the bottom for their portion of free food, writhing in the sand. As they did so, our guide dived down into their midst. He reached out and grabbed the tail of a smaller shark, placing a hand behind its head. This one was about three feet long and it twisted in his arms as he brought it up, strongly enough to break his grip, at which point he pushed its head away from him and it flashed away. Beneath was another shark, larger at about 5½ feet long. He wouldn't try to pick this one up, I thought, but he did. Our guide had spent his childhood on the island diving for lobsters and catching sharks to sell at a market – he knew what he was doing. He used the same technique as before, grasping the tail and putting a hand behind the head, much like someone might hold a snake. Then he quickly turned it upside down, at which point it became meek in his hands. We could see the mouth and extended fang-like teeth jutting from the underside of its head, around which was pallid white skin. Reaching out to touch it, we found the skin had a rasping, leathery texture, quite firm and dry. Then the shark was released and it swam powerfully away through the water.

We turned around to see another guide behind us with a stingray balanced in his outstretched, horizontal arms. The ray was large enough that the edges of its wings rippled over the edges of his parallel arms. The tail was free, but the guide was careful not to let it come too close. The ray had a different feel, quite spongy and soft. These close encounters were spellbinding, even if the ethics of such practices were slightly dubious.

Afterwards the guides took us on a couple more snorkelling tours, pointing out various fish as we swam along. We saw a large parrotfish and a flounder that lay flat against the sand with its two eyes disconcertingly looking straight up from the middle of its back. But the best encounter was saved until last. Swimming along in a straggly line, we heard an underwater cry from one of the girls in the group. She alerted us to the magnificent sight of a huge green conger eel, fully five feet long, with a large dorsal fin rippling along its back. It had been swimming towards the girl like a giant sea serpent, but then it turned contemptuously and took cover in a coral hole, from where it glowered out at us with cold, black eyes of hatred and a mouth that hissed open to reveal rows of vicious teeth. No one felt like a hands-on experience this time!

On another day we kayaked around the cay. This turned into a storm-dodging exercise as black clouds raced towards us, sending us scuttling for cover in the mangroves. In between, we glided serenely along, stopping to look at the flora and fauna on the way. A little nature reserve harboured a range of plants, which our Canadian guide pointed out as having a range of medicinal properties. One had black sap which would bring out nasty boils if it so much as touched the skin. Apparently the Mayans used to flay their prisoners and tie them to this tree as a punishment. Then there was the tree with red bark that hung down in strips from the trunk, nicknamed the 'tourist tree' because it was red and peeling. We had to concede the aptness of this as our legs were still smarting from our snorkelling trip.

Overhead, frigate birds cruised the skies, rarely bothering to make the effort to move their sickle-shaped wings, which gracefully sliced through the air as their long forked tails streamed out behind them. Brown pelicans came to visit, flapping more ponderously but still able to wheel and dive into the waves in search for fish to fill their over-size gullets. Large blue herons noisily made a fuss about leaving their treetops, dangling their ungainly thin legs underneath them. More serene ospreys perched quietly on the mangrove branches, waiting for the sight of easy prey. Iguanas – up to three feet long – were lying camouflaged on the branches, basking in the sun. Salt-water alligators stalked the shallows and boa constrictors hid in the undergrowth. We saw thin lines of splashes where something under the water was breaking the surface and hurried after them to catch a glimpse of eagle rays gliding away from us in the shallows. There were jellyfish and strange algae in the shallow seagrass that waved under the water and then, finally, in amongst the mangrove roots, a male seahorse, 'pregnant' with youngsters. The male seahorse is a fish, but is also the only species in the world where the male becomes 'pregnant'; it is the female who inserts her eggs into the male's pouch, which are fertilised and hatch two to three weeks later. This one had its curled tail clasped around a stick and was poised handsomely upright, its thin tube-like nose sticking out in front of its face – a delightful sight. Our guide again knew what she was doing here; she was working to train other locals how to protect these precious creatures, an example of local ecotourism in action. Unfortunately, Hurricane Wilma had torn away much of the sea life from their normally sheltered harbours and this seahorse was the very first to return.

As the rain showers turned the waves choppy and blew spray in our faces, we hurried back to safe harbour ourselves. There was a sense of vulnerability, even though these were small squalls. Our guide certainly wasn't taking any chances as we hugged the shoreline and sheltered between mangrove roots. The expression she used was, 'I'd rather be in here wishing I was out there, than out there wishing I was in here.' We realised that we wouldn't want to be on the island at all if a full-blown storm came through.

As it was, the wettest we got was back in Belize City, while standing beside the road waiting for our onward bus. In the hot, humid air we quickly became unpleasantly drenched with sweat. It was time to head northwards into Mexico again and take a twenty-hour bus journey directly to Mexico City. After our experiences in Guatemala, Mexico now was able to really impress us with its efficiency and relative modernity. The large, clean bus station had a decent toilet where we could change out of our sweaty clothes, and a smart little café to grab a bite to eat. The ticket office was perfectly straightforward and there were uniformed officials supervising the whole station. It was a far cry from the chaos of the Xela market-side road or the grubby, poky bus station that we passed through in Guatemala City. So it wasn't too long before we had come full circle in Central America. From Mexico we headed further south, flying all the way to Lima, the capital of Peru.

Part Three
Peru, Bolivia, Chile and Brazil

Chapter 16: Lima to Cuzco

Lima was one of the three cities in which we had booked accommodation over the Internet prior to arrival. This was mainly because we arrived there at 2 a.m. and neither of us fancied roaming its streets at that time. The following day we intended to explore the sights of Lima and arrange our onward travel. On the previous occasions that I had been to Lima, undertaking voluntary work in the shanty town of Zapallal some 40 km to the north of the city centre, I had never found the city very attractive. It has been estimated that one third of Peru's 24 million inhabitants live in Lima, 4 million of whom survive in the shanty towns that spread over the sandy hillsides on the edge of the city. We met a friendly teacher during the one day that we spent in Lima who spoke to us about these poor communities, where new arrivals from the countryside sometimes have to live in cardboard boxes. The shanty towns grow faster than the government's ability to provide roads, water, sanitation or electricity. In places there wasn't enough money available to operate a cash economy, she said, so communities barter amongst themselves for goods.

We had met the teacher whilst sitting on a bench in a supermarket car park, wondering quite how we had ended up there. Our intention had been to leave Lima on an early bus to the lovely colonial city of Arequipa, but when we arrived at the bus station we found that all the buses were full. In fact, the only two seats we could get were to Cuzco, leaving at 7 p.m. that day for the twenty-hour journey. Without any good reason other than serendipity, we had taken those two seats and then began to wonder what to do with the rest of the day. We consulted with a taxi driver outside the bus station. His opinion was that the upmarket coastal area, where most tourists hang out, would probably not amuse us for more than an hour or so – with which I agreed. This gave me a degree of confidence in his judgement, which turned out to be unwarranted. He recommended to us a plaza whose name I didn't recognise. But no doubt it would have colonial buildings to look at, a park to sit in, maybe a museum or two nearby – or so we thought. Off we drove, around the corner to a large modern shopping plaza. This is what he thought would suitably amuse gringo tourists for hours on end, but he couldn't have chosen anything further from our desires.

Still, we went in and were surprised to find that the mall was upmarket and very chic, with prices in the fashionable shops that were comparable to those in Europe. It was full of well-dressed, sunglass-sporting young and middle-aged

European-looking people. I looked in vain for an Indian face amongst the shoppers, but everyone exemplified upper-class, rich Liman society. When I had been in Lima before, my only contact with this set had been with a group of privileged medical students who spent their holidays in places like Italy – and who claimed not to have known of the desperate conditions that existed within the shanty towns.

Much of the migration to Lima resulted from the vicious guerrilla war between the communist 'Shining Path' group and the army from the 1970s to the 1990s. Both sides were capable of freely murdering individuals who were believed to support the opposition. Some 30,000 people died and almost a million people fled from the crossfire into Lima, which in 1993 was ten times larger than Peru's second city. Lima had been the pre-eminent city in the country, indeed the continent, since its founding in 1535 by Francisco Pizarro, who called it the 'City of Kings'. The Spanish conquistadores, led by Pizarro, needed a coastal port to ship their gold back to Europe, so they shunned the inland capital city of the indigenous empire that they had conquered – Cuzco of the Incas.

Lima's coastal location, however, proved a weakness when José de San Martin arrived in Lima with Chilean, English and American sailors to liberate Peru and declare independence from Spain in 1821. The South American independence liberators had stories that rival those of the conquistadores several hundred years earlier. San Martin, for example, had previously led an army over the Andes from Argentina in order to liberate Chile. In Peru, it took until 1824 and an army under the leadership of Simon Bolivar to finally defeat the Spanish forces.

Simon Bolivar had studied in Europe during the period of Napoleon's victories, before returning to his native Venezuela and fighting for independence. He was defeated twice but at the third attempt he gained victory and independence, which he followed up by liberating not just Peru, but also Colombia, Ecuador and Bolivia. He merged these countries into a single union called 'Greater Colombia' under his rule, but was to be bitterly disappointed that his hopes for pan-Americanism ultimately failed.

Our overnight bus journey to Cuzco took us away from the coast and up into the hills and mountains of southern Peru. It was long but beautiful, with the morning views being among the most spectacular and evocative of any trip on our world travels. At first it was just a relief to be on a bus that was not frozen by overenthusiastic air conditioning. We drove south along the arid coast, past the carpet of twinkling lights that receded over the desert hillsides into the distance, giving us an indication of the scale of Lima's size. We then turned east, falling asleep as we climbed upwards. Travelling from Lima to Cuzco can present difficulties for some people: the start is at sea level but the journey finishes 3,250 m higher, enough of a jump in altitude to cause breathlessness and headaches.

The Andes are the longest series of connected mountain ranges on earth, being 8,000 km from north to south, but they are quite narrow, less than 350 km wide. In Peru, the desert coast is on one side and the Amazonian equatorial rainforest on the other. In the morning we awoke to find ourselves still driving across ridge after ridge of Andean mountain chains. Bold white glaciers starkly contrasted against the black peaks in the distance. In between were empty, imposing grasslands where lamas walked in herds, coloured tags through their noses. Our road wound around itself as it snaked slowly up each valley to a high altitude pass and then down the other side, only to have to begin climbing yet another hillside.

In the valleys were small dark brown fields that had been freshly ploughed, separated by hedges of cactus with broad 'leaves' and yellow flowers. Teams of oxen were yoked together to do the ploughing; we saw just one motorised tractor during the entire journey. Some fields were being harvested by hand, the potatoes being dug out or the wheat scythed. In one village fresh drains were being excavated by a team of people. In most cases, we saw work being shared between a small group of people. Alongside the men in the fields were women wearing typical red blanket-like shawls and black bowler hats. Mud brick houses with terracotta roof tiles stood in ones and twos beside the road. We saw piles of mud bricks everywhere, drying in the sun under the shelter of grass covers.

Claudia was by now feeling the combined effects of a long bus journey and the high altitude. One of the perks of our bus ticket was that the attendant came around the bus offering a morning cup of tea to all the passengers, who were variously wrapped up in blankets, knitted shawls and woolly hats. Claudia gratefully accepted a cup of coca tea, which is a popular high-altitude drink that is supposed to relieve the effects of sickness. It is made from the leaves of the cocaine plant and can work wonders.

As we neared Cuzco the mud turned from dark brown to a reddish colour, and with it so did the houses. Just before the city was a flat plain, obviously richer and more densely populated than the valleys we had passed through. When we reached the end of this plateau, we looked over the edge and saw Cuzco beneath us. It was a sea of red/brown houses and rooftops sheltering in the bottom of a broad basin, enclosed by similar brownish coloured hills. On one of the hillsides was a typically Peruvian piece of landscape graffiti, written in gigantic letters made out of white stone: *Viva el Peru*. After the sparse buildings of the mountain valleys, it was quite dramatic to look at an expanse of houses – a city. The earthy colours were very soothing to the eye; it was a pretty city despite its dirt roads and mud brick houses. And after a few days soaking up its cultural riches, we would think that it was one of the loveliest places that we visited around the world.

When the Spanish arrived in Cuzco in 1533, a letter was sent to Charles V back in Spain saying:

> This city is the greatest and finest ever seen in this country or anywhere in the Indies. We can assure Your Majesty that it is so beautiful and has such fine buildings that it would be remarkable even in Spain.

The Incas had occupied the valley from about 1200, but it was not until the mid-fifteenth century that Cuzco as an imperial city began to be constructed, complete with gold-lined temple rooms and life-size gold statues. According to the historian Peter Bakewell, the rulers of the Incas were given the title 'Sapa Inca' and over time the tradition began of preserving their dead bodies as mummies, which were worshipped, housed in elaborate palaces and even taken on visits to one another. All these riches and rituals had a financial cost, and it has been speculated that the pressure to acquire more wealth was one of the reasons why the Incas expanded their empire so dramatically. By 1500, it stretched for 4,500 km, from the present day Colombian border to central Chile.

Almost unbelievably, the Incas were conquered by a group of 168 conquistadores, led by Francisco Pizarro, in 1532. Clayton and Conniff describe how Pizarro, having landed in Peru, invited the Sapa Inca to a meeting in the centre of a southern town called Cajamarca. With 5–6,000 armed Incas camped just outside town, the Spaniards ambushed the Sapa Inca with an onslaught of horses, cannons, trumpets and swords. Reputedly, 2,000 Incas were killed but only one Spaniard was so much as injured. The Sapa Inca was captured and was asked why he had allowed himself to walk into a trap. His reply was that it had actually been his intention to capture the Spanish instead. He offered to fill a large room with gold and silver as a ransom for his release, which was agreed to. The room was duly filled – but the Spanish kept both the riches and the Sapa Inca, putting him to death in 1533. The leadership of the Incas continued to be passed between relatives, some of whom led resistance against the Spanish from the true 'lost city' of the Incas – Vilcabamba, west of Cuzco – until the last Sapa Inca was captured and killed in 1572.

The central square of Cuzco was now a Spanish colonial construct, predictably enough. At one edge of the plaza was the familiar blocky large cathedral with two imposing bell towers on either side of it. A slightly different twist from other colonial squares we had seen was the existence of a similarly ornate but slightly smaller *La Compañía de Jesús* church on an adjacent side of the square. The open layout of the plaza was very attractive. There were no trees to obscure the views from one side to the other, and everyone could see the central fountain and the colourful flower beds nearby, perhaps while sitting on one of the nearby benches. By night, the scene was lit up with a soft amber glow, the cathedral being particularly prettily highlighted.

In Cuzco, the combination of stone walls made from blocks carved to fit one another as precisely as correctly placed jigsaw-puzzle pieces – with up to twelve sides per block – and Spanish colonial balconies overhanging the narrow cobbled streets was quite charming. Walls three storeys high were whitewashed and windows and balconies were painted blue, the result looking like a Greek painting. The reddish roofs with their neat lines of curved tiles added another layer of attractive character to the buildings. Wandering through the streets could be slightly confusing, as narrow roads merged and twisted, sometimes entering small squares with well-kept grassy lawns at their centre, but most roads eventually ended up back at the central Plaza d'Armas.

Our hotel was a fair way from the city centre, which is perhaps why it offered us a good deal on its rooms. After spending too long walking into town on our first evening in search of food, but failing to find any nearby eateries that offered more than 'bistek' or other carnivorous fare, we eventually hailed a taxi to take us to the Plaza d'Armas. As the taxis – typically Daewoo Tipos, for some reason – all had a fixed 3 soles (US $0.95) evening fare for local trips, we soon got into the habit of jumping in and out of them to go backwards and forwards. But never did we take the same route twice to or from our hotel, as each driver chose his own favourite rat run. Once, our taxi could only manage to splutter its way towards the nearest petrol station, giving out just as we reached it. The driver put in only 5 soles' (US $1.60) worth of petrol, which I took as an indication of his operating margins. The cost of petrol was unusually high, at 12 soles (US $3.80) per litre. Around the world one of the most common connecting threads was complaints about the high cost of fuel, hurting taxi drivers, boatmen and farmers all the way from South America to Asia.

One unfortunate aspect of our hotel was that we managed to lose a piece of Claudia's underwear in the laundry there. When we enquired about this, a large and fierce washerwoman emerged from a back room, vehemently denying any possibility that she had mislaid the item. She had, after all washed everything carefully by hand. We entered into a pantomime 'yes you did' – 'no I didn't' scene for a while, but that got us nowhere, to Claudia's frustration. As was so often the case, there was nothing we could do except forget it and move on.

Cuzco was, thankfully, less spoiled than the Mexican and Guatemalan honeypots we had seen. Somehow it had retained its low-key, quietly impressive Andean character. Much of the city had little to do with tourism; it was definitely a city that was busy enough in its own right not to worry overmuch about visitors. In some ways it was a remote mountain city, but this didn't insulate it from the impact of globalised modernity. I was quite surprised to learn that virtually every house had a DVD player, imported cheaply from Bolivia and used instead of CD players for playing music. Children were increasingly addicted to playing online computer games in the Internet cafés around town.

Five years ago, one 'profession' available to people in Cuzco was as a typist. With a table, chair and typewriter, people could simply set up their stall on the street, and anyone who needed a formal letter written could verbally describe what was required and wait for the result to be punched out. There used to be a whole street of typists operating like this in Cuzco. Now there are only two typewriters remaining – the Internet cafés with PCs, word-processing and printers have taken over.

Religion was changing too. Catholicism has traditionally mixed very well with indigenous religious practices, with most people practising both. Offerings were also still given to the land, to mountains or to trees in order to have good fortune. But apparently into this mix have come an increasing number of evangelical Protestants from other South American countries or the USA, who are aggressively critical of the indigenous practices. Interestingly, perhaps, Muslims have not yet even entered the scene.

Coming from Central America, we found the mix of normal life with a relatively informal tourist industry in Cuzco very appealing; it seemed to us to create a sense of dignity. At the same time, it was very easy to be a tourist in the central areas. Around the Plaza d'Armas were small tourist shops selling a variety of trekking clothes, postcards, tours and travel tickets, Internet access and photo processing. We stocked up on ponchos, first buying the same cheap plastic kind as all the locals had to hand. When it rained, the streets were turned into a kaleidoscope of moving pink, yellow and blue colours. These ponchos turned out to be little more than bin bags, however, and just as effective at keeping us dry, so we bought another pair made from slightly higher quality material, which kept us more or less comfortable throughout the rainy seasons in Peru, Brazil, Fiji and Nepal.

Along one end of the Plaza d'Armas there were expensive restaurants, complete with traditionally poncho-clad musical groups churning out '*El Condor Pasa*' on their long panpipes and guitars – one of the few places where such stereotypical music of the Andes could be heard. These were also places where guinea pig, a Peruvian speciality, could be eaten, sliced in half lengthways, roasted and served on a plate with head and feet still attached. Looking for evening meals, we could step away from the Plaza d'Armas restaurants to find that the cost of a multi-course meal would drop in proportion to the distance away from the square. From having to pay 30–40 soles (US $11) per head, we could find four-course meals for 10 or even 2–3 soles (US $0.80). Although the options on the cheaper menus were more limited, the quality of the food was still good and musicians still toured around with their panpipes, dressed in ordinary jeans at this budget end of the market.

It wasn't hard to find bargain places; touts bearing menu cards would patrol the streets, flocking around any potential customer, the first tout trying to drive away rival newcomers whilst simultaneously shepherding the tourist towards their establishment. There was a friendliness, a sense of humour and a respectfulness about these encounters that removed any intimidation. The touts had a personal touch too, as we discovered when they stopped for a chat and a smile, willing to give advice to us freely. In Cuzco, more than in most other places, we felt that tourists were still seen as people rather than as dollars, and we were treated as individual guests. It was refreshing and very pleasant.

Chapter 17: Machu Picchu

Cuzco was the capital city of the Inca Empire and around it were many Inca ruins, the most famous of which lies at the end of the Inca Trail: the forgotten city of Machu Picchu. Before going there, however, we visited several smaller temples that were strewn through the fields above Cuzco, culminating in the hilltop walled temple of Sacsayhuaman. This impressive ruin contained some of the best examples of Inca masonry, with huge blocks weighing up to 130 tonnes that are perfectly shaped to fit others as snugly as if they were a single entity. The temple was destroyed following an Inca rebellion against Pizarro and some of its stones were used to build Cuzco's cathedral. In the sunshine it provided us with a superb view out over the city below, nestling in its valley. Our tour had been by horseback – the first time that Claudia had ever ridden a horse.

We hadn't anticipated this adventure, but came across a young man called Paulo on the outskirts of Cuzco who offered us the opportunity with his family business. He told us that his grandfather could only speak Quechua, the language of the Incas and the traditional local language of the Quechua population. Paulo, on the other hand, could only speak Spanish. We learned later that this was representative of a cultural trend in and around Cuzco, driven by a prejudice against Quechua and 'country' people. They find it harder to get anything other than basic manual labour jobs in the city. Young adults even change their surnames to indicate a less rural background when they are applying for jobs. At the university in Cuzco, the Quechua language course had to be cancelled the previous year as there was insufficient interest. It was suggested to us that within another generation or two Quechua might have ceased to be an everyday language even in the Cuzco valleys. To us, it seemed sad that when so much is made of the Inca ruins, one of the strongest remaining aspects of their culture might now also be passing into history.

As it was the wet season in Peru – it always seemed to be the wet season everywhere we went – we were given the chance to walk the famous Inca Trail to the city of Machu Picchu at a bargain price, which surprised us because we had expected that places would have to be booked months in advance. Nevertheless, we declined it. The cultural landscape may have been the best that Peru had to offer, but the prospect of walking amid 500 other people was enough to put us off. Not even the saleswoman could disagree with this. The Inca Trail was also quite expensive. A couple of years ago the charge to walk it had been US $25, but this year it had doubled to US $50 and the next season was forecast to be US $100 – a serious amount of money in a country like Peru.

Instead of the Inca Trail we chose to walk an alternative five-day route that still finished at Machu Picchu, in the company of eight other European travellers, a local guide and three porters. Although we didn't see the same archaeological features as on the Inca Trail, the landscape and vegetation that we passed through were varied and interesting. The trek was named after a mountain called 'dangerous snow', which had glaciers plunging down its rocky faces, looking distinctly unappeased by the few sweets and coca leaves that our guide buried close to its base as an offering.

At night we camped in tents provided by the trekking company, some of which were decidedly ropey. The first evening, in a place called 'night sickness' because of its altitude, we had the slightly odd experience of eating our meal under the shelter of a large tent which was being stopped from being blown away by our three porters, who were each holding a corner down. Outside, our tents were all tied to one another in case one blew away. That night the thunder crashed and rolled all around the mountains, keeping us awake.

All our luggage was carried on the backs of two horses, which would be pushed along the paths at a canter by the porters. We instantly became the porters' 'friends' – in fact, we instantly became everyone's friend in Peru, *amigo* being a common term of familiar address there. It was a bit of luxury for us to have our camp food prepared for us and to be provided with hot drinks, popcorn and biscuits after each day's trekking through the rain. We ate our meals sitting outside dark stone, mud brick and straw huts, with chickens, turkeys, pigs, cats and even horses wandering freely beside us. When the mist swirled around it sometimes seemed as if we had stepped into the middle of a Scottish glen a few centuries ago. It also seemed as if the hygiene standards came from then, quite disconcertingly so at times.

The effects of this were too much for the stomach of one poor chap from Sweden, who spent the best part of two nights running backwards and forwards between his tent and a hole-in-the-ground toilet, stark naked in case of uncontrollable accidents before he reached the toilet. In the evenings the local children were glad of the opportunity to practise their football skills on small patches of flattish rock-strewn grass, in bare feet, in the dark.

Our trek took us across high altitude mist-shrouded meadows, through mossy forest – our guide called it the 'eyebrow of the Amazon', which was as close as we got to the real thing – and past small patches of coffee or banana crops. The coffee beans were small, round and berry-like, usually green but they turned red when they were ripe, reminding me of holly berries against the green leaves of the small bushes. Flocks of green parrots whirled in unison above us; they apparently eat the coffee beans. We also saw hummingbirds once or twice in the forests, but little else.

Because of the rains, the rivers we had to cross were dangerously swollen, potentially enough to prevent our packhorses from following us. Sometimes we took off our shoes and socks, rolled up our trousers, and picked our way through the turbulent streams, which seemed quite tame when we later came to wider, deeper, stronger rapids. These were bridged by the simple construction of poles laid between the banks. Usually there were a couple side by side, but sometimes we had to balance our way across a single broomstick-like pole, as the waters cascaded down waterfalls just below us. The horses had to plunge their way into the torrents, pulled from the front and pushed from behind, making quite a dramatic scene. Our final river was broad, swift and deep, so we crossed it by means of a hand-pulled cable car – more of a wooden crate really – suspended on a pulley beneath a wire stretched between the fifteen-metre-high banks.

This was quite an entertaining prospect, until our guide informed us that not long before three children had fallen out of the crate into the river below and all had drowned. He also pointed out a nearby village that was perched higher up the valley side. It had been sited on the lower banks until the river flooded and swept through the village, causing enough death and devastation for the inhabitants to relocate the entire village on higher, safer ground.

Farmers were struggling to make a decent living around Cuzco, which was partly why young people such as our guide looked for work elsewhere. Traditionally, a small household would grow crops to eat or exchange and animals such as pigs and chickens to trade – all within a barter economy. But now in Cuzco it was possible to buy imported vegetable crops very cheaply, which was undermining the local system. The remote farms that we saw had few or no crops being grown – most of the ones that were there had been planted directly into landslides, where the work of forest clearance had been already done by nature. The farms were the kind of places where children walked every day down the valley and up the other side, 1½ hours' journey each way, just to get to a morning's worth of school.

One way that farmers here could manage to get some cash income was through tourism. They maintained trekking paths through their forested valleys and in return had an opportunity to sell drinks. This was enough of an incentive for them to wait patiently by a muddy path in the pouring rain, in the hope that someone would walk past and buy something, perhaps a beer or the yellow soft drink popular with Peruvians called 'Inca Cola'. Seeing these people and how they lived made it easy to appreciate how tourism can have a direct and positive impact on people's lives.

Another beneficiary of tourism was the small town of Aguas Calientes, which happened to sit just beneath Machu Picchu. It levied a tax of US $1 for every tourist passing through, which could be as many as 2,500 per day. This allowed it to provide a fair degree of local employment. Our guide explained that his parents were farmers, but now he was a tour guide – earning 30 soles (US $9.50) per day – his brother was a security guard in Aguas Calientes and his sister worked in a hotel there. They were living case studies of how tourism can affect livelihoods; it was a story that we would find repeated all over the world.

After having travelled alone for more than two months, it was strange to be thrown for a few days into the company of an assorted mix of German, Swiss and Swedish tourists, but we all managed to rub along OK, helped along by a few beers along the way. Having seen how casually money was drunk in this way, it was a little disheartening to note how little was later dispensed as tips to our porters – barely the price of a drink each. It was impossible to know how our tips might have been used, but amidst all the indulgences of international tourism, ultimately it is the transfer of money from wealthy countries to poorer ones that can help to justify the existence of the industry as a force for development. Few opportunities can be more immediate and direct than putting cash into the hands of an Andean porter; and it galled us to see money being spent liberally enough on beer but then being withheld from locals to whom it would surely have had more value.

Before we walked into Aguas Calientes on the last afternoon of our trek we had to walk for two hours through a narrow, steep-sided valley that curved right around the base of an imposing mountain. The dark slopes were forested, but rose high enough for mist and clouds to swirl around above us. Just before we reached the base of the central mountain we were told to look up. Ahead of us, high above, was a rocky cliff face at the top of the valley side. Across this face of rock was scratched a continuous straight line, from one side to the other; and just visible, like little boxes perched at the very edge of the cliff, were some buildings. This was our first glimpse of Machu Picchu. The scratched line across the cliff was one of its entrances, the Inca Bridge path cut into the cliff. The path didn't seem feasible from below, but we were to discover that Machu Picchu defies reason and expectations.

The historian-explorer Hiram Bingham who would eventually 'discover' Machu Picchu eloquently described his impression of the surroundings in 1911:

> I had entered the marvellous canyon of the Urubamba below the Inca fortress. Here the river escapes from the cold plateau by tearing its way through gigantic mountains of granite... I know of no place in the world which can compare with it. Not only had it great snow peaks looming above the clouds more than two miles overhead; gigantic precipices of many-coloured granite rising sheer

for thousands of feet above the foaming, glistening, roaring rapids; it has also, in striking contrast, orchids and tree ferns, the delectable beauty of luxurious vegetation and the mysterious witchery of the jungle. One is drawn irresistibly onwards by ever-recurring surprises through a deep, winding gorge, turning and twisting past overhanging cliffs of incredible height.[4]

Bingham probably had a more romantic trek than us along this particular section, for we were following the route of a railway line. For several hours we had to adjust our steps to the sleepers between the tracks, which became extremely tedious. Incidentally, on the way back to Cuzco we took a ride on this train, which was an exciting prospect. It turned out to be the most bone-shaking, body-rattling, noisy and uncomfortable train ride that we would take anywhere.

While exploring the valley, Bingham met a local farmer who told him about ruins on the nearby 'Old Mountain', which in Quechua was called 'Machu Picchu'. Bingham described how he persuaded the farmer to take him there:

[He] shivered and seemed inclined to stay in his hut. I offered to pay him well if he showed me the ruins. He demurred and said it was too hard a climb for such a wet day. But when he found I was willing to pay him a sol, three or four times the ordinary daily wage, he finally agreed to go. When asked where the ruins were, he pointed straight up to the top of the mountain. No one supposed that they would be particularly interesting, and no one cared to go with me.

At the top of the slope they found a family living amongst the ruins, using the rich terraces for farming. An eleven-year-old boy finally escorted Bingham to one of the most incredible archaeological discoveries in history.

We had our first shower in four days and spent a night in a hotel bed in Aguas Calientes before setting off early one morning to visit Machu Picchu for ourselves. To reach it, we climbed a steep zigzag path that took us upwards through sweaty forest and thick mist. As we gained height, we were treated to glimpses of atmospheric views across the valley, showing the cloudy mountain summits all around.

At the top of our climb, we found ourselves sitting on the rocky edge of a small cliff, with our backs to the walls of a stone house, full of anticipation. In front of us was a thick veil of white misty cloud. We had to wait impatiently for it to clear, which it gradually did, first through shifting holes that gave us tantalising glimpses of the famous panorama below. We were sitting over a drop down to a flattish ridge that ran away from us, longer than it was broad. At its far end rose the dark shape of a steep triangular peak, like a rhino's horn sticking up at the end of its

---

[4] Bingham, H, *Lost City of the Incas: The Story of Machu Picchu and its Builders*, Duell, Sloan & Pearce, 1948.

head. The ground literally fell away on all three sides of the ridge, down into the huge semicircular gorge that we had walked along the previous day, beyond which were further mountain ridges and peaks. Just the spectacular physical geography was dizzying enough, but as we sat and watched we began to see the stone walls and green terraces of the forgotten city emerging from the clouds. This was a magical experience, making it look at times as if Machu Picchu was floating in space; its existence here seemed to require us to suspend rational belief. We were seeing a fairy-tale city through the mists of time.

The ridge had the shape of a long, thin bowl, raised at its sides and lower in the middle. Through it ran a grassy avenue, lined on either side by hundreds of stone-walled buildings of a tan brown colour. The houses were roof-less empty shells, their regular shapes forming a series of box-like squares in long regular lines. They varied in quality between smaller and poorer buildings on the outside edges of the city to the perfectly carved stonework and more elaborate design of the chief's house – which even had a hole-in-the-floor toilet – and the nearby Temple of the Sun. It is estimated that Machu Picchu housed about 800 people. The buildings continued right to the very edge of the precipices on either side, as if almost into thin air itself.

No one is really sure what the Incas were doing up here, in their remote outpost of Machu Picchu. Possibly it was a kind of seasonal retreat for local leaders, although an abundance of temples, sundials and spiritually important sites also point to it as having been a religious centre of some sort. Also unclear is why it was suddenly abandoned by all its inhabitants, presumably connected to conflicts with the conquering Spaniards. But abandoned it was, never to be discovered by the Spanish invaders, which accounts for it being the best-preserved Inca city in existence today. Perched on an inaccessible mountain ridge, its existence was virtually unknown for centuries.

The city was a sublime feat of human engineering. To build any houses at all the land had first to be terraced into levels, supported by huge boulders and series of smaller terraces cascading around the sides, almost dropping down the cliff faces themselves. Walls and doorways all sloped inwards in traditional Incan earthquake-proof designs, although over time subsidence has led to some cracking of the walls. Complicated channels were constructed to provide irrigation, culminating in a Temple of Water at the top of one of the slopes. There were even separate areas for farming and extensive series of terraces on the hillsides, reaching 300 m from top to bottom, for which soil had to be brought up from the river valley far below. Pens were built to keep herds of llamas and alpacas, the former used as beasts of burden and the latter for wool and meat. And all this packed into the compact area of the mountain ridge, an almost impossible location.

After wandering through the pathways of the city, we returned to our original vantage point to have lunch and to absorb the beauty and splendour of the city and its setting. The initially deserted streets below us were filling up with long lines of tour groups, adding hundreds of moving dots of colour to the picture. Some groups stopped just below our perch to take photographs and to be told by their guides about the history of the city. Several times we heard explanations for the different buildings, and each account was different from the one before. Somehow, it was perfectly appropriate that Machu Picchu remained a mystery. In many ways it defies ordinary comprehension. One of these is the tangible harmony between the city and its surroundings, producing a deep sense of calm and peace.

We loved it there and could have sat for hours. In fact, we did sit there for hours. If the Grand Canyon was the outstanding natural feature of our trip, for us Machu Picchu was the premier man-made wonder of the world.

Chapter 18: Lake Titicaca

Probably the worst misjudgement of our planning was the time that we had given ourselves in South America. We had wanted to travel overland from Lima all the way to Patagonia, and then return to Santiago for a flight to Rio de Janeiro in order to visit Brazil. Unfortunately, we had also booked a flight to Fiji whose date couldn't be changed, and so we were stuck with just eight weeks between arriving in Lima and leaving Rio de Janeiro. It was nowhere near enough. We could have given ourselves six months, or indeed the whole year, to potter around this diverse continent. But we hadn't, and so we raced from Cuzco to La Paz, through Bolivia into northern Chile and then south to Santiago. We had just enough time to make a few choice stops along the way, the first of which was at Puno, still just inside Peru. It was easy to book a bus out of Cuzco to Puno from one of the numerous small tourist offices around the Plaza d'Armas. The most expensive was a luxury coach that drove through the day, stopping at several tourist sites on the altiplano. The cheaper version – and the one that we chose – was an overnight bus.

Generally we felt that overnight travel was cost- and time-efficient, but we often paid for it in other ways. We found our seats on the bus at 8 p.m. and then sat and waited for it to leave until 11 p.m. The journey was terrible, being both cold and jarring and wasn't helped by either the fact that Claudia's seat – which soon became my seat – was broken, or that an incomprehensible Chinese action movie was being shown until 1 a.m. We were exhausted on arrival into Puno at 5 in the morning, not in the best frame of mind to be faced with a tout, even if he said it was his birthday. He waited patiently until we had gone to the toilet and had some breakfast from the bus-station café, and so afterwards we let him take us to a hotel.

Puno had the gritty feel of a frontier town. It was dusty and busy, as if built without gloss by pioneers in a harsh environment. Infertile hillsides were not far away, the town gradually spreading outwards over them with every additional drab brick box-house that was tacked onto their slopes. Puno had a railway line, a particularly evocative presence that seemed to signify the arrival of modernity – an achievement in itself in this remote outpost. The only use that we saw of the tracks, however, was as a spacious pathway for pedestrians and stallholders. Elsewhere, handcarts and pedal tricycles bumped their way through narrow streets, on the lookout for customers and passengers. Woolly hats and thick coats were the order of the day: the nights were often freezing at this high altitude of 3,856 m. We didn't explore much of the town – not that there was a great deal to see – because we were efficiently ferried from hostel to harbour and back by a series of tourist minibuses.

Puno sits on the bank of Lake Titicaca, which is the highest navigable lake in the world. Inca legends say that the Quechua people originated there, and it is still known as a sacred lake; if a fisherman falls into the lake, it is traditional not to rescue them as their drowning is seen as an offering to Pachamama, the Earth goddess. Lake Titicaca is now home to a group of people called the Uros, who are famous for living on floating reed islands. About 600 years ago the Uros left solid land to find security for themselves, living at first in canoes, then in houseboats and finally on reed islands. Traditionally they survived by trading fish and birds for other goods in the markets onshore – although not frogs, as these were considered sacred. More recently some of the Uros left the islands and returned to dry land in places like Puno, which diminished their numbers. Then, as tourism grew, so did opportunities to make a living again and now the island population is increasing once more.

There were about twenty-five floating islands when we were there, with about half of those open to tourist visitors. The signs of prosperity were shown by the number of motorboats, corrugated metal huts and even solar panels owned by the islanders. We took a trip out on a boat to see how people live on the floating islands, which turned out to be an interesting insight into what must be one of the more peculiar lifestyles on earth, even if it did live up to its reputation as something of a tourist circus.

The islands were found within a vast reed bed, which had channels cut into it so that it could be navigated by boats. The islands themselves were squarish platforms about 50 m wide, totally built from natural materials. Mud and roots formed a thick foundation, on top of which reeds had been placed in a layer some 4 m deep. The whole structure sat in the water, with the topmost reeds just above the water line. They looked like a thick bed of straw, and felt like it too. The platforms were secured with vertical stakes and anchored so that they stayed in one location. Reeds were also used to build round or square houses, with perhaps a dozen houses collected together on each platform. Some looked like tepees or wigwams, while others were square barns with two large reed mats draped across their tops for a roof, folded down and tucked in neatly at the edges. Pigs and ducks lived on the floating islands, too, and there were even little vegetable plots.

The two islands we visited were like a kind of living museum. The houses, cooking pots, grinding stones and so on were all laid out on display for visitors to take photographs of, as indeed were the people themselves. Enormous women wearing brown bowler hats squatted on the reeds, their long black hair plaited into two pigtails that hung down their backs. Pink cardigans over white blouses and bright blue or green billowing skirts completed the picture. The ladies sat beside small stalls of artefacts such as pots, jewellery or paintings, turning a part of their island into a little tourist market. That, after all, was the deal: come and take photographs freely, but only because you are paying us for it. We were told not to give out sweets or other presents, but, instead, if we wanted to help the people more, we should buy their souvenirs.

Around the world, attitudes to donations have changed significantly. Ten or more years ago it was customary to take small gifts as presents for people whose villages and lives we passed through – preferably practical gifts like pens or paper that could be used by children in school rather than sweets, it was thought. Sweets are still frowned on, doing little more than causing tooth decay – although that doesn't stop small children in Peru asking for a *'caramelo'*, indicating that they still receive them often enough to make it worth their while asking. But nowadays the prevailing advice, from the Americas to Thailand and India, is very much not to give out any free gifts at all. The fashionable way to help is to purchase handicrafts, in the hope that this will support a sustainable and self-respecting local industry.

We found one of the rare examples of sustainable tourism on a proper island that was further out into Lake Titicaca, called Taquile. At least, it appeared to be sustainable, through its careful management. Tourists visited in droves to see people in indigenous clothing and traditional farming practices on Inca-era terraces, on an island that could have come from the Greek Mediterranean. Rocky coastal inlets nestled beneath semi-arid hillsides dotted with sparse trees, while small fishing boats harboured offshore on an azure blue sea. We were led from the harbour up a flight of stone steps, in a straggly line that became increasingly spread out as we coped in our different ways with the effects of the altitude and thin air. There was no flat land visible, as the whole island seemed to consist of hillsides, but absolutely everywhere had been turned into terraces for farming, still being intensively used today.

As well as the crops, the people on the island kept sheep and used the wool to knit colourful clothes. Along the path we were passed by small flocks of white sheep being herded by ladies who carried small spinning tops. It seemed as if no one could stop spinning or knitting for an instant, if their hands were free. Even the men and the youths were knitting while they walked or lounged against old stone archways, looking very smart in their traditional black trousers and black waistcoats over a white shirt, topped off with bright gnome-like hats that were, of course, knitted.

We were allowed to walk along the path to the village, where there was a museum and a single shop. Here each of the hundreds of knitted items for sale had a code tagged onto it which revealed who the knitter was. When the item was sold – for a strictly fixed price – then that person would receive the profit.

It was well organised and seemed to have the effect of removing cut-throat open competition amongst the villagers for the tourist dollars. The same applied to eating: part of the deal about visiting the island was that lunch would be bought from one of the family restaurants, but each tour group had to be allocated a specific restaurant by a village elder, who ensured fairness throughout the village.

After lunch, our group was led down another stone-stepped path to a second harbour, where our boat was waiting to take us away. Our whole visit had been carefully managed to provide us with a controlled experience, while ensuring that the villagers received fairly distributed benefits and kept a large degree of their privacy. The more we travelled around the world, the more we recognised how valuable the system that had been established on Taquile was. The key seemed to be the fair organisation by the village elders; there was clear ownership and control of the entire process by locals. It seemed a shame to read later in a guidebook that some travellers disliked the touristy feel and tried to visit independently, so that they could have a freer and more 'genuine' personal experience. In such ways are carefully constructed collective boundaries broken down by individuals.

Tourism and travelling is ultimately a self-centred pursuit, which all too easily can be extremely selfish. As uninvited – albeit paying – visitors to another community, other people's homes, it is surely important to respect boundaries that have been established to protect the integrity of the community. Taquile seemed to offer a far better model than the unrestricted tourist industries in countries like Guatemala and, as we would later see, Thailand.

Chapter 19: La Paz and the Bolivian Highlands

The bus journey from Puno to the Bolivian capital of La Paz – the highest capital city in the world – took us over the Andean altiplano, passing through drab valleys of small fields and terraced hillsides, beside deep blue lakes and through a couple of small towns. There was a pervasive sense that this was a harsh place to survive in. The altitude with its thin air, the freezing climate and the sheer remoteness of these places were bad enough, but there was also a starkly evident lack of modern technology. The farming way of life appeared to have been barely touched by modernity. It looked a simple and primitive existence, changed little, if at all, for centuries. The people we saw were the very picture of labouring peasants who grow just enough in small fields to provide for their own subsistence. Each small mud brick cottage with its straw thatch – or, if it was lucky, a corrugated metal sheet for a roof – had a few patches of fields around it and several animals nearby. There were no fences or hedges anywhere, no trees to break up the landscape. Just the odd painted mural of the side of a house depicting political election symbols of a panpipe or a llama.

Long-haired donkeys stood tethered beside the road, and sometimes a couple of horses waited patiently beside a house. Small groups of cows or oxen lay in the rough grass between the ploughed strips, where one or two men could be seen digging away by hand. Women sat in the grass too, with their bowler hats on, keeping an eye on their cows or flocks of half-a-dozen white sheep. Sometimes they were even taking the sheep for a walk, bizarrely holding each animal by a separate long lead. The old women walking along the roadside seemed to have been shrunk, so tiny were their frames. They were permanently bent from the years spent in the fields, needing a stick held out in front of them to stop themselves from toppling forwards. When it rained, large puddles and small rivulets sprang up quickly outside people's doors, turning the earth into wet mud. These were sad sights, revealing the true nature of life here, of toil and poverty, hardship and suffering.

Bolivia is the poorest country in South America with the exception of Guyana. Average income per capita is about US $2,800 a year, which amounts to less than US $8 per day. A staggering 64 per cent of the population live below the poverty line. It is a high-altitude, land-locked country, which means that transportation costs for trade are very high, just like we would see towards the end of our journey in Nepal. It hadn't always been like this: a strip of northern Chile used to belong to Bolivia, providing coastal access and rights over valuable nitrate deposits. But in 1878 a dispute over taxes paid by Chilean companies escalated into a full-scale war between Bolivia, its ally Peru, and Chile. Despite heroic resistance, Lima was overrun in 1881, and in 1884 Bolivia signed a truce that handed all of the Bolivian coastline to Chile. Bolivia had lost its nitrate and copper reserves. Its silver mines, particularly Potosi, which in 1592 had produced 202,000 kg of silver, had already been plundered by the Spanish. But Bolivia still owns the second largest natural gas field in South America and 70 per cent of the world's iron and magnesium.

As La Paz drew closer the landscape became even more bleak and monotonous, yet with an almost unique quality that still stands out in my memory. Flat treeless plains of pale brown tufted grass and darker brown patches of fields ran unbroken for miles until reaching snow-capped mountain backdrops. With so much space, the people who lived here had spread themselves out across the plain. Darker brown mud houses with the odd shiny grey roof were literally dotted across the landscape as far as the eye could see. Occasionally the faded colours of a line of washing were strung between buildings; often a small group of cows were clustered close to the house, and sometimes a pig could be seen rooting up the ground by the front door. Otherwise, nothing much was moving and little seemed to be happening. It was as if the very harshness of the environment was slowing everything down, imposing its own rules and rhythms and suffocating efforts to progress and develop.

Gradually the number of red-brick walls and houses began to increase, each with its own regular quadrant of land. A large roadside sign advertised the selling off of the plots for development, right on the very edge of La Paz. There were no commercial housing estates, just individuals buying an area and gradually building their homes within it as best they could. Closer to the city were slightly older districts that had already been developed; these were roughly built areas of red-brick housing that were evidently poor. By the roadside sat women in colourful skirts and knitted woolly hats, hoping to sell something from the bundles of wares that they laid out. We continued on towards the city, totally unprepared for the sight that was about to greet us.

The houses we had been passing were sited on a plateau that is at an altitude of 3,600 m (11,800 ft). It stopped abruptly at the edge of an immense, jagged, crater-like valley. From the road, which dropped down the edge, there was a stupendous view across the valley to a beautiful panorama of white-topped mountains spread along the far side. Filling the bottom was the city of La Paz, its thousands of red-brick box-like houses swarming up the steep sides and spilling over the top. A cluster of blurry grey high-rise towers far below indicated the centre, but they were dwarfed and swallowed by the crater and its overflowing mass of urbanity. La Paz had a setting fit for the most ambitious Hollywood science fiction movie.

Despite the glamorous location, however, La Paz cannot be described as being particularly pretty at street level. The tight, narrow streets that squeezed between eight-storey buildings, always running either uphill or downhill, were busy and noisy. Cars and *collectivos* – minibuses running as public transport – crowded the roads, and the pavements were full of market stalls and pedestrians. At times it was a slightly grotty, chaotic mess of overcrowding but at others it was a colourful melting pot where indigenous traditions met globalised modernity.

Voluminous women still sat by the roadsides, their large frames wrapped up in brown, white and black checked or lined shawls and wearing their ubiquitous brown bowler hats tilted at an angle on top of their black plaited hair. Potatoes or other foodstuffs they had to sell were kept in blue plastic sacks beside them on the pavement. These loads were typically carried in a large multicoloured striped blanket of striking pinks, blues, yellows and greens, which was thrown over their back and held by two ends knotted around their neck. When the rain came, the fat ladies huddled lower, pulling the blue plastic over them for as much protection as they could get. There were dozens of these women on the streets trying to make a living by selling their goods.

The army was making its presence felt, too, with numerous men in green uniforms, black boots and black padded jackets loitering on corners. It was slightly ominous, as if trouble was expected. In fact, recent protests in La Paz were over and it would not be until Kathmandu that we felt again the tense apprehension associated with street violence and its suppression by military force. Here it reminded us that however easily we passed through countries as tourists, with relatively safe passage as foreigners, political unrest was for many people very close and real – often without the security of accountable police services or just legal processes.

We found La Paz, for all its unregulated chaos, to be an easy place to get around and get travel plans sorted. There were plenty of eateries and hostels catering to backpacking tourists; we found a comfortable hotel that conveniently provided Internet access. We had realised that there was no way we could travel overland to the southern tip of Chile in the time available, so we splashed out on domestic flight tickets that we could book online, courtesy of the excellent airline, LanChile. We also took advantage of the shopping opportunity to provide ourselves with warm alpaca gloves and hats, in preparation for our visit to Patagonia.

After a couple of nights we had to be on our way again, winding up out of the crater and onto the Bolivian altiplano, heading further south and west on what would become one of our worst overnight bus journeys. We were in for a long drive, through inhospitable country that was dry and desert-like, mostly just rocky with few plants. Somehow odd smallholdings still managed to exist, with small strips of fields and a motley collection of animals. For the first time in Bolivia we saw llamas in large numbers, proudly holding their heads upright as they stood beside the houses amid the cows and donkeys. We drove through the afternoon and into the night, changing buses once which gave us our only chance to visit a toilet. The huge tank-like vehicle with monster wheels we then had to board should have given us a warning about what was about to come. It was just our luck to find that we had been given yet another pair of uncomfortably broken seats, but then again maybe all the seats were like that.

Off we lurched into the darkness, unable to see the road but feeling it all too clearly. The 'tank' rattled slowly on, over bumps and into ruts, bouncing us for long stretches when the dirt road was corrugated and pitching us around as it rolled from side to side when the road deteriorated into potholes. It was hard to believe we were not off-roading it through the desert. Only once did we get an idea of what a horrendous track we were driving along, and that was when the bus attempted to ford a river but ended up grounding itself on a boulder in midstream. In the middle of the night, everyone had to pile off the bus – I doubt that anyone actually had to be woken up, as it was impossible to sleep on this journey – and splash through the mud and water to the safety of the bank. We stared into the bus headlights as it backed off the rock and tried a different path, lurching so horribly to one side that I was convinced it must tip over, but the driver held on and it made it through. The 'road' was more like a 4WD adventure track – an extreme off-road rally course: not much fun in the middle of the night in a suspension-less bus with broken seats.

The town we eventually reached at 5.30 in the morning was as desolate as its location. Even in the full light of day, Uyuni had all the appearance of a ghost town. The streets were bleached from the burning sun overhead and a stiff wind blew through, carrying leaves and seeds with it. The town was washed out, windblown and apparently deserted. There were plenty of houses around and painted wooden advertising boards stood on the pavements, indicating that there should have been shops, offices and restaurants, but the wooden doors were all shut and padlocked from the outside. The only people around were a couple of other lonely gringos sitting at a table in the tiny excuse for a park. Down the road a bit further on we did come across a sad little market which was feebly attempting to give off signs of life, the stall-holders huddling idly under the shade of their shelters. It was a Sunday, and so the following days were a little more lively – but not by much. The sight of a 'train graveyard' on the outside of town, with several engine hulks rusting into oblivion, did little to change our initial impression of empty desolation.

The reason that we had come to this lonely outpost was because it was the starting point for tours into the Salar d'Uyuni wilderness. As such, it was fully equipped with hostels, tour offices, banks and money changers. There was even an immigration office where travellers going on into Chile – like us – could get their passports properly stamped. We weren't too surprised to find that in this little office of two small rooms, the official at the first desk could put a sticker into our passport but not actually stamp it; that complex, highly technical operation needed the services of the second official at the second desk. At least it gave them both something to do. Having come through a desert to get to this godforsaken spot in the middle of nowhere, it felt as if we were about to venture out into no-man's-land.

Fifteen years ago, when tours first started here, it had cost US $1,500 to hire a 4WD jeep and driver who could cross the country without roads or tracks, camping rough each night. Now we paid just US $75 for our three days, still in a jeep but following established dirt tracks and staying in comfortable, if basic, bunkhouses with kitchens, bathrooms and – most of the time – electricity. The last point was significant for us, as we carried digital cameras whose batteries needed charging, especially after days of endless photo opportunities.

The attraction that draws tourists by the jeep-load was the surreal scenery of the volcanic highlands, including the largest salt flat in the world, Salar d'Uyuni itself. When we drove onto this salt lake we were faced with an immense expanse of perfectly flat blindingly bright whiteness. It was literally all just salt, in a crust seven metres thick. The salt was being dug out by locals, to be piled into trucks for export all over Bolivia and South America. Right in the middle of the vast white expanse there was a hotel, made completely from bricks of salt, with salt tables and salt chairs. It had the imaginative name of 'Hotel del Sal' and seemed a lonely place to spend a night. Which was just what one of our party had to do, on her own, because in typical Bolivian fashion our driver had spent so long driving around Uyuni before leaving that she had missed her tour's connection and would have to wait for a pick up the next day. In the middle of an empty salt lake that stretched until the very horizon, she didn't have many other options.

As we continued in our jeep, black shapes started to appear in the distance, gradually taking form as small hills fringing the lake. The closest one turned out to be an island made of ancient coral. The salt flat was actually an old seabed whose waters had evaporated away to leave all the salt behind. The island was covered with the bizarre sight of tall green cacti growing out of the almost bare rock. These cacti were 20 ft giants, with fat furry stalks and stumpy arms, looking like malformed scarecrows. The image of these strange life forms on the coral island, under a brilliant blue sky, with the flat white expanse as a backdrop, was possibly the weirdest natural sight that we encountered on our travels. It only became more bizarre when we looked out from our hilltop vantage point to see a cyclist setting off out across the salt flat. At first glance this seemed even more absurd than the cyclist in Death Valley, but on second thoughts the cool high-altitude temperatures and pancake-flat terrain made it quite practical, if unusual. When it rained, apparently, the entire surface would be covered by 10–20 cm of water; a vast saline puddle that made driving hazardous, but which produced the most beautiful reflections. Oddly for us, it was dry for our visit, so all we saw was the white shimmering glare.

Our journey continued away from the salt flat into the dry, rocky, lifeless hills. Only where there was water did small, compact villages spring up, with mud brick houses and mud brick walls lined into regular streets. One even had a pretty stone chapel, complete with a solitary belltower. There seemed to be nothing else around in the semi-arid hills and apparently no way of producing enough food for sustenance. Even when they were pointed out to us, I couldn't make out the fields of quinoa on the brown hillsides. We did, however, come across a large herd of llama one evening, coming back into a village for the night, and often we saw pairs of the smaller, wilder vicuñas running away. Once we had to take a diversion along an old, narrow track to visit a medical clinic, because a Japanese girl in our little multicultural group was feeling ill, struggling to adjust to travelling here. This was quite common, apparently.

In Puno and again here we heard the local opinion that rich tourists were too soft to cope with water that wasn't out of a bottle. Perhaps there's some truth in that. The gulf between the cosiness of homes in the USA, Europe or Japan and the reality of life in places like this never seemed wider. On our barely used track we passed a man who thumbed for a lift. He was wearing ski goggles for his eyes and sandals on his bare feet. It wasn't long before he got out again and walked off, carrying just a small blue cloth bundle over his shoulders. His journey was 40 km long, he had told us, and he wasn't even carrying a bottle of water.

We toured around a series of five saline lakes in the desert, each a unique palette of different colours created by minerals within the water. These blue, green, red, pink or white bodies of water, one of which had steam gently rising from its surface, frequently lay under the shadow of bare volcanic cones that looked like giant sand dunes turned into stone. The unearthly panoramas of stark colours and sweeping shapes were weird and beautiful at the same time. To make the scenes even more peculiar, flocks of pink flamingos stalked their way across the shallow waters, sometimes taking to the air with ungainly flaps and gangly legs dangling beneath them before turning into graceful silhouettes in the sky. In between the lakes we drove through valleys of nothing but rock and sand, triangular hills on either side coloured delicious shades of browns and reds, as if the colours had been mixed into a marbling effect using the hills as a canvas. It was all bone dry, totally empty, stark and surreal. Virtually the only other living thing we passed on these high passes was yet another pair of cyclists packing up their tent. We had to wonder at their sanity.

These highlands were volcanic in origin and were still geothermally active – an active volcano in Chile was not far away. One of the lakes had a thermal spring, allowing us to sit wrapped up in woolly hats and gloves while dangling our bare feet into waters of 28°C, looking straight at a 6,000 m high volcanic peak that rose directly up from the lake shore. Other tourist groups joined us and some set out little picnic tables and chairs nearby, complete with tablecloths.

Somehow everything here was touched with an air of surrealism – but it couldn't detract from the almost perfect artistry of the lakes and their reflections of snow-capped mountain peaks. The only time this was obscured was during a sunrise visit to boiling mud pools and hissing fumaroles. At 4,300 m altitude we walked around belching pits in half-darkness, as steam and sulphurous gases swirled all around. We could barely see where we were walking until the sun rose, casting eerie rays of light through the thick clouds.

After that, it wasn't far to another long, beautiful lake with an exquisite backdrop of snow-capped mountains, which marked the end of our jeep trip. We were transferred to a minibus and driven past a lonely hut isolated in a deserted valley. This was the Bolivian border post. Our already stamped passports were checked, but the two guards were far more keen to get their hands on the newspapers belonging to our driver, who duly handed them over. And so we left Bolivia behind and began the long descent into Chile.

Chapter 20: Northern Chile

Entering Chile from Bolivia provided a superb illustration of the geographical structure of much of the western coast of South America. In the morning we had been at 4,500 m in altitude, on high plains rich in geothermal activity, surrounded by 6,000 m peaks. Soon after we passed out of Bolivia we found ourselves poised right at the edge of the Andes, with conical volcanoes to either side of us standing like a guard of honour. Snow gleamed white against their dark profiles and ice etched vein-like cracks into them as if they were on the verge of splitting open in a new eruption. In front of us the land fell away in one long, smooth, continuous slope all the way to the coastal desert below, a full 2,000 vertical metres lower. An impeccable tarmac road swept down out of the mountains, in a statement of Chile's modernity. We joined it from the Bolivian dirt track and rolled downhill towards the Chilean border post, passing yet another mad cyclist sweating his lonely way up. If all his papers for Bolivia weren't in order, it would be a long way back down again to Chile.

At the bottom of the slope sat the small town of San Pedro de Atacama. This was literally an oasis in the desert, where palm trees were growing beside dusty streets and whitewashed houses. It was just like my imaginary picture of a stereotypical Mexican border town, complete with decorative sombreros and cacti. All that was missing were mustachioed cowboys with pistols underneath their ponchos. Instead, we found that we had re-entered the modern world – this was nothing less than a tourist resort within the Atacama Desert. It had proper toilets and iced water; there was not a trace of indigenous clothing; everything was Westernised. We could use credit cards and US dollars again; we were given receipts; the bus office used a computer to book our seats and print out proper tickets. In Bolivia, when we had booked a bus our seats had been crossed out by pencil on a paper diagram and tickets had been written out by hand. That had been the paper age – but Chile was in the computerised age. It took some readjusting to and we were to experience a form of culture shock for the rest of the day. In my experience, for some reason culture shock is always worse this way around, when moving from the basic to the affluent.

We had no desire to pay the kind of prices that were being asked in San Pedro and so, after buying a cheapish meal in a restaurant, where we were given safe water in a clean glass – another novelty – we continued on our way by bus across the Atacama Desert. Apart from the odd abandoned mining operation, a few crumbling mud brick settlements, a passing train and – no surprise any more – the obligatory lone masochistic cyclist, there was nothing but rock and dust. The pebbly, hilly grey desert continued all the way to the shimmering Pacific Ocean, dropping down again at the end to meet the sea.

The Atacama Desert is the driest desert in the world, fifty times drier than Death Valley. In some places where there are weather stations, there has never been a recorded drop of rainfall. All the way up into Peru, even to Lima, the coastal strip is barren, rocky and dry. The reason for this is that the air is already too cold to hold enough moisture to form raindrops, having been chilled by the icy sea that comes from southern Antarctic waters and the deep depths of an offshore ocean trench. So fog is usually the only relief for the Atacama Desert, providing enough wet condensation to feed the life that struggles to exist there. The cold ocean currents are very rich in nutrients, however, and support huge numbers of sardines and anchovies, which generate an important industry for Peru. The seabirds that feed on the fish create another: guano, up to 30 m deep on offshore islands. This is rich in nitrates and can be used as a fertiliser. In the nineteenth century, guano was one of South America's most valuable exports.

At the Pacific Ocean we turned southwards towards Santiago. Our original idea had been to travel the entire length of Chile overland, but despite the excellent bus services we rapidly realised that the distances were far longer than they had at first looked on the map. Chile is actually the longest country in the world. It was also turning out to be very different in character to our expectations. The city of Antofagasta was typical of the succession of northern towns that we hopped between on our way to Santiago. It is the main settlement in northern Chile – one of the places which used to be Bolivian – and receives an average of 1 mm of rain per year, but has been known to have not a drop falling for forty years. Despite the existence of a central square with its obligatory cathedral, a mock Big Ben clock tower and profusion of flowering bushes, Antofagasta did not appear to be a historical town like so many we had seen since arriving in Mexico City. It was the opposite: modernity was being proclaimed everywhere. The red-brick buildings were not functional square blocks, but had definite architecture and design. The high-rise towers, the banks, even the brilliantly white ornate cathedral, all had a kind of style about them. The roads were not only clean and well maintained, but the traffic was paying attention to road markings and traffic lights, without a chaotic cacophony of beeping horns. There were no handcarts and no three-wheeled tuk-tuks; we only saw one cycle-rickshaw. In their place were smart, shiny, gleaming cars that processed sedately through the streets. Instead of dilapidated minibuses tearing past with touts hanging out of the doors, here were small coaches professionally painted with company logos.

People were dressed in jeans, summer dresses, business suits or low-cut T-shirts. They wore high heels, white trainers or brown suede shoes. We saw briefcases, mobile phones, even ladies with dyed and styled haircuts. In the park were flocks of pigeons, rather than stray dogs. The broad shopping streets had modern art sculptures outside the open air cafés, and a proper Father Christmas with a bulging sack over his shoulder was walking up and down. Christmas decorations were brightening up the fashionable, trendy shops and the strains of familiar carols were leaking out into the street. This was Chile, but it could so easily have been Europe. Claudia found it reminiscent of southern Italy, clearly modern and developed, but still not quite able to mask an appealingly 'rough and ready' character around its edges.

One of the few cultural quirks we encountered were groups of gypsy-like women and young girls who passed through streets and parks as if blown on the wind, begging for money with a haughtily proud air. Tall and slim, with gracefully upright postures, they were eye-catching in their long flowing skirts and reddish hair. But they were also dishevelled, even dirty, as if they had been sleeping rough for a while. Hand on hip, they would defiantly accost passers-by, repeating mantra-like stock phrases – '*Una monesita por un pansito por mi niño a comer*', meaning, 'A little money to buy bread for my child' – before sweeping haughtily onwards and disappearing around a corner.

Despite there being many open air cafés and restaurants in Chile, it was hard for vegetarians to get a decent meal. Helpful waiters offered us vegetable sandwiches or avocado-on-toast, but however tasty these were, they wouldn't fill me up. As it turned out, in all our time in Chile we only ate a meal out twice, and those were both at the same fast-food counter in a bus station in Santiago. It was common for hostels and guest houses to allow use of their kitchens as self-catering facilities, and where they didn't, we simply cooked on our little gas stove in our hotel rooms, washing up in the bathroom sink. Supermarkets were as European as everything else, so we had no problems at all buying food. One of the benefits of being in Chile was the availability of a good bottle of wine, which we took full advantage of in the evenings.

Often we found ourselves eating picnic sandwiches – usually avocado, tomato and a creamy white cheese – on park benches, in high streets, or once while getting sunburned in seconds at the very pleasant beach in La Serena. There we were interrupted by a man who asked us whether we were interested in going on an excursion. Our response was that we couldn't afford it. He looked at our meagre ration of dry bread that we were dipping into a pot of butter and sympathetically said, 'Oh, you're on a budget.' Indeed we were.

Chile was, like Mexico, proving too expensive for us again. As ever, it was the travel costs that were pushing us over our budget, particularly as we couldn't spare the time for 'non-travel' days that would have helped spread these costs out.

One place that stood out as being different from the modernising northern cities was Valparaiso, a harbour town close to Santiago. This confusing melee of buildings was built somehow on top of no less than forty-five hills. The most significant of these were more like ridges running down to a coastal bay from the higher hills behind, incised by several steep ravines. Any roads, therefore, had to either curl around the front noses of the ridges or run straight along their tops. Joining these necessarily disconnected roads together were numerous little alleyways between houses – flights of steps, really – and fifteen funicular elevators. These distinctive features of Valparaiso were very short railway lines running up and down the slopes, with single brightly painted box carriages ferrying passengers up and down between the crowded houses.

The slopes were crammed full of houses until a fair way back into the hills, where they gradually petered out. Some were neat, pretty places reminiscent of English seaside cottages: wooden houses gaily painted in blues and reds. But most buildings were more like those of a *favela*, poor wooden shacks that squeezed into available spaces on the hillsides by building treacherously outwards from the steep slopes on precarious-looking stilts. We tried to follow a detailed map that marked every single little alleyway and path twisting between the houses, but we never managed to follow the route for very long before getting lost in the maze.

At the bottom of the hillsides, beside the sea where the land was flatter, were the wider, more ordered streets of the 'old town'. Some of the buildings here were exceptionally large, looking like grand Victorian warehouses, four or five storeys high, painted in pink and yellow. Where they were being maintained they looked impressive, but where they were shabbier they appeared more like Dickensian London dockland warehouses, musty and half derelict. Valparaiso was full of character, with plenty of different places to explore. It was once home to the poet Pablo Neruda, who had aptly captured something of the quality of the town when he said that anyone walking the stairways 'would have travelled the world.'

Valparaiso was also to be the only place in South America where we were ripped off as tourists. This was only by a taxi driver short-changing us – we should have picked up on the signature pause, the chance for us to discover the 'mistake' before he left – but nevertheless it was a surprise to us that it should have happened in comfortable Chile. As we travelled through the country, though, we heard about other thefts from travellers, far more so than we had done in either Peru or Bolivia.

One incident left a poor American girl stranded without her wallet on arrival at a bus station in Santiago, with no means to go anywhere else until we came along to help her out. At times like that, travelling alone in a foreign country must be intimidating. Another Australian girl we met had been unfortunate enough to miss one of her pre-booked around-the-world flights in northern Chile. She had assumed that she could just skip that particular flight and catch the next one, but arrived at the airport to be told that when one flight had been missed without prior notice, every other single flight on the ticket was automatically cancelled too. It took her three days of tearful pleading at the airline office to have them reinstated. Not a pleasant experience – but it turned into a very useful traveller's tip for us when our turn came to skip a flight from Bangkok several months later.

Chapter 21: Santiago and Patagonia

Central Chile was a green and pleasant land, with the soothing sight of vineyards in its valleys. This was the setting for the capital, Santiago, which had a picturesque backdrop of snow-capped mountains. We found Santiago an easy city to explore, coming to know it well after passing through its airport no less than seven times. In the commercial centre was the main square, full of benches under the essential shade of trees, with pigeons flocking all around and small groups of passers-by gathering beside impromptu street preachers to join in prayers and receive blessings. It was edged with a cathedral, modern glassy tower blocks, and a huge Christmas tree that had been adorned with coloured baubles. The surrounding streets were all modern, either affluent shopping parades or expensive hotel and office quarters. Local cafés sometimes had a 'stand up' theme: men in pinstripe business suites could be seen leaning against a bar as they slurped their cappuccinos, served by girls wearing such disturbingly skimpy dresses that it was hard to tell whether they had a skirt around their waist or not.

Further out in the city were several large parks, easily accessible using the efficient metro system. These were popular with locals, the paths being full of joggers, cyclists, prams and elderly strollers. One park was situated on a hill, rising 300 m for a fine view out across straight roads and a small cluster of tower blocks nearby. At the top of the hill was a statue of the Virgin Mary overlooking an open air auditorium-style church, shaded by palm trees and with Taize music playing discreetly all the time. It was all very dignified, despite the public setting.

Further down the hillside was an equally well-managed swimming pool, where families sunbathed on the grass between dips to cool off. We joined them one sunny afternoon, enjoying the diversion from sightseeing. Business, shopping, religion, relaxation: all seemed to have their place in the city, each well provided for and respected alongside one another. Santiago had a sense of maturity; it felt competent and at ease with itself. It may not have had the chaotic character of La Paz or the vitality that we would find in Rio de Janeiro – in fact, it seemed distinctly plain by comparison – but it was safe, efficient and prosperous.

We chatted to an elderly journalist in the central square one day, who was pleased to have an audience for his carefully received English pronunciation. He was proud to see Chile as being like Europe, claiming that 85 per cent of the population was 'European'. In fact, he chose not to use the more correct term 'mestizo', or of mixed European and indigenous ancestry. But this is nevertheless significantly different to Argentina or Brazil, for example, which have far higher proportions of indigenous populations. Immigrant Europeans apparently integrated themselves well into the indigenous population in Chile, perceived as beneficial traders and farmers rather than imposing colonisers. Indeed, in the 1850s the Chilean government invited Germans to come to the country to help clear southern forests for pasture. Chileans still retain evidence of the immigrant cultures in their language. English words like 'lunch' and the literal Spanish translation of 'elevenses' – *onces* – had been in use within the memory of our friend, while in southern Chile we discovered that the German words *Ja*, *Kuchen* and *Strudel* were widespread.

Our familiarity with these terms didn't help us much as we struggled to understand Chilean Spanish. It was far harder to understand than the Spanish in Peru, or that spoken by Spanish tourists. Chileans seemed to rattle words out with the speed of a machine gun, whilst at the same time running the words together by dropping their endings. Simple examples were that '*buenas dias*' was compressed to *buendia* and '*gracias*' became *gracia*. Our difficulties were a shame, the more so for me as I singularly failed to impress Claudia with my knowledge of Spanish, of which I had previously been quite proud.

We happened to be in Chile during their lively presidential election campaign. Billboards and posters were everywhere, up to fifteen A-frame boards clustered around each other on the pavement corners. Girls in T-shirts emblazoned with party slogans handed out leaflets in the streets or marched colourfully past with streamers, balloons and banners. At times it seemed more like a student election on a university campus. The campaigning was very much about the character of the candidates and from all that I could see or hear was typically very thin on policies. It was all quite familiar, really! The personality-driven slogans included such gems as 'Firm and Fair', 'The anchor for the future', or 'A northerner like you'. Practical policies were summed up by more catchphrases, from the ever so appealing 'Work, work, work' to the ambition that Chileans should 'have their feet on the ground but their eyes looking to heaven'.

The television advertisements were even worse, each containing the apparently essential elements of slushy shampoo advertisement-style pictures; lots of people from all parts of the country saying that they would definitely vote for this candidate; and images of the candidate appearing presidential, even if in one case it took a blatantly fake podium speech to a grand but empty hall. All good fun. In the end, we were able to watch the election results come in – it had been a very close contest between essentially left- and right-wing candidates – and to hear the winner's speech over a couple of bottles of champagne supplied by the jubilant manager of our hostel.

The President Elect of Chile – Michele Bachelet – began by saying, 'Who would have believed ten, even five years ago that a woman would be president?' Yet there she was, making a point of addressing '*amigas y amigos*' or '*señoras y señores*', emphasising the feminine form to show how important gender balance was to her.

Feminism may have a very long way to run yet before equality is achieved in South American countries, but it seemed Chile was making significant progress. It was also following in the wake of Venezuela and Guatemala by electing a left-wing president, as did Peru and Bolivia soon afterwards. South American politics seemed to be developing a strong sense of regional identity and solidarity, expressed in such things as mutually beneficial trade deals between countries. This regionalism felt embryonic in South America, but when we reached South East Asia we gained the impression that regional cooperation was on the verge of becoming a strong political movement around the world.

We had to fly south from Santiago to Punta Arenas in order to visit the renowned Torres del Paines National Park, in Patagonia. The only alternative to the flight would have been a three-day coastal voyage, which, although it would have given views of the Chilean fjordland and glacial scenery, was just too long for us. We were later told that this experience was highly dependent on the boat captain's inclination to draw attention to features during the voyage. As it was, the flight over the southern Andes was a real treat for me. Out of the window I saw great tongues of furrowed glaciers carving their way between snowy mountain peaks, streaked with dark lines of moraine, their snouts ending abruptly as they calved into the waters of ribbon lakes. I had wanted to visit these glaciers ever since my studies at the University of Edinburgh, preferably en route to Tierra del Fuego and Antarctica, and they didn't fail to impress.

Tierra del Fuego had been named by Magellan, after he had seen indigenous people lighting fires to keep themselves warm in 1520. He had probably encountered a tall people called the Selknam, who have since died out. Other tribes used canoes to travel the coasts hunting sea lions or lived inland feeding off rhea and guanaco. These local people were largely displaced and killed off by European settlers who established Punta Arenas in 1848 as a port during the Californian gold rush, with sheep ranching being introduced soon afterwards. Wool became the principal source of wealth for the region, which prospered until the Panama Canal was opened and ships had a new short cut between the Atlantic and Pacific Oceans. Virtually all trade now is in the seasonal tourist trade, whether staying in Punta Arenas or Puerto Natales, 200 km to the north.

The Patagonian countryside in between the two towns was particularly atmospheric. A combination of slate grey waters, lush green grassy meadows and snow-streaked mountain peaks formed what was to my mind a classically Chilean landscape. There were also great tracts of forests, so strange that even Tolkien could not have dreamt them up. They were half dead and half alive, dense tangles of thick stumpy trunks, twisted limbs and spindly branches, all bent and gnarled like hunched old women. The live trees had a dense dark green foliage of tiny leaves in tight horizontal bands, but the dead trees were bleached white skeletons, as if their outstretched, grasping forms had been petrified whilst trying to escape the clutches of the pale green moss that was smothering them in a mournful shroud, clinging on despite a scouring wind that tore it sideways. Where the forest thinned, single trees stood on the skyline looking as if they were caught in a permanent wind tunnel, every branch turned sideways like a head of hair being blow-dried.

Amongst and beneath these trees ranged cattle or sheep, and riding the fence lines or herding cattle along the road were occasional gauchos – the South American cowboy – complete with ponchos, wide-brimmed hats and three or four dogs. Where the land was higher it turned into empty expanses of bleakness, something like the North York Moors but with white-blossoming sage instead of purple heather, and little to see except sheep and fences. Sometimes I spotted the odd bird or two: an eagle on a post looked like a scrawny old headmaster with its black mortar board headdress; several yellow-necked ibises poked around in the ditches and marshy grass; and just once or twice I caught sight of the large brown ostrich-like rhea, standing surprisingly well camouflaged beside the road.

Often in Patagonia we were reminded of being in Scotland. The towns were certainly reminiscent of Scottish coastal towns, perhaps somewhere in the north-west, like Ullapool. Both Punta Arenas and the slightly more northern Puerto Natales were similar, although the former was larger and had more than just tourism about it. The main difference between the two seemed to be that Punta Arenas was surrounded by bright yellow gorse bushes, while in Puerto Natales the verges were bedecked with purple and pink lupins. Their houses were typically made of wooden boards and corrugated iron, all pointy shapes from various arrangements of triangular architecture. Despite being brightly painted in a range of colourful hues, a corroded, weather-beaten appearance pervaded the towns. Shopping streets provided a mix of practical handyman type stores for locals, souvenir shops for tourists and sporty outdoor stores for those going mountaineering.

Most distinctive, though, was the indefinable quality of the air and light, which is ultimately what made it so like Scotland. It was an artist's light, both soft and dramatic. When we looked out of the window, hearing the constant rattle of draughty frames, we knew that outside the wind would be chilly enough to make us gasp, and more than likely squalls of rain would sting salty pellets against our faces; but there was a freshness, a sense of space, that always called us outside to be a part of it. And after the aridity of Bolivia and northern Chile, we didn't mind the rain.

Accommodation was highly variable in these towns, ranging from established high-class hotels and guest houses to home-stays with families who had opened up a couple of back bedrooms in their basic houses. As we disembarked from the bus on arrival in Puerto Natales, we were handed a cheap business card from a loitering lady, which we stashed in a pocket as we set out to find somewhere on our own. Unfortunately, all the better places in the centre were full, so in desperation we pulled out the crumpled business card and followed its directions across town to where the tarmac ran out and the houses looked distinctly run-down. The upstairs of our home had been crammed full of bunk beds separated into rooms by flimsy cardboard partitions. Also staying there were a group of American students and a couple from Ireland. Downstairs was a tip, full of piles of bedding, bed frames, cluttered tables and a sedentary grandmother. When we asked if we could use their kitchen, we found a poky, filthy little room, where we had to shift piles of dirty laundry off chairs to sit down, move dirty pots to cook or wash up, and clean away old food and oily tins to find a greasy patch of counter. It was disgusting – afterwards we had to laugh to think that we had actually cooked and eaten a meal there.

The landlady was almost as shocking as her house, with a head of badly dyed orange curls and an aggressive saleswoman attitude. She offered her services as a travel agent to us, trying to sell us tickets to various expensive places regardless of whether we wanted to go there or not. We were more than relieved to escape her clutches after one night. Later on we saw her at the bus stop, touting for more guests. She asked us if we wanted to return to her house. No chance. 'Book another trip?' We almost ran away.

By contrast, we stayed several nights in a friendly guest house in Punta Arenas run by the most welcoming host that we encountered anywhere during a year's travels around the world. Each morning the young man laid out a vast spread for breakfast on the kitchen table, cooking us fried eggs and offering us slices of his mum's home-baked cakes. We watched *Star Wars* films on his TV, used his Internet to email home and chatted to him over meals. It was like being in a warm, friendly little home. He didn't even seem to care how much we paid him for everything at the end; he enjoyed meeting people and sometimes would simply close up to go trekking with guests for a few days if he felt so inclined.

One morning he organised an outing for us, a visit to a nearby penguin colony. It didn't seem like much at first as we walked out across a flat piece of moorland beside the grey sea, wrapped up well in our Bolivian hats and gloves in an effort to keep out the biting wind. But when we saw our first penguin, black and white as if in a dinner jacket, standing bolt upright with its head inclined at an attentive angle to enquire what was happening on its patch, and then jerking stiffly from side to side as it waddled towards us, we couldn't help but be captivated by these charming birds. They looked half comical as they tottered around, flipper-like wings straight down beside their sides, but also half serious with their intent, almost intelligent stares from fixed beady eyes. Some stood guard beside the entrances to their underground burrows, others lay on the grass in sociable groups, while yet more went to and fro across the beach, where they flopped on their bellies into the waves.

They were a delight to see and these couple of hours became one of our fondest memories from Patagonia, an unexpected treat. How often it would be that way: the much anticipated Torres del Paines National Park was our reason for being here, yet it turned out to be something of a let-down.

The National Park is focused on a group of granite mountains that have been eroded into distinctively shaped towers and ridges. Various trekking routes around the peaks exist, each of different lengths, with the most challenging being the seven to ten-day full circuit. We opted for a five-day trek that took us along one edge, walking alongside a long blue-green lake that was lined with white pebble beaches, green bushes rich with vivid red and orange flowers, and the steep flanks of the mountains, which rose up from the black rock of blocky cliffs. Looking across the ribbon lake with lines of rounded brown hills in the background, much of the scenery retained its Scottish feel, although the sight of herds of pretty brown and white guanacos, with the males keeping alert watch on the hillsides above their harems, reminded us that this was, after all, Patagonia. We were well equipped with our winter clothing from La Paz and wet-weather ponchos from Cuzco, having been told tales of endless torrential rain and depressingly thick mud. In the event we found ourselves stripping off to T-shirts and applying suncream in beautiful spring-like conditions.

The trek was therefore pleasant, more like an easy hike through pretty lowland countryside instead of the mountainous experience we had expected. After several hours of walking beside the lake one day, the views even began to get a little monotonous. At one point we looked up at a snowy peak beside us to see three black birds slowly circling, riding the thermals from the cliff face, picked out against the tops of pure white snow. We romantically assumed that the birds were condors, which was briefly exciting. At times we left the lake behind and climbed uphill towards the mountains through valleys of beech trees, their leaves a beautiful pale green as the sun streamed through.

These short incursions into the mountains revealed that above the black stone cliffs was a layer of creamy white rock, creating a stark visual contrast. It was into this cream layer that the famous Torres were sculpted, three vertical pillars of white rock cut out of a thin ridge. One path took us to the only viewpoint that looked directly at the Torres from the top of a moraine boulder field, with a blue-green tarn lying serenely in between. It was very picturesque, especially with bright blue skies behind – a staple image of postcards and calendars – but after a few windy minutes there was nothing else to do but turn around again and retrace our steps all the way back to the lakeside. On another occasion we hiked up into a bowl-like valley that was ringed with mountain peaks, including the back side of the Torres. It was again a pretty panorama, but not extraordinary, let alone 'mind-numbing' as our guidebook had described it.

Before getting to that particular viewpoint, we had to camp in a beech forest beside a raging torrent of a river, which thundered out of the mountains, while avalanches crashed down mountain slopes like giant powdery waterfalls. Here people were pitching their tents close to one another at a crossroads of the paths. There was coming and going at all hours of the day and night, with some trekkers crawling in after dark having misjudged the distances between campsites. Others were up and off before dawn, hoping to reach a vantage spot in time to catch the first morning rays. There was a complete range of hikers on view, from overdressed mountaineers who found their technical winter equipment an unnecessary weight on this springtime stroll, to inexperienced tourists carrying hired tents whilst wearing jeans and strappy vest tops. The majority of trekkers, apart from the ubiquitous group of noisy Israelis, were from the USA. It was the first time that we had seen so many Americans since leaving Mexico. Apparently this Torres del Paines trek was 'the Big One'. We met one guy who had come here ahead of some of the renowned national parks in his own country, including the Grand Canyon. We couldn't help feeling that he had missed out.

At this campsite we met up again with the Irish couple who had been staying at the same awful place in Puerto Natales as us. Their impression of the place was even worse than ours, as they had bought gas canisters from the freaky lady. One had lasted only a day and the other nearly exploded in their faces when they first tried to light it. Their stove turned into a fireball – a real hazard in a campsite with tinder dry forest litter and a gusty wind to fan flames. We read in a local paper about a recent forest fire that had devastated the beech forests. The article describing the fire was not entirely reassuring:

> ...during the first 48 hours, the firefighting team consisted of two dozen teenagers, armed only with shovels and without any logistic assistance...the following Monday evening the wind returned and Patagonia became a living hell. On Monday, 56 hours after the fire was declared, the local authorities

finally performed the first aircraft flyover and had a proper assessment of the real situation... the main reason is that there are no resources for it...

We learned elsewhere that the budget for all of Chile's national parks was US $5 million per year, which compared to US $20 million per year for Yosemite National Park alone. In Patagonia, travellers were bemoaning the rises in entrance fees, with Torres del Paines' rumoured to become a staggeringly prohibitive 250,000 pesos (US $475). Just as with Peru's Inca Trail, it was the environmental damage caused by the sheer weight of hikers, as well as the potential revenue stream for the country, that argued for price rises as a mechanism to limit numbers. These arguments had failed to win over the budget travellers that we met, however, who saw such world highlights fast becoming a preserve solely of the rich.

Only on our last morning did we see the Torres del Paines as they had been reputed to be. We had both caught a cold and were advised not to bother with the trek up to the snout of a glacier, so we finished our trek with a short walk around the lake shore to a catamaran port. This final corner of the park was truly beautiful. Over our shoulders the panorama of the famous ridge just got better and better; all around were red-flowered bushes, white and orange butterflies and heather-like plants that smelled of honey; ahead of us were the peaceful waters of the lake and its shore. The catamaran ride finished our trek perfectly, with a complimentary cup of hot chocolate to drink as we cruised in front of the best view in the park. The entire length of the ridge was spread out beside us, gouged into cavernous glacial troughs, with sheer cliffs and narrow ridges in between. This view had been a long time coming – in the end, we needn't actually have trekked anywhere at all – but at last these were the dramatic Torres del Paines in all their glory.

Nevertheless, it wasn't enough to change our sense that the National Park had failed to live up to our previously high expectations. Yet again, the hyperbole had only led to an anticlimax. The Torres were an unusual feature, but it had been a very long way to travel for the brief photo opportunities. When we reached the Himalayas in Nepal, we would discover the joys of proper mountain trekking amid truly spectacular scenery.

Having reached the southern tip of Chile, we now had to turn all the way around and return to Santiago. We did not have the time to do proper justice to the southern reaches of Chile and Argentina, which was a real shame. Our race across South America took us instead to Rio de Janeiro and Brazil. We didn't have long there either, especially considering that Brazil is the fifth largest country in the world. But we didn't need very long to realise that the Brazilian character was qualitatively different from any other place we had visited. It was a beautiful country, full of beautiful people.

Chapter 22: Rio de Janeiro

We were tired when we arrived in Rio de Janeiro. Our hectic schedule had meant travelling pretty non-stop ever since arriving in Lima, and now we were finding that the mere thought of another bus or plane journey was off-putting. Travelling might not exactly be a hardship, but the mental and physical fatigue of always adjusting to new places and having continuously erratic daily routines should not be underestimated. We needed a rest, to stay somewhere for more than one or two nights. Perhaps it was just as well that our plans to fly to the Amazon were foiled by the discovery that we had arrived during a peak season – Christmas and New Year – which doubled the cost of flights there. We were faced with the options of spending more of our limited funds, which would almost certainly force us to return home early, or missing out on visiting one of the places we had long wanted to see. Right back at the beginning of our journey we had promised ourselves that we would not spoil this precious time by endlessly chasing down sights. Now was one of the times to remind ourselves of that promise. We turned our backs on the Amazon, leaving it for another day. This gave us time to fill in and around Rio de Janeiro. We decided to take it slow and have a holiday for ourselves over Christmas and New Year, and as we did so, we fell under the spell of Brazil's charms.

Brazil is the country with the most Portuguese speakers in the world today. This is in some ways an anomaly within South America and is largely due to a historical misjudgement. In 1494 Spain and Portugal divided the Atlantic into separate zones for their exploration. Portugal's area was east of a line that was assumed to be well beyond the continental coastline. In 1500 the first Portuguese sailors landed on Brazilian shores, thinking that they must have found a new island. A year later another expedition arrived, carrying an Italian called Amerigo Vespucci. On his return to Italy he published details of a new continent which was from that point forward known as 'America'. Brazil's territory now extends well west of the 1494 line, but this was due to Spain's inability to challenge Portuguese explorations up the Amazon river in the mid-1600s.

By the sixteenth century the Portuguese had already begun to exploit Brazil's capacity for producing sugar cane; by 1650 Brazil was exporting about 30 million kilograms of sugar per year. This industry needed manpower, which unfortunately came in the form of slaves. Tens of thousands of native Indians were initially enslaved, but by the 1620s they had virtually all been replaced by people from West Africa. It is estimated that between 3 and 5 million Africans were taken to Brazil as slaves. They were also used to work the gold seams that were discovered in the first half of the eighteenth century, including the richest gold mine in the world at Minas Gerais. The gold rush led to the expansion of a coastal town called Rio de Janeiro, which happened to be close to the mines. It became the capital of Brazil and remained so until 1960, when the government decided to build a totally new, carefully planned, capital city further inland called Brasilia.

Once we had mentally slowed down, we relaxed into Rio de Janeiro's famously laid-back way of life. In some ways the city looked and felt like New York. Its streets were lined with high-rise blocks of apartments, fairly tatty and with air-conditioning units sticking out from the windows. Smart cars and bright yellow taxis clogged the roads, stop-starting between traffic lights on every street corner. Local shops had a 'corner store' feel, with small cafés, chemists or grocery shops lurking behind nondescript doorways. Some parts were a little worn, but this was more than compensated for by the essential element that made Rio such an enjoyable place. The people were wonderfully warm and friendly. Children with skinny arms and legs played football in the roads, watched over by parents who leant leisurely against their door frames, gossiping with one another and sharing exchanges with passers-by. Women with prams waited patiently on pavements before crossing. The cars didn't hoot at everything in sight. There was no aggressive rush and no stress. Of the major cities we visited, only Sydney could compete with Rio's relaxed and friendly atmosphere.

The dress code about town was as laid-back as the people, quite different to the smartness of Chile. Outside our hotel, people walked to the shops in dressing gowns and slippers as if the street was just an extension of their home. Men often had nothing on but shorts and flip-flops, which became slightly disconcerting in downtown shopping streets when we started to see overweight middle-aged men whose naked bellies rolled over the front of their far too small 1970s-style swimming trunks. Women usually preserved their modesty by wrapping a colourful sarong around their bodies, but not all the time. It was not uncommon to see slender, long-legged girls making their way elegantly along pavements wearing nothing but skimpy bikinis. With temperatures of 32–36°C and high humidity, we understood why dressing down was more comfortable, as we dripped with sweat.

One of the good things about Rio was the food. We were surprised but nevertheless very pleased to hear our first hotel owner's offer to use their kitchen and so off we went to the nearest supermarket and bought a stock of pasta and sauce. However, the landlady omitted to inform her staff about this, which nearly resulted in an argument with the clerk on duty that evening. He reluctantly let us into the kitchen, where we had to make do with industrial-sized catering pans but neither utensils nor cleaning materials to be found anywhere. We tried hard to be discreet and careful, and it was all going fine until I opened a jar of tomato sauce and it exploded over the kitchen, spraying the room and ourselves in a gooey red mess. Perhaps that was why they didn't normally allow guests to cook in there.

Next we tried out the local restaurants and found that they either served huge portions – always a winner with me – or took the form of self-service bars. This was a novel idea to us, but one that seemed eminently sensible. We could wander in off the street, take a plate and help ourselves to whatever we wanted from the wide selection of salads, fruits, potatoes, fish, cooked meat stews, boiled eggs and lentils. The plate would then be weighed before we sat down to eat, and on the way out we paid for the meal according to the fixed price per kilogram of food.

Breakfast in our second hotel was even more of a treat. A long counter at the back of the little dining room was full of platters and plates holding an astounding array of food. Sliced pineapple, water melon, honeydew melon, papayas, avocados, kiwi fruit, oranges, apples, bananas, grapes, fruit I didn't recognise, nuts and raisins, breads, cakes, puddings, pancakes, omelettes, boiled eggs, yoghurts, cheese, meats, biscuits… and back at the tables, more breads, coffee, hot chocolate and fresh orange juice. We piled plates high and indulged, which set us up nicely for the day's exploration of the city.

Nowhere in Rio was very far from the beaches, which seemed an integral part of ordinary city life. The coastline had a shape like a backwards 'L', with long stretches of sandy bays extending along both sides of the city. One of these formed the famous Copacabana district, supposedly an exclusive location for the super-rich. It didn't come across as particularly glamorous, apart from the fronts of hotels that opened out onto the beach-side road. But the setting was quite dramatic. A long, curving bay stretched away to either side with a wide strip of white sand before perfectly breaking waves. Behind was a line of tower blocks that followed the curve of the bay, and over their tops were green forested hills, including the famous Sugar Loaf at the far end of the bay.

The beach was filled with people wearing very little, relaxing and playing on the sand. Volleyball nets had been set up for the public to use, mostly for the popular craze of foot-volleyball. There was a sporty open-air buzz that reminded us of California, but it was equally acceptable just to laze about on the beach. Strolling up and down the sand were hawkers with their boxes of soft drinks or armfuls of wrap-around cloths, but they weren't pestering or annoying anyone. It was an easy place to while away a few hours, watching the world go by. Not many people were actually going for a swim, as the water was too chilly – just a quick duck under the waves was about all that anyone managed. But even on an overcast day the beaches were still busy with joggers or sunbathers, as if a day in Rio wasn't really complete without paying a visit to the beach.

Not far inland of Copacabana was the city centre. It took a while to realise why we found it slightly disorientating – there was no singular central plaza, unlike virtually all previous South American cities we had seen. Here the centre was a fairly dense network of busy streets lined with shops and offices, much like many city centres in Europe. In an Internet café we had to queue for a computer because the place was full of young men in office suits and ties shouting at each other as they played arcade-style combat games. This didn't come across as an entirely healthy pastime, but the sight of young men or boys playing these violent games was a ubiquitous feature of Internet cafés all around the world.

Nevertheless, access to the Internet provided us with a means of making arrangements to hold a wedding in New Zealand, and even to invite one or two guests. Thankfully, our celebrant-to-be was game enough to agree by email to marrying an Englishman and an Austrian who were travelling around the world but promised to pass though Wellington on a certain date!

As we explored the streets of central Rio we passed lots of shops stocked with white dresses, which was the traditional colour to wear for New Year's Eve beach parties. Claudia's mind, however, turned to wedding dresses. 'Just a look,' she said, as we went into one shop. 'I don't like this much, but I'll try it on anyway, just to see if the cut suits me.'

I waited while the shop assistant took some accessories into the dressing room – and then she beckoned me forward. There, looking like a radiant angel to my eyes, was Claudia in her wedding dress. She had never looked prettier. To find a wedding dress from start to finish had taken about ten minutes, which must surely be some sort of record. And maybe it was just coincidence, but the next few streets were full of jewellery shops. It took two or three to find a pair of rings that suited us. Suddenly we were all set for a wedding. Rio, we thought, was quite a romantic place to go shopping.

Like Brazil in general, Rio contained great extremes of inequality. By one measure, Brazil was the fourth most unequal country in the world. The poorest 20 per cent of the population own just 2 per cent of the country's wealth, while the richest 20 per cent own 64 per cent of it. In Rio de Janeiro the richest 1 per cent was even said to own more than the combined total of the poorest 50 per cent. Some of the city may have been extremely wealthy, but never very far away – literally – were areas at the other end of the income scale. 15 per cent of the city's population lived in poverty, one third of them in a *favela*. There were 180 different *favelas* – communities of illegal housing – squatting on the hillsides and in the valleys that surround the official city districts. The richer areas nearer the coast were clearly visible from the hillsides, and in many cases the *favelas* ran right to their edges. *Favelas* were often too big for the government to try to evict people from, so there was a policy of trying to integrate them into surrounding neighbourhoods. Water and electricity services were being provided through local 'associations' who also offered postal services, health care and citizens' advice.

We joined an organised tour to one of the most notorious *favelas*, called Rocinha. It was one of the largest *favelas* in Brazil and one of the most developed. It contained an estimated 100,000 people – with five schools, two banks, a samba school, four radio stations and a local cable TV station. The houses were almost falling over one another, connected by narrow passageways just like those in Valparaiso. Many of the houses were well established; some had been constructed to a relatively high standard by workers who migrated from the north-east of Brazil, initially in the 1940s. Electricity cables hung above the paths like lengths of black string, collecting in great tangled bundles at central posts which Claudia aptly described as 'cable salad'. Each house had an electricity meter, but the wires had frequently been reconnected to avoid paying bills. Washing lines draped clothing over the alleys, while potted plants and the odd caged canary brought a little life into the claustrophobic maze. Blue plastic tubs set on every rooftop collected rainwater. There were barely any roads into these *favelas*, so everything had to be manually hauled up and down the steep slopes – from bricks and mortar to waste and rubbish. There was only one main road into Rocinha, which was full of motorbikes acting as cheap taxis for journeys up and down the hillside.

In some ways the *favelas* seemed just like any other urban neighbourhood, albeit poorer and more chaotic. Eccentric they certainly were, but we didn't have the impression of miserable slum conditions, except at their edges. Indeed, the relatively good views afforded by houses on the hillsides had made some places within them fairly desirable for middle-class types, who took advantage of the cheap prices. Our guide even told us that some buildings had been turned into bed and breakfast accommodation. We had a look inside one tall, thin apartment block – some were seven storeys high – which had rooms furnished with plush carpets and wooden furniture, kitted out with modern hi-fi equipment.

The wider streets of Rocinha were lined with shops just like in any other district; we were told that the owner of one delicatessen actually lived in Copacabana. In the windows of houses were informal signs advertising clothes, DVDs or food for sale. Work wasn't easy to come by, so many people from the *favelas* worked in the service sector in the city, as maids or cleaners in private homes or in supermarkets and hotels. One of the reasons that our tour was allowed into Rocinha was because it was bringing another income stream – from paying tourists. There were even little shops and stalls selling home-made arts and crafts to visitors. However, beyond the external appearances of relative normalcy, there was a dark side to life within many Brazilian *favelas*.

Drug barons were in control of everything that happened inside Rocinha. I asked our guide how influential they really were, what with all the apparently independent shops and other enterprises. He replied that nothing happened unless the gang leaders allowed it: they had total power. We were only allowed in under the escort and supervision of young lads who maintained a watchful eye on us, keeping us within clear limits and not allowing photographs in certain places. The drugs trade in Rocinha alone was reportedly worth US $3 million per week. Young people who get involved in the drugs trade here often don't live beyond twenty-five years old. Of the 102 people killed every single day in Brazil, 90 per cent live in city *favelas*. Police didn't venture inside Rocinha much, tending to maintain a watchful presence on the outside. When they did go in, it was usually in groups and with guns, carrying out swift and dangerous raids. A form of street honour upheld by the gangs did, however, tend to ensure that little internal crime occurred within the *favelas* – apart from when conflict erupted between rival groups. Only two weeks before we visited Rocinha there had been a shoot-out on the streets that killed a gang leader, changing the balance of power.

Rio's districts nearly all follow the shoreline because they are hemmed in by hills whose slopes provide homes for the *favelas* and whose tops are covered in coastal rainforest. The forests within Rio were the largest city forests in the world. We decided to walk up to the top of one hill to get the view from the Christ the Redeemer statue, whose pure white outstretched arms overlooking the city and its coastline is one of the iconic images of Rio de Janeiro. The hill was just over 2,300 feet in altitude, with the statue adding another 100 feet to that. We had to get a bus to the foot of the hill, from where a little train ran visitors up to the top and down again. There was also a queue of taxis offering to drive people along the road that we intended to walk up. The idea of walking was something of a novelty to everyone else. One taxi driver offered us a price of ten reals (US $5) to drive up to the statue. We said we wanted to walk and he couldn't quite believe it. 'But it's nine kilometres!' he protested, 'and you are on holiday!' Still, he pointed us in the right direction.

Soon afterwards we passed a lady crossing the road, who helpfully asked us whether we were looking for the train station. No, we were walking. 'But it is a long way and it is dangerous,' she told us, clearly a little worried. We pressed on. Next came a man whose reaction was, 'It will take you two hours. It's twelve kilometres – you are crazy!' He offered us a price of twelve reals for the journey in his car.

Upwards we went, finding our way through the roads that twisted around the outside of a small *favela*. A group of lads were hanging around a barrier across the road at one of its entrances. And sure enough, there was a police car loitering just around the corner. One of the older youths came down to us and offered us fourteen reals for a lift. He too was of the opinion that we were mad, but gave us accurate directions that skirted around the edge of their territory.

It was a long walk, but was pleasant enough along the winding road, and good exercise – something that can be hard to get whilst travelling. The forest was thick, humid, mossy and lifeless, but we did get one or two good views across the *favelas* and the city. When we got to the top we walked past the railway station, a couple of restaurants and several tourist shops before emerging at the foot of the statue, behind its back. It was looking out over a drop all the way down to the coast, a very impressive view of the curving bays of the city, with high-rise blocks in front of them and Sugar Loaf just behind. We were just in time, as all too soon grey clouds swirled in, surrounding us and totally obscuring all the views. So we left, this time taking a ride on the train. We were glad we did, for at one of the stations halfway up the hill there was a samba group on the platform. They started playing for the people in the carriages and soon every Brazilian inside the packed train was singing along with them. As ever, it was a delight to be in the midst of such Brazilian joie de vivre. We were to experience more of this over New Year, but Christmas would come first.

Chapter 23: Ilha Grande and Paraty

Although I felt that we could have spent a couple of weeks in Rio alone, we wanted to see just a little more of Brazil. We met other travellers who had endured mammoth bus journeys to reach places further west or north of us, but we personally couldn't face any more overnight trips for a while. Instead, we drove along the coast and out to an island that was full of idyllic beach-lined coves and coastal hills covered in rainforest. This wasn't what we had originally planned, but Brazil turned out to be one of our favourite beach destinations. The island of Ilha Grande was popular with all sorts of holiday makers, so there was plenty of accommodation to choose from. We started off in a campsite, until the attraction of the bare ground and communal facilities wore off as we were plagued by sand and ants – although thankfully not the dengue-fever-carrying mosquitoes that we were warned about by health posters.

In the sweaty heat the attractions of air conditioning also grew on us, so we moved into a cosy guest house, which had freshly painted wooden fences around a pretty garden and a constant stream of hummingbirds flying across the paths to hover at special feeders just feet away from our eyes. We were delighted by it all, and took great pleasure in relaxing into unaccustomed luxury. The village was everything that Cay Caulker hadn't been. Here we really could wander about barefoot, over stone-laid walkways, along neatly swept wide sandy paths and between the carefully tended gardens of impeccably maintained guest houses. Beyond the village there were over one hundred beaches, should we want to explore them. Some were attractive to divers and snorkellers, others were more for sunbathing and swimming.

The closest formed a succession of small gently sloping sandy bays with barely a swell disturbing the shallow waters. The sun was so hot and intense that we just had to go into the water to get some relief every now and again. Every single fair-skinned person whom we saw was burned red somewhere or other. We found that even with factor 15 suncream on, it only took fifteen minutes in the sun to burn. So we sought out the shade of palm trees, where we would read or play chess, gradually getting warmer and warmer until it was time for another dip. Travelling can be such a hard life!

To reach the more distant beaches involved either a short hike over the hillsides or a boat trip around them. We chose the walks, to give us some exercise, getting hot and sweaty as we climbed up muddy paths through the coastal rainforest. These short hikes were semi-tropical jungle experiences to remember. Mossy trees had vines and creepers hanging down everywhere and fresh green plants growing from every available branch. Towering stands of bamboo sprouted beside us, their stalks as thick as my wrist. Often we were nearly overpowered by the stench of rotting durian fruit, which is a sickly sweet football-sized brown fruit, renowned throughout the tropics for its pungent smell. Some people thought it was a delicacy, but when we tasted it in South East Asia we were not impressed. It had a flavour somewhere between overripe papaya and rotten cabbage. Unfortunately, at that particular time it was being offered to us by some ladies who had invited us to share their lunch – Claudia bravely swallowed several pieces and tried to look appreciative.

In the smelly forests of Ilha Grande, at one memorable point we stopped for a drink of water and a nearby movement of leaves caught my eye. Hanging in the branches was a bright green snake, slowly lowering its coils from twig to twig. It was a little unnerving to see it, not knowing what else might be lurking in the trees. But the only other creatures we encountered were an iguana that clawed its way off the path in front of us, and huge black flies, more like giant moths two inches long, which irritated us by buzzing around our heads. Our reward for these intrepid jungle adventures were long, empty stretches of beach around the coast, where we could relax in peace.

We could hardly notice that Christmas was upon us on the island. There were a handful of lights twinkling in some trees and a nativity scene had been set up outside the church, but there wasn't really any festive spirit. The Brazilians were probably saving their energy for their big event – the New Year's Party. So we gave ourselves ten reals (US $5) and half an hour to buy presents for each other and treated ourselves to a Christmas dinner in an expensive restaurant. This turned out to be disappointingly ordinary, not helped by the quality of the wine. Several times we had sampled Brazilian wine and on every occasion – this included – we decided that it was awful. With the meal having been a bit of a let-down, we returned to our guest house to find the leftovers of a feast that had been a present from the owners to their guests. They had come looking for us several times that evening, but we weren't there and had missed out on a seasonal banquet.

For New Year, we returned to the mainland and moved further south along the coast to a small colonial town called Paraty, which had been founded in 1667. In the nineteenth century it had been the second or third most important port in Brazil, because it was at the end of a gold trail that led from the mines inland to the coast. After this route was diverted by a new road to Rio de Janeiro, the trail continued to be used to take slaves to sugar and coffee plantations, as well as to the gold mines. In the mines, slaves were considered to have a 'useful lifetime' of just seven to twelve years. Today, the Old Gold

Trail has become a tourist attraction. It has been turned into a leafy walk passing beneath small banana trees, with flocks of screeching green and red parrots flying overhead and bright blue butterflies the size of saucers flitting between yellow and white flowers. Although we had missed out on the equatorial rainforest of the Amazon basin, Brazil's coastal rainforest proved to be a real treat for us, with its vivid flora and fauna becoming a rich part of our experiences.

Paraty itself was left largely undisturbed after the gold rush stopped, and so it has managed to retain its Portuguese colonial character, to the extent that the entire centre has been declared a national historic site. This was a small area of gridiron patterned streets that were cobbled and totally closed to motorised vehicles. The one- and two-storey colonial houses were now largely restaurants, curio shops or art galleries. The fairly plain, almost Puritan chapel-like churches were the dominant buildings. It was charming in a gentle, slightly twee, Cotswolds-type way, half catering to beach holidaymakers and half aspiring to be posh and arty. The 'real' town lay inland of the historical centre, while to one side, across a river, were beaches full of picnicking families and a sea so warm that it felt like a muddy bath.

On New Year's Eve we visited a nearby beach that had been turned into a kind of Glastonbury-by-the-sea. Tents filled every available space between the sandy roads, little guest houses, cafés and, of course, the beaches. From out of the tents streamed a continuous river of brown bodies, wearing nothing but bathing shorts and bikinis, all heading to the sea. The youth of Brazil were on holiday for an all-night party. The beaches were gorgeous: wide arcs of golden sand beneath verdant coastal rainforest. Bold lines of white surf ran up the bays, bathers rising and falling in the water with the waves. Everywhere was packed with people, sunbathing, swimming or surfing; promenading, preening and displaying their bodies. The Brazil we saw was a beach nation; it was as if Brazilians were naturally at home on the sand.

Back in Paraty, we headed down to the seafront at about 11 p.m., joining a throng of hundreds of people moving slowly but steadily in the same direction. Virtually everyone was wearing something white. Some had a white top, others white trousers, others were completely white. The girls in particular were all dressed up in dainty skirts and summer dresses. This was a family occasion, with people of all ages out together. There was no trace of rowdiness or disorder. Until we reached the beach I didn't see a single can of beer, and then only one or two. Quite a few people were carrying small bottles of champagne; a couple of lads in baseball caps passed us holding champagne glasses delicately in their hands. At the beach the mass procession ground to a halt, forming a crowd in front of a large concert stage. The stage was dark and silent, but that wasn't stopping the Brazilian bodies from swaying, their hips rolling to an unheard rhythm, everyone expectant and happy. Adult men were moving in anticipation just as much as the young girls.

Then the lights came on and a samba band started playing, with two bikini-clad dancers jerking and thrusting energetically on stage. The minutes ticked past and I could tell midnight was nearing when I saw a lady at the corner of the stage with a stopwatch. The music continued playing but the crowd made up its own mind about when to celebrate, helped by some premature fireworks bursting down the beach. With a cheer, champagne bottles were shaken, corks popped, and jets of champagne were sprayed everywhere. Everyone was wet, laughing, hugging and kissing each other. The joy was spontaneous and moving. And then the fireworks began. The crowd 'ooohed' and 'aaahed' as burst after burst lit up the sky, gradually building up to a finale of golden stars cascading down in ribbons. It was 2006 – *Feliz Ano Novo*! And as soon as it was over, many people began to trail home again, as the samba band played on. It was not until halfway back that I realised we had only seen four policemen all evening. There had been no need for Claudia to leave her jewellery at home; it had been a beautiful celebration from start to finish.

The next day we left Paraty and returned to Rio de Janeiro, where we found everything closed, including most public transport. Unfortunately we didn't know this until a pre-paid taxi from the bus station had already dropped us outside the nearest metro station, which was locked shut. We found ourselves stranded in a slightly dodgy area of Rio with no idea what to do next. A passing Peruvian rescued us – it seemed a miracle that a Spanish rather than Portuguese speaker should be passing just when we needed him – and he directed us to one of the few open metro stations.

Our time in Brazil was over too soon. It had been a heart-warming, interesting, relaxing time from start to finish – the perfect holiday. As we left, we agreed that this was one country that we really wanted to return to. We had only had a taste, but it left us hungry for more. As it was, we had to turn our faces west again, back across the continent to Santiago and then out into the Pacific Ocean. We had a once-in-a-lifetime opportunity to look forward to: a visit to Easter Island. As a child I had read Thor Heyerdahl's accounts of his adventures on the island, mapping the locations of the enigmatic Moai statues and hypothesising about their mysterious creation. More than anywhere else in the world, Easter Island was a place where we expected to encounter people with an exotic culture, a fascinating place full of intrigue.

Chapter 24: Easter Island

Easter Island is the remotest inhabited island in the world, 2,000 km from the next centre of population and 4,000 km from the Chilean mainland. Its people, who call themselves, their language and indeed the island itself 'Rapa Nui', proudly describe it as being at the 'navel of the earth'.

It was created from a now extinct volcano that rose 10,000 ft from the ocean floor. There are three separate craters on the island, one at each corner of a roughly triangular shape, about 17 km long and 10 km wide. In between are low hills and flat land; around the edge the sea crashes into jagged black lava cliffs, conveying a sense of wild remoteness.

The most famous image of Easter Island is of its Moai stone statues. Their characteristic shape is of a broad torso supporting a large angular head, hewn out of a single chunk of grey volcanic rock. The tallest is 33 feet high and has a weight of over 80 tonnes. Around 887 of them had been carved and then carried to sites all around the coastline of the island. Some had been transported six miles across the island, probably by being rolled on wooden logs. Some Moai were erected in straight lines on square cobblestone platforms; five, seven or even fifteen could be seen standing side by side in a formal row. A few still had red hats on, one or two stared out from gleaming white eyes. Surprisingly to us, almost all had originally faced inland. Most Moai now are in various states of repair, such as heads with great chunks smashed off by the occasional storm waves that can break over the island. Many look abandoned, half-buried or even lying face down amid the rocks.

We had expected the statues to invoke a sense of awe, imposing, even intimidating. But really they just fitted naturally into the landscape, becoming a kind of familiar feature of the island. They were large, being on average fourteen feet tall. But their size wasn't intimidating – it would be hard to be dominating when set into a semi-wild, rugged landscape with the vastness of the ocean behind. Indeed, the statues had an almost comforting, benevolent presence with their human appearance. A certain enigmatic quality attached to them, certainly, but they were more normal than we had expected, not appearing as a breathtaking wonder. They seemed to be keeping watch over the island, quietly and motionlessly standing guard.

Later, when we were in a New Zealand museum, I was surprised to see a small wooden statue that was carved with extremely similar features to those of the Easter Island Moai. It was a traditional Polynesian carving and as such was believed to contain a spirit within it – so it couldn't be photographed. Although the exact function of the Easter Island statues is unknown, they almost certainly had similar properties. As well as being symbols of power – perhaps indeed representing ancestors who watched over small settlements – they probably were believed to hold the same magical spirit.

The Moai were carved out of the side of one of the volcanic craters, at a site now just called 'the quarry'. It appeared as a small hillside, sloping down to the flatter centre of the island and the empty shoreline. Stone heads poked out of the grassy ground at all angles, as if half-submerged and waiting to be rescued. Further up the slope, where small rock ledges protruded near the rim of the crater, half-cut statues could be seen everywhere. Here they looked as if they were literally growing out of the rock, in various stages of completion. We had a couple of hours of fun exploration one morning, poking about amongst the statues on our own. As the low morning sun began to burn through the clouds, it bathed the statues in a warm glow, silhouetting their shapes against the sea and sky. When the sun rose higher and the sky became a clear blue, it was time to cycle the 12 km back to the only village, virtually from one end of the island to the other.

We had with us two dogs who had followed us out of the campsite in the early morning. We quite enjoyed their company on the empty roads, slowing down so that they could slake their thirst in shallow puddles – but by the time we had reached the quarry they were obviously hot and tired. On the way back we had to guiltily leave them far behind, struggling along the road in the midday heat as we raced back to return our bikes before noon. It wasn't until much later that afternoon that we were relieved to see the first dog make it home, crawling under the shade of the house for a long sleep. The second must have arrived sometime in the evening, for it was there next morning.

The previous day we had hired our bikes for twenty-four hours with the intention of cycling all around the island and stopping off at various sights along the way. Cycling was a popular way of sightseeing, although there were only a limited number of tarmacked roads. We made it to the far side of the island, beside a very pretty white sand beach that was fringed with palm trees and watched over by a photogenic row of Moai. After a short swim there we set off again, but immediately one of Claudia's tyres burst on the sharp volcanic grit. We were stranded and had no idea quite what to do – it was the end of our afternoon's sightseeing. It took the help of a typically friendly lady selling souvenirs to arrange a lift back in a partially full tourist minibus, whose driver told us that ten years ago it had taken a two-day trip on horseback to get around the island. Nine years ago the roads had been sealed, and now jeeps run the island tour in three hours.

The nature of Easter Island surprised me, as we walked and cycled around its various paths. With images of a treeless landscape in my mind, I was prepared for an empty desolation befitting the loneliest island in the world. But almost everywhere was surprisingly green, mainly because of introduced eucalyptus trees. Grasses were growing well in fields beside the roads and shrubs formed little hedges. Dragonflies buzzed beside us, birds darted from the verges and hawk-like birds perched on the fence posts. From out of the woods, the rocky beaches and the roadside verges stepped numerous fine brown horses. There are now 3,000 horses on the island, usually semi-wild and causing significant amounts of erosion. Another introduced pest was the ant population, which apparently arrived only six years ago but had since spread literally everywhere, because they have no natural enemies on the island.

It may be that the island as we found it was beginning to look something like its condition several hundred years earlier. With fresh water and fertile soil, the island once had abundant palm trees and grasses. The Rapa Nui people had no problem growing sweet potatoes, sugar cane and bananas. With plentiful sea life around, including porpoise and turtles, and the birds from what was probably the richest seabird breeding site in Polynesia, the island was able to support a population that once reached somewhere between 7,000–20,000 people. Contrary to Heyerdahl's imaginative but largely erroneous work, the original inhabitants had come from Polynesia – although how the South American sweet potato had arrived was still a mystery. People had certainly been on the island since AD 318. They developed their own writing and specialised in the manufacture of huge stone-carved statues called Moai, which were carved largely between 1100 and 1600.

But by 1877 there were only 110 people left alive on the island. The causes of the catastrophic decline of the Rapa Nui population and culture are still disputed. It may have been that the islanders caused their own downfall; cutting down trees may have deforested the island to such an extent that by around 1400 the whole ecology collapsed and people began to starve. Within this ecological theory are suggestions of inter-tribal wars in the seventeenth century, between Swiftian groups of 'Long Ears' and 'Short Ears' – referred to in island legends – and events such as the overturning of statues and people living in caves. It was even rumoured that islanders resorted to cannibalism, which may not have been unusual for Polynesian cultures.

After this dark period, the population may have recovered to about 3,000 by the time Europeans entered the scene and began to wreak their own destruction, causing the population to crash again. On Easter Sunday, 1722, a Dutchman arrived at the remote Pacific island and gave it its European name. During the nineteenth century, Peruvian and Spanish slave traders and whaling ships made more than fifty incursions onto the island. Despite fierce fighting, hundreds or even thousands of islanders at a time were carried off as slaves, including the king and priests. The ravages of smallpox were brought to the island, decimating the population still further. In 1864 missionaries arriving at Easter Island found a scene of social collapse among the hundred and eleven survivors – and within three years had converted all of them to Christianity. The truths of the Easter Island cultures and history were all but lost, largely confined to stories and legends.

But the sorry history was not yet over. In 1888 Chile annexed the island and penned all the remaining population within the confines of their village for nearly one hundred years, while the island was rented to a company for sheep farming. This probably caused the final deforestation of Easter Island. Only in 1960 was the population freed and the island and its people given a chance to begin their recovery.

The closest we got to experiencing the Rapa Nui culture for ourselves was to hear its language still being spoken by our campsite hostess, who was Rapa Nui herself. The locals used their language partly as a means to distinguish themselves from incomers. Even the population was globalised, with only about half of the 4,000 islanders being native. The rest were mainly Chilean, although a good handful came from places like Tahiti, Europe or the USA. The children from the island managed to get around too: one lady we met had children in Miami, Paris and Monaco. It was hardly a remote island out of touch with the rest of the world. Our landlady told us that there still were three traditional healers on the island who dispensed medicines, and that meals cooked in earth ovens were still being prepared for tourists, but virtually all the other traditional customs that had been rejuvenated by the local population seemed to be crammed into one week-long annual festival, perhaps something like a village fête.

During this festival there are competitions in body painting, canoe racing and so on. Pictures of men and women wearing little but grasses, animal skins, body paint, masks and headdresses, which are sold to the world as the image of Easter Island, come from this event – but we saw nothing like that, and those images didn't really fit the island that we found. Incidentally, one famous tradition that is unlikely ever to be restarted even during the festival was that of the 'bird-man cult'. Paintings of the swirling character, symbolic of Easter Island, could still be seen in caves within the rough lava cliffs, but the best representations were on the modern carvings and paintings of houses and shops in the village. The 'Birdman' was a title given to the first person each year who managed to swim across shark-infested waters to a little islet offshore and return with a tern's egg, unbroken of course.

We had been warned by our landlady in Santiago that we would have to pay high prices to stay in a tourist resort on Easter Island. But we found a simple campsite on the edge of the village, next to the coast, that was in the process of being established and therefore not mentioned in our guide book yet. The only village on the island was a fairly sleepy place, with just a few tarmac roads and a smattering of dirt lanes in between. Well-kept houses were spread out, with enough space for tended gardens that blossomed with flowering bushes and shrubs. Everything was within easy walking distance. There were a couple of grocery stores, a little market, a pub by the harbour and a post office. We became familiar with the post office, visiting it several times in the hope of receiving a Christmas present sent by my mother from England. It didn't arrive in time, but must have done so eventually, for it was later sent all the way back home again. Postal services around the world must surely be one of the most understated and yet truly magnificent achievements of human communication. We would finally get to open our Christmas presents in Europe some nine months later!

Alongside the close-knit character of the village that seemed typical of an island community there was also a strong tourist economy. Many offices advertised tours around the island, Internet access, and cars or bikes for rent. Expensive hotels and chalet-bungalows were much in evidence, with more being constructed all the time. Globalisation had arrived here in more force than we would ever have imagined. Aeroplanes were now landing twice a day, one in each direction between Santiago and Tahiti. This was seen as a good thing, because the planes brought more tourism and therefore more employment, which was needed on the island. They also brought more chances for the islanders to go shopping on the mainland. Our landlady had been to Santiago several times over the past few years, always coming back with three suitcases stuffed as full as she could manage with shampoo and foodstuffs; items that were unavailable or too costly on Easter Island itself. It must surely rank as one of the longest shopping trips in the world!

It was suggested one morning that the people at our campsite could cook freshly caught fish in a traditional earth-oven meal, with the help of our hosts. The idea was passed around the various German, Japanese, Italian and Irish guests, and Claudia set out to the market to buy a fish before they were all gone. The fish was a couple of feet long and was sold at inflated tourist prices. Back at the campsite, multilingual Chinese whispers about the meal continued throughout the day, eventually resulting in everyone giving up on the idea and leaving Claudia stuck with a huge fish in the fridge. This wasn't much good to us, but the others graciously helped Claudia out at the dining table that evening. And so even our attempt at sampling a traditional meal was foiled.

Right across the Americas we had witnessed a tidal wave of globalised culture that was washing through every locality, swamping their distinctive characters with a repetitive mix of English pop music, blue jeans and

European-style shirts, Internet cafés, pizza, pasta and beer. A macro-scale homogeneity seemed to have spread virtually everywhere we went, always familiar and often provided in a practical and efficient manner. Partly this was because global travellers are quick to take advantage of – and indeed sometimes demand – 'home from home' comforts. The tourist industry provides Westernised hostels and restaurants, because these are the sort that make money. One of the ironies of travelling is that taking advantage of such home comforts probably undermines the very local cultures that tourists have purportedly come to experience. Jeep tours provide glimpses of an outside world through glass windows, before returning to globalised restaurants and bars where travellers can bemoan the lack of 'authentic culture'. Local people do change quickly too, as they embrace the improvements to quality of life that globalised modernity, perhaps led by the tourist industry, can bring.

This is the process of development, both economic and social, taking advantage of ever greater access to the wider world. Tourism will only accelerate that development – although not always sustainably – as it provides jobs and wealth to people, often in places with precious few alternatives. But in an additional irony, it may also turn out to be the only thing that will preserve pockets of indigenous culture that would otherwise be lost from one generation to the next. Tourism can give displays of traditions a tangible monetary value. Many tourist attractions that we saw – 'cultural' photo opportunities at a price – seemed to be just shows, stage-managed for the tourist industry. This was the case from Peru to New Zealand, from Fiji to China. Perhaps one of the reasons that we felt the force of globalised development more acutely on Easter Island than anywhere else was because there was so little traditional culture left.

Once we had visited the quarry and the perfectly bowl-shaped volcanic craters with their green lakes inside, we began to run out of things to do on the island. A week there was perfectly long enough – those at the campsite who had come for two or even four weeks, perhaps in anticipation of exploring the historical mysteries of the island in depth, were now thinking exactly the same thing. Some took to fishing to pass the time, managing to catch several bright red and blue tropical fish, even a small swordfish, from around the rocky shoreline, which were all barbecued in the evenings. We took advantage of the time and an Internet connection – exploiting the modern communications that had reached even the remotest village on earth – to write our own wedding vows and email them to our wedding celebrant in New Zealand. One of the advantages of our wedding plans was that we had almost total freedom over the words in our ceremony. We will always treasure the opportunity to have made it so personal, inspired by the peaceful and remote environment of Easter Island.

Our stay had turned into a campsite holiday, in a place that just happened to be littered with Moai statues. It was perfectly pleasant, but not at all what we had expected. So much about Easter Island was different to how we had imagined it to be. We were very glad to have visited it and to have had the opportunity to see the Moai first-hand and close up; it had been gentle fun exploring the island; but now we were ready to move on again, across the Pacific Ocean to sample the delights of Fiji, New Zealand and Australia.

Part Four
Fiji, New Zealand and Australia

Chapter 25: Fiji

Unfortunately for us, our particular package of flights meant that on leaving Easter Island we had to return all the way to Santiago and then turn around again, crossing the Pacific Ocean to Auckland before catching a more local flight to Fiji. If only we had registered for a frequent flier scheme before these flights, we would probably have earned at least a free journey, but we didn't realise that different airlines ran a joint programme until Australia. We had lost more than half of all our potential Air Miles, to Claudia's eternal chagrin. As it was, we were lucky not to be rerouted via Sydney to reach Fiji, as most of the passengers on our cancelled flight were. Finally we arrived in Nadi Airport, on the island of Viti Levu. We found ourselves in the basic lobby after dark with nowhere to go, and so asked in a tourist information office about accommodation, to be pointed in the direction of a uniformed man. As he led us deeper into the airport I saw out of the corner of my eye a sign saying 'Accommodation Office' and remembered the guidebook advice about ignoring the tourist office agents and going directly to that office instead – too late. Sometimes it seemed just too rude to turn around and walk away from a tout, even if he was taking us in the wrong direction.

Perhaps we were too tired to make the best decisions: another of our hindsight maxims would be that late at night when just arrived in a strange place is not the right time to commit to any plans beyond finding a bed for the night. Still, there we were. We went up to a dark little office, ready to have our tout's favourite resort pushed at us. Not really knowing all that much about Fiji, we told him that we would like to visit both beaches and trekking areas, which should have been reasonable. Both the largest island – the 'mainland' of Viti Levu – and scores of outlying islands have plenty of beaches, although the main trekking hills are only found in the north and east of the mainland. Not that this geography was of any consideration to our new friend.

He courteously showed us a range of enticing leaflets for island resorts on the two main groups of islands. These are west of Viti Levu, strung out in an approximately north-south chain, the further northern ones being more unspoiled, exclusive and expensive. Eventually he found one that managed to fit inside our price range, a backpacker resort on the nearby southern island of Mana. Apparently it was one of the larger islands, we were told, with beaches and hills to walk in. He even told us to be careful in case we got lost on our treks, which later was to become a somewhat rueful joke to us. We didn't know any better and took his word for it. The boat journey out to the island was expensive, enough to prohibit us from going further out from the mainland to visit other islands. We committed ourselves to being stuck on Mana for six nights – even this was at the very limit of our budget – despite more guidebook advice to avoid precisely this in case the first resort was unsuitable. It was actually pretty easy to island-hop once getting somewhere, but we didn't know that yet either. We couldn't complain; the tout arranged all transport and made all bookings in advance for us, including a bed in a nearby hotel for that first night. It was only on the way out of his office that we noticed the name of our resort painted onto the office window. He hadn't exactly given an unbiased recommendation.

This being Fiji – a world-class professional in the tourism business – everything worked as we were promised it would. We were ferried by complimentary buses to and from the hotel and the ferry terminal, and were even met personally on arrival in Mana, with a characteristically loud cry of *'Bula!'* The Fijian notion of service was second to none. Everything was well organised, services were all joined-up, and everything was conducted in a genial but efficient manner. Tipping had been discouraged, so the friendly help on offer was genuinely complimentary. Additional frills were even added just to make the holiday experience more memorable: traditional music groups were playing at the airport, at the ferry terminal, on the ferry itself and then again on Mana Island jetty, for no other reason than to provide a welcome. The male guitarists wore blue skirts and tropical shirts, somehow carrying off the white or red flowers tucked effeminately behind their ears.

From the ferry we saw hints of the paradise that Fiji claimed to offer: its tourist board described itself as being the home of '333 unspoiled islands in the tropical South Pacific'. We did indeed pass perfect miniature islands of pristine white coral sand beaches encircling stands of green trees, surrounded by a sea that was coloured various shades of blue, ranging from the enticingly pale coral shallows to the deep, darker ocean. Their names were a roll-call of romantic destinations: 'Treasure Island', 'Honeymoon Island', 'South Sea' and so on. The island used for the Tom Hanks film *Cast Away* was here too. Out of anywhere on earth, this was where the archetypal deserted tropical island exists. These were storybook places, where family chiefs still handed down their titles from father to son as if they were unexplored and untouched by Europeans.

Fijians were historically a fierce, warlike people who engaged in brutal inter-tribal conflicts. In 1643 Abel Tasman was the first European to travel to the islands, but declined to land as he had heard about the cannibalism that was practised there, which died out as the Fijians embraced Christianity in the mid-1800s. Captain Cook found in the late eighteenth century that Fijians were much feared by Tongans, who prized the Fijians' finely carved wooden weapons. We admired a display of these once, assuming that they were ceremonial paddles or pointed decorations. This elegant impression was somewhat tarnished when we were told that they were all crude but effective bludgeons and spikes, carefully designed to gouge out eyes and beat heads into pulp. We brought one home anyway, with a turtle etched into its blade, which we were told was a symbol of good fortune.

Fiji had been under British rule from 1874 until its independence in 1970, during which time the population was swelled by large numbers of indentured labourers from India, who worked on sugar plantations. Today ethnic Indians make up 44 per cent of the population and ethnic Fijians about 51 per cent. There has often been political tension as these two groups seek a fair balance of power, including several military-led coups.

All that violence and strife seemed a world away as we cruised past the islands to the somewhat unlikely accompaniment of John Denver and 'Country Roads'. When we arrived at Mana, we could see that it was indeed slightly bigger than many of the other islands, large enough for a long bay to run along the side of a low, grassy volcanic ridge that formed the spine of the island. The sea around the jetty was pale blue, discoloured in patches by brown weeds in the shallows. There didn't seem to be much of a beach – for the good reason that there wasn't much of a beach. Our resort did its best, though, raking up sand each morning immediately outside its doors. This accumulated enough for a volleyball net to be stretched across the little patch, although the game could only be played at low tide if it wasn't to become water-volleyball.

Our little resort was in the middle of the bay, which deteriorated at either end into a rocky foreshore as it curved around the ends of the island. To one side of us were the wire fences of a far more expensive resort, consisting of secluded chalet-style huts in a setting of palm trees and grassy lawns. Proper roads led from it to a simple airstrip that ran across the island, on the other side of which was an even more exclusive wedding-and-honeymoon resort, right on the island's sunset tip. This was the kind of place that we had once thought about getting married in, when we were back in England. The logistics and cost had put us off then, but at least we could now have a look over the fence at what might have been. In the end, New Zealand offered not only a far easier process but also the company of relatives and friends – and we still managed to have our service on a beach, even if it turned out to be not quite such a tropical setting.

We stayed in a little wooden hut – or *bure*, to give it its Fijian name – which was the farthest of a cluster that made up our small, very basic resort. It was right on the edge of the houses and shacks that formed the local village, complete with a Seventh-Day Adventist school next door. The village was set within an open grove of fruit and flower trees. Washing was hung between the trees, and plastic barrels had been set up to catch rainwater. This wasn't quite the romantic image of a paradise resort, but it brought us closer to real island life. Everything was a bit makeshift and rudimentary. Electricity was turned off during the day and our drinking water came from the rain buts. Sand got absolutely everywhere, as did ants, which marched in long black lines across the floor of our *bure*. At night came killer mosquitoes and giant bats with bodies the size of pigeons and wingspans of perhaps 1.5 ft. They flapped slowly over the dark trees, spookily at first, although after a while we found their languid presence somehow reassuring, familiar and unthreatening.

The ridge of the island ran upwards from behind our *bure*, with a path leading us directly to where our adventurous hill treks were supposed to have taken place. The island, we quickly discovered, was about as wide as the airstrip. It went up from the sea on one side of the ridge to its thin crest and then straight down to the sea on the other. It took us fully ten minutes to walk from coast to coast: there wasn't much time or space in which to become lost. Still, we had a week to explore every corner of the island, which became our own Robinson Crusoe experience. Not that there was a lot to discover. The coastline was mostly rocky and any sand in between was usually strewn with seaweed, broken coral or the modern detritus of plastic water bottles and single flip-flops. The fenced-in resort had laid claim to the only decent stretch of beach, so we scrambled around the rocks to make use of its pretty deckchairs and thatched shelters. No one else was there and we ended up with a beach to ourselves – a very nice beach at that. It was made from fine white sand, with just the odd lump of painful dead coral or squelchy patch of seaweed. The sea was warm, the waves gentle, the sun strong, and a row of green palm trees lined the beach. We had found our tropical beach holiday.

The friendly staff at our resort did their best to entertain us during a couple of evenings. After their day's work as barmaid, diving instructor, cook or porter, they all came together to put on a show for the handful of backpacker guests. This was genuine Fijian hospitality, all part of the tourist service that in our experience was second to none. The staff put on grass skirts and worked through a series of traditional dances from Fiji, the Cook Islands and Tahiti, although I couldn't tell much of a difference between them. The plump girl always waggled her bottom furiously, perplexingly, and the bronzed, oily men energetically knocked their knees together and pumped their arms in the air. The dancers laughed their way through and we applauded their efforts.

On another evening the entertainment was a crab race – the 91st International Mana Crab Race, to be precise. A white chalk circle was marked on the floor. One by one the contestants – small hermit crabs found on the beach, each with a number painted on their shells – were held up and auctioned off. One loud Englishman entered into the spirit of the contest by trying to up the bidding, but only ended up with more crabs to his name and less drinking money than he had bargained for. When they had all been bought, the crabs were released in the middle of the circle. They were off, racing to be the first to cross the line. Surprisingly, most actually made a beeline towards the edge of the circle, probably heading for the dark shadows beyond. The Englishman had picked his share of winners, which he found again the next morning on the beach outside, hiding in their little shells with their white numbers still on their backs. Most of the people staying in the resort were young and English, commonly on their way to or from Australian working holidays.

Something we hadn't accounted for was that we would arrive in Fiji during the rainy season. On the rainy days when the sky was a uniform grey, the gutters never stopped dripping, and the water barrels overflowed to form large puddles in the sand, there was nothing much to do except sit on the damp wooden benches overlooking the wet beach and let time pass. The mornings were filled by waiting for lunch to arrive. Swallows huddled on the top of the beach volleyball posts, bedraggled but resigned to patience, just sitting around the same as everyone else. In the shallows of the sea squatted three siblings, the younger sister no more than a tot, pulling in a fishing line. Washed by the lapping waves they cleaned and gutted their catch one fish at a time, throwing the finished meat into a blue pot. They had eight to ten fish in all. They were in no rush, no hurry; there was time to break every now and again for a playful roll in the surf.

Just as they were leaving, a dark, fat Fijian emerged somewhat improbably from beneath the waves like some great dark monster from the sea, with a snorkel and mask on his head. In one hand he held a metal spear and in the other was a long string of fish. He threw a couple of these to the staff in our resort and continued along the shore to the village. And with that the excitement of the day was over.

The coral reefs in Fiji offered excellent diving and snorkelling – there was even a dive shop beside the entrance to our resort – but the best sites were far out from our island. Only one small reef edge was close enough to the shore to be accessible without a boat. We were able to hire snorkels and swim leisurely over brilliant blue starfish, past large blobs of jellyfish that appeared from nowhere to hang silently in the water, and through numerous shoals of small tropical fish that hardly bothered to drift sideways out of our path as we approached. Pecking at the large orange plates of coral was a large parrotfish, the old grandfather of the reef. Off the edge of the reef, where nothing interrupted the infinite vastness of the blue water, we saw a squadron of small squid arranged in a perfectly straight line as if conforming to an army drill pattern. This was a semi-magical world, silent and wondrous, as coral reefs always are. Once we were thrilled to see a slender reef shark gliding right underneath us, coming out from the bottom of the reef and stealthily, eerily, disappearing into the blue.

On our last night we were treated to the sight of a beautiful Fijian sunset. After the bright sun had fallen beneath the horizon, the entire sky began to colour, starting furthest from the sun but eventually spreading everywhere. It was a bright yellow first, then changed into a gleaming gold, then pink, and finally became a vivid, deep red. The sea reflected each of these colours like a mirror, so that the entire world in front of us was painted with an extraordinary wash of rich beauty. It was a memory to treasure, one of those unexpected but priceless moments of joy and wonder.

The Manhattan skyline, New York

The Grand Canyon, USA

The Zócalo and cathedral of Mexico City

The Avenue of the Dead, Teotihuacán, Mexico

A Mayan temple pyramid at Tikal, Guatemala

The forgotten Inca city of Machu Picchu, Peru

The Atacama Desert, Chile

The Torres del Paines National Park, Chile

Rocinha, a favela in Rio de Janeiro, Brazil

A Fijian island tropical paradise

View towards Mount Aspiring National Park, New Zealand

Cowboys in New England, Australia

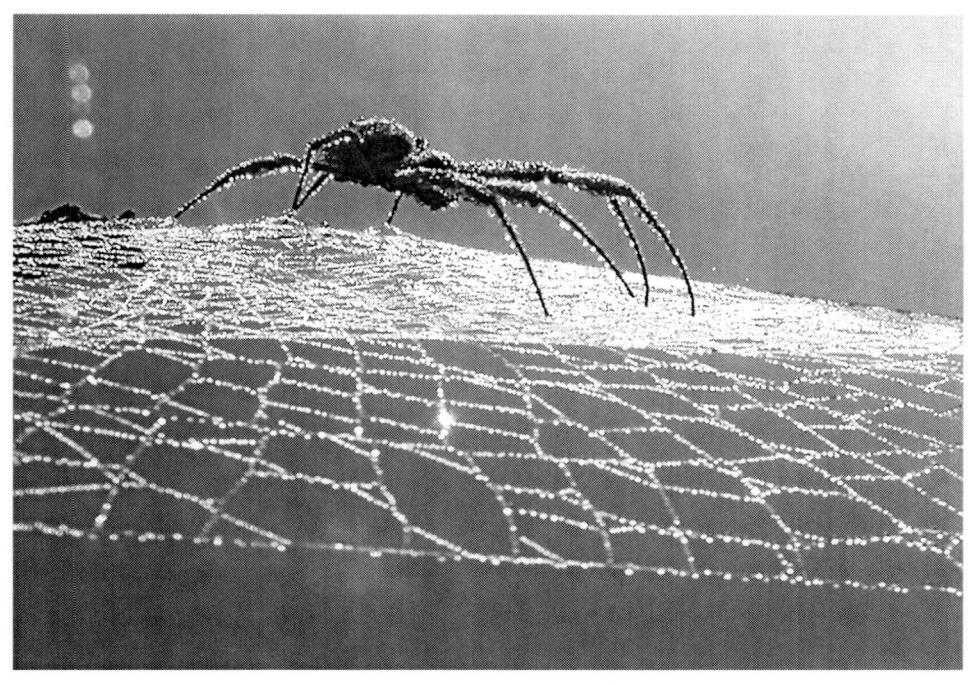

Early morning frost, Australia

The Petronas twin towers, Kuala Lumpur, Malaysia

A reclining Buddha statue, Thailand

Rice paddies at dawn in Thailand

Going to market in Cambodia

Angkor Wat, Cambodia

Motos in Vietnam

Sorting a fish catch at Mui Ne, Vietnam

Buddhist monks collecting alms in Luang Prabang, Laos

Naxi women in Lijiang, China

The Great Wall of China

Central Hong Kong

The Buddhist stupa of Bodhnath, Kathmandu, Nepal

A Nepali rickshaw driver

Mount Everest

The Taj Mahal, Agra, India

Women carrying water in Rajasthan, India

A camel ride at sunset, Rajasthan, India

Chapter 26: New Zealand's North Island

I had visited New Zealand some ten years before and had left with the idea in my head that this would be a great place to come to live. In many ways the country was again a pleasure to be in, not least of all because of the Kiwis themselves. Here we found the world's friendliest bus driver, for example, who chatted to passengers as he let them on and off, even taking the trouble to call another driver just to check that one couple had successfully made their connection.

Auckland was the main terminus for visitors to New Zealand, rather than the capital city of Wellington. It was also the largest city in the country, with one third of the population. It was a clean, white, gleaming city, with shiny bright tower blocks and fashionably dressed people, trendy bars and cafés. Very modern and very chic, and just a little bit sterile. The people were so well behaved that they calmly waited for pedestrian crossing lights even when there were no cars in sight. It was a low stress kind of place, complete with waving palm trees and green parks outdoors, where inside a government office a clerk would call everyone 'mate' as he processed them. But being on a budget made Auckland expensive for us; the youth hostel alone cost us NZ $70 (US $52) per night, for a small bedroom with two beds, shared bathroom facilities, and use of the functional, spartan communal kitchen.

This was the epitome of the worldwide trend that eventually discouraged us from using international youth hostels by preference, something that felt to me like betraying an old solidarity. The youth hostels of my childhood were family places, where members were welcomed as kindred spirits and efforts were made to make the hostels homely and comfortable. Sometimes this is still the case, for example some of the smaller hostels we stayed at in the USA, but by and large the YHA appeared to have changed its priorities and was aiming for the more profitable family hotel market, where – most sadly of all – every extra service had a charge attached.

Auckland was a sailing city, the image of sparkling clean white yachts filling its harbour and dotting the waters between offshore islands perfectly fitting the city's classy character. Not having the time to wander too far away from town, we took a ferry to nearby Waiheke Island. Here, just to add to the impression of Auckland's playboy prosperity, property prices had risen 97 per cent in three years. On the bus to Whakanewha Regional Park the guy sitting in front of us was a kindly ageing gentleman who engaged us in conversation, being more interested that Claudia was from Austria than anything else. Outside it was raining hard and before he jumped off the bus he told us that he was going to collect his car and give us a lift to the park. And so he duly did, which was a much appreciated gesture. We had to detour past the petrol station and then a bottle shop first, but we wound up driving into a campsite that was marked 'closed'. He seemed unperturbed by this and showed us to a patch of overgrown land, claiming it was ideal and trying to reassure us by saying, 'If anyone comes, just tell them I put you here and you'll be fine.'

We were more sceptical: somehow I didn't quite fancy trying to explain to a ranger that 'some random guy from the bus whose name I can't remember gave us permission'. Once the friendly chap had left us alone, we scouted around a bit and found an information board that showed us where the proper campsite was, not too far away. This turned out to be a fine place, near a beach and close to a series of local walks that were a welcome reintroduction to the exotic nature of New Zealand vegetation. Native palm trees shared the forests with giant tree ferns just as tall, their circular pattern of fronds looking like something from a primeval swamp. As was so often the case in New Zealand, it would have been little surprise to us to see a dinosaur's head looming into view, bending down to munch on the ferns. The plants – and the peculiar birds they sheltered – were one of the features of New Zealand that made it such a distinctive country.

On the island were remains of Maori pits, dug into the earth to store sweet potatoes, and ruins of fortified settlements called *pa*. The Maoris, who are thought to have arrived around AD 1,000 in New Zealand, were prone to inter-tribal wars in 1642, which was when Dutchman Abel Tasman – him again – voyaged to New Zealand, the first European to do so. He didn't land because his sailors from the vessel *Zeehaen* were attacked by several canoes of Maori, as recorded in his journal:

> We saw seven more boats come from the land... those in the canoe which was nearest us, called and waved their paddles...what their meaning was we didn't know... they began to paddle vigorously... they struck the *Zeehaen*'s cockboat with the stem of the canoe so that it lurched violently to the side. Whereupon the leader in this canoe of rogues struck the quartermaster, Cornelis Joppen, in the neck several times with a long, blunt pike, so fiercely that he fell overboard. Whereupon the rest of them joined in with short, thick pieces of wood and their paddles, overpowering the people in the cockboat and in their violence killed three men from the *Zeehaen*. The fourth man, through the heavy blows was mortally injured... we shot hard with muskets and cannon but although we did not actually hit them, they nevertheless hurried back and paddled for the land out of shooting range.[5]

---

[5] Rendition courtesy of Brian Hooker www.findingnz.com

The Maori population in New Zealand at the time of the arrival of Europeans was primitive – basically an advanced stone age culture – and its general health was believed to have been in a poor condition. In the early nineteenth century, northern Maori were provided with muskets by Europeans, which only fuelled their conflicts. Often the weapons were traded for embalmed heads, which traditionally were presented to the family of the decapitated person. The musket trade aggravated tribal violence, because warriors sought to collect more heads just so that they could acquire more weaponry. In the midst of a degenerating situation, not helped by the presence of European settlers, the British brokered the Treaty of Waitangi in 1840. This was eventually signed by 500 Maori chieftains, who accepted their allegiance to Britain in return for the protection of the rights that this status should have brought. The Treaty was partly intended to prevent hundreds of immigrants stealing Maori land, but it also gave the British government a pre-emptive right to purchase land. Even today, Maoris are pursuing land claims through the courts, in the hope of compensation.

One of the delicate issues facing countries like New Zealand and Australia that have an indigenous population which is – in the modern era and jargon – an ethnic minority, is how to provide a degree of positive discrimination as recognition and compensation for past wrongs, whilst simultaneously trying to treat all minority groups fairly. In New Zealand one apparently successful strategy has been to incorporate Maori land ownership and rights into modern settlements that establish joint management of lands for the country's benefit.

One such settlement in 1998 was to the Ngai Tahu, the tribe whose lands cover the South Island: Mount Cook would subsequently be called by its tribal name, 'thus restoring mana (status, prestige, integrity)' and in return the tribe gifted the mountain to the people of New Zealand. The settlement also 'acknowledges and redresses injustices suffered by Ngai Tahu over a period of 150 years that affected its economic, social and cultural development' and included a public apology for 'the suffering and hardship caused by the 1840 Treaty of Waitangi', gave the Ngai Tahu the right of first refusal over any sale of Crown property, and provided a cash settlement of NZ $170 million (US $128 million).

In 1985 the Maori language was declared to be a 'national treasure' which had to be protected under the terms of the Treaty of Waitangi. Two years later Maori became a national language and the government adopted a policy of writing all official signs bilingually in English and Maori – despite the paucity of Maori readers. In a condition that echoes the decline of Quechua in Peru, the last generation using Maori as their mother tongue are grandparents today. Efforts such as a Maori radio station and the teaching of Maori in schools hope to revive the language. The impression we had of Maori culture in general was that while there clearly was a proud and significant Maori population which was working hard to preserve its identity and to redress historical discriminations, their traditional culture was dominantly found in museums and tourist attractions. That having been said, these did put on impressive shows, transporting visitors into a Polynesian world of dance and costume.

After a couple of days on Waiheke Island, we took the opportunity to explore more of Auckland's twenty-one regional parks, many of which were within a few hours' drive from the city centre. We loved visiting several of them in our somewhat ropey hire car. The parks were often located near beaches and away from main roads, each with its own little campsite. They were wonderful for families looking for safe outdoor weekend breaks. And the Kiwis certainly knew how to camp in style. They stayed in tents that were more like houses, with dining shelters and shower cubicles, picnic tables and chairs, hanging gas lights, even gas BBQs and fridges. There were paddling pools, washing lines and drying racks, store tents and children's tents. Camping was not a small affair, particularly when several families came together. Cars and trailers, even small boats, further filled up the campsites – but there was a well-managed booking system to prevent them getting overcrowded.

One of the things we had to do in Auckland was to apply for a marriage licence. This entailed completing a single A4 page of information, signed to say that we weren't breaking any laws, and paying our money. Nothing more than that. This was a far cry from the multiple documents required by other countries before even starting the process. One had even asked us for proof that we hadn't been married before – something that seemed particularly difficult to achieve. Here in New Zealand, we simply registered that we were going to do something that we were freely allowed to do, a lesson in simple, practical efficiency that we appreciated.

Once we had our license, we set off southwards through North Island, together with a friend from Austria who had come out for our wedding. We met Martha off the plane after a very long journey, and one of the first things she said was, jokingly, 'I hope you're not going to tell me we have to get into the car and drive for a bit.' Unfortunately for her, we did, for we had to make progress that day if we were to stop off at some of the sights of North Island on our way south. With admirably little complaint once she realised we were serious, Martha curled up in the back of the car. She subsequently refused to sit in the front passenger seat except when Claudia took a turn to drive, which apparently had something to do with my having passed my driving test literally a few days before leaving for the USA.

Rotorua was one of New Zealand's tourist honeypot locations, mainly because it was a hot spot for geothermal activity. Driving into town there was a smell of sulphur hanging in the air, pervading the whole town. Smoke could be seen gently wafting up from behind clumps of trees in small parks, which on closer inspection turned out to be a series of hot springs and mudpools – the Rotorua version of duck ponds and fountains – set within neat lawns and pretty flower beds. Somehow the exotic was normalised as we strolled along the pathways with perhaps only a little more care than anywhere else. And outside the town even more serious activity was taking place.

Within a forest were spouting geysers and whole areas of bleached, acrid moonscape, now turned into rather expensive tourist attractions. Craters and caves rimmed with bright yellow sulphur crystal deposits were leaking wafts of rotten-egg gas into the air. Lakes with temperatures of 74°C became toxic baths, bright green and bubbling, rimmed with shelves of orange deposits that looked as if they came from another planet. And best of all, boiling mud pools large enough to row across were gurgling, burping and spitting great dollops of thick grey-brown ooze into the air. The mud seemed alive, constantly noisy and always active, as if were an unnatural organism that had just swallowed a meal and was gradually digesting its remains. Close encounters like these were what could help make a visit to New Zealand special: there aren't many places in the world where geothermal activity creates its own theme park.

Rotorua's activity was just a part of what is called the Taupo volcanic zone, which contains several volcanoes, some active and potentially explosive. Mount Ruapehu at the southern end of the zone is one of the most active volcanoes in the world and the largest active volcano in New Zealand. It last erupted in 1996, but trivially compared to the 1886 eruption of Mount Tarawera, which blew out a hole some twelve miles long and three square miles in volume. In fact, the most violent eruption in the world over the past 5,000 years was the one that expanded the crater that now holds Lake Taupo itself, in AD 181. It removed 100 km^3 of rock and produced an ash cloud that was visible from Europe and China. And even this was smaller than the eruption that first formed the crater 26,500 years ago, which ejected some 800 km^3 of material, so that even islands 800 km away were coated in 11 cm of ash.

Today the southern volcanoes of Ruapehu, Ngauruoe and Tongariro collectively form one of New Zealand's most famous landscapes. The closest we got to them was spending the night in a small campsite on their western edge, where we treated Martha to our own particular brand of camp cooking, which I called 'one-pot meals'. In fairness, there was more of an emphasis on nutrition than taste or presentation, so it wasn't long before Martha went shopping herself for food. The cloud was down, making the brown slopes of heather and bog, shrouded in a grey, damp mist, look more like a bleak Scottish moorland than the land of Mordor, as they had been seen in the *Lord of the Rings* films. Unfortunately we didn't have time to walk between the volcanoes, which had been described as the best one-day hike in New Zealand. We were in a rush to reach Wellington to attend a wedding for which we couldn't really be late – we were to be the bride and groom.

In Wellington, which was more like a regional town, we were again struck by the friendliness of New Zealanders. This wasn't an over-the-top geniality, but simply people treating each other as individuals. They took the time to help one another, to share a few companiable words. The world was considerably brightened up by people generally being nice to each other, something which made a huge difference when it was the norm. Every shop we went into had staff and customers who were not stressed, rushed, overworked or behaving like remote automatons. And this was in the centre of the capital city. Another reason for New Zealand being special.

Wellington is a hilly place at the southern end of North Island, renowned for its windy weather. Flimsy-looking wooden board houses dotted steep wooded hillsides, which had been pushed up by an active geological fault. The high number of earthquakes was one of the reasons for many houses having been built from wood. The city centre was built on land that had been raised two metres out of the sea in 1855 by the most powerful earthquake ever recorded in New Zealand. Nowadays the city centre was a bit of an odd hotchpotch of architecture, varying in style from the sublime to the ridiculous. It was suggested to us that it resulted from thirty different people having been tasked with creating modern buildings, but not told to consult one another in the process. Nowhere was flat or straight except right down on the harbour, where an attractively modern waterfront had a succession of relaxed cafés and bars.

We were blessed with a few days of glorious sunshine in Wellington in the run-up to our wedding day, where we were joined by, among a couple of others, my sister and her Australian partner. Poor Martha, who had been bravely coping with conversations in English whilst trying to get used to the Kiwi accent, now found herself in the company of a rural Australian. I think the best that can be said of their conversations was that they involved mutual confusion dosed with much goodwill, and were the sources of great amusement for the rest of us.

After buying some bottles of champagne and half a dozen plastic flutes from a local supermarket, pretty much all that we had to organise was a bouquet of flowers. In the same shopping precinct as the supermarket, lo and behold there was a small flower shop, almost bare at the end of a week. The highly professional but more than slightly astonished young lady behind the counter told us at first that the flowers she had left were really not fit for a wedding; we persisted because the wedding was the next day! Out the back she eventually found six red roses, and we ate ice creams as a perfect posy was magically created. The next morning – our wedding day – we went to the botanical garden for a picnic amongst the flower beds, feeding pigeons as a game of cricket was played in the nearby sports ground. It was lovely not having to worry about organisational details; instead, we could simply savour those precious moments.

My hope had been to get married on a beach as the sun set. The advice from our celebrant had been that sunset would not be such a good idea – this was 'windy Wellington' after all – but a beach was certainly possible. It was called 'Princess Bay', which sounded quite romantic enough to us. We didn't see it, however, until we arrived in the afternoon for our ceremony. Pulling off a road that ran around a small headland, we stopped in a car park overlooking a small stretch of grey sand between rocky outcrops, on the side of a choppy bay with houses spread along the far side. The skies had been grey all day, threatening rain, and here the chilly breeze was stronger. We shook hands with our chirpy celebrant, who pulled out a folding wooden table and portable CD player from the boot of his car. Claudia took the player in one hand and I took a chair in another, and we strode out onto the small beach ahead of the small party of family and friends who had journeyed to be with us. It wasn't quite the traditional entrance for a wedding, but then wearing flip-flops was not altogether usual either. Shivering slightly as our hair was blown across our faces, with the sun valiantly trying to shine through to us, we were married. It was a beautifully personal and very happy ceremony, followed by a glass of champagne from our plastic flutes and bare-footed dancing on the beach to the strains of The Carpenters' 'Top of the World'. From now on, we were on honeymoon – a 7½-month long honeymoon – the first few weeks of which we would spend as a threesome with Martha as we continued our travels around New Zealand's South Island.

Chapter 27: New Zealand's South Island

Driving around New Zealand was a popular way to 'see' the country. Our hire car had already driven 220,000 km and when we commented on this we were told that another was still going with 400,000 km on the clock. With relatively few route options in New Zealand, there was a degree to which this method of sightseeing risked becoming an exercise of spending long hours looking out of a car – or worse, a bus – window trying to get from Tourist Location A to Tourist Location B, en route to Tourist Locations C and hopefully D. The whole country at times could feel like a giant drive-through theme park, with commercial tourist-trap stopovers breaking up journeys before we reached the more impressive highlights. We saw some tour brochures that ran trips all around New Zealand in two weeks, which seemed to us like utter madness; stopping for a five-minute photo opportunity before heading on to the next sight couldn't possibly do justice to the country's offerings.

To be fair, there were often many possibilities to linger and sample numerous adventurous activities, something that New Zealand was justifiably famous for. In one place we stayed we could have walked on a glacier, horse-trekked through forest, gone white water rafting, jet boating, canyon swinging, helicopter riding, and even para-bungee-jumping, whatever that was. Unfortunately for us, the cost of everything, everywhere, seemed to start at a minimum of NZ $100 (US $75). The helicopter ride cost NZ $180 (US $135) for 30 minutes, which may well have been good value for a helicopter, but was outside our budget. Right at the very end of our stay I came across a quote from the tourist authority in New Zealand saying that it did not mind being perceived from abroad as a high-cost holiday destination, for the very reason that it is a high-cost destination. Not a good place for backpackers, then. Actually, several times we were told by locals that tourist sites were known to be overpriced with an emphasis on commerciality, which matched our impressions – especially having come from Fiji.

On South Island our journey took us through the vineyards of Marlborough to the exquisite coastline of Abel Tasman National Park, and then to the inland town of Murchison. This was a route which roughly followed the old path taken by Maori moving south in search of greenstone on the west coast. Explorers, pioneers, miners and then farmers followed the trail, eventually turning the area into a mix of lowland dairy and hillside sheep farming. Murchison was the central town in the area. It extended perhaps

200 m in each direction out from its centre. I counted about one hundred houses in the cluster that could be called the town. Among these, at the lone crossroads, were a café, a grocery shop, a hardware store, a second-hand goods shop and a museum. There was a souvenir shop too, but it was closed. However, if there happened to be someone who desperately wanted a souvenir, then in the door window was a sign with the owner's phone number on. She wouldn't take very long to arrive if she lived 'in town'! I learned in the museum that in 1987 the county had an area of 3,657 sq km for a population of 1,370 people. This was not a place that could be called overpopulated! One of the features throughout New Zealand was that there were very, very few houses, although most of the landscape had been cultivated or used as pasture for sheep or cattle.

The second-hand shop was fascinating. It consisted of three rooms filled by rows of counters that were overflowing with ornaments, magazines, records, books, kitchen utensils, pots and pans, carpentry tools, tree saws, scythes, African carvings and hundreds of salt-and-pepper shakers. There was even a wall stacked with empty glass bottles. Every basic household item that one could want must have been somewhere in there, and plenty more besides that no one would ever want. It was a treasure hunter's dream, surely full of antiques, where everything looked musty, covered in a thin layer of dust and grime. With three people to feed using our little camping stove, we bought a cooking pan, knife and bowl from the sharp little old lady behind the counter, all for the bargain price of NZ $5 (US $3.77). As we were leaving the lady checked that we had picked up our coats, saying, 'Don't leave anything behind.' Or they would surely end up for sale somewhere on her shelves, we thought to ourselves.

We travelled on down the west coast, past scenery that reminded us of the Californian Route 1. White waves crashed into black rocky headlands, spraying a veil of mist over the sandy bays in between. We were increasingly in the shadow of the Southern Alps to our left, which run the length of South Island. The mountains are rising relatively rapidly, but are also being eroded quickly by one of the highest rainfall rates in the world. This creates glaciers that plummet down the mountains, of large enough volume and speed to be flowing through rainforest before finally melting away, which is a very unusual combination. To cross the Southern Alps from the west coast to the broader eastern side of the island, there were basically two options. One route passed between the mountains at the northern end and the other did so at the southern end. We chose the southern route, on the way to the Fiordland National Park.

The pass we took was named after the Haast River, which was broad and shallow as it flowed through a wide flat valley between towering forested slopes that rose up into the clouds and presumably to even higher mountain peaks. Waterfalls dropped out of the clouds all the way along the road, creating splashes and streaks of vivid white that sliced into the dark green background. The Haast Pass then climbed through a reasonably dramatic gorge, topping out into a series of flat, brown grassy plains between steep valley sides. We had a perfect view over one of these plains for lunch, watching some fly-fishermen whilst being attacked by clouds of midges. The plains had been attractive for early settlers and tourists too, apparently having been stocked with deer for hunting. They must have seemed then like some kind of Garden of Eden in the midst of the hostile forest and mountains.

Dropping down the far side of these plains we were treated to our most spectacular views yet, of two huge deep blue lakes with long panoramas of mountain ridges alongside their lengths. These were truly beautiful features and were crying out to be stopped beside, for their magnificence to be appreciated and their calm presence enjoyed. So we pitched camp on the shore at one end of Lake Wanaka. When I asked the manager of the campsite which place he recommended for our tent, he replied, 'You've driven in the gate – it's all good!' He was right.

From the shore of the lake we could see across into Mt Aspiring National Park and its snow-clad peaks. Willow and plane trees provided shelter and atmosphere. The sun was beating down, even making swimming in the lake a possibility. Children with their families were enjoying a holiday where they could run around and – as children do – throw sticks and stones at one another as a game. As Martha went for a dip in the lake, Claudia and I walked up a nearby small mountain to have a better look at the surrounding landscape. From the top, the view was worth every step of the climb, a vista right across this very attractive part of New Zealand. It was surprisingly dry and grassy, the forests all having been left behind with the rain on the western slopes. We could see many valleys, peaks and ridges, all virtually deserted and therefore just waiting to be explored.

The history of Lake Wanaka reads like a snapshot of the history of much of South Island. Maori hunter-gatherers lived or travelled through the area, hunting birds like the moa and gathering plant roots and shoots. The now extinct moa grew up to 3.7 m tall and weighed 200 kg, just one of several flightless birds in New Zealand. The Maori greatly prized greenstone, which could be found along the west coast of South Island, and Wanaka was on a crossroads of their trading paths. European explorers entered the area in the 1850s, searching for farmland where they could run sheep. Interestingly, they found wild potatoes here, a plant that was indigenous to South America. Either Polynesians had visited that continent and returned here, or perhaps Chinese explorers had carried the plant across the oceans on their great world voyages of the early fifteenth century. Hard on the heels of the sheep farmers came gold prospectors, who opened up the landscape still further. By 1880 development had reached a point where tourism was possible, with steamer boats crossing the lake. Wanaka was firmly on the map as a scenic location.

Wanaka was an ideal base for an activity holiday, although not everyone there wanted it to become another version of Queenstown, which was notorious for being the brash adventure sports capital of the world. The location of Queenstown itself was even prettier than Wanaka's, set on the sides of another lake but this time enclosed by mountain ridges. Unlike just about anywhere else in New Zealand, Queenstown was full of traffic, queues, people, hustle, bustle. And it was still growing – there was evidently quite a bit of building going on. When we were there it was almost full up with tourists: in the tourist information centre the available beds in town started at NZ $120 (US $90).

We drove on to Te Anau, where we stocked up with provisions and investigated walking possibilities in the Milford region. The south-west corner of South Island forms the largest national park in New Zealand, called Fiordland after its characteristic landscape. It had only one highway entering it, which ran all the way to the famous Milford Sound, but there were plenty of long and remote walking trails. We decided to do the usual thing and drove in our car the impressively scenic 119 km to Milford Sound. Along the road were plenty of small campsites in meadows, beside rivers and on lake shores, and so, despite all the tourism tearing up and down the road, we were able to find our piece of solitude. We swim, cooked on a beach and looked out across the night-time stillness to a beautiful, shadowy, starlit panorama of sleeping mountain tops.

Further along the road to the Sound we stopped to walk one of the advertised short hikes that were accessible from the roadside. This was worthwhile purely from the experience of climbing up through the rainforest – or rainjungle, more like. Actually, it was silver beech forest, thick with greenery, stuffed full of both giant and slender trees, and with a dense carpet of ferns erupting over the forest floor. The trees all dripped with moss, coating every trunk and hanging from every branch. Indeed, the whole forest reeked of dripping, running water: it just oozed wetness, even though we were walking up on a totally dry day. This was a Jurassic kind of forest, where dinosaurs were surely skulking behind the ferns, just out of sight. Some people still hope that moa continue to survive somewhere in these remote, wild valleys, and here that idea seemed far more plausible. At the top of the jungle we reached a lake, like a giant version of a corrie tarn. It was remote and peaceful – tranquillity itself, apart from the small plane that buzzed over our heads on its way to Milford Sound, a warning of things to come.

By the time we arrived at Milford Sound it was late afternoon and the skies had cleared to give us a postcard silhouette of Mitre Peak, which rises to 1,692 m above the water level. The Milford Sound fjord is 15 km long, with cliff-like walls on either side of it that are up to 1,200 m high. It also receives around six metres of rain a year, enough to create a layer of fresh water on top of the otherwise saline sea water. We parked and walked along the shore at its near end, with a beautiful view down the fjord between the mountains. A magnificent setting like this deserved to be peaceful and quiet, but instead we were at first surprised and then irritated by the noise and disturbance around us. First it was boats, setting out and returning from their harbour, and then planes started their tours from Milford Sound's own airport. One after the other they flew low over our heads, circling up the Sound and back again. One, two, three, four, five – each following the other at intervals of approximately forty-five seconds, putting five planes in the sky at once in addition to the boats on the water. Over a considerable time period we counted only one seven-second slot when we considered it to be quiet. The rest of the time there was a continuous noise from engines. This was such a shame, for it wrecked the atmosphere of what was otherwise a truly beautiful location.

At such sightseeing spots, whenever there was emphasis on enabling large numbers of people to drive up, take a photograph, spend their money and then give way to the next in line, it seemed that the attraction had its peace shattered by the crowds and facilities. We would see the same phenomenon again at Uluru in Australia. The result was that more magical atmospheres that are an essential ingredient of natural beauty were more often to be found in quieter corners rather than the most famous locations.

From the west coast of Fiordland we drove back across South Island to the east coast town of Dunedin, through a landscape that reminded me first of the Scottish Lowlands and then of the Yorkshire Dales. Rolling hills of thin grassland, with craggy rocks exposed by incised river gullies, were blanketed in green fields that one after the other were stuffed full of thousands of sheep, which had been brought down from higher ground for shearing. The first sheep in New Zealand were introduced by Captain Cook in 1773. By 1982 there were 70 million sheep, although the figure today is only about 43 million – which still makes twelve sheep for every person in the country! And after this drive, we could believe it. The further we drove, the more the Scottish heritage of this part of New Zealand was revealed in its place names. Dunedin is actually a version of the Celtic name for Edinburgh, but there was another Edinburgh here anyway. Even the street names within the villages read like an index of British towns, although St Andrews – which advertised its 'world-famous golf course' – managed a different take by using the names of famous authors.

The attractions in this part of the country, apart from the typically rural scenery, were mostly wildlife. Seals, sea lions and, most of all, seabirds. This was the only place in the world where the albatross – the bird with the largest wingspan on earth – nests on a mainland. And with another tourist location came the obligatory visitor centre, offering a choice of tours for a hefty charge to see one bird sitting on a nest. Sometimes, when it was windy, the car park was just as good a place to see the albatrosses surfing the air currents over the cliff tops, but as the weather was calm when we were there we saw nothing but a few seals rolling in the waves below.

So we went to see yellow-eyed penguins instead, which Martha found particularly cute. Her name for them, 'Pingus', has since stuck. We sat in a tiny hide beside a small cove for a couple of hours, peering out at nothing much except a lazy seal basking in the late afternoon sun. Then, suddenly, we spied a little head bobbing in the surf, which stood up to totter out of the waves as a yellow-eyed penguin. We saw a grand total of two walking quickly across the weed-strewn sand before they disappeared out of sight. And that was that. Not quite the same as our Patagonian penguin-fest, but even these little birds were able to conjure up a peculiar fondness. It was well worth the wait.

Slightly further north came the Canterbury Plain. It was flat and intensively farmed, reminding me of my home Cambridgeshire. Christchurch was the major city in this part of the world – just about the only sizeable place in South Island – and seemed to have been styled on Cambridge too. Or perhaps that should be Oxford, as it had a pretty little river called the Avon meandering between grassy banks, beside willow trees and under collegiate-style wooden bridges. There were even punt rides along the river on offer. Christchurch was founded as a deliberately diocesan settlement by a Bishop of Ipswich and about fifty brave settlers in the mid-nineteenth century, many of whom indeed came from Christ's College, Oxford. Not that anyone would have guessed. Today, it was a typically relaxed New Zealand small city, pretty and clean, with a smart but sleepy shopping centre adjacent to the dominant cathedral. It was about as cosmopolitan as it got south of, well, Auckland. We dropped Martha off at the airport and our threesome became two again.

For our final taste of New Zealand, Claudia and I turned inland again towards the eastern flank of the Southern Alps. Moving leisurely between small campsites and holiday parks, chatting to locals and fellow campers, swimming in rivers and going on walks that immediately took us into forest or up hills, we had a delightful holiday. It was perhaps only marred by an incident with my wedding ring – or more precisely the losing of it – at a particularly serene campsite. I looked down at my hand one morning and found that the ring wasn't there. We turned out everything in our tent and hunted all around, but couldn't find it. It probably came off whilst swimming in the little brook, we thought, and so we spent many happy hours peering through the freezing cold water at the pebbly bed, searching every square centimetre, but all to no avail. Claudia was very good about it, and after reporting the loss to the local police, we went out to the local cinema in the evening to cheer ourselves up. Here we were treated as honoured guests by the friendly owner, who reserved for us the red, slightly threadbare, but very comfortable sofas that formed the front row.

As we travelled westwards towards the Southern Alps, we came across my favourite of all the different landscapes that the country had to offer. The mountains rose in a spectacularly jagged white and grey line that ran right across the horizon. In front was an aching expanse of flat straw-coloured ranch land, broken up by fences and small rivers with slender autumnal yellow-leaved trees lining their banks. These landscapes had a scale that was only comparable with the vistas of the Sierra Nevada, but here were also great lakes that stretched towards the mountains, enhancing a flatness that only ended abruptly at the base of the sharp peaks. The waters of the lakes were an almost disturbingly bright cobalt blue, as if artificially coloured by paint powder. In fact it was the powder from glacial erosion in the water that gave them this strange yet beautiful colour. From the unusual blue to the clear, bright whiteness of the snow-capped mountain peaks behind, the sight was as splendid as any we had seen in New Zealand, which says something.

One road ran right along the side of one of these lakes towards the highest mountain in the country, Aoraki/Mount Cook – to give it its official post-1998 name – at 12,316 ft high. With the intense blue water alongside the road, grey pebble beaches, empty brown hills in the foreground that receded into great jagged hulks of snow-covered rock faces and ridges, and glaciers streaming down the mountainsides, this was one of the world's great roads, going nowhere but ever closer towards the rising wall of the Southern Alps. It was empty and remote, invoking a sense of extreme challenge and adventure that was only enhanced by the few ranches in the area, pioneer settlements if ever there were any.

There was only one significant town in the area, which had been built as temporary accommodation for workers on a large reservoir project. However, the inhabitants decided that they didn't want to leave and ended up purchasing their land and homes. So now there was a town where before there had been none – and it was all set for further growth, advertising itself as a new tourist destination. New Zealand has a justifiable reputation for the quality of its landscapes and its environmental record but I couldn't help wondering if one of its biggest challenges will be deciding when and how to limit the tourist industry, in order to conserve the very attractions that draw so many people to the country. New Zealand was beautiful, but for me it had not been the tourist attractions that made it so.

Chapter 28: Sydney

Sydney is the premier city in Australia, but like Auckland or Rio de Janeiro it isn't actually the capital of the country. That didn't stop it feeling as if it was – full of cosmopolitan self-confidence and at ease with itself. Over half of the population of New South Wales live in Sydney, including over 200 different nationalities. We ultimately decided that Sydney was our favourite city around the world, combining attractive features of other world cities. Like London, its different districts managed to contain very different characters, although always with the same underlying laid-back Australian atmosphere. It was almost as modern and functional as Auckland, almost as clean and tidy. And the importance of its beaches to city life made Sydney feel like an upmarket version of Rio de Janeiro. It was casual, cool and full of interest.

The famous harbour came across as a relatively small part of Sydney, the chic preserve of sightseers and the city's elite. Here were the iconic Opera House and Harbour Bridge, at opposite sides of the docks. The smoothly arched bridge – the widest and highest of its type in the world – dominated the harbour in a dark grey metallic kind of way, a sight made less attractive closer up by the rows of barbed wire strung along the top of the pedestrian walkway. For some reason it was a popular pastime for Sydney-ites to jog across the bridge, jammed in between wire fences and next to lanes of traffic. Just about the only reason we could find for being up there was to get the best views across the harbour to the Opera House. Despite it being constructed from segments of a sphere, that building seemed to defy all rules of visual symmetry.

Quite why the jogging didn't take place around the other side of the harbour, along the pleasant waterside paths and through the elegant botanical gardens, was a mystery to us. Had the joggers done so, they would have found themselves in the company of all sorts of unusual flora and fauna: trees of all sizes and shapes; whirling flocks of green parrots; tame white parakeets; colonies of flying foxes suspended upside down from the branches of trees overhead, their black leathery bat-like wings wrapped around their large furry bodies; and the characteristic bird of Sydney, the white ibis, stalking every park with malevolent beady eyes on the lookout for any scraps of food that could be rudely snatched with their long curving beaks.

Along the docks, we were impressed by the way Sydney was managing to successfully integrate its history and heritage with modern, high-class urban living. Alongside the gigantic cruise liner and gleaming buildings could be found remnants of original nineteenth-century houses, with the stories of early settlers engagingly described.

Captain Cook landed at Botany Bay in April 1770, and on 26 January 1788 eleven ships brought 1,400 soldiers, convicts and settlers to Sydney harbour, which was named after the British Home Secretary of the time. Not left out of the publicised history of the city were the roles of Aboriginals, who had lived around Sydney for 40,000 years before Cook arrived. We saw some ancient Aboriginal rock-art on flat stones on the coast of southern Sydney: scratched outlines of animals that were fading with age. Their original significance appeared to be totally unknown, although intelligent guesses about eating places or trading posts had been proposed. What impressed me was not the carvings themselves, but the fact that they were evidently considered a valued part of Sydney's heritage.

Just like in Rio, much of city life seemed inseparable from the beaches. The equivalent of Copacabana in Sydney would probably be Bondi Beach. Although this was shunned by many sensible locals, it was worth visiting just for a look at the extreme end of urban beach culture. The beach itself was typical for Sydney, comprised of a long curving bay with white surf rolling onto a wide beach of flour-soft sand. The powerful surf was dangerous for swimmers, with lifeguards constantly vigilant for those in danger of getting caught in strong underwater currents as they enjoyed being bowled over by waves and spat out in the shallows, totally disorientated and breathless. At 7.30 a.m., as the sun was beginning to gather strength, the beach was already busy with early-morning joggers, strollers and surfers catching their first waves of the day. By midday the sand was choked with topless sunbathers, their already well-tanned bodies turning periodically for that perfect all-over browned look. This was serious sunbathing, paralleling the intensity of the surfing and fitness training all around. We joined them for half a day before deciding to continue our explorations of Sydney.

At the southern end of Sydney's coastline was Cronulla, a highly desirable suburb with million-dollar luxury waterfront properties. Open air cafés on the high street and ultra-rich cars cruising ostentatiously past made a point of advertising the available wealth. On the beach, elderly bathers indulgently relaxed in a concrete swimming pool built into the ocean, the very picture of Victorian upper-class holiday-making. We hadn't seen affluence like this since California and hadn't seen so many national flags on show since New Hampshire. We didn't know whether this was a sign of patriotism, or nationalism, or worse. Cronulla had been the setting for recent race riots, when extremist right-wing nationalists clashed against people of middle-eastern origin, some of whom had been harassing women on the beach. It was quiet again now, but still there were those flags in the windows.

Another less pleasant side of Sydney were the budget hostels beside the beaches that we stayed in. In fact, our accommodation experiences here were actually worse than anywhere else in the world. The hostels appeared to cater to – and be inhabited by – student backpackers and grunge-surfer types who clearly didn't care much about their living conditions. In one YHA, the staff had resorted to withholding kitchen utensils until the mess in the kitchen was cleaned up. This was despite the fact that they employed live-in cleaners, whose own dormitory was in such a state that the spare beds could not be let out. In another hostel, we were welcomed by a slanging match between the staff, given a grotty room which contained a bed in pieces on the floor, and then a second bedroom that reeked so foully that we couldn't believe a cleaner had been near it for weeks.

Closer in to the centre of Sydney, the hostels were often little better, full of semi-dressed, semi-hungover students who seemed to think that they were still at home and could live in as slovenly a state as they wished. Unfortunately, the culture of the hostels appeared to be to acquiesce with this idea, rather than undertake the work of imposing common standards that might have gone some way to meeting basic health and hygiene standards. Not all the places were like this, of course, although to find one of a decent standard required searching and pre-booking. There were several to choose from in the Kings Cross district, which was backpacker central for Sydney. It had a very bohemian air, with tattoo parlours and fast-food outlets mixed alongside elegant old houses and tree-lined pavements, plus a dash of modern urban architecture in spacious parks and newly renovated buildings. One of the best hostels we found had a friendly Swiss owner, who one day gave us directions to the jewellery shops in town.

We had searched for a replacement wedding ring in New Zealand with no success and now hoped for better luck in Sydney. Pompous jewellers at the exclusive end of Sydney's shopping malls sniffed to us that any ring had to be manufactured to order, unless we were prepared to take a ring from within the shop itself, which would naturally have a reduced price on account of it being 'soiled'. We left these shops and made our way through seven or eight more until, in the very last store that anyone knew of, we found exactly what we were looking for. This shop had three rings on display – and in a sale as well – of the very same design as the ones from Brazil, defying another stuffy claim that such a ring couldn't be purchased in Australia. One of these three was even a perfect fit, slightly smaller than my original wedding ring. Our perseverance had paid off, and I for one was very relieved.

Sitting on rocks looking out to sea we opened another small bottle of pink champagne and played again 'Top of the World' from our little cassette recorder. Having reached Australia, we felt that we were safely halfway around the world and all was going well. We were ready to leave Sydney and begin a taste of wilder Australia in the nearby Blue Mountains.

Chapter 29: Blue Mountains

An attractive feature of New South Wales was the number of parks that have been created in the wilder areas of the state, in and around the rugged topography of the Great Dividing Range. Probably the most famous wilderness area near Sydney was the Blue Mountains, a World Heritage Area that contained no less than seven national parks. The mountains were actually more a neck of upland plateau that had been dissected by broad valleys, with sides lined by sheer escarpment cliffs and bases thick with eucalyptus forest that created a blue-green haze when seen from a distance. Roads and railways wound up to touristy settlements such as Katoomba. This small town had rows of bungalow houses – many sporting bed and breakfast or art gallery signs – running all the way from the railway station and inevitable pub opposite right to the edge of an escarpment precipice. Here an extensive car park and visitor centre backed onto a place called 'Echo Point', from where hundreds of people at a time could lean against railings and look out across the Jameson Valley to hills and cliffs that were miles away on the other side of the valley's expanse. The sight was one of extremes of vertical drops and horizontal plains, edged by sharp lines of brown sandstone cliffs and with a blurred green carpet spread between.

Tall, skinny eucalyptus trees exposed their shiny white fresh bark where the older red-brown skin had peeled off in great strips, as if sunburnt. These were all colloquially called 'gum trees', but then had individual names like 'stringy bark' or 'blue gum'. In between were scraggy tea-tree bushes, with just the odd tree fern growing beside rivers that found themselves suddenly in mid air, plunging as waterfalls into nothingness. White galahs, with pink flashes under their wings, screeched noisily as they wheeled from tree to tree, and high-speed green parrots streaked through the branches. To one side the cliff line stuck out in a small promontory of three vertical pinnacles called the Three Sisters. This had to be the single most photographed spot in the Blue Mountains, although the backdrop didn't have the definition seen elsewhere. And along with the hordes of tourists were modern facilities, including cable-car rides and multi-sensory walkways along the cliff edge.

From the car park we heard the droning sound of a didgeridoo, which was suitably evocative at the edge of this vista. Had this been Scotland, no doubt there would have been bagpipes being played by a mock Highlander in full kilted regalia. Here in Australia, the musician was a huge Aboriginal figure, who stood at the centre of a little huddle of predominantly oriental tourists.

He was not just tall, but also had a significant beer belly protruding from above his red cloth skirt. The only other clothing he wore was a complete animal pelt draped over his back, tied around his neck with string. His dark skin contrasted with the streaks of white paint he had daubed on his body. Most impressive was his fearsome face: a great shaggy mat of long black hair obscured most of its features, with beady eyes and a flat, stubby nose just visible. These had been daubed in white paint too, covering up any remaining features. He appeared like a great unkempt bear as he towered over the tourists.

They often caught sight of him from a distance, judging from the audible shrieks of delight. Going towards him, people simply stared in wonderment at this figure, who agreeably posed for photos as long as dollars were thrown onto a rug spread out before him. Once people were standing next to him, they stopped being intimidated; even the reticent, demure Asian ladies collapsed into giggles at their predicament as he respectfully embraced them in an enveloping bear hug.

We camped one night near to Echo Point, right on the edge of a cricket ground. In the morning a game was in progress, although the only way that we could tell was the occasional sound of a ball being thwacked by a bat. Mist had totally enveloped both us and the players, who unfortunately were fully kitted out in their whites. They continued undaunted, the clouds thinning every now and again to reveal ghostly players. It was all just a bit surreal. But then, the Australians were as passionate about their national game of cricket as the Kiwis had been of their rugby.

Our tent happed to be sited next to a couple whom Claudia was sure she recognised. 'Didn't we meet you on Easter Island?' she asked the girl, to her mild consternation.

'No, we're French,' the girl replied, thinking Claudia had asked if she lived in Ireland. But in a little while, after the couple had conferred, they suggested that we might well have seen each other before in South America – they recognised our well-pitched little tent from somewhere. 'Yes, Easter Island!'

It was a small world – but the international backpacker trail wasn't actually all that varied, so we weren't too surprised. The coincidence provided us with a lift to the National Park office, where we needed to find out about campsites down in the Grose Valley. We were helpfully given maps and told about routes and water supplies. The rangers were very informative and friendly – but not a word was mentioned about potential encounters with spiders or snakes. Which was probably just as well.

The descent down the cliff face had once been thought to be an impossible route. Seven months of labour had nonetheless created an improbable path, clinging somehow to a sheer rock face, under overhanging walls that were covered in mosses dripping a curtain of water. In some places steel handrails provided a degree of security but at others there seemed nothing between the slippery stone steps and a slide off into the abyss which plunged down just inches away. Small lizards had no sense of fear as they scuttled out of our way, headlong over the edge. Our extreme position provided us with beautiful views out across the valley, bounded on each side by receding lines of escarpment cliffs that were just like the one we were precariously descending. This tricky little path was even more dramatic than the Bright Angel Trail within the Grand Canyon had been, but nowhere near as long. We quickly dropped down to the base of a waterfall, at the foot of a 150 m high curving amphitheatre of bare rock. The wind was blowing up the face and catching the water drops in mid air, twisting them into a fine spray that swirled around until it vanished into nothing, not a single drop reaching the ground.

Along the valley, following the riverbeds, the surrounding views were disappointingly obscured by dense trees. Instead, our attention was caught by the animals and birds of the forest. Butterflies were constantly fluttering away as we passed, black-winged with yellow and orange markings. Gecko-like lizards were harder to spot, but we could hear them as they rustled quickly away through the leaves. At one point an angry two-foot-long dragon stood its ground as we rounded a corner. It had frightening spines raised like hackles along its back, trying to scare us. It succeeded, for the shock of suddenly seeing it gave Claudia quite a fright.

Birds were all around, but they were shy and hard to spot, either small wrens darting for cover or parrots streaking overhead. We disturbed three large black macaws with yellow crests on their heads as they were concentrating on their meal, holding pine cones in their craggy claws so that their cross-billed beaks could tear out the seeds. When they noticed us they flew off in a very disgruntled manner, offended by our presence. They continued to circle overhead for a while, calling to each other with each pass and slowly flapping their wings like giant black bats. When we reached the campsite, under a stand of tall, thin gum trees, we were quickly joined by a pair of crows, who perched in nearby branches and kept each other company with self-pitying mournful bleats. Kookaburras gave us a welcome too, with their loud imitations of screeching monkeys: *hoo-hoo-ha-hee-hee*.

Wildlife continued to provide the entertainment in the quiet solitude of the bush. Often it was just leeches, cockroaches, ants or flies, but not always. As we made our way along a path to the river, we stopped in our tracks at the sight of one end of a black snake just feet away in the undergrowth. While we watched, its head slowly began to slide from side to side several feet up in the branches above. Its body looked like a sleek, glossy branch, as thick as my wrist. Gradually it reached out to rest its head and neck on a higher twig, then heaved along its length, pulling itself upwards. As it stretched out we were entranced by its size. On the ground it would have been about five feet long, but hanging in the tree it would easily reach to eight feet or more. So there were snakes around here too – long ones. Our state of blissful ignorance had been shaken. The answer to the issue of whether there were more around came soon enough: we had to step over a small brown snake, which was more disturbing. I knew from a prior visit to Australia and another close encounter that brown snakes were the ones to be avoided. We could only take the advice that we helpfully offered to a passing trekker who was also concerned about the risks: 'Just don't get bitten by one.'

It wasn't just the snakes that we had to worry about. Suspended between branches, approximately head-high in the centre of webs that reached five feet or more across open space, were scary yellow-and-black-legged spiders. These webs could easily be imagined to have been set to ensnare passing humans. Somehow we didn't fancy testing the toxicity of the spiders, an especially spooky thought during night-time calls of nature. Later on, in another part of New South Wales, we would get close up to even more creepy-crawlies: black snakes gliding through the grass; the small but notoriously painful redback spiders; large but harmless tarantula-like huntsman spiders; and the poisonous golden orbs, sitting in the centre of webs hung out like mantraps in the bush, just like those we were encountering here in the Blue Mountains. As we learned more about the various risks these posed, we also found out about other natural dangers in Australia. It seemed to us as if the countryside was alive with animals just waiting for the chance to eat ignorant humans. I found a thick, large book ominously entitled *Australia's Dangerous Creatures – Understand, Avoid, Survive*. A section of its contents list read as follows:

> Animals that can wound: kangaroos, cassowaries, emus, wombats, quolls, thylacines and feral cats, lizards, pythons, feral pigs, water buffaloes, rats, dingoes, feral dogs, insects, birds, crocodiles, turtles, crabs, octopuses, squids, stingrays, bivalves, eels, barracudas and gropers, billfishes, seals, whales, sharks.
>
> Animals using venom: snakes, sea snakes, spiders, caterpillars, scorpions, centipedes, bees, wasps and ants, platypus, blue-ringed octopus, cone shellfish, crown of thorns starfish, sea urchins and sponges, bristle worms, fishes, jelly-fishes, hydroids, sea anemones and corals.

In case those lists weren't off-putting enough, the details about the wildlife in Australia made for some scary reading. Here can be found the world's biggest crocodiles, up to seven metres long; the world's only poisonous octopus; and the world's only jellyfish capable of killing healthy adult humans – just happening to be the world's most deadly marine stinger. There is even a 15 kg crab, with a pincer 45 cm long. And of course 2,000 species of spider, almost all venomous to some extent, including the world's deadliest, the Sydney funnel web.

One type of brown snake has enough venom to kill on average 100,000 mice, I read, although statistically it was not the deadliest species. That accolade belongs to the taipan, which is aggressive enough to bite repeatedly. One of these had killed a four-year-old boy in ten minutes. And with the description of this particular snake in the above-mentioned book came a story of heroism. There had been no antivenin available for the taipan until 1950, when a knowledgeable man spotted one in a Cairns rubbish tip. He caught it and put it in a sack, preventing witnesses from killing it even though it had already bitten him. He must have known the fate that awaited him. Before he was paralysed, he ensured that the snake would be sent alive to the serum laboratories. He died the next day, but the result of his actions was that there was an antivenin within five years. Incidentally, shark attacks apparently are so rare in Australia that they are statistically negligible. Since 1957 they have killed at a rate of less than one person per year. That's all right, then.

Back in our tent in the Blue Mountains at night, we could hear crashing noises in the bushes around our campsite. These weren't snakes, but there was definitely something large out there. The next evening, in the dusk, we saw what these fearsome monsters were: bush wallabies, to our relief and delight. One lolloped into clear view, just across the glade from us, as we sat eating dinner on a log. With its pointy nose and peaked ears facing directly towards us, it looked almost intelligent, as if about to wish us a cordial 'G'day'. Perhaps it was waiting for us to start the conversation, because after a while it just hopped away, noisily snapping twigs as it went.

After a couple of isolated days, containing several close encounters with snakes and spiders, we felt that perhaps it was prudent to quit while we were ahead. We made our way out of the valley, up a different path which had a steepness grade of 1 in 2.5 – pretty steep, for a footpath. It felt even steeper with packs on our backs. But once safely at the top, another fantastic lookout reminded us of just how spectacular this country was. It was certainly on a par with the national parks that we had seen in the USA. And yet, with the exception of Echo Point, we found it to be surprisingly undisturbed and relatively undeveloped. Perhaps Australians knew more about snakes and spiders than we did.

Chapter 30: New England

We travelled further north along the Great Dividing Range into New England. This was rural Australia, a very different world from the urban centres, and we found ourselves amongst people who still followed the spirit of the larger-than-life characters in their folk tales and country ballads. Here were whip-cracking, bull-riding, bronco-bucking cowboys complete with obligatory blue jeans, checked shirts and foot-tapping country-and-western music. It was an old-timer's land, where traditional values were still important and a man wasn't dressed if he went outside without the appropriate hat. Strangers were called by their first names until they earned respect, and men usually didn't shake a woman's hand. It was a place where a promise was expected to be as good as any contract, where a man would go out of his way to help a neighbour in need, and where goodwill and honesty allowed people to deal simply with one another. In a world where all too often urban modernity has overrun such values, it was thoroughly refreshing to see and hear these people live out their principled lives along codes of honour. It was a hard-working place, where men were men and where a beer or several after a day's physical labour was the Australian equivalent of an English cup of tea.

Early pioneer settlers had found it easier to travel along the highlands and plateaux of the Great Dividing Range, and a railway and highway still followed the inland route. Small mining settlements, some still looking like collections of tin shacks, had been built in the remote hills. The miners had been looking for sapphires and other precious stones, as well as metals like tin. Sheep farmers had moved in too, occupying land that had traditionally been Aboriginal hunting grounds, which led to several nasty conflicts between these groups. For example, in 1937–8 there had been several murders of shepherds by Aborigines near the town of Inverell. The workers of a sheep station had retaliated by rounding up and killing twenty-eight Aborigines in what has become known as the Myall Creek Massacre. Australian law acquitted the sheep farmers of mass murder, but public outrage caused a retrial under British law, after which seven people were hanged.

This was all well documented, but other incidents were not, perhaps because the timescale of European settler history was short enough for events to be too close for comfort. There was an unmarked lookout called Bluff Rock overlooking the highway, where in 1844 an Aborigine tribe had been driven to the edge by European settlers. No one was yet willing to say whether the tribe fell to their deaths voluntarily or whether they were thrown over. Several other landmarks in the area had been named after a 'bushranger' called Captain Thunderbolt – the real life Australian equivalent of a Robin Hood character – who was celebrated as a local legend after having lived a dashing life of gentlemanly bravado, escaping the police on stolen horses many times before being finally shot. In a book we also came across the story of Black Tommy, the Aborigine equivalent, who was virtually unknown locally.

We visited a horse sale one morning. Driving into the field behind a children's playground, this at first appeared more like a local country show than the regional, or indeed national, event that it was reported as being in the media. Temporary stables housed rows of horses, being groomed by their owners or stable boys. Pinned to the doors were notices that listed the virtues of the horses, such as the competitions won by their sires. It was noticeable how many of these notices were hand-written and misspelled. We couldn't distinguish which horses were good or bad, so we wandered off to take a seat on the wooden benches that lined the show ring. We felt conspicuous in our lack of apparently compulsory jeans, boots and hats. Dandy cowboys sat perched on the top rails of fences, absolutely the stereotypical image from Western movies. The sale itself did little to dispel this impression, with riders in fancy black outfits putting their horses through their paces around the ring while a couple of auctioneers tried to rouse some enthusiasm from the crowd.

'I'm not afraid to ask 6,000,' one would start. '…5,000… will anyone bid 4,000? …I'll take 3,000… 2,000…'

Eventually, more out of pity than real desire it seemed, a hand would go up and the auctioneer would pounce, launching into a continuous barrage of unintelligible numbers and gobbledegook, taking one bid after another until everyone's interest dried up. Then with a final drawn-out flourish it was, 'Going, gone, gone… last chance, any more, gone… final takers, no more, gone… all gone… *Sold!*'

Sometimes the bidding simply wasn't high enough and the second auctioneer would step in. His contributions were always along the lines of, 'Look, I know you don't think she's worth more, but I'm telling you that really she is and you trust me, don't you, so someone should offer more for her!'

All this dealing was taken very seriously by the impeccably behaved people, on their best behaviour for a public outing. After several hours with no sign of the end in sight, it was time for us to wander off, through the children's park and towards a pub for an Australian beer.

We drove back to the east coast and to Brisbane, a city without an obvious character but with a highly developed transport system. A broad, meandering Thames-like river was crossed by several stylish bridges and fast-moving catamarans. Along its banks ran cycle paths and roads that were built into a three-dimensional, multilayered, interchanging, fly-overing network. It looked very futuristic. The city had the feel of being invested in and well run; it was clean and orderly, practical and efficient – and so there is not much more to say about it.

While we were there, Queensland was hit by Cyclone Larry, the worst storm in twenty years. Its wind speeds had been estimated to be 290 kph, but as the relevant wind gauges had to be read manually, more accurate measurements had not been practical to take. We kept up to date with progress by watching the television news programmes, which became a subject of interest in themselves. Having failed to get to the best locations, reporters held interviews with locals on the telephone. The owner of a caravan park, who was lying underneath his mattress at the time, became the 'mate' of the broadcaster. On one prime time morning news programme, the newscasters referred to him as a 'poor bugger,' someone that 'sounded like a real tough dood'. Meanwhile the damage was such that 'no one can believe the amount of destruction'. The banana and sugar cane plantations of Queensland were indeed badly affected, losing 80 per cent of Australia's banana crop. Some settlements also suffered extensively.

All of which afforded a perfect opportunity for self-congratulatory adulation of the great Australian character. 'What makes Aussies really great is the way we rally around.' 'What a gutsy lot we are as Australians.' 'Talk about the Aussie spirit – it's just amazing, isn't it?' 'Australians are really good at this sort of thing.'

It became so sickly that it was off-putting to watch the news at all. This event only confirmed our opinion that the television news programmes in Australia were even more introverted than those of the USA. The reports were dominated by subjective and emotive reporting, designed to appeal to the 'personal angle' but which ended up obscuring any objective information. And it all reinforced my perception that part of the Australian psyche consisted of an inferiority complex, which continually had to be overcompensated for. This explained to me why justifiable pride in their successes, such as notable sporting achievements, were sometimes overblown, as if in an attempt to inflate the Australian ego.

We were finding it difficult to visit places along the east coast, such as the numerous national parks, without a hire car. Further north were the Great Barrier Reef and Cairns, but we had to swallow the bitter pill of finding these places just too far away and too expensive for a visit – rather like the Amazon rainforest had been. The central east coast of Australia seemed to be the perfect location for student backpackers, with its hostels and beer-and-beach tourist culture, but that was not us. It was time to head inland and to visit Uluru, one of the many world-famous sights of this huge and very diverse country.

Chapter 31: Uluru

Once Australia had separated from South Africa 95 million years ago, it was barely disturbed by further tectonic processes. Long rivers drained from the western flank of the Great Dividing Range into its hot interior, only to evaporate from vast lakes from which no water ever flowed out. Today, Australia has the lowest average elevation of any continent and is also the flattest. It sits and it bakes. 70 per cent of the country has an arid or semi-arid climate. In its deserts the rainfall is highly erratic, with long dry periods followed by thunderstorms and flash flooding. We were told that there were only two types of explorer who visited the interior of Australia: lucky ones and unlucky ones. The lucky ones found water in the rivers, lush grasslands and beautiful scenery, which they reported back in places such as Adelaide, encouraging other farmers to try their luck in the outback. The unlucky ones found dust, sand and searing heat, and failed to return to warn everyone else.

Only 6.5 per cent of the land is suitable for arable farming. Australia is the driest inhabited continent on the planet and, because of the scarcity of its natural resources, like water, it is officially classified as an over-populated country. This is despite it only having an average population density of six people per square mile, compared to over 630 people per square mile in the UK. Places such as Sydney are increasingly aware of their vulnerability, potentially made worse by climate changes that have brought decreasing levels of rainfall during the past twenty years. Water conservation was a frequent theme in bathrooms and kitchens that we saw. This didn't stop Australians having the highest energy consumption per capita in the world and being one of the few countries that refused to sign the Kyoto Treaty on gas emissions causing climate change.

Alice Springs is almost right in the centre of the continent, 1,200 km from the nearest ocean and 1,500 km from the nearest major city. We had booked flights in and out of Alice Springs in order to visit the 'outback' and to see Uluru – or Ayers Rock, to give its out-of-fashion European name. True to our lack of planning, our flights were originally only three days apart, which would have been disastrous. Coincidentally, and very fortunately, we had had to change the dates and were forced by availability to give ourselves a week there. We hadn't realised it, but Alice Springs is actually some 400 km from Uluru.

Even before we had landed, the landscape around Alice Springs reminded me of the East African scrub: the sparse, wiry bushes that gave the flat land a uniformly mottled appearance were a kind of indecisive compromise between bare earth and lush grass. Gum trees provided dappled shade from an intense sun, while their dried leaves on the ground sheltered armies of scurrying ants. Beside the roads on the outskirts of town were narrow paths that had been worn into verges of thin yellow grass, exposing an ochre-red soil. The roadside walkers were Aborigines, with strikingly black skin. They were dressed in ill-fitting and faded clothes, wearing just flip-flops or even going barefoot, giving an overall impression of impoverishment. At sundown we saw groups of Aborigines collecting beneath trees, standing or sitting together as if they were destitute outcasts.

The contrast with the centre of town was startling and even unsettling. Bar one man shuffling along the road, two teenagers cycling on the pavement and a couple in a car, everyone in town was white. The clean little shopping centre and the supermarket were not places of mixed race, despite Aborigines making up 17 per cent of Alice Springs' population in 2001. The town, however, was actually something of a centre for Aboriginal art. This may have been partly due to a famous local character called Albert Namatjira, who had acted as a guide for a visiting Melbourne painter in 1934. Namatjira learnt how to use watercolours and became recognised in his own right for his paintings – he even met Queen Elizabeth in 1954. Being an Aboriginal at the time, he was not allowed to vote, to own land or to buy alcohol.

Only in the 1970s was the law on land ownership changed; only in 1992 did the Australian High Court rule that Aborigines could have a valid claim to land that they had inhabited before the European settlers arrived. The public face of Australia was now making a real effort to reconcile Aboriginal culture and people with the rest of the population, as we had seen in Sydney, although the private face of the racial divide was often unsettlingly different from the public one. Reconciliation can't have been an easy task, considering both the character of many white Australians that we met and the mainly hunter-gather nature of traditional Aboriginal culture. As the Alice Springs Town Council website describes:

> The traditional culture and economy of the desert Aboriginal people are probably as different as it is possible to be from the contemporary Australian culture and economy. The culture of the desert combined a very simple technology with an incredible level of skill in its use, an encyclopaedic knowledge of the landscape and its ecology, a profound and rich religious life tied to that landscape and the world's most complex kinship system. It is a monument to the human intellect and spirit and most likely the only culture that would have survived for so long here in one of the world's harshest and demanding natural environments. It is also at one end of the world's cultural spectrum. In almost every respect the culture brought by the European newcomers in the nineteenth century is at the opposite pole.[6]

---

[6] www.astc.gov.au Alice Springs Town Council website 2007

Alice Springs had grown up as a staging post for camels making their way north or south across the outback, and then became a telegraph station. 'Alice' was the name of the postmaster general's wife; there was a permanent waterhole within a dry riverbed; and so the town got its name. We went out to have a look at the telegraph station and the spring, which were just outside town. There wasn't much to see except an old building and a sandy watercourse. We were more excited by the wallabies that hopped onto the lawn in the dusk, and by pink parrot-like galahs that flew to and from the fence posts.

The five-hour drive to Uluru in a hired car was fairly uninspiring, because the vista of scrubby vegetation hardly changed at all. Sometimes it was more woodland, at other times more grassland, sometimes there were even minor undulations of old sand dunes underneath the vegetation, but that was pretty much it. The roads were virtually empty. On the whole of our return journey I counted only five other vehicles in our lane – which made waving to other drivers a welcome diversion. The drivers of clapped-out campervans seemed to be the most friendly, perhaps because they had traversed half of the continent in virtual solitude before reaching here.

Despite the warning signs, there were no kangaroos to be seen. The only companionship was provided by eagles near the road. We did see a cow after about 100 km and then several miles further on a few more – quite exciting! Near the turn-off from the main north-south highway there were a couple of service stations which advertised attached campgrounds and tourist services such as camel rides. We managed to see emus here, but only because they were inside a paddock. They stank, really very badly, and were surrounded by swarms of flies, so many that Claudia was quickly driven back to the car. Actually, flies often forced us to retreat inside the car – and even there we were never fully able to escape from them.

That was all there was until we reached the Uluru Resort Complex. This was a purpose-built, suits-all-needs large-scale tourist resort, the only place that we could stay overnight in the national park. We pitched our tent in the campsite, this being by far the cheapest option, and set out to discover Uluru. The visitor centre informed us that Uluru is the remains of sands that were once eroded from nearby mountains and deposited in great alluvial fans. These deposits hardened into sandstone and were tipped at an angle so that their end stuck out from the surrounding layers of younger sands. The rock was so hard that its edges had held together rather than weathering away, which is why Uluru has such strikingly sheer sides emerging vertically from the sandy soil. It is the largest monolith on the planet, 1.5 miles long and with surprisingly proportionate dimensions.

The most significant feature of Uluru, however, is that it stands all alone. There was nothing else for miles, just flat outback – and then this great orange-grey lump sticking up from nowhere. It was very distinctive – despite, at the end of the day, being just a big rock. The best times to see Uluru, apparently, are sunrise and sunset, when the rock can be turned a rich red colour. So at 5 p.m. we set off, parking with a perfect view of the rounded hulk of rock, next to hundreds of other people pouring out from minibuses and coaches. Our own black shadows lengthened in front of us as the sun dropped, obstinately remaining a disappointing yellow colour. The rock face therefore changed from brightly lit brown to softer brown with just a tinge of orange before darkening into shadow. The show was over, and along with all the others we headed back to the campsite before it became too dark: our car insurance had a 'no night driving' clause.

The next morning we tried again, but a similar event occurred. Our typically fond experiences of sunrises were times of calm and stillness as the world gradually awoke. We had hoped that having Uluru in the foreground would heighten the atmosphere. It might have done, if it were not for the lines of cars and chattering people hugging mugs of warm drinks. The best view turned out to be behind us, of the sunrise itself and a pretty fan of half-lit clouds. The sheer number of people coming to witness an event had taken away its essential quality. But then quite suddenly, as if moved by a single mind, everyone else left. Within ten minutes we were literally deserted, standing totally on our own beside the roadside and wondering what had happened. It was now our turn to brew a mug of coffee and quietly enjoy the scenery. We reflected that it might have been worth watching sunrise from the sunset viewpoint, where we could have seen the silhouette of Uluru against the clouds, in relative peace and quiet. As we had the whole day ahead of us, we decided to make use of it by first walking the 8 km circuit around the base of Uluru, despite the heat and the flies.

Uluru and its surrounds contained a number of sites that are sacred to Aborigines. Their stories and legends incorporate certain features of the rock, and some places are reserved for teaching their children about Aboriginal laws and customs. The analogy with a place of worship, such as a cathedral, seemed ever more appropriate to us, as we began to appreciate its importance for the indigenous population. About 200 Aborigines still live in the national park, although none depend on their traditional lifestyle for subsistence any more. The park is jointly managed by local Aborigines and appointed park rangers, which to all appearances was a great success. A balance had also been reached between the Aboriginal culture that still existed and the demands of tourists. The Aborigines appeared keen to preserve their integrity rather than prostitute their culture for commercial gain. For example, photography of people was not encouraged, and certain sacred areas were off-limits for tourists. This hopefully resulted in a greater level of respect and understanding from tourists.

Indeed, the longer we spent at Uluru, the more its relevance to the Aboriginal community – rather than its physical presence – impressed itself upon me.

Having said all that, it was a shame to see evidence of other people's opinions about the significance of Aboriginal customs. When we paid for our park ticket we were given a leaflet which asked us not to climb the path to the top of the rock. Various reasons were given for this, including: the tourist route crosses a ceremonial path used by Aboriginal elders which is of 'great spiritual significance'; the path itself was difficult; and as custodians of the land, Aborigines would feel 'a great sadness' if anyone got hurt. The point, ultimately, was that Aborigines refrained from climbing the rock themselves and they asked tourists to do likewise. This was explicitly stated on further signs at the Cultural Centre and again at the base of the walk: 'Please Don't Climb', and 'If you worry about Aboriginal law, then leave it, don't climb it'. In the nearby Kata Tjuta hills, climbing on the rocks was prohibited, but here at Uluru the national park website explained that:

> Anangu have not closed the climb. They prefer that you – out of education and understanding – choose to respect their law and culture by not climbing. Remember that you are a guest on Anangu land.

And so, slowly but surely, making their ant-like way up and down Uluru was a steady trickle of tourists. These people had been left a choice and were choosing to disregard local wishes. It was an example of the reality that, at the end of the day, tourism is essentially an exercise in self-gratification and this was a blatant illustration of how insensitive that motivation could be.

There were flies by the very irritating thousand around Uluru and Kata Tjuta. Some people chose to wear green head-nets for protection and respite; we tried to put up with the irritants, desperately waving our hands to get rid of the swarms. Typically, we would walk around with as many as seventy flies at a time all over our backs and arms, driving us to maddening distraction. Strange that no one had mentioned the flies to us beforehand, when we talked about visiting Uluru. Wildlife continued to be a dominant feature of our Australian experience. Centipedes fifteen centimetres long with claw-like legs stalked through the grass. Bizarrely spiky lizard-like animals called thorny devils stood motionless on the roads, as if just waiting to be squashed by passing cars. These creatures actually absorbed water through their skin, so that they could take full advantage of any condensation in the desert. There was a bit of excitement in camp one morning when the couple next to us were packing their tent away. They discovered to their intense discomfort that a very scary large brown hairy-legged spider had taken up refuge underneath their groundsheet. The thought of what might have happened sent shivers down our spines as well as theirs.

After we had completed our walk, we decided to cool off and avoid the flies by heading for the resort's on-site swimming pool. Here, dark sunglasses were a common accessory whilst swimming and two people even had their leather cowboy hats on in the pool, their rims dipping into the water. One of these was a bubbly Welshman who was excited about his grand scheme to emigrate to New Zealand. He was on his way home, but only to get his things together and come straight back 'down under'. We met him again on our return to Alice Springs, as we were checking into our nice hostel, looking forward to a meal and another swim. We were told to wait in the lobby, while our room was being cleaned, and there we found our friend preparing to leave. He was gathering together all his souvenirs, including his pride and joy, a large didgeridoo wrapped up in brown paper.

To pass the time whilst we waited, we booked seats on the shuttle to the airport for the next morning. Claudia had the sense to check on the time of our flight, just in case, and then blinked. The date – was today. The time – was in a couple of hours! We hurriedly re-packed and boarded the same airport shuttle as the Welshman. Halfway to the airport he discovered that he had left his precious didgeridoo behind, so the characteristically matey driver obligingly turned around and they were happily reunited. We all made our flights, leaving us thankful for a chain of events that had prevented us from being stranded in the middle of Australia and missing our connection to Singapore. Suddenly we were on our way out of Australia and into Asia, our fourth and final continent.

Part Five
Singapore, Malaysia and Thailand

Chapter 32: Singapore

Singapore was a city first and last, despite it actually being an island that extended beyond the urban area. In fact, Singapore is composed of one major and sixty minor islands, in total nearly 700 km^2 in area. Over 20 per cent of this is forest or nature reserves. But the city is home to 4.5 million people; it has the fourth highest population density in the world, behind Monaco, Macau and Hong Kong. All along the 20 km long road from the airport to the centre we saw plain apartment blocks ten to fifteen stories high, one after the next, in a nearly continuous row several blocks deep.

The city centre had many individual skyscrapers and other strikingly modernist buildings that were spread out enough to create a pleasant airiness. This was enhanced by plenty of green spaces and wide pedestrian walkways. Singapore was a very comfortable, accessible and safe city. Everything in the centre was clean and orderly, partly because of ubiquitous fines for misdemeanours. Riding a bike through a pedestrian underpass would incur a fine of Singapore $1,000, for example. We saw a T-shirt emblazoned with the nice slogan 'Singapore: a Fine Country' to make the point. Large colonial buildings still dominated the quarter around the old dock, their mock-Grecian columns painted starkly white.

On a Sunday morning we saw cricket being played on the pitch that maintained its presence in the shadow of church spires and glossy high-rise office towers. Singapore had a strong feeling of being a rich colonial settlement, a world within a world. On the banks of the river were glamorous urban waterfront redevelopments, such as quays lined with restaurants that offered the widest range of international cuisine we could wish for, from Moroccan and Mexican to Indian and Italian. Waitresses there used hands-free walkie-talkies and palm-sized touch-screen electronic organisers. Quaint wooden barges ferried tourists to and from their hotels along the riverside. Nearby, children flew the latest toy: radio-controlled motorised kites that could perform aerial acrobatics as if nothing was impossible. There was a definite sense of the high-tech about the city, without it being brash.

If transport was an indicator of development, then Singapore was doing well for itself. Shiny modern cars, coloured monochrome shades between black and white, processed in an orderly fashion along the roads. There was an odd red or blue taxi in between, but we didn't see a single tatty car. There were only a couple of scooters and just one or two cycle-rickshaws for tourists.

Pedestrian crossings were modern, the metro system ultra-modern. In many ways it could be compared to a European city, more so than any other Asian city we saw. On a passing bus there was even an advertisement for Marks & Spencer.

Singapore had been chosen for a settlement by the British in 1819 because of its strategic geographical location. It lies close enough to Malaysia to be connected to the mainland by a causeway and a bridge, while on the other side is the strait that separates the Malay peninsula from Indonesia. It therefore sits right on the coastal trading route between the Middle East and China. The British operated it as a free port, which grew rapidly to dominate South East Asian trade. In 2005 it was the busiest port in the world and was rated the most business-friendly economy in the world. Singapore's per capita income in 2005 was nearly US $27,000.

As Singapore prospered, it became home to a rich ethnic mix, and this is still one of the distinctive features of the city. Signs on the streets were written in four different languages, although English appeared to be the most 'official' language and seemed to be the preferred medium for business. A family of market traders, who we met illustrated a trend in the adoption of English: the grandfather couldn't speak English, but his daughter could manage a stilted, pidgin version, and her son was fairly fluent. An impressive feature of Singapore was the way it had preserved its sense of history and heritage through public information boards:

> Much of early Singapore in the mid-19th and early 20th century was built by thousands of coolie labourers. Mostly from southern China, they sailed to Singapore on crowded junks. Upon arrival they were sold to the highest bidder...the men shared wooden beds and there was hardly any proper sanitation or fresh water. Sickness, violence and opium addiction were rife. Commonly called piglets, or *ju zai*, coolies were treated no better than beasts of burden.

Now the network of neat backstreet roads in Chinatown was a colourful and bustling market area. Orange and yellow umbrellas sheltered the street stalls and red Chinese 'balloons' hung down from orange-tiled pagoda-style shop roofs. At night it turned into an elegant oriental festival of lights and people. Each shop appeared to be in charge of the covered pavement in front of it, creating tidy but ever-changing walkways. Artisan stalls, tailors and dressmakers, masseurs, alternative therapists and electronic shops were common. The pungent odour of incense filled the air from sticks that were burning in front of many doors.

Little India had an altogether different character and flavour. Serangoon Road was the dominant thoroughfare, with smaller alleys disappearing behind it. It used to be the only north-south road, named after a river and the white storks which lived there. The grazing land had initially attracted Indian cattle farmers to settle there. Now the road was a noisy, busy line of shops and stalls literally spilling into the sidewalk and road. Bollywood music blared from the CD stores, sweet fragrances intoxicated our noses, whilst our eyes had to contend with the visual clutter of bright yellow and red garlands, cut-price jeans, glitzy jewellery shops, restaurants and vegetable stalls. It wasn't easy to push our way along the streets; it wasn't particularly pretty; but Little India was certainly vibrant and intense. In the side streets there was even more clutter. Parked trucks, mountains of fridges or computers and cardboard boxes were strewn around – it was chock-a-block with things that may not have actually been rubbish or litter but which still gave the impression of dirty untidiness. All of which was nothing at all to the real thing, as we would discover when we eventually reached Delhi itself.

One of the fascinating things about Singapore was that its different quarters each preserved their own distinct cultures and languages, being separate characters within a single unified city. It was a diversity that created an engaging, stimulating mix. But always the authoritarian hand of the government lurked in the background. We were told over an Indian dinner with a couple of chatty businessmen that one of the reasons why there was remarkably little ethnic tension in the city was that unrest would simply not be tolerated. The current state was described to us as a 'benevolent dictatorship' in which the population was not entirely happy, but put up with it because the government had continued to deliver prosperity and stability. Besides, significant criticism was not possible. Singapore was 'a police state' where 'the government controls everything'. There was also still not complete freedom of expression, and the government strictly controlled civil organisations. More people were executed in Singapore in proportion to its population than anywhere else in the world – it had mandatory death penalties for, among other things, drug trafficking.

Singapore had also been at the centre of the advocacy of the concept of 'Asian values', which purportedly describes a different philosophy from the individualistic materialism and social decadence of the West. As well as the supposed acceptance of authoritarian governments that claim to know better than their people, an example of this in practice was the deficit in pension provision in Singapore, justified because it was the duty of Asian families to care for their elderly. However, just as we would be hard pushed to identify a set of characteristics or values for European societies, so the Asian countries we visited seemed, if anything, to contain an even greater diversity of peoples and opinions. Just about the only constant as we travelled was that the cultural mix was ever changing, like an artist's palette of colours. Indeed, the cultures within Singapore itself and the individual people we met seemed to exemplify this.

Nevertheless, it was interesting that every now and again the theme of 'Asian values' cropped up. It was as if governments of South East Asia at times deliberately highlighted the difference between their behaviour and that of the immoral West in order to cast themselves in a more positive light. We would see this most clearly in Malaysia. The extent to which the Malaysian government played a role in shaping behaviour – acting as the moral guardian of the country – was illustrated by news that local governments were being allowed to impose their own regulations on 'antisocial behaviour'. This included hugging or kissing in public, the latter offence of which could receive a 250 ringit (US $73) fine or a spell in prison. These behaviours were explicitly described by media commentators as being Western in origin and therefore not acceptable to Chinese or Indian cultures.

As we were leaving Singapore, our taxi driver said gracefully, 'Thank you for visiting Singapore.' This was a typical comment that characterised much of our very amenable experience there. We took a very efficient cross-border train from Singapore to Kuala Lumpur, the capital of Malaysia. At a railway station just after the bridge between the two countries, the train stopped to allow all its passengers to file off and be processed through immigration controls. It was all very straightforward – quite unusual in our experience of border crossings, but again perhaps typical of Singaporean and Malaysian efficiency.

Chapter 33: Kuala Lumpur and Penang

As soon as we crossed into Malaysia there was a noticeable lowering of living standards. Smart apartment blocks were replaced by single-storey houses in a range of conditions. Some were more elaborate, with coats of paint over plastered walls, while others consisted simply of breeze blocks, wood or corrugated iron sheets. On view from the train window were the margins of society: dilapidated huts and shacks; dirt yards where goats, chickens and the occasional cow lived alongside the houses; rotting piles of discarded waste and scraps of litter strewn around. This was dirty, poor living. Under a road bridge were homes that needed no walls or roofs, the bridge sheltering an open-plan kitchen, sofas, chickens and even a car. Working in allotment plots beside the railway tracks were men wearing conical straw hats, the archetypal image of Vietnamese peasants, which would become so familiar there.

Despite the patches of poverty, the majority of the scenes from the train were of endless palm oil plantations. These dark trees were gloomy and foreboding, their overlapping fronds stretching into the distance, covering and obscuring the gently undulating topography. It was no surprise to learn later that Malaysia is the biggest producer of palm oil in the world. Sprinkled liberally about the edges of the plantations were banana trees, coffee bushes and rubber trees. Malaysia is also the world's largest exporter of rubber gloves, with 60 per cent of the global market. Once or twice I glimpsed some natural forest from our train, thick with green branches hanging down and creepers growing up; a living jungle that contrasted with the desert-like emptiness of the oppressive plantations. 60 per cent of Malaysia was covered by forest, which makes an area about the size of the UK. Some of it is 130 million years old and may be the oldest forest in the world.

On the train the signs were still bilingual, although Malay now took precedence over English. This didn't stop people on the train all conversing in English. It was amusing for us to see official Malay words that had been created as phonetic imitations of their English equivalents. So for example, one *notis* was written '*Kaunter Tiket*: Ticket Counter'. When we reached Kuala Lumpur's *tren stesen* alongside other *komuters* we had to find a *Teksi* to take us to our hotel. Later, for some *aktiviti*, we visited a *galeri* and a *muzium* before eating in a *restoran*.

There had been a return to the Singaporean-style modern apartment blocks on the outskirts of Kuala Lumpur. Development within the capital city reflected much of what we saw throughout the country: old poverty alongside new wealth. There was a grimy side to some of the city streets. Roads and pavements were neglected; litter was on the ground; beggars and hawkers were prowling beside the street stalls and restaurants that colonised tiny alleyways. But Kuala Lumpur – or 'KL' as it was colloquially referred to – also contained a futuristic clutch of glistening tower blocks, at the heart of which were the twin Petronas Towers.

These were the symbol of modern Malaysia, its pride and joy. When they were built they were the highest buildings in the world, at 452 m high, but they now merely claim the title for the highest twin towers. They are two tall, thin, unusually shaped columns of shiny silver metal and blue tinted glass, standing side by side, continuing up and up into the skies. They have eighty-eight floors, connected by a horizontal bridge at the 41st floor. Standing at the bottom it was impossible to make out their size: they were merely a colossal, gleaming hulk of pristine modern architecture. From further away it became more clear that surrounding tower blocks were merely half the height of the twin pinnacles. This difference in relative heights was shown even more emphatically from the midway bridge, which gave a view out over the city, already higher than virtually everything else in sight.

In the lower reaches of the towers were such things as a concert hall and a perfectly pristine five-floor shopping centre, full of stores with names like Versace, Laura Ashley, Cartier and Armani. In fact, there were no less than 222 different stores in the centre – not that I was bored enough to count. Actually, Claudia wasn't shopping; there also happened to be a first-class medical centre, where a skin disorder on Claudia's arm that had resisted a couple of weeks' treatment with antiseptic cream was diagnosed as being ringworm, a common ailment in sweaty climates. With the correct cream, it duly disappeared.

It was difficult to reconcile the displays of the latest in elegant fashion in the stores, all split-tops and revealing dresses, with the world outside the towers. Although many posters around the city were advertising a globalised teen culture of baseball caps, baggy jeans and skimpy tops, in KL and across the country people were typically far more demure and modestly dressed. Characteristic of this were the many Muslims – 52 per cent of Malaysia's population was Muslim, as all Malays officially have to be – and particularly the women. The frequently worn headscarves were sometimes matched with a traditionally elegant dress, although they just as often accompanied trendy jeans and short-sleeved tops. These fashions mixed with many others – the head-to-toe black burqas ironically attracting attention rather than deflecting it – but it was only the foreign tourists who dressed in revealing clothes like miniskirts and strappy tops. With everyone else dressing both conservatively and stylishly, we couldn't but wonder whether these Western tourists were ignorant or simply didn't care about local opinion. They flattered neither the individual nor Westerners in general. Maybe it was this all too obvious indecency that helped encourage Asian governments and societies to protest against Western morals and behaviour.

Another notable characteristic of Malaysians almost everywhere was their courtesy. Nearly everyone made a point of being polite and welcoming. Thailand has often been credited with being 'The Land of Smiles', but after travelling there too, we considered Malaysia to be the rightful claimant to this title. It was a relaxed and friendly society, with clear boundaries that demonstrated the value of respectfulness. It was not done to throw litter on the floor, or to be rude, and so on. Courtesy was a national trait that was encouraged by such things as posters in the metro saying 'Aren't we courteous?' above seats reserved for passengers with special needs. For foreign visitors, this made for a very comfortable experience. Perhaps this was why we saw more tourist families with children in Malaysia than anywhere else in Asia. I also liked the concern shown by a newspaper report concerning a forthcoming National Toilet Summit in Kuala Lumpur – as well as the idea of a World Toilet Organisation:

> ...to educate the public about the importance of clean commodes...public toilets have long disgusted residents and tourists with their lack of basic items such as toilet paper, soap and sometimes even toilet seats...the meeting would bring together local officials and international experts on toilet management, including the founder of the World Toilet Organisation.

It was hot and sticky in Kuala Lumpur. We sweated our way through the days, Claudia suffering from headaches, until the inevitable late afternoon thunderstorms cleared the air for the evening. Our hotel room was in Chinatown, opening right onto the central market. Because our room had a small unopenable pane of glass in a wall, euphemistically called a window, we were in a 'deluxe' suite. The main road outside our hotel door was a traffic thoroughfare by day but a street market by night. During the day there was space to walk past the stalls that were selling thousands of fake branded watches, copies of any DVD ever made, cheap clothes, leather bags, fruit and flowers. At night cars were banned and the stalls multiplied until there was barely any room left, making progress only possible by squeezing between stalls and shoppers. We saw a group of young men selling CDs from a table in the middle of the road, who panicked as shouts went up further down the street – warnings that the police were on their way. The men literally fled, grabbing as many CDs as they could before disappearing into the crowd, the table still standing where they had left it.

Night-time was when Chinatown was at its most colourful, literally. The red lanterns overhead were turned on, becoming bright yellow globes strung out like giant Christmas lights. Neon signs blazed out yet more yellow and red and the streets took on a festive feel. The balmy temperatures and crowds of shoppers added to the relaxed atmosphere. It was a good time to claim a table at one of the restaurants whose tables had suddenly erupted into the roads. Their incognito waiters lurked amid the crowds, arguing over their patches of turf and looking for an opportunity to pounce with a menu and drag unsuspecting victims in off the street.

The menus were all pretty much the same, however, and the food not particularly great. Whatever vegetable was on offer, it would inevitably come swimming in grease, having been quickly poked around a wok in what passed for a stir-fry. White rice was available by the bucket-load, a compulsory part of virtually every single meal in South East Asia. The food came in bowls, with ladle-like spoons to transport it to a personal plate, from where chopsticks took over. Getting the knack of eating came quickly, but the taste couldn't be said to be hugely appealing. We found that it was best washed down with a bottle or two of local beer.

I bought a new watch at the market, a fine-looking piece with a brand name emblazoned on it. The strap was just what I wanted for travelling, hard to pull off my wrist and unlikely to break. Perhaps the way that the seller calmly retrieved one watch from his display that was not working and replaced it with another should have been a sign that his stock was not entirely reliable. Another indicator might have been the 10 ringit (US $3) price tag. But then, that wasn't a lot to lose in any case. So I had my new watch and proudly wore it for at least a couple of days. This was enough time to discover that it not only ran slow, but also had a tendency to stop completely every now and then. When I looked to see what the time was, the best I could tell was that it was definitely not earlier than the time shown. In fact, it was generally a fair bit later. It was not the best way to ensure getting to stations on time, as we discovered once while eating lunch in a park before catching a bus. Using my new watch, I was quite relaxed at having plenty of time left, whilst beside me Claudia was getting ever more impatient. When we consulted watches my leisurely half an hour instantly became a two-minute dash for the bus – which of course turned out to arrive late anyway.

The more touristy Central Market of Kuala Lumpur provided for the higher quality souvenir and handicraft trade. Most interesting to us was artwork of a dot-paint style, adorned with swirling circles and lizard graphics, that looked identical to the Aboriginal art that we had seen in Australia. Yet we were told that these paintings came from Borneo. And in a corner of the shop, even more surprising, was a collection of genuine didgeridoos, again from Borneo. This suggested to us that a cultural link must have existed at some point between the Australian Aborigines and the tribes of Borneo. Actually, the origin of the indigenous Australians is not clear. Some probably did indeed arrive from South East Asia, most likely via New Guinea, at around 40,000 BC.

Malaysia was a country formed from a collection of different ethnic groups, each with their own traditions, customs and cultures. There are eighteen different tribes of indigenous Malays, some of whom still live as blowpipe-wielding hunter-gatherers in the forests. Along the coast are different fishing communities; inland are a variety of farming groups. Malaysia's unusual geography and political divisions contributed to a sense of a country that wasn't entirely coherent. On the western Malay peninsula are nine sultanates, two states headed by governors and two federal territories. On the island of Borneo to the east, there are two more states and one more federal territory that belong to Malaysia courtesy of their history as British colonies.

As well as people from Indonesia who had settled on the Malay peninsula, significant numbers of Chinese and Indians had migrated into the cultural mix, bringing their own religions, architecture and commercial enterprises. Right across South East Asia we would encounter the impact of these two ancient civilisations and vast countries. Through the centuries their influence had been felt, and is was clear to us that it continued to be so. As we progressed, it seemed fitting that our world journey would end with visits to these regional superpowers, first China and then India.

In order to visit the places with reputedly the finest architectural examples of Chinese influence in Malaysia, we took an overnight train and then a 6 a.m. ferry ride to reach the island of Penang, in the north-west corner of the country. Georgetown was founded here in 1786 by the British East India Company, from where it became a centre for the spice trade as well as for tea and cotton coming from India and China. As a piece of trivia, Georgetown was where Jodie Foster filmed *Anna and the King*, after Thailand refused permission to film it there. Not that the modern Georgetown had the look recreated for that film, of course. In old Chinatown, the roads were lined with typical Chinese style two-storey buildings, originally constructed by Chinese labourers. The top floor comprised the living quarters, and nearly always overhung the pavements, supported by roadside pillars that created a sort of covered passageway underneath. The ground floor was the family-run commercial shop, often completely open to the street and closed at night with a metal shutter that was rolled down and secured to the floor with a large padlock.

The architecture of these buildings also contained elements of Portuguese design, such as delicate wooden window shutters, because many of the coastal towns along the western coastline of the Malay-Thai-Burmese peninsula had originally been Portuguese trading posts. Sometimes there were touches of Dutch and English influence too. Neoclassical columns and other decorations reflected the European vogues of the period. These old houses reeked of being once grand but had now faded from their former glory. Their paintwork was peeling off the walls, shutters were broken, many looked shabby and almost derelict. The old Chinatown houses gave an impression of degeneration that modern Georgetown never fully managed to counter.

Despite this, we found it interesting to wander around the backstreets looking at the outward signs of ordinary life. Slightly more modern buildings were decked out with Chinese writing, red lanterns and joss sticks. Walking wasn't easy, because there was rarely a stretch of pavement that didn't resemble an obstacle course. Different shops each had their stretches of pavement at different widths and heights, their pillars at different distances from the walls, and their goods placed erratically into the footpath. Our best option was to walk outside the rows of parked cars, trying to ignore passing rickshaws, scooters and cars in the hope that they would dodge us instead. We did try taking a tourist rickshaw one morning, partly out of sympathy for the driver. But we felt very strange being pushed around the streets whilst he huffed and puffed, suffering the looks from people walking beside us. We decided that however sweaty and haphazard it was, walking was preferable.

In the more central roads, we found shops selling familiar high street merchandise, the globalised household goods that were available everywhere around the world from Mexico City to, well, here. Chinese temples appeared at intervals between the shops, ornately decorated with multicoloured dragons and other beasts on their roofs, and with flamboyant markings painted all around their entrances – a real taste of the orient. Some of these temples were family-owned, which must have represented quite a status symbol. There were also Hindu temples and a mosque in close proximity, with Christian churches slightly further afield. Penang, like Malaysia in general, had a very mixed society, its culture and history being full of varied flavours.

From Penang we travelled inland to the Cameron Highlands for a taste of a totally different part of Malaysia. It had been a long time since something surprised us as much as seeing giant red plastic strawberries along the roadsides. Somehow I hadn't associated Malaysia with strawberries, but in the Cameron Highlands we found 'pluck-your-own' soft fruit farms, along with tea estates that offered perfect cream teas, scones and all.

Chapter 34: The Cameron Highlands

After leaving Penang we had out first sight of flat paddy fields that were prettily coloured bright green with the tender shoots of new rice seedlings. Then we drove up through forested valleys stuffed with ferns and undergrowth, before reaching the upland area of the Cameron Highlands. Between low, rounded hillocks were suddenly grey patchwork quilts of plastic sheeting stretched over bamboo pole frameworks. These were plots of intensive agriculture, Malaysian-style. The area had become rich by supplying 'winter vegetables' to the rest of the country, including strawberries, flowers, cacti and cucumbers. At 5,000 ft altitude, the temperature range here was usually between 10–25°C all year round. As well as the plants, a booming tourist industry thrived on the cooler highland temperatures, which provided a welcome respite from the otherwise hot and sticky equatorial climate. This was where Japanese and Singaporeans came to stay in fancy hotels and play golf, or where Malays visited for weekend breaks.

The roadside settlements were a mixture of primitive street stalls and glossy hotels that looked like Swiss ski resorts. We passed a golf course and then a very convincing mock Tudor building, complete with black beams, whitewashed walls and rose beds around the garden path, bizarrely called 'Ye Olde Smokehouse'. The longer we spent in the Cameron Highlands, the more it seemed to us a quaint, eccentric kind of place, with something totally unexpected around each corner. It was a jumble of assorted attractions, something like a sweet box full of brightly coloured surprises, much like the pink, yellow and blue apartment blocks on the hillsides around us. It may not represent stereotypical Malaysia, but its eccentric, harmless charms grew on us as we stayed there.

Along the main road of our small resort town we found the usual tourist bric-a-brac of restaurants and shops selling a little of everything but nothing in particular. In doorways sat people advertising themselves as 'Tourist Information' but who were nothing more than a front for tour operators hoping to enlist customers. All sold the same tours, offered as pick 'n' mix bundles. We could choose from a number of visits to surrounding jungle, fruit and flower farms, an indigenous village, or large, wealthy tea plantations. Before sampling those, however, we dined out on the local cuisine, called steamboats. These turned out to consist of a bowl of water sat on a portable gas ring, with several plates of uncooked food on the side, such as noodles, mushrooms and unidentifiable greens – at least, these were the vegetarian option. It was a cook-your-own meal, which I thought kind of defied the object of going out to a restaurant. And it proved to be an exercise in frustration as we struggled to handle the hot, slippery food. Delicacy wasn't a skill that we had acquired yet with chopsticks – and quite why a tiny china bowl the size of an egg cup had to be used instead of a decent-sized plate, I didn't know. An Indian meal the next night served in dollops on a banana leaf was far more to my taste and style, demonstrably more practical as well as being environmentally friendly.

One day we woke to a fresh morning with the birds singing and the sun streaming in through our window. It was one of those Spring-like mornings when the air was chilly and slightly damp but deliciously clean and fragrant, just calling us to run outside and feel the dew between our bare toes. We didn't quite do that, but we set out for a walk through the jungle, more properly called montane rainforest. We started off following a well-used trail, which gradually deteriorated into a questionable path. Beside it thin, spindly trees stretched up to the light, next to bigger ones with broad, splaying roots and wild banana trees – there were twenty-seven varieties of banana here, by the way – which obscured the sun with their giant leaves. Bright green ferns, white orchids and other plants sprouted from branches and crevices; vines and creepers hung in coils all over the place; white and pink carnivorous pitcher plants lurked in dark corners. Fallen branches and tree trunks lay everywhere, some rotting, some mossy, all damp and slimy. Leaf litter was spread over the ground, except where the path exposed brown, slippery mud or equally treacherous rocks. There was a constant noise from insects and birds, but otherwise no animal life was visible except for the occasional cloud of flies and the odd large and pretty butterfly. Once the lurking fear of getting lost, or stepping on a tarantula, or putting a hand on a snake, or being bitten by some exotic flying beast had passed, our hike settled into a routine exercise in avoiding slipping or tripping over.

Malaysia is actually home to some incredible wildlife – we saw stuffed versions of it in a museum – from giant crocodiles to pygmy elephants, rhinos, tigers and orang-utans. Unfortunately, the precious forests are threatened by the conflicting interests of loggers and palm oil or rubber plantations. Only 11.6 per cent of Malaysia's forests are still pristine, largely because many are managed for timber production. Sadly, Malaysia's deforestation rate is increasing faster than any other tropical country; since 2000 it has lost 0.65 per cent of its forest – an area of 140,000 hectares – every year.

At the end of our path we emerged onto a road that wound past vegetable gardens that looked like large-scale terraced versions of backyard allotments. Local families were allowed to lease a strict two acres of land for a four-year term, forcing them to be productive or lose the opportunity. Productive they were: three hundred metric tonnes of vegetables were produced every single day in the Cameron Highlands. We wandered into a flower farm, where what looked like marigolds and cucumbers were being grown in dense rows under plastic sheeting and intense light bulbs. The flowers were exported to places like Japan and Singapore, apparently. A group of workers, wearing gardeners gloves and conical hats, emerged out of curiosity to look at us. They grinned and passed unintelligible comments between themselves, asked whether we were married, and then waved us on our way. Everyone we passed was very friendly and helpful, always responding in kind to a smile and a 'hello'; the Cameron Highlands was a fun place to go exploring.

The three tea plantations there were a different scale of industry. One was owned by a Scottish family, the other two by Malays. Combined together, they grew a total of 8,000 hectares of tea. Row upon row of green waist-high bushes carpeted the hillsides, neatly picking out the rounded contours. Hundreds of workers came from Indonesia to pick the tea leaves, earning about 30 ringit (US $8.79) per day. A single tea bush would be picked every three weeks and pruned every three years. We were shown around one plantation by a young Indian whose grandfather had come to Malaysia as a tea picker, but whose father was a shopkeeper. With the third generation being a tourist guide, this was a familiar global story of development. 50 per cent of the population in the Cameron Highlands was Indian, 30 per cent was Chinese and only 20 per cent was Malay, making for a usually trilingual population. One of the reasons our guide gave for the success of the immigrant populations was that they value education, and will persist at their schooling, recognising it as a ticket to increased wealth.

In a shop window on a main road our attention was caught one morning by signs that advertised a forthcoming sale of newly built apartments. The pictures showed smart, modern blocks with low suburban fences, neat lawns, and expensive cars in the driveways. These images would have fitted perfectly into the design portfolio of property developers in places like California. They represent an idealised 'dream home' that was apparently a global aspiration. And just around the corner, there they were, in real life. Smart white blocks, low fences, lawns and bushes – the works, complete with glossy jeeps parked outside. This was clearly a Malaysian dream, too.

From the Cameron Highlands we returned the way we had come, towards Penang. Rather than going onto the island again, we stayed a night in the coastal town of Butterworth. As we wandered its lonely streets in the rain and the dark, searching for somewhere to stay, we reflected again on how quickly tourist facilities drop away once the standard tourist trail is left. We had to put up with a night in a dodgy Chinese hotel, but had the satisfaction of a pleasant meal in a nearby eatery, where the staff and customers seemed happy to see foreigners and tried hard to please us. In the early morning we made our way back to the railway station and continued north to Thailand in a superb air-conditioned train that had started its journey in Singapore.

The last scenery of Malaysia that we saw from outside the window was beautiful, a dream-like rural landscape. At first the land was flat, with just a few pale blue shadows of featureless hills in the distance. Stands of ragged, un-kempt trees and bushes broke the skyline, sometimes as dark green silhouettes of palm and banana leaves. Fields beside the railway were marked out by lines of small low-lying mudbanks. In between, water flooded the square plots, reflecting light like flat white mirrors. In some fields fresh green shoots of rice were pushing through the water; in others thick dark mud lying underneath was still exposed. On overhead wires perched birds, many and varied, including kingfishers and storks. Sporadically we passed workers in the fields, standing knee-deep in water and mud. They worked the rice paddies with shovels or ploughing machines that looked like portable water-wheels, churning through the mud. And then, as we reached the Thai border, looming hulks of forested limestone rose up out of the plain. These isolated towers and cliffs were like features from a fairy-tale world, looking surreal and yet with a dignified presence. Sadly, we gradually left this pretty corner of Southern Thailand behind as we were carried northwards, eventually arriving at the town of Hat Yai.

Chapter 35: South Thailand

Thailand was immediately different from Malaysia. Hat Yai was a city of concrete buildings, brash and noisy, with an intensity that was more reminiscent of Guatemala. Even before disembarking the train we had been plagued by young touts who accosted every potential tourist: 'Where are you going? Hello – you – where you going?' After our conversations had been repeatedly interrupted by this aggressive touting, we gave increasingly irritated replies, which caused most of the touts to move on to softer targets. There was an abrupt rudeness about this kind of exchange that left a bad taste. So we relented and gave one young lad the more humane response of 'Songkhla', which we immediately regretted. Instead of a pleasant personable interaction, all we received was, 'Follow me, come, follow me,' and the tout jumped off the train, looking over his shoulder to see if we were following him out of the doors.

He acted not only as if he now had a personal claim to our custom, but also as if we had given an agreement that he could organise our affairs for us, by the simple act of being less than rude. It was at times like this that I felt inclined to simply turn and walk in the opposite direction, but on a station platform there was little choice. Once outside the station we found him waiting for us by the entrance. 'This way – here, you!'

He tried to shepherd us across the road and into a taxi, which would no doubt have resulted in our being charged an extortionate amount. As politely as we could, we told him no, that we were going to get a bus, thank you. 'Yes, yes. Here! Bus-taxi!' was his final attempt at getting us into his car.

We found our way across a corner of town to where we had hoped would be a bus station, despite the efforts of taxi drivers who hung out of their windows and shouted at us, 'You – where are you going?' We walked past a row of sewing machinists, each sitting at their individual tables on the pavement intent on their tasks. Motorcycles weaved past, some offering lifts as a form of cut-price taxi service. Vans that looked like miniature cattle trucks with benches in the back were also new forms of public transport to us. Coloured advertising signs hung from the blocky buildings overhead, dwarfed by large gold-framed portraits of the Thai royal family looking magisterially over the lively chaos below. It was hectic, just a bit crazy and quite rough. There was also barely any written English visible – another difference from Malaysia.

We reached where we thought the bus stop should have been and walked completely around the block, sure that we were in the right place but increasingly frustrated at being unable to see any bus station at all. Eventually an amused group of scooter-taxi men in orange bibs indicated that we should wait by the side of the road, confirming that this was indeed the 'bus stop' even though none of the buses zooming past gave any indication of stopping. Nevertheless, they could be stopped here, as the men demonstrated on our behalf.

Spotting the bus to Songkhla coming a little way back – we wouldn't have known where any of them were going – the men ran out into the traffic, waving to attract the attention of the driver. He pulled over towards us and we were literally pushed into the still swiftly moving bus by our laughing helpers. We were grateful for their assistance, feeling not just a little helpless and inadequate, and we were relieved that the ticket collector on board was friendly towards us too, despite the communications barrier. It took the assistance of two passengers to work out where we wanted to get off. Everyone helping us seemed to wear an expression of amused patience, which was reassuring as we were struggling to make sense of what was going on. Travel was often about periodic whirlwinds of activity and confusion, between which were quieter times during which we would cross our fingers and hope that we were headed in the right direction. And take the time to look around and absorb the sights of the country.

There was a lot of green outside in Thailand. Green rice, green grass, green trees. Numerous hump-back Brahmin cows stood knee-deep in marshes with knotted ropes pulled through their noses. We passed two herds of water buffalo in the fields; large, powerful animals with fearsome horns that curved in a scimitar-like way from their thick skulls. Dried mud was peeling off their broad backs; they had obviously been enjoying a mudbath recently. The oldest houses I saw out of the bus window were wooden plank or even woven bamboo mat boxes on stilts, set in individual plots within the lush greenery. These had usually been updated or replaced by concrete and brick buildings in the same style, often unpainted and still looking pretty rudimentary. Sometimes a wall had been built between the stilt legs to provide a garage or perhaps more downstairs rooms. The most modern, stylish, expensive houses – of which there were a smattering – seemed to have done away with stilts altogether. These were pretty bungalows or large family houses, which would have been attractive anywhere in the world.

We had chosen to stop at Songkhla solely because we had travelled far enough for one day and we didn't fancy staying in Hat Yai. Songkhla was a small coastal resort, popular with locals. It sat on the edge of a peninsula and so had beaches along two sides, which were pretty white strips of sand shaded by palm trees. Not many people were swimming here, but Muslim families picnicked on grass underneath the trees. Hawkers walked past with eggs or fruit in baskets that were suspended from the two ends of a flat bamboo pole balanced across one shoulder. An orange-robed Buddhist monk sat on a bench by himself, absorbed in a book. It was a gentle, peaceful place where everyone smiled a genuine 'hello' to a pair of foreigners.

The main form of transport was by motorcycle, and these were used by everyone from petite girls in tight-fitting jeans holding an umbrella as a sunshade, to an old man carrying a poodle as a passenger, or a family of four squeezed together on a single bike. At road junctions the already slow-moving traffic would pull to a halt and all the motorbikes would weave to the front of the queue, collecting in a massed huddle, ready to pull away in unison when the lights changed. They looked as if they were starting a slow motion road race. Motorbikes – or 'motos', as they were called here – would rapidly become a distinctive feature of South East Asia, being the ubiquitous all-purpose utility vehicle. Beast of burden, family car, fashionable icon, taxi, mobile kitchen, sales vehicle – they could be and were put to all sorts of uses.

On the top of a hill overlooking the coast of Songkhla was a Buddhist stupa. This was the first Buddhist religious building that we encountered on our travels, to be the first of many wats and stupas right across Asia. It looked a bit like a giant yellow ice cream cone turned upside down, with long red and orange sashes wound around it, catching the breeze. Green trees, bougainvillea bushes, brass bells and incense sticks beside it all created a harmonious and contemplative atmosphere. Somehow the simplicity of the stupa made it more accessible to us than the colourful Hindu temples we had seen in Singapore and Malaysia. We sat for a while, looking out at the view and appreciating the calm around us. We even pulled a couple of numbered sticks out of a pot and read our fortunes – but quickly forgot what they had actually said.

As we walked down the hill through the trees, we passed several gold statues of the Buddha, each housed in its own little shrine. Some were grotty and others were pristine, each invariably dressed with a sash of yellow or orange and sometimes wearing a garland of flowers. Most of the houses on the streets below also had shrines outside them; small temples on poles that looked something like oriental bird tables. All of these shrines contained incense sticks and offerings, such as small plates of fruit or flowers, even a glass of tea or a Fanta bottle complete with a straw. One morning we watched a lady in a café laying out her offerings on a shelf behind her counter. She brought her hands together, whispered a few words and bowed her head. It was a short, simple ritual, but moving in its sincerity and gracefulness.

On the hillsides of the town lived half-tame troops of monkeys, which had become something of a tourist attraction. People would give them offerings of food, buying bananas and nuts from any one of numerous stick-wielding sellers. But the monkeys had been provided with more than just free food. There were ropes suspended from the trees across the road, providing a safe monkey-crossing. And there was a 'fun park' created especially for them, complete with tyres hanging down, metal climbing frames, even a slide into a tank of water. As we watched, the monkeys spurned the slide in preference for launching themselves from swinging ropes into the water, falling fully ten feet with a huge splash. They climbed out bedraggled but cool, clearly having great fun.

Songkhla turned out to be one of our favourite places in Thailand. The very fact that barely any English was spoken was an indication of how unaffected by international tourism it was. Particularly in retrospect, that very fact made it appealing. As we moved further north, the places that we would visit were at times swamped with foreign tourists and often the worse for it; we would look back on Songkhla with ever more affection.

Southern Thailand was not, however, as peaceful as the impression given by pleasant places like Songkhla. The southern provinces housed a Muslim separatist movement which had resorted to violent tactics in order to have its voice heard. Daily killings were frequently reported in the papers. Schools and teachers were being particularly targeted; while we were there we read about one violent attack that left a female teacher in a coma. Schools were being periodically closed over safety fears, while several murders of workers in rubber tree plantations had made many people too scared to work. In the past 2½ years, almost 2,000 people had been killed in southern Thailand. Perhaps it was no coincidence that Songkhla and Trang were centres of protests during the 2006 parliamentary elections. The saga that followed the boycotting of these elections was only resolved many months later with a coup that ousted the unpopular prime minister.

After numerous military coups during the last decades of the twentieth century, this was the first in Thailand for fifteen years. The King played a back-seat role during the political dispute, refusing to exercise his own authority but instead insisting that a judicial process be followed – until an army commander took unilateral action. It was fascinating to see how central to life in Thailand the longest-reigning monarch in the world was. From the giant family portraits to local aid projects funded by the King, his presence permeated life throughout the country. Perhaps this was similar to the level of influence over society that the British monarchy used to have. The genuine respect and affection for the King was incredible. He was beyond reproach, a benevolent and wise father-figure for the entire country.

We returned to the main transport route up and down southern Thailand at the large town of Trang, not far north of Songkhla. There was a mix of cultures here too. Shrouded Muslim girls shared the pavements with barefoot Buddhist monks in orange robes. It was more modern than Hat Yai, with shiny new Australian-style pickups on the roads, large banks, shops and restaurants. There were also several Internet cafés, although here they didn't call them that – these were 'games shops'. At the night market, the stallholders were more interested in watching the Tottenham game on portable televisions than working, whilst the sports pages of newspapers were preoccupied with the twists of the English Premiership.

Looking for a cheap meal the first night we arrived in Trang, we turned right outside our hotel door and walked in a big circle for about twenty minutes before arriving at a couple of eateries not fifty yards to the left of where we had begun. We sat down at a typical place, open to the road and full of tables. Waitresses were buzzing around and at the back several cooks were busy amid clouds of steam. They were all too busy to pay any attention to us, despite most of the customers having taken an interest in our presence. Just as we were wondering whether we had better walk out and try again, the couple seated at the table next to us took it upon themselves to get us served by a waitress, offering at the same time to help us translate the menu. It was a typically generous gesture; in Songkhla and now here, virtually everyone reciprocated a smile with instantaneous delight and was genuinely friendly towards us. The waitress asked us if we wanted our meal 'spicy' or 'not spicy'. We requested the latter, but even then found that the food was so hot that our mouths were still burning two hours after the meal, despite all the rice and beer that we had tried to dilute it with.

In these local eateries we didn't have to ask for rice. Indeed, it wasn't even on the menu. It just came automatically with every meal. The Thai invitation to have a meal could be literally translated as being invited to 'eat rice'. Thai breakfast was curry and rice. Somehow we always expected to have a mound of rice heaped before us, but were constantly surprised by the tiny cupfuls; rice was often used as a filler, to be eaten after the other more favoured courses of a meal. Time and again we had to fill up with more rice, as the portions of food were often small – we joked that this was why the Thais were all so little.

The following night we chose another restaurant, which was otherwise totally empty. The waiter was pleased to see us, bowing a gracious welcome. He produced a menu, which stumped us as it was all in Thai and we hadn't brought our dictionary out with us. Its translations didn't always help much anyway, as the spoken languages in South East Asia depend significantly on the intonation of the sounds. No such equivalent exists in English, but here one word could have several meanings according to its tone or pitch. We found it almost impossible at first to hear these differences, let alone reproduce them. Often we would hazard a word to be met with a totally blank expression. In

Vietnam we were taught how to say 'hello' but were then warned that when pronounced in the way that we did, the word actually meant 'I want porridge'.

Here our waiter had a few choice words to help us along. 'Rice?' Yes. So far so good. 'With pork, or chicken, or shrimp, or fish?' No, no meat. 'No meat? Shrimp?' No, but how about fish? 'Fish! For you only? And for you, chicken? Not chicken? Pork? Shrimp? What do you eat?'

Claudia had the bright idea of pointing to the leaves of a pot plant, which the waiter stared at for a while before the link dawned on him. His face brightened – yes, they could do vegetables. 'With rice?' Of course.

Later on in Trang's food market we came face to face with the pork, chicken or shrimp that we might have chosen, making us thankful that we hadn't eaten any. The market was inside a large warehouse, where bright strip lights hung from the ceiling over roughly built tables and stalls laid out with produce. Silvery fish glistened on slowly dripping beds of ice, hosed down by women in plastic aprons and wellington boots who were gradually turning the floor into a vast dirty puddle. Fresh squid, shrimp, prawns and crabs were all heaped in plastic bowls, often festering in a strange black liquid. In another section meat was on display: raw pink cuts hung from metal hooks, dripping red blood into plates of tripe or liver. Plucked yellow-skinned chickens were strung up by their necks, feet dangling limply in mid air. Some had already been dissected, their different anatomical parts carefully separated into a pile of heads here, or a bowl of feet there. The same fate had been applied to pigs a bit further on. The plate of trotters was strangely unappetising to me, but then so was the intact head next to it. The fruit and vegetable section gave us some relief, their bright tropical colours professionally arranged in attractive displays. But even here were wobbling mounds of black jelly and a pot of giant black beetles. Delicious!

Chapter 37: Thailand Beaches

We hit Thailand's international tourist trail at the west coast seaside resort of Krabi. In this busy riverside town there were suddenly familiar brand names, like Kodak, Coca-Cola and HSBC. There were also pizza-and-pasta restaurants, English bookshops, souvenir shops and tourist offices. On the streets were plump white European girls, their stomachs bulging out from between too-tight tops and miniskirts. Our hostel happened to be run by a European and his English-speaking Thai wife. This globalised blend had inevitably diluted the local culture: whenever 'Westernisation' increased, local features diminished proportionately, as we would soon see in the larger tourist resorts. Here in Krabi, however, the local flavour was still just about holding its own – enough for us to enjoy seeing daytime shopping pavements turned into evening entertainment venues, for example. A carpet would be laid down on the street, low tables and cushions set out and a TV placed on a table at one end, making an impromptu cinema.

The main attraction of Krabi was the surrounding scenery. It offered jungle, mangrove forests, beaches, coral reefs, caves, limestone towers and cliffs. Visitors could go kayaking, hiking, visiting fishing villages, elephant riding, rock climbing or caving. The offshore island of Ko Phi Phi was reputed to have some of the most exquisite beaches in the world, with tourist resorts that had price tags to match. Not for nothing were the Leonardo diCaprio film *The Beach* and scenes from the James Bond film *Goldfinger* located near here.

On a tip from another traveller, we took a boat ride to visit beaches that were on the mainland just outside Krabi. The excursion was worthwhile just for the showcase of coastal scenery. Mangrove trees crowded the shoreline where they could get a toehold, at the edge of thick green forests that covered low, rounded hills. Offshore islands had a similar hulking green presence, and here and there vertical swathes of hard whiteness jutted up from the hillsides – limestone towers, forming striking cliffs and pillars out at sea. We cruised beneath some of the rock faces into a bay of palm trees, mangrove roots, white coral sand and imposing white cliffs that hemmed everything in from both sides. A cluster of moored boats and half-built resorts couldn't detract from a setting that was almost too striking to be real. But even this paled in comparison with the beaches we were to find on the other side of the little headland.

There the sea was a shallow green, receding into an enticing blue further away from the gently sloping beach, which was made of a perfectly soft white sand, feeling like powder between our toes. The sun blazed down from a blue sky, making the colours even more intense. Halfway along the beach a pillar of white rock jutted up from the waves, smoothed into bare rounded forms at its base but angular and sprouting with green trees higher up. Nearby a wooden boat rocked gently in the waves, tugging at its mooring rope. More boats lay offshore, waiting their turn to ferry groups of holidaymakers to and from the beach. A handful of bathers lazily lolled in the water or stretched out under the shade of the mangrove trees lining the beach. It was a picture-postcard idyll, the prettiest beach that we would see anywhere in the world.

When we returned to the first bay, the tide was out. Instead of waves lapping to the base of a sandy beach, a wide expanse of mudflat had been exposed, strewn with bits of broken shells and pieces of coral. It all looked distinctly less glamorous than when we had arrived. The boats were waiting on the other side of the mud, leaving us with a dirty and painful walk to reach them, and then we had to negotiate a reasonable fare back to Krabi. Once that had been decided, our boatman had only one thing to say to me during the journey. 'Football? Chelsea? Liverpool?'

As well as being muddy, we were sweating from the heat. Although we refrained from dousing our faces and necks with talcum powder to absorb our own moisture, as local women and children often did, we did gradually get into the Thai habit of having up to five showers a day. Sometimes this required a bit of agility in hotel bathrooms, as the shower heads were often placed directly over the toilet. Water was sprayed onto the bathroom floors, which dipped slightly towards drainage holes in one corner. Often the sinks didn't bother with separate drains; any water just emptied through the plughole and fell straight onto the floor, splashing any legs standing in front of the sink in the process. One thing that we hadn't expected about budget bedrooms was that they often didn't provide more than a single sheet on the bed, probably on the reasonably accurate assumption that the nights were too hot to use a cover anyway. So we made good use of our thin sleeping bags, which were turning out to be one of our more useful belongings, also acting as blankets on night buses or trains and clean covers on dirty beds.

From Krabi we moved northwards, still on the west coast of Thailand, to visit Ko Phuket, Thailand's largest island. This was the location of the biggest coastal tourist resorts in the country, beside the beaches at the edge of the island. Our bus stopped first in Phuket old town, in the centre of the island, and so we took the opportunity to explore the town before making for the beaches. The walk into town from the bus station put us off right from the start. The roads were dirty and smelly, full of traffic that gave no quarter to pedestrians. But it took us a little while to realise something more significant.

The famed Thai smiles had vanished. Lounging groups of moto-taxi riders studiously ignored us as we stepped around them and women gave us hard glares as if accusing us of wrongdoing: our reception felt like one of resentment and unwelcome.

The buildings in the old town had the same crumbling Sino-Portuguese architecture as in Penang, but thick bundles of black wires suspended between telegraph poles made the place look less attractive. We stayed in the oldest hotel in town, which was showing its age. The mouldy walls, cracked mirror and cobwebs on the ceiling of our bedroom all seemed to reflect the condition outside. And yet even this place was full. German tourists were here in large numbers, as they had been everywhere we had travelled, with the exception of Fiji. Indeed, Germans frequently appeared to constitute the majority of all tourists – it was incredible how widespread and numerous they were. As time passed we learned to respect their sensitive behaviour and knowledgeable attitudes. Here in Phuket town there were bookshop shelves filled with German language books as well as the internationalised English editions. The old town was sufficiently touristy in general for local eateries to have stopped advertising in Thai: their menus now offered 'European Food'.

The coastline of Ko Phuket was one of the places that had been badly hit by the Boxing Day tsunami of 2004. It was estimated that 5,300 people were killed across Thailand, 250 of them on Ko Phuket. In the reportedly worst hit location in Thailand, Khao Lak, there had been one hundred hotels before the tsunami. Only four were left standing after it hit, and as of May 2006 only fifteen had been rebuilt. In the months that followed the tsunami, tourists had understandably stayed away, which had the effect of causing severe unemployment and even local migration towards Bangkok. Apparently people from Korea, Taiwan and Hong Kong had refused to return, believing that the resorts would be haunted by ghosts. Even offers of free accommodation didn't bring the Asian tourists back. The Europeans were the first to return, seven months after the tsunami, and now it was believed that Phuket's tourist industry at least had fully recovered. The only signs that we could see of its impact were new blue signs on the beaches warning of the danger of tsunamis and pointing the way to higher ground.

We headed for the beaches in one of the small trucks – I thought of them as cattle vans – that formed the public transport system here. It dropped us off on one of the quieter southern stretches of beach, which ran for miles northwards towards the biggest tourist resorts that catered for package holiday crowds. Even Kata Beach seemed to stretch forever along the coast. The adjacent road was full of shops, restaurants and large resort hotels. Every second shop appeared to be a tailor, making cut-price Armani dresses and suits. And everywhere was strangely quiet, to the point of feeling deserted. Cafés were full of plastic chairs and tables, but no one was sitting at them. Hundreds of empty blue and purple loungers were laid out next to each other right along the length of the beach, with matching sunshades forming an artificial wall behind. Only a handful of bodies were visible, usually elderly couples so brown and wrinkly that they looked as if they had been pickled in vinegar.

The sand itself had barely a single sunbather, partly because it was too hot. The only movement on the beach was the criss-crossing of bathers moving between their loungers and the sea. Even there only a few people splashed lamely in the shallows. The waves were choppy and the red flags were flying – there would be no swimming today – so we wandered up and down the sand. From previous experiences, I had confidently expected at some point during our travels to meet someone we knew from home. It was just a matter of when and whom. As it turned out, it was here on Kata Beach and it was a hairdresser from Claudia's home village, which was a pleasant surprise.

Everyone on the sunloungers, exposing their skin to the sun, was European. Sometimes the girls lay there topless. There was something disconcerting about seeing visitors to another country paying absolutely no regard to the morals of the host population. If any Thai women were to go swimming, they would wear at least a wrap that fully covered their body. We heard the opinion of one Thai that the flaunting of naked flesh is considered to be uncivilised. Small wonder that it is tempting for Asians to believe that their set of values is morally superior to those of Westerners.

The only locals that we could see around were sitting in the shade beside the road, passing the time until they summoned up the energy to do another round of hawking. They were all fully dressed, with hats and bandanas around their faces to protect themselves from the sun. The impression I had was that these were workers in a business park, who would come to do their shift and then go home. The business was, of course, tourism – the beach, the restaurants, the shops and the hotels. These resorts seemed to be places where locals no longer lived as such, but instead catered to the package holiday industry and earned money from it.

After a few days on Ko Phuket we decided to continue our journey northwards, towards Bangkok. The main transport routes – using buses and trains – went up the east coast, so we had to first take a bus across the peninsula on a typical Thai journey. Inside the bus, music was played loudly the entire time, an odd mixture of Thai pop and English folk tunes. The bus driver sat amid a colourful array of garlands of flowers and religious icons, obscuring his view out of the windscreen. Outside, the landscape was at times incredible, particularly when we passed through an area of limestone hills and forest, which formed cliff-like ridges that curved around each other, creating a maze of giant stone amphitheatres. In places over the white rocks draped thick nets of vines and creepers, trailing down until they stopped where caves began, whose entrances were in turn decorated with great fang-like stalactites.

On reaching the small town of Surat Thani, we wondered where the bus would stop until we saw the railway station out of the bus window and promptly jumped off. We needed to get a train ticket for the next day and find a hotel for the night. It wasn't hard to find the latter: as we watched the bus drive away, a man came running towards us, hurriedly pulling on a shirt so that he would appear respectable, and offered to guide us around the corner to a hotel. We checked in and returned to the train station, only to discover that all the trains northwards were full for the next few days. We booked the next available tickets and found ourselves with time to kill. The obvious place was the nearby island of Ko Samui, another very popular holiday location and the premier resort on the east coast.

If Ko Phuket had been a business park, then Ko Samui was a theme park. The main resort at Chaweng was not as large as Patong, and Ko Samui even claimed that it could avoid following the over-exploitation that some of Ko Phuket suffered from. But Chaweng's smaller strip packed far more of a punch than Kata Beach did on Ko Phuket. The main road was set back a little from the beach and so suffered from development on both sides. It was a tunnel of denationalised commercialism, with the same names repeated all the way down: McDonald's, Starbucks, Pizza Hut, Häagen Dazs, Tesco's, Boots, Levi's, Burger King. There was the usual mix of cheap imitation shops selling CDs, clothes, leather bags, sunglasses and designer suits. In between were ATMs by the dozen, Internet cafés and travel agents. Neon lights and colourful signs were crowding each other out – this was a brash strip that was, to us, more intense than anywhere since Las Vegas. In fact, it seemed to be the 'Sin City' of South East Asia, complete with middle-aged European men – usually overweight and not particularly handsome, it has to be said – being partnered by slender, pretty young Thai ladies.

Almost everything was written in English first, then German and only lastly in Thai. Restaurant menus were only in English; they served European food, and their staff didn't bother attempting to speak Thai. Some even had taken to advertising local food as being 'Exotic Thai', which particularly appalled Claudia. It seemed to be the epitome of the way in which these tourist resorts colonised areas and converted them into something that was alien to local customs and traditions. This was Thailand – but it wasn't easy to tell.

The beach itself, however, was as pretty as Thailand is famous for. White sand curved in a huge arc beside a blue-green gentle sea that was too shallow for much swimming. Palm trees waved in front of the entrances to one resort after another. It could well be the setting for an ideal beach holiday, if all one wanted to do was sweat in the sun, stroll into the sea for a paddle in the cooling water, and then drag oneself back to the lounger for another spell. And if one didn't mind sharing the beach with hundreds of others doing much the same. The beach was cluttered up with jetboats, deckchairs, loungers, sunbathing bodies and hawkers who were indefatigable in their diligent approach to every single person on the beach, trying their luck with cloth, food, drinks, ice creams, jewellery. Although we could appreciate its attractions, it wasn't too our fancy and after a couple of days we were glad to return to the mainland and our overnight train to Bangkok.

Chapter 37: Bangkok

We approached Bangkok in the 28-bunk overnight compartment of our sleeper train, arriving at the outskirts of the city just as dawn was breaking. In the early morning light we saw what must have been one of the worst faces of Bangkok. Beside the railway track were dozens of small, flat rooftops made of corrugated metal, crammed together on top of walls made from grey wooden boards. The scene looked like rows of grotty garden sheds packed closely together. Only, these sheds were actually the rough hovels of a shanty town. They were dark; there was no lighting of any kind. Narrow walkways between the shacks had been made of short, uneven pieces of wood that were cobbled together into makeshift platforms. Through the gaps in these walkways I could see glimpses of something black and glistening. It was water. The whole place was built over water, on some kind of marsh or lake. Everything from the houses to the walkways was built on stilts; the floors of the houses were barely above the water level. The dark, dank, claustrophobic place seemed to be a fetid, smelly, rotting, insect-infested nightmare. What a place to live in! And what a contrast to the area around our first hotel in the centre of the city.

Siam Square was the face of upmarket, modern, affluent, trendy Bangkok. It was more a small grid of enclosed streets than an open square, with all its entrances controlled and traffic restricted. Here were rich young city slicks going out for a pizza or a Chinese meal, to catch a movie or to browse through the fancy shops. There was not much Malaysian decorum either; the young were racily dressed with bare shoulders and small skirts, as if flaunting their modern confidence, proud to show it off. Around the square were newly built shopping malls, all air conditioning and smooth elevators, with large advertisements in the windows that had English-only catchphrases and slogans. And going past the front of Siam Square, above a main road, was the Skytrain – Bangkok's futuristic version of an elevated metro system. It was very efficient, even if not very pretty from below. The Skytrain ran on a huge grey concrete flyover that was supported by hundreds of thick concrete pillars descending from beneath the line like an array of giant insect legs. The road underneath it was choked with noisy cars, motos and three-wheeled tuk-tuks, which formed endless queues at traffic lights.

On the pavement, under pedestrian bridges or in the shadow of the concrete legs, were dingy little stalls selling pineapples or newspapers. Wooden carts with fruit were even being pushed through the traffic by people trying to eke a living in the melee. Claudia initially loved being able to pick up a slice of fresh fruit as we walked around, until she heard that they were sometimes cut and washed in the shanty towns and was told about the effects they could have on the stomach! From then on, we only bought fruit when we could see it being cut in front of us. Within Siam Square itself were little alleyways running between some of the buildings, a bit like Arabian souks. These provided available space that could not be wasted in crowded Bangkok; they were somehow fitted with long, thin kitchens that laid out bowls of food in a buffet-style service. A single row of chairs and tables had been set against the walls, where the well-dressed city workers stopped for a bargain meal – perhaps the Bangkok equivalent of a sandwich bar.

There were possibly more contrasts in Bangkok than in any other city so far. It was full, full of people, of traffic, of buildings, of noise, of fumes. It was busy, vibrant and eccentric – it could be fun. But it could also be hopelessly confusing. We were staying in the centre in order to be closer to the embassies, where we hoped to get visas for various Asian countries, primarily Vietnam and China. We had the address of the Chinese Embassy and even found its location marked on a map at the nearest Skytrain station. But finding the building itself proved impossible.

The system of road names and numbers seemed designed to prevent anyone from working out where a building actually was. Often streets were described with reference to a main road, as in 'the third road off that main road'. But it was difficult to tell on the ground at which point in the sequence any particular road was, especially for foreigners new to this game. And particularly when both side roads and main roads had a habit of changing their names into something totally different. Even when we were fairly sure that we had found our road, by a process of elimination, we couldn't figure out the system of building numbers. We found out later that the incoherent codes usually referred to the plot number of the original building site!

We eventually gave up after we had returned to the Skytrain station and asked the help of a friendly worker there, who clearly had no idea where anything was either, but suggested heading way out to another station just in case what we thought was the house number was actually the number of the side road. We didn't fancy that idea, so we decided to try to find the Vietnamese Embassy instead.

This time we knew we were getting close when we passed shops that advertised the arranging of Vietnamese visas. And then we met a young man and walked straight into one of Bangkok's famous scams, although it was so well done that we didn't realise it until weeks afterwards when a fellow traveller in Cambodia told us his story and the penny dropped. The smartly dressed man, apparently just passing by, addressed us in English. He had noticed us looking at the shops but advised us that these were expensive – he could recommend another one for us. Besides, he told us, the embassy was closed today as it was a public holiday and anyway was only open during the mornings. This line was a familiar one to me that immediately made me sceptical, but he continued with his smooth story: he worked in a bank and had only stopped to help us because his parents had wanted to get a Vietnamese visa recently and had tried several shops themselves. The ones here were close to the embassy, but they were very expensive and they would rip us off. His parents had used one that he could recommend to us, which had offered fast service and was perfectly reliable. It was even registered with the tourist authority, so we could trust that it would handle things properly.

He marked its location on our map for us and warned us not to get ripped off by tuk-tuk drivers; the fare there should only be 20 baht (US $1). This was accurate, confidence-building advice, but our new friend went a step further and helpfully hailed a passing tuk-tuk driver, negotiating our fare for us and giving directions to the driver. We were quite pleased to take advantage of serendipity and local knowledge, so off we went. The resulting travel agent did indeed have a large white sign above its door saying 'TAT' – Tourist Authority of Thailand. Inside the staff were all smartly uniformed; it was apparently respectable and we no longer had any reason to doubt the sincerity of the smartly dressed bank worker.

The lady in the office would be happy to arrange visas for us, any visas we wanted – even the Vietnamese, Chinese and Laotian all at once. But having them done in ten days would cost extra. Having a 45-day Chinese visa would cost extra. Paying the increasingly large fee with a visa card would cost extra. The resulting bill was exorbitant, only slightly less than we would have paid for the visas in Europe and way too much for Bangkok. Still, we needed them and so swallowed and paid up. The lady was as good as her word, with the slight exception that the Chinese visa turned out to be only valid for thirty days, for the very good reason that the Chinese Embassy didn't give any 45-day visas. When we collected our passports a fortnight later, our additional fee for this had mysteriously vanished with the lady, who was no longer in the office, and there was nothing that the other staff could – or would – do. They did, however, reassure us that we could extend our visa when we reached China and wouldn't have to pay anything if we told the Chinese officials that we had already paid for it in Bangkok! As if!

After laughing at all the tuk-tuk drivers who asked tourist rates of 100–200 baht for a 20–40 baht journey, we found our own way back across town and to the notorious backpackers' ghetto of Khao San Road, instead of Siam Square, now that we had our visas. Suddenly here were dozens of travel agents who were offering visas at half the price of what we had just paid. They also had

'TAT' signs outside, despite looking decidedly less trustworthy. The 'TAT' signs weren't really worth the boards they were painted on, apparently. Looking at the prices, we knew that we had been ripped off, but believed at the time that it was just the tourist office taking spontaneous advantage of a pair of tourists. Actually, it was a common ploy in Bangkok for smartly dressed men to loiter around likely corners, waiting for the chance to put visitors into tuk-tuks and send them to their dodgy offices. Part of our bill had undoubtedly gone to the helpful 'banker'. But what was done was done; an essential part of a traveller's philosophy has to be the acceptance that sometimes deals are won and sometimes they are lost. It's all part of the same game. And always, always, prices will be cheaper just around the corner; one has to be content with a price that was good at the time. Fixed prices were rare in most countries that we travelled through, and so we had to learn to accept the concept of flexible pricing – all just part of the experience. As, it seemed, was falling for at least one scam whilst in Bangkok.

Khao San Road perfectly fitted my preconceived image of Bangkok. It was a street cluttered with colourful market stalls that squatted underneath rows of bright signs advertising the wall-to-wall tourist shops and hostels behind them. A few odd taxis or tuk-tuks slowly made their way along the road, beeping their horns at the mass of pedestrian traffic thronging everywhere. Street vendors tinkled their own bells to attract attention, pop music blew out of shop doorways, there was noise and movement everywhere. From ghetto-like backpacker dormitories to low-end hotels set back from the road; or from smart tailors to the stalls outside their doors selling fake ID cards of just about any description – we particularly liked the look of the International Press cards – everything on this chaotic, bustling, noisy road was there for the tourist industry. There wasn't a Thai in sight who wasn't selling something.

The street was packed with young travellers wandering aimlessly up and down. This was backpacker central, in its intensity not dissimilar to the Ko Samui strip, but without any package holidaymakers, multinational companies or fancy restaurants. Khao San Road was all about budget travel, the dregs of the industry, cheap and tacky. Here were travellers who would swap stories about how little they had spent on accommodation or on food, and furtively tell each other about which secret island was the latest in the succession of undiscovered paradises soon to be trashed by all-night parties. The multitudes of flowing skirts and vest tops, shorts and sandals, tattoos and Rastafarian hairstyles all gave us the impression of being within a hippie festival. Purple and yellow campervans parked on side streets only confirmed this idea. Khao San Road was a tourist phenomenon, but its appeal quickly wore thin. Far more pleasant areas could be found just around the corner, quieter and slightly more upmarket. And it was here that we had the first of our two rice-free meals in what would be nearly three months of South East Asian travel – a pizza, in the company of young Thai couples treating themselves to a night out.

We stayed for a couple of nights in a cheap hotel that happened to have a small swimming pool on its roof, about the size of a large bath tub, and with water that looked a bit like old washing water. With not much space to swim, this was the place for conversations with fellow travellers, even if some people do just talk for the pleasure of hearing their own voice. One such conversation revolved around the possibilities for deportation or imprisonment if caught with drugs in Thailand. After a verbose American had given his opinions to everyone within earshot – no one reclining in the bath tub could escape hearing – he was somewhat squashed by the reality of a contribution from a quieter Australian, whose friend had been given a ten-year prison sentence in a Bangkok jail.

Since 2003 the Thai authorities had stepped up their fight against drugs, leading to several thousand deaths within a couple of months. The prime minister at the time said, 'Drug dealers and traffickers are heartless and wicked. All of them must be sent to meet the guardian of hell, so that there will not be any drugs in the country.'

The interior minister described the official approach to drug traffickers. 'They will be put behind bars or even vanish without a trace. Who cares? They are destroying our country.'

From Malaysia to Vietnam, the authorities made it very clear that illegal drug use was not desired and would be dealt with harshly. Vietnam in fact had one of the harshest anti-drug codes in the world, with an estimated one hundred people being sentenced to death there every year from drug-related offences.

Khao San Road was near the bank of the river that flowed through the city. Pretty much all of the main sights of Bangkok were along its bank, making the river a convenient transport artery. Elegant longboats with outboard motors, brightly painted in red, blue and yellow stripes, zipped past slow-moving chains of overladen barges in midstream, whilst more sedate ferries cruised up and down between frequent stations, often packed full of all kinds of city folk. We boarded a ferry one morning, intending to travel to sites further down the river. The journey started well enough, for the boat crossed the river to another station, but there everyone streamed off and we were told to follow suit, paying for the pleasure on our way out. We watched as the ferry re-filled with passengers and returned to exactly the point we had started from. With nothing of interest on the other side of the river except a small playground, we returned too via an adjacent bridge to try again with a different kind of boat. We got the hang of the different coloured flags on the ferries eventually, and enjoyed using the river as a leisurely form of highway.

Many ferries had signs that indicated 'Reserved space for monks', often with huddles of orange-robed Buddhist monks standing underneath. Many of them were teenage boys, perhaps accompanying their elders to one or other of the many wats that were visible from the river. These wats were some of the prettiest buildings in Bangkok, with slender three-tiered rooftops of shiny orange and green tiles, culminating in elegant golden spires. They contrasted with the huge silver tower and cables of one particular suspension bridge that spanned the river, Bangkok's version of the Petronas Towers. Along the riverbanks were also a wide variety of buildings, ranging from exclusive hotels and modern skyscrapers to wooden houses standing on stilts over the water. These waterfront dwellings were often enlivened by semi-naked children splashing in the river, or women washing clothes by hand in the brown water. This was our first sight of lives that were intricately linked to the waters of a river, but throughout the countries of South East Asia we would come across more riverbank cultures that were integral to both history and everyday life.

A good example was the Damnoen Saduak Floating Market. That is to say, it would have been perhaps ten years ago. It became possibly the most famous image of Thailand, and indeed perhaps South East Asia – photographs of it are still commonly seen in Europe today – which almost inevitably resulted in a tourist boom that pushed out virtually all the traditional commerce. The market now survives on the cash from the 300–400 tourists per day who visit in high season. The market is not far outside Bangkok, in a very flat landscape that is riddled with rivers, canals and ditches running everywhere like a network of arteries and capillaries. Fields seemed to have been literally dug out of the surrounding water, their soil piled up into thin rows that were planted with vegetables and fruit.

The area was rich with coconut palms, banana trees, mangos and much more besides. Houses had to be built on stilts, for even now floods periodically cover everything with water. With so many waterways, the main form of transport was by narrow boats that plied up and down the channels, carrying people or produce. Some farmers literally had no road access at all.

In order to get around we had to hire a small boat and a friendly local guide. Travelling on the water was a delightful experience. Luxuriant foliage all around was often perfectly reflected in quiet, undisturbed backwaters. We saw a lady taking her grandchild to school in a boat; another chugged past with a row of monks inside it; women would kneel on the steps of their houses to wash themselves or their clothes; in one place we saw several bags of sweets hung from the banks, to be taken by passers-by in celebration of a local marriage.

And so we came to the floating markets, which were exactly what they sounded like: markets on the river, where trade was carried out directly between boats – or at least used to be. When we reached the main market area we were greeted by stallholders on the banks selling tourist souvenirs such as fabrics, soapstone ornaments, handbags, postcards, candle holders, even little wooden giraffes. A couple of times the stallholders reached out as we cruised past and held us alongside so that they could show us their wares – we literally became a captive market. We were taken to a large shop, where instead of expensive souvenir shopping we wanted an early morning coffee. We really wanted the traditional Thai coffee made with condensed milk, but here they only sold instant Nescafé. As we progressed we began to pass boats that were laden with goods for sale, mostly catering to the tourist market. A fair few offered drinks and snacks, such as 'coconut pancake'. Only one or two had piles of fruit in the middle of their boats. These were the pictures that had made the Floating Market an iconic image, back when the river was clogged with colourful fruit of all shapes and sizes. Today, the hats being worn by the ladies and men were more of a feature, almost like a kind of uniform on the river.

The market was a pretty sight though, quite novel for us, and thankfully the only other tourists we saw so early in the morning were a boatload of Thais and an Indian family. Actually, there were other floating markets in the area that still exist much as they always had done, without the influx of tourists. It was just that getting to them was that much harder. After the rural tranquillity of this watery world, returning to Bangkok was something of a shock to the system.

The city was preparing to celebrate the King's sixty years on his throne, with many people dressing in royal yellow T-shirts and waving flags outside the Grand Palace complex. The palace had been built from 1782 onwards and was the residence of the Kings of Thailand until the early twentieth century. Adjacent to the official palace was an open square that was crowded with over one hundred buildings, a fantastic place, surely one of the most luxurious religious sites in the world. Colourfully grotesque statues, conical white stupas, gold spires and red-and-green roofs, all sumptuously and ornately decorated, were only the eye-catching sideshows to the dazzling central temple buildings. Their walls had not just been painted with patterns in gold leaf, but some were entirely gold-plated. Nowhere else in the world did we see such an incredible display of glittering gold and riches.

Somehow, between all the tourists with cameras, there were Thai people finding space to kneel with dignity at altars and shrines, placing candles, incense sticks and bouquets of white lilies as offerings. To these people, the opulence – and the crowds – all around seemed an irrelevance to their devotions.

Close by the palace was another famous Buddhist icon, called the Reclining Buddha. The statue was, like so many others, gold-plated, but this one was a giant 46 m long. It lay within its own wooden barn-like wat, looking very much like an image of an outsized Gulliver in Lilliputian accommodation.

Leaving this wat, we passed a lady who wanted to sell us a paper parasol, painted with oriental designs for the tourist market. We didn't really want it, but she persisted. In fact, she followed us down the road, every ten yards dropping her price as if that was the only reason that we were walking away. When she reached 100 baht (US $3), a bargain price, I suddenly turned around and said, 'Yes, all right then.' She looked a bit startled, as did Claudia, but it was a deal and the parasol sits in our lounge to this day.

A better place to pick up souvenirs in Bangkok was the huge weekend market. This was large enough to need maps showing the different thoroughfares which subdivided the hundreds of covered stalls into theoretically thematic areas. Little alleyways criss-crossed their way though the bazaar, past a myriad different goods on sale. From reptiles and puppies to wooden carvings, clothes, plants, furniture and food, there was surely something for everyone – even the 200,000 people who visit each weekend. Going to the market was a popular outing for many young Thais, by the look of it all. Apart from the density of the crowds it was a surprisingly well-organised and orderly place; not like the madness of shopping in Bangkok's Chinatown, which we sweated through one afternoon.

Chinatown was chaotic and polluted. The roads were clogged with noisy traffic, forming a stop-start nose-to-tail stream of taxis, tuk-tuks, motos and vans, always with more vehicles trying to cut in from side roads and pedestrians tentatively dodging their way across the roads. The sides of the roads were further cluttered with mobile stalls, usually trying to sell food – fried quail eggs, roasted corn-on-the-cob, battered squid – but generally just getting in everyone else's way. Goods spilled out of shops to pile up right across the pavements, leaving only a narrow, hazardous path for pedestrians to walk through. Side streets were little more than passageways, impossibly filled with stalls on each side. Shoppers struggled to push and squeeze between everyone and everything else. Just when it couldn't get any worse, a cart would be wheeled past, or a moto come crawling through, beeping its horn vigorously in an effort to clear a path ahead.

The stalls were selling large quantities of watches, hats, CDs and calculators, repeated over and over again. Scarily, there were also many stalls selling arrays of vicious-looking long-bladed knives that ranged from smaller hacking machetes to four-feet-long ceremonial curved blades in scabbards. And bizarrely, who should be looking at these with interest but a group of orange-robed teenage Buddhist monks – a picture of brutal violence and pacifist compassion juxtaposed. Somehow, this exemplified the nature of Bangkok, which was all about a crazy kind of diversity and contrast.

For a change of pace – and a breath of fresh air – we ignored the warnings about thefts on the overnight buses from Bangkok to the northern town of Chiang Mai, and booked a ticket from our hotel. Our bags, minus all valuable items, were loaded into a walk-in hold, which was therefore accessible from inside the bus should anyone care to enter it at 3 a.m. Which someone duly did: on arrival in Chiang Mai, one fellow passenger checked her bag and was sure that it had been rifled through, as had Claudia's on closer inspection. Nothing had been taken – we always, always kept our valuables to hand – but we decided to take the train back when we retraced our steps about a week later.

Chapter 38: Chiang Mai

Chiang Mai is Thailand's second city, its capital of the north. Most tourists stay in or around the old town at its heart, which had been built to prevent the Burmese from capturing it – a strategy that had not been successful. The old town formed a city-within-a-city, bounded by a moat and sometimes the remains of a wall. Although outside the old town was a typically modernising, chaotic Thai city, inside the moat existed a different world. Here were quiet lanes that meandered their way between lush gardens and sleepy hostels. It was a return to the leisurely pace of expat life and foreign-owned businesses. We heard a couple of stories of people who were longer-term residents here: a man who owned several properties on the south coast of England and had sold one to finance living here for a while; another who had made enough money gambling to live here for five years. If one had the means and inclination, Chiang Mai would certainly make a good place to hang out. The cafés and restaurants consistently served up the best cuisine in Thailand, particularly notable for their delicious yellow, green and red curries. Vegetables in a cream curry sauce was also delicious – as was the new dish of sweet mango rice. Not so appetising were the whole peeled frogs, skinned and sliced open along their bellies.

Chiang Mai was also distinctive for its wats, which were on virtually every street corner. There were nearly as many wats here as in Bangkok – over 300 in Chiang Mai compared to 400 in the capital. One day we tried to take a tour of Chiang Mai and its wats by hiring a tuk-tuk. We were offered a reasonable price for a couple of hours and set off, pleased with the bargain. But it wasn't long before our driver pulled over. He asked us whether we wanted to go and see umbrellas being made. Despite our long-held fascination with this intricate process, we declined his offer. Just do what we have arranged, thank you very much. The driver persevered – everyone goes to see the umbrellas, he said. Presumably to be pressured into buying one, I thought. This cynicism was fully justified when the driver showed us where he wanted to take us on our map. The supposed umbrella factory was right in the middle of a handicraft shopping centre on the outskirts of the city. We definitely didn't want to go there.

Finally the driver tried his trump card, but it was one we had heard before. He told us that the wats were all closed because it was a religious holiday and they would only open after 3 p.m., which coincidentally gave us just enough time to visit the shopping centre. We were having none of it, so he eventually drove us to the nearest wat, dropped us at the entrance and drove off without us. We never did see him again – but at least we hadn't paid for the tour in advance. We walked around the city instead.

Some of Chiang Mai's wats were old, some were wooden, some were large and others were small, but all were ornate and highly decorative, with plenty of opulent gold leaf and several gold Buddha statues of various sizes. Often dragon-like serpents lined the steps into the temples, guarding their entrance. Large double doors were among their most impressive features, lavishly furnished with gold patterns or pictures and set within door frames that were full of rich paintings showing scenes from Buddha's life story.

Inside, the temple buildings were usually very simple open spaces, with the doors at one end and a grand statue of Buddha sitting at the other. This icon was often surrounded by an array of smaller statues, arranged in height order. On the floor in front of them were usually offerings of flowers or bowls of fruit. Outside, there would be more statues set in alcoves around the temple walls. Most of the temples were set in grounds with grass lawns and plenty of trees, making them green and attractive places to visit. Some compounds, especially the older ones, had stone statues of elephants encircling the bases of their white stupas. The tallest of all was a pagoda that dated back over 600 years. It was a brick and stone construction that looked reminiscent of a thin stepped pyramid. It was 80 m tall, but half of it had collapsed during an earthquake in 1545 and it remains a partial ruin. In one wat we saw a nice poster with cartoons illustrating 'Do and Don't' for ignorant Western tourists:

> Do display polite behaviour in places of worship. Don't climb upon the Buddha image to take a photograph. Do wear shoes while walking around the compound of a Buddhist temple but don't wear them inside the chapel where the principal Buddha image is kept. Don't display affection for another person in public. It is frowned upon in the Thai society. You may hold hands, but that's as far as it goes in polite society. Don't touch the head of another person, even in a kindly gesture. Thais regard the head as the highest part of the body both literally and figuratively. It's considered rude to point your feet at a person. Don't point your foot to show anything to anyone, but use your finger instead.

As we saw all the offerings of food and flowers inside the wats, we wondered how these fitted within a religion that follows the doctrines of Buddha, who explicitly stated that his image should not be revered like a god. We wanted to find out and so stopped for a drink at tables within the grounds of one wat which advertised a 'monk chat'. Signs pinned to the trees warned against entering into a conversation with monks who didn't have an official card. When a cigarette-smoking young man in an orange robe nearby called across to us and asked if we wanted to 'chat', I was therefore a little sceptical, but Claudia was keen to talk with him.

The monk was about to meet a friend of his at the museum, he said, and so he suggested that we join them there. Stubbing out his cigarette and offering us chewing gum, he led the way at a rapid pace. At the museum we found a small group of several tourists and a couple of teenage monks waiting for us. We were shown inside and told to sit and wait in a room, which we presumed would be shortly followed by a discussion about Buddhism. Wrong: we were shown a video about the history of Chiang Mai, followed by a tour of the museum's galleries. This was all very well, but it was not what we had in mind, so we left the group to it as they headed for the second floor and a doubtless fascinating review of the building's history.

We never did learn about the relevance of all the offerings, but we did discover that Buddhist monks used to be cremated on altars in the shape of a mythical being with the body of a bird and the head of an elephant, which was believed to carry the deceased monks to heaven. That didn't seem to fit my understanding of Buddhism, either. Eventually we learnt that Buddhism had often simply merged or coexisted with traditional animalistic beliefs and religions, much like Catholicism had in South America.

One of our mornings in Chiang Mai was taken up with a visit to a hospital in order to have my inflamed ear examined. Being ill in a foreign country must be one of the things that fully brings home the potential isolation and vulnerability of travelling abroad. Thankfully, here the hospital was very efficient. A succession of young nurses speaking good English checked my weight and blood pressure as part of the registration process and after a short wait my ear was examined and I was prescribed ear drops, which thankfully resolved the problem. The final bill came to a very reasonable 288 baht (US $8.80), albeit with a breakdown of charges that we couldn't completely account for:

Outpatient medication	88.00
Nursing and Midwifery charges	40.00
Outpatient care	60.00
Procedure	100.00

Many people visit Chiang Mai in order to trek through the undeveloped hill country nearby, which is part of a swathe that runs from northern Myanmar right across the north of Thailand and into Laos and Vietnam. This hill country was home to several related groups of people referred to as 'hill tribes', who are usually among the poorest citizens of their countries. Many of the Karen tribe in Thailand were refugees from Myanmar, having been persecuted by the regime there. Over 100,000 Burmese Karen had moved into temporary villages on the border since 1996; the Myanmar State Peace and Development Council – the official name of Myanmar's government – had reportedly cleared villages in a 5-km radius around its new capital of Pyinmana. Myanmar was very much the black sheep of the ASEAN countries, perceived as the most destabilising and problematic country of the region. As we read in newspapers of political discussions about regional cooperation and free trade zones, even a single currency, there were frequent references to the inability of ASEAN to bring Myanmar into line. We had assumed that travel there would be far too difficult to consider visiting, but in Vietnam we bumped into one guy who had found it both accessible and enjoyable.

Some of the Karen women from one tribe were famous for having unusually long necks, around which they wore up to thirty-seven brass neckrings, which actually depress their collar bones, giving the appearance of stretched necks. Another tribe went in for ears that had been grotesquely stretched by the weight of metal rings, which gradually widened and stretched holes within their lobes. The Karen used to be very poor, living in little more than refugee camps, until tourism came along. Now they were able to build better houses and to buy mobile phones, a reflection of their improved conditions. But we were told by a tour operator that over the twelve years of trekking in the area, tourism had created several negative effects, such as dependence on handouts, inequality within tribes, and the turning of people and culture into tourist attractions – just like the Uros on Lake Titicaca had been. Apparently the 'long neck' tribe was at risk of shaping itself purely around tourist desires and the income that could be generated by appealing to visitors.

In trekking, as in other aspects of tourism, Thailand seemed to have led the way in showing how not to do things. There was much discussion in the national press about the impact of uncontrolled tourism on both the environment and the culture of Thailand. There was a clear sense that in some places they had made a real mess of it. Later on, in neighbouring countries like Laos, we encountered growing tourist industries which were concerned not to repeat some of the mistakes of Thailand, and instead to put in place more sustainable management before tourism got out of hand. At least now in Chiang Mai there was significant awareness of these issues and lip service at least was paid to attempts to avoid some of the negative consequences of tourism. One simple measure was for treks to stay at several houses within a village rather than just one, so that the income could be spread more fairly.

Our three-day trek took us into a couple of Karen villages, but mostly we walked through upland hill farming countryside. There were two kinds of rice being grown in the hill areas. 'Wet rice' was grown in the terraced rice paddies during the wet season. While we were there the paddies were being ploughed by machines, instead of buffaloes. In some fields there were patches of rice seedlings growing, looking like dense cress seedlings in corners of muddy puddles. We would later see in Laos how these bright green seedlings would be thinned out and replanted in neat rows across all the freshly ploughed paddies, one seedling at a time, all laboriously by hand. The other type of rice was called 'jungle rice'. This was grown on hillsides, on newly cleared patches of forest, in a form of primitive slash-and-burn agriculture.

The hill farmers used to struggle against a lack of official recognition by the Thai government. They had no land ownership and no citizenship. So they supplemented their income by growing poppies for heroin. It was bad for their children and bad for the villages; they suffered from high rates of addiction and consequent criminality. But the government had more recently been handing out land titles to villagers, allowing them to buy seed and guaranteeing prices for their crops. So now the people farmed rice, cabbages, potatoes and even flowers as cash crops. They still kept buffaloes, but these were only for meat and for sale. The King of Thailand had a special fund which paid for the education of one child in every three, which was how our guide, who came from a Karen village, had been able to go to school. He then went to university, where he learned Thai and became an English teacher, before changing to earn his living as a tourist guide. And yet, just like our guide in Peru, he insisted that he would return to live in his home village, saying that he missed the jungle and wanted to help the children of his village to get an education too.

The village houses were traditionally made from bamboo. They were boxes on stilts, with the floor and the walls made from split bamboo and the roof made from interwoven leaves or straw. It took about a month to build each one, which then lasted for one year. We weren't surprised, therefore, to see that most houses in the village had metal roofs or wooden plank walls; the villagers were making improvements as and when they could. What did make me look twice, however, were the shiny satellite dishes that seemed even more incongruous here than elsewhere. And under the raised floor of one house there was a line of stickers showing football players – Liverpool FC players.

It occurred to me that when these people had gone, there would be little or no trace of there having been a house there at all: it would be hard for archaeologists to reconstruct houses or villages from these simple, natural lifestyles. Just the odd metal pot or pan perhaps – or satellite dish, I suppose. In fact, with the rice paddies being divided amongst villagers like the old strip farming system of the Middle Ages, and everything being centred on farming, involving long hours of manual toil in the fields, I wondered if this was as close as we would get to a window into what medieval villages in Europe might have been like in the past – apart from the Liverpool stickers, of course.

As part of the deal for staying in the first village, soon after we arrived we were surrounded by a group of children all clamouring for us to buy their necklaces. They were only just ahead of their mothers, ladies dressed in traditional clothes and carrying armfuls of hand-woven cloth which they meticulously laid out for us to see. As the rain began to fall, we bought a couple of scarves and then helped to pack everything away again.

The next night we stayed in a place that was as remote and basic as anywhere we saw around the world. Two bamboo huts had been erected on the bank of a river in the middle of the forest. The nearest house was four kilometres away, although there were some small rice paddies closer than that. One hut was for us to sleep in, just a room with mats and blankets on the floor; the other was where our hosts lived their primitive lives. When we arrived the lady of the house was fishing. She tried to cast a net weighed with stones into the river, but this didn't meet with much success in the swollen, turbulent, brown water. So she picked up a circular net, like a sieve, and waded up and down the banks, trawling in every little nook and crevice for fish. When she found one, she put it into a cloth bag hanging at her side.

After nearly an hour, she had a small bowlful of sprats, nothing we would ever consider doing anything with. But it made for a dinner of sorts. By candlelight outside, our guide demonstrated to us how to eat the large flies that were being attracted to the flame. He held them by their wings and bit their bodies off. They were little more than snack food, he said, but very tasty. People here ate everything. Spiders could be deep fried, and cobras were put alive into bottles of potent 'rice wine' to make it even more formidable. Our guide couldn't think of a moving organism that was not used in some way for food.

Beside and underneath the buildings there were a dog, several scrawny chickens and a tiny kitten. Occasionally the chickens poked their heads into the main house, strutting inside for a few moments to have a look around and a peck before being shooed out. All light came either from a gap between the walls and the roof or through the doorway, as there were no windows. Inside the single all-purpose room was a little wood fireplace set into the floor, its smoke drifting out literally through the straw roof. In a corner by the door stood a simple bamboo-framed shelf unit. On its three shelves were stacked a number of white tin plates and bowls; a couple of old plastic tubs with kitchen utensils and cutlery in; two metal bowls; a blackened kettle; a frying pan; two woks and two black pots. The only other kitchen implements were a wooden chopping board and a large pestle and mortar. Leaning against the shelves was a grass sweeping brush.

At the other end of the wall was a sack of rice hanging next to a wooden rail. The rail was the family's wardrobe: it held three pairs of jeans, a couple of T-shirts and a blanket thrown over it. In the opposite corner to the shelves were a pile of grey woollen blankets and grubby pillows. Three bamboo mats were laid out over the bamboo floor. That was all there was. Nothing else existed in the hut. The single room was the kitchen, the dining room and the bedroom; the family ate their meals sitting cross-legged on the mats and then lay down on them to sleep, with the blankets pulled over them.

Into this remote setting walked two young women who turned out to be the wife and sister of our guide, bringing our food. They were wearing tracksuit trousers, T-shirts and baseball caps. One had a large wristwatch and the other wore a friendship bracelet and a blue rubber wristband, the kind which had been fashionable in England before we left. It was more than slightly odd to see these trendy young women who would not look out of place in a modern city sitting at home in such a primitive house. They had walked several miles to come here, along narrow muddy paths beside the river, and later they would make their way home, after dark. We also met the daughter of our hosts, briefly. She was sixteen years old and pregnant, but had already been divorced from her forty-five-year-old Thai husband. They had been married for one year.

It was usual for Thai men to pay money, perhaps 65,000 baht (US $2,000), to the parents of a girl in order to marry her. If a girl became pregnant before marriage, she would be shunned until she had married, given birth and then taken a black pig to a village elder, who would hold the pig while the father clubbed it to death as an apology and appeasement. After that everything could go back to normal. Only two generations ago it was common for families in these villages to have twelve children, but now it was more usual to have only two or three, partly because there were the costs of education and more fashionable clothing to consider in the modern world. In the past, we were told, people used to be happy to just have rice.

Our trekking package also included a short elephant ride and a trip on a bamboo raft. In contrast to the elephant ride, which turned out to be more uncomfortable than exciting, the rafting was something of an adventure. A raft consisted of long bamboo poles lashed together, buoyant enough to support half a dozen passengers sitting in two rows of three, albeit half-submerged. Our punter stood at the front with another bamboo pole, balancing on the shifting raft as he pushed everyone along. His philosophy was 'no wet no fun' as he raced everyone else down the river, trying to overtake the many other rafts making the same touristy journey. Thai girls, who were normally so reserved, had great fun taking the liberty of splashing us with water, squealing with joy as we returned the favour. Sometimes the journey was quite genteel, where the river was broad and calm, but often the raft had to be manoeuvred deftly around submerged rocks, past overhanging trees and large boulders, through channels barely wider than the raft, down white water rapids and even over one cascade three feet high that had a sign beside it saying 'Get out of raft for safety'. We clung on to the poles, risking having our fingers sliced off by passing rocks or rafts, while trying not to slide off the slippery raft into the water.

This task was made more difficult for us by our punter, who was so keen to show off his talent that he lurched the raft this way and that, tipping its edge up out of the water so it lifted over boulders like a car on two wheels. As other people fell in and tried to avoid colliding with oncoming rafts, we merrily sped past them all. At one point we even saw an elephant in the water ahead, before it submerged and vanished from sight, only to re-emerge just beside the raft, so close that I brushed my fingers along its hairy side. Some of the younger Thais had life jackets on the rafts – Thais were not good swimmers in general – but a helmet would have been a better idea. Somehow I had the feeling that this form of extreme punting would never be allowed in the UK.

Chiang Mai was as far as we went in Thailand. We returned to Bangkok to collect our visas and then took a bus eastward to the Cambodian border. It was raining during our journey and I was surprised to see how quickly the roads began to flood. Soon after we had left Thailand it was hit by even heavier storms. In the north of the country this caused flooding and mudslides, exacerbated by the effects of deforestation. Thousands of villagers had power and food supplies cut off. Fifty-one people died and the damage was estimated at 100 million baht (US $3 million). In one district up to 80 per cent of the orchards were destroyed. It brought home again how vulnerable people can be, often at the mercy of unpredictable natural hazards.

Part Six
Cambodia, Vietnam and Laos

Chapter 39: Angkor

Cambodia was as different to Thailand as Guatemala had been from Mexico. People streamed across the border on foot, hauling hand-drawn wooden carts loaded up with boxes and sacks. The sight was like something from history, before the invention of motorised transport – and it wouldn't be the only time in Cambodia that we were to have this impression. As we walked between immigration offices we were latched on to by touts who wanted us to take their bus or their pickup. We tried to work out which transport deals were the reasonable ones, haggling as we went, with little success. This border crossing was notorious for scams – with good reason, as we were to find out soon enough. Our aim was to go directly to the town of Siem Reap rather than break the journey halfway, particularly as we were being quoted more or less the same steep prices for any journey.

We eventually opted for the cheaper deal of a ride on a pickup and followed our favoured tout to a vehicle, which already appeared to be carrying a full load. We climbed onto the back, sitting on top of bags and sacks, next to half a dozen other patiently waiting people. Then our wheeling and dealing tout changed his mind and we clambered onto another vehicle, then to a third. This final one was just as full as the first had been, but additionally had a bicycle tied to the back so that it stuck out horizontally beyond the rear bumper. Eleven passengers perched on top of their belongings; one man even had to squat outside the trailer, somehow balanced on the frame of the bike. Our tout demanded that we pay the fare in advance – never a good idea – so that he could pay off various people. He assured us that we had paid for the complete journey to Siem Reap and then asked us for a tip, which we declined on the basis that he would doubtless have already pocketed a significant cut of the fare for himself.

We lurched off, feeling vulnerable and unsafe as the pickup bounced through potholes and jolted off the road to avoid colliding with oncoming lorries. We also had to negotiate horse- and donkey-drawn carts on the dusty roads, as well as a few other pickups and the usual motos that we were familiar with from Thailand. Vehicles blew up dust as they passed us and disappeared into the distance behind a reddish cloud. Bicycles wobbled along either side of the tarmac and people walked along the dirt verges. Chickens, dogs and children were running in and out of the road. Litter was strewn all along the sides of the roads, which was to my mind always a good indicator of development, or in this case the lack of it. Cambodia at first sight appeared poorer than any other country we had visited.

The landscape was nothing but flat expanses of fields for miles, the fen-like emptiness broken only by dark lines of hedgerows and houses that were strung out in a single line alongside the road. These houses reminded me of those we had seen near Tikal in Guatemala; they were little more than shacks on stilts. Their frames were made from wood and their walls were either wood or simple bamboo mats. Most of the roofs, however, were corrugated metal. Everything was coated in a layer of red dust, from the leaves of trees to the walls and floors of the houses.

Immediately beside the road was a ditch, broken up into a series of ponds by causeway-like paths running to each house. Water in the ponds was a fetid, festering green or brown colour. Often the houses had been built right on the edges of these ponds; we saw people washing in their waters. These were depressing sights of miserable conditions and rural poverty. As if to make it all worse, we drove past a sign that showed a broken machine gun. Underneath the writing stated that guns were not needed any more. It was a sobering reminder of the horrors that this country had had to endure.

When we reached the edge of the halfway 'town' of Sisophon, a young man jumped on the back of our pickup and immediately tried to befriend us in English. We drove into the central square and there we stopped. Our bags were transferred onto another pickup, laden with fruit. It transpired that not only did we have to change vehicles here, but we were being asked to pay another fare. While we were discovering this, via our new 'friend', the first pickup drove off without us. When we pointed out that we had already paid the full fare to Siem Reap, he shrugged and asked us innocently where the first driver was. We had been left stranded.

Claudia was all for finding somewhere to stay in the town for the night, as it was getting late, but I was focused on getting out of there. We were assured that we could trust the new driver, who coincidentally just happened to be the father of the English speaker – a discovery that didn't improve our perception of the whole affair. But at least the new pickup contained a couple of rolled up rugs that we could sit on. With a final rejection of the plate of black beetles that a lady was persistently trying to sell us, we set off once again.

The journey progressed from bad to worse. The tarmac road ran out, turning into an endless sequence of ruts and craters. We had to slow down, which only made the journey take longer. And then darkness fell, so we slowed even more. The ride was no fun: it was painful and exhausting – and we didn't particularly like being in the middle of the unknown at night. There was no electricity here; only the light of wooden cooking fires penetrated the blackness from the roadside houses. The only bright spot of the journey was being offered some small yellow fruit, called *pniel*, by the two Cambodian ladies who were travelling with us. They each wore a traditional chequered scarf around their face, to keep the dust out of their hair, eyes and mouth. It turned out that we were sitting on their fruit.

Their home was off the main road, down a side track, where in the darkness we helped to unload a dozen large jackfruit the size of footballs, several sacks of potatoes, baskets of orange fruit, bags of *pniel* and the carpets. The ladies and their family were grateful and seemed to be inviting us into their homes, which for a moment was a tempting prospect. Prudence and practicality prevailed and we continued on our way again, now alone in the back of the empty pickup. We quickly discovered that without padding underneath us the ride was even more bouncy and painful than before. We clung grimly on and wished for it all to end.

Over five hours after leaving the border, a distance of only 105 km away, we finally reached the tarmac and lights of Siem Reap, to our great relief. We drove past a succession of grand hotels with fancy driveways before our driver pulled up at the side of the road. He clearly wasn't interested in taking us any further – and we weren't impressed with being dumped at random in a strange town, caked in dust and grime, tired and sore. Miraculously, a smiling young face appeared out of the darkness and in a smattering of broken English offered to take us in his tuk-tuk wherever we wanted to go for the princely sum of US $2. We went to a hostel and took the last available room there. We were so grateful to the tuk-tuk driver that we happily took him up on his offer to take us around the ruins of Angkor in a couple of days' time – and he turned out to be one of the loveliest people we ever met. But for now we crawled gratefully into a hot shower, followed by a soft bed.

As it happened, we learned from other travellers that even if we had taken a bus from the border we would still have faced a long, uncomfortable journey, which might have ended up in a worse situation. Some buses deliberately stop for a couple of hours just to ensure that they arrive in Siem Reap after dark, thus leaving their passengers little alternative but to stay at the hotel of their bus driver's choice, which could often be outside town. We even heard the story of one bus that broke down on the journey, after dark. Replacement transport was eventually arranged, consisting of a minibus and several motos. None of the passengers were willing to take a solo ride into the unknown on the back of a moto, so they somehow all piled into the minibus. But none were allowed to get in until they had first agreed to stay at one particular hotel in Siem Reap.

Despite this less than encouraging introduction to the country, the people of Cambodia soon cast their charming spell over us, repairing any damage. The Cambodians we met were almost always softly spoken, calm and gentle people.

As we walked around the roads of Siem Reap we often received inquisitive glances from men or women passing on bicycles or shopping at market stalls. Children would call out 'Hello,' laughing and waving, while young girls giggled shyly when their curious eyes met ours. From grown men on motos to female construction workers wearing yellow hard hats, everyone returned our smiles instantly. Maybe not as openly as in southern Thailand, but even more appealing for their soft, shy manner.

The reason that expensive tourist hotels existed in Siem Reap – it even had its own airstrip and not just one but two ATM machines – was that it was the gateway town to the most famous of Cambodia's treasures. The ancient city of Angkor had been the centre of the Khmer Empire for over 500 years, from AD 800 to around 1350. At one time the Khmer Empire stretched from the Vietnamese coast across to Myanmar, and from Malaysia to northern Laos. As Dawn Rooney records, at the end of the twelfth century, the city of Angkor was grander than any contemporary city in Europe. Chinese visitors called it 'opulent' and 'rich and noble'. Angkor was 310 km^2 in size – comparable to New York – and may have had over 1 million inhabitants. Just one of the monasteries within Angkor was fifty-six hectares in area and was home to 98,000 people. But as neighbouring Thai forces increased their power, the city was threatened, and in 1432 the capital was moved to Phnom Penh. Angkor was left to the care of monks, until it was all but abandoned to the jungle in the seventeenth century. It gained the attention of European archaeologists in the nineteenth century, but when the Khmer Rouge came to power it became off-limits until a decade after the regime fell.

Cambodia only opened up to tourism in 1998 but with the help of Angkor it is now well and truly a major global tourist attraction. In 2005, 1.5 million tourists had visited Cambodia, and in the first three months of 2006, 40,000 people had been to see Angkor Wat. Angkor Wat is the most famous of the buildings within the city of Angkor and is the largest religious building in the world, covering 1.9 km^2. Its walls run for 5.5 km, outside which is a 200 m-wide moat. It was all built in the twelfth century as a temple to the Hindu god Vishnu. Later on our travels, in India, we would come across an eleventh-century temple complex that looked surprisingly similar in architectural terms, if on a far smaller scale, to Angkor Wat. India's influence had reached right across South East Asia to Cambodia from the fifth century onwards, replacing previous cultural ties with Indonesia.

We approached Angkor Wat through a forest drive, which brought us alongside a square canal-like moat, with a dirty dark grey wall on its opposite side. Halfway along the moat, opposite a gaggle of bright food and souvenir stalls parked beside the road, there was a stone causeway across the water.

Looking down the causeway, we could see the long boundary wall and behind it in the distance, just poking above its top, were several grey oval-shaped towers. It took a while to appreciate that this was our first sight of the world-famous Angkor Wat itself. As ever, over-hyped expectations had only led to something of an anticlimax. One of our guidebooks contained all of the following descriptions:

> ...one of the most inspired and spectacular monuments ever conceived by the human mind ... extravagant beauty ... majestic monuments ... one of humanity's most audacious architectural achievements ... the world's most spectacular temples ... monuments unrivalled for scale and grandeur in South East Asia ... the traveller's first glimpse ... is a mind-blowing experience, matched by only a few places on earth such as the Great Wall of China or the Taj Mahal ... the immense Angkor Wat ... will send a tingle down your spine as you first cross the causeway.[7]

We felt no such thing. Part of the reason was the sheer scale of the complex. From the outside wall it was 350 metres across open space to reach the main temple, so it was hard to appreciate that the central tower rose an impressive 65 m high. The best views of the entire structure were from a distance, because closer in the different sections lost their perspective and increasingly obscured one another. A small lake in the grounds, which we found by accident in search of an early morning coffee, gave the best view of the whole building – its five towers all visible at once from this slightly angled perspective – with the bonus of a reflection too. The picture was indeed imposing: Angkor Wat was a brooding mass of stonework, large in both width and height, its dark bulk nonetheless conveying a sense of grandeur and of elegant, proportioned form. But our experience was that it didn't compare to the Taj Mahal for poetic beauty, or to the Great Wall of China for mind-blowing scale.

Once inside the building itself, I was reminded of being inside a Scottish abbey, looking out from the archways of a stone cloister into a central open courtyard. Only, this was a cloister on a seriously large scale and decorated with delicate patterns on virtually every surface. Geometric patterns, reams of text, repeated images of bare-breasted women linked arm in arm – all of these were carved in relief from sandstone blocks. These carvings were one of the distinctive aspects of Angkor Wat and a feature that I felt did deserve a reputation as among the world's finest: there were thousands of bas-reliefs and the precision of their carving was immaculate. Unfortunately, the carvings were deteriorating, literally crumbling away as if being slowly eaten.

---

[7] Harding, P, & Richmond, S, *South East Asia on a Shoestring*, Victoria, Lonely Planet Publications Pty Ltd., 2001. Reproduced with permission from South East Asia on a Shoestring © 2001 Lonely Planet Publications

The centre of this outer courtyard – the first of a sequence of three ever-higher rooms and corridors – was the Gallery of a Thousand Buddhas. It contained many recovered stone statues that frequently had limbs amputated or had even been decapitated, although those mutilations hadn't stopped the statues from being tenderly wrapped in orange cloths. They looked like pitifully maimed sentinels, watching eerily from the shadows over a central Buddha image, which in contrast was surrounded by lights, flowers and incense sticks. After the original wooden city of Angkor had been destroyed by forces from Vietnam in 1177, it was rebuilt in stone by a Buddhist king tolerant enough to allow Hindu shrines in his temples. The next king, however, was a strict Hindu again and had thousands of Buddhist statues destroyed – the remains of some of which we now saw around us.

Behind the Gallery of a Thousand Buddhas, up some steps, was Angkor Wat's second courtyard, again ringed with cloister-like archways, but this time with a square pyramid at its centre. Forty steep, narrow stone steps climbed the sides of this pyramid at an angle of 70°, leading up to a platform that supported the third and final ring of column-lined corridors or passageways. We were apparently free to scramble around them at will, paths even leading in and out of the windows as they navigated around areas of broken masonry. The handful of men sweeping the stones next to Buddha statues didn't seem to mind. This was the highest gallery, where once only the king and the high priest had been allowed to step. It supported the five towers of Angkor Wat, one at each corner and the highest in the middle. These were multi-cornered shapes that reminded us of London's landmark 'gherkin' tower – but more accurately were representations of lotus buds, ornately carved. Reaching 31 m above the stone passageways underneath it, the central tower was an impressive sight, although I had to kneel with my face pressed to the floor to get a decent view of it.

The temple was filling up with tourists – one of whom decided that Claudia was as worthy a subject for a photograph as the surroundings, to her delight – and so after a couple of hours of exploring stone corridors we had seen enough here. We returned through the wall and across the causeway, against the flow of hundreds of incoming people, to our patiently waiting young driver.

He was such a delightful man; we would have liked to have been able to talk more with him, but he was only just learning English. He was from the north of Cambodia, and had moved first to Phnom Penh and then to Siem Reap in search of work. He was an electrician by trade, but that paid even less than tuk-tuk driving. His tuk-tuk, by the way, was a motorbike without its back wheel. Instead, its body had been welded onto a two-wheeled carriage. When it began to rain, he pulled a plastic sheet over the frame as protection for us and then continued, until the rain turned into a torrential downpour, deluging him on the motorbike seat. We pulled up under a suitable tree and huddled under the shelter, passing the time waiting for the storm to pass by playing cards.

It was a drive of about one kilometre from Angkor Wat to the next significant building and beyond that a further two kilometres to the next. We passed some cyclists touring around, which must have been hot, wet and tiring work. At the gates of the walled palace of Angkor Thom there was an alternative possibility: riding on the back of an elephant for a few hundred metres, photogenically past 108 large stone statues of gods and demons and then through the 23-metre-high stone gates. Somehow the size and majesty of the stately elephants complemented the grandeur of the ancient setting perfectly. Looking back, this was a scene that again linked Angkor to India, where such images were – in Rajasthan at least – almost commonplace.

At the very heart of Angkor, literally, was Cambodia's national temple, called the Bayon. It surpassed Angkor Wat for me, not in scale or grandeur but as a place of fascinating intrigue and interest. The outside of the Bayon formed a square with four entrances and column-lined corridors that were similar to those at Angkor Wat, only here they traversed piles of debris, fallen stone columns and blocks of masonry that looked like Roman ruins strewn around the compound. There were 7,000 different stone pieces on the ground, some of which had once belonged to a library building. Restoration workers had identified 2,000 potential pieces of the jigsaw, but after two years of investigations had only positively located thirty.

At the entrance was a sign which asked visitors to show respect whilst in the temple, including 'no shorts or bare shoulders'. European women streamed past, the clear majority wearing strappy tops with very bare shoulders. How such insensitivity doesn't cause more offence I don't know. Time and again our impression of fellow tourists dropped; almost everywhere we saw a lack of cultural respect, as if concerns over dress and behaviour simply didn't apply to Westerners.

Once inside the doorways I couldn't make head or tail of the Bayon's layout. There seemed no identifiable geometric pattern to the maze of corridors and towers, although plans showed that originally it had been a regular sixteen-sided shape. Today was a riotous jumble of stonework, made even more confusing by the discolouration of the stones. Grey blotches of all shades, shapes and sizes worked like a camouflage pattern, making it hard to distinguish edges and shapes. Everything blurred into a two-dimensional mess of masonry. We weren't the only ones to find it confusing. As one guidebook explained, it defies adequate description by words or photographs, needing to be experienced in person to comprehend – or to be adequately bewildered:

> The Bayon remains one of the most enigmatic temples of the Angkor group. Its symbolism, original form, subsequent changes and additions have not yet been

Angkor

understood. These aspects leave us today with a complicated, crowded plan that challenges both archaeologists and historians...the layout of the Bayon is complex due to a maze of galleries, passages and steps connected in a way that makes the levels practically indistinguishable and creates dim lighting, narrow walkways and low ceilings.[8]

The most distinctive features were the fifty-four 'gherkin'-shaped *prasads* that rose out of the jumble, again defying order or symmetry, except that the tallest were in the centre. Also, within the jumble of corridors, at every corner and against every skyline, were no less than 173 giant 'smiling faces' carved out of stone. Looking like cherubic gargoyles, they gazed across at each other, their enigmatic expressions suggesting that they knew the answers to the Bayon's riddles, but they had been frozen in stone for eternity.

Littered across the vast area that had been the city of Angkor were numerous other large and complex ruins, with enough stone corridors and walls to satisfy any budding archaeologist. We found it hard to get a sense of perspective, either for the whole city or for the individual buildings. Partly this was because they were in ruins anyway, but also most of the buildings were only on one level and so the view from any one place was often limited to the next stone doorway. Even the advertised viewpoint of a hilltop temple could only offer an indistinct sight of Angkor Wat's towers rising above the surrounding treetops. Forest had obscured much of the sense of a complete city – and it looked as if restoration was going to take a long, long time. In some buildings huge trees had grown over the stonework, their tentacle-like roots snaking between the blocks and forcing them slowly apart, gradually but remorselessly tearing the constructions into pieces. It was as if a timeless force was being driven to destroy the works that had temporarily had the effrontery to be built in the forest, but whose days of reckoning had now come.

In some ways the stone ruins within an encroaching forest reminded us of the Mayan ruins, although on a very different scale. Perhaps this was why one temple at Angkor caught our eye particularly: a steep stepped pyramid, the only one of its kind in the city, which was uncannily similar to the style of the pyramids at Tikal. There were so many places to look at in Angkor that it would take days to see more than just a handful. By the end of a long nine-hour day of exploration, we were becoming saturated by stone walls, steps, doorways, corridors, pillars, blocks, rubble, broken statues and fading carvings. It was all just too much to take in at once.

Amid the ruins were numerous hawkers and beggars, including children of no more than three years old who were selling postcards with an American-accented 'two for one dollar' catchphrase. And as was often the case in Cam-

---

[8] Rooney, D, *Angkor*, New York, Odyssey Publications Ltd., 1994, p.162

bodia, it was hard to escape the terrible impact of the war years. Musicians sat beside paths with signs saying that they were all victims of landmines who didn't want to beg but had to find a way of earning money somehow.

There are thought to be up to 6 million landmines in Cambodia. Over 40,000 Cambodians have suffered amputations since 1979 as a result of landmines, which is an average of forty a week over a twenty-year period. In 2005 there were 359 casualties from landmines, of which more than half are usually fatal. Today, however, more people die from unexploded ordnance – bombs and shells left over from the fighting – than from mines; in 2005 there were over five hundred casualties from unexploded ordnance. According to the Cambodian Mine Action Centre, 'almost all the UXO victims are poor villagers who break the bombs apart because they need the metal to sell'. Since 1992, CMAC have destroyed 310,990 anti-personnel mines, 5,573 anti-tank mines, over 1 million unexploded ordnances and over 332 million fragments. It is estimated, however, that at the current rate of progress total clearance may take another hundred years.

Cambodia seemed to us to be a country that was struggling to develop economically. It is one of the poorest countries in the world: in 2005 the GDP per capita was US $2,500; the average life expectancy is fifty-six years; the infant mortality rate is one of the highest in the world; two thirds of the population don't have access to clean water; more than a third of the population live on US $1 or less per day, and 77 per cent live on under US $2 per day. Its infrastructure is also terrible, with rivers being used heavily as a transport system and its roads often becoming impassable during the wet season. All this poses certain challenges to travellers, which is perhaps why most tourists who visit Cambodia seem to do one of two things. Either they go straight in and out of Siem Reap, on a flying visit to see Angkor Wat, or they cross east-west en route between Thailand and Vietnam, via Siem Reap and Phnom Penh. A coastal resort town was increasingly popular in the south-east, but that seemed to be more or less the extent of tourist trails in Cambodia. After leaving Siem Reap we decided to detour slightly and prolong our stay in the country in order to see the second city, called Battambang. It turned out to be one of the best decisions of our entire journey.

Chapter 40: River Journey

We drove out of Siem Reap along a dirt road that turned into a raised embankment across a flat landscape of rice paddies, vegetable fields and then just wild bushes. Motos were about the only traffic on the road, often laden with bags and boxes. Men did the driving and their wives sat behind them, squeezed behind or underneath the loads of fish and vegetables that were being taken to market. Along the way we passed houses that had been built on stilts to bring them level with the causeway, some 12–15 ft above the fields. These houses were little more than square boxes on legs, made from wood and bamboo mats. Fishing baskets dangled beneath their floors and children or adults squatted in the dark doorways. This seemed to be as basic living as we had seen amongst the hill tribes in Thailand. People were barefoot in the mud, dressed in dirty and ragged clothes. There was nothing to indicate how they survived here, beyond perhaps catching fish somewhere in the marshes.

We stopped where the road reached the beginning of a newly dredged canal, which contained water that looked just like thick green pea soup. A little collection of canoe-like boats were moored at its edge. The road continued over a rickety wooden bridge and alongside the canal, making this place a kind of transport junction. Feet and wheels had churned the ground up into a sea of wet mud, through which the passing motos slid and slithered. A few huts were gathered beside the bridge, sheltering a kind of café and two fruit stalls. One of these was selling green saucer-sized seed-heads, which contained seeds that children in tatty T-shirts liked to extract and eat. They threw the green pulp away into the mud beside all the other garbage there. Several people were hanging around, doing nothing in particular. Men were barefoot, wearing dirty shirts and caps. As we waited and watched, I thought again that this striking scene could have come straight out of the Middle Ages, a universal picture of daily hardship and toil in poor, miserable conditions. The significant difference, of course, was that now petrol engines and motor vehicles had replaced hand-drawn wooden carts.

Eventually we boarded a narrow boat and chugged off down the canal to start our eight-hour boat journey – travelling by river was just as practical as by road in Cambodia. Soon we passed into a shallow lake that was so big that the water seemed to go on forever, until it must surely drop off the end of the world. This was Tonle Sap, the largest freshwater lake in South East Asia. It was also something of a geographical phenomenon. The river that connects the lake to the Mekong River usually flows west to east, draining the lake into the Mekong. But during the monsoon season, when the Mekong is swollen with water, the river level can rise above the level of the lake and cause the flow to change direction, which used to be the occasion for a great festival in Cambodia.

The Tonle Sap River then floods the areas around the lake, making them fertile lands for farming and fishing. The fisheries of Tonle Sap actually provide a livelihood for over 3 million people, generating 75 per cent of the inland fish catch of the entire country. On the lake we saw men in little canoes, hauling in their fishing nets. We also saw houses that had been built in the middle of the lake. Indeed, a whole village existed on stilts, surrounded entirely by water. This was the first of many 'floating villages' that we would pass, most of them strung out along the sides of the river that we chugged into after the lake.

Floating houses on the river were actually built on rafts of bamboo poles, several layers thick. Entire platforms rose and fell with the swell of the water, banging into the bank or straining at their mooring ropes. The houses themselves were essentially not much different to those we had seen earlier on dry land, although many had TV aerials sticking out of their roofs. Inside their open doorways we could see pots hanging from walls and wood fires burning in metal stoves made from oil drums. Outside, clothes were spread out to dry, and an occasional flower pot sat on the platforms.

Beside the houses were pens, like small prison cages made from bamboo poles, either floating or half-submerged. Crammed inside these pens were pink pigs and even live crocodiles. On the dry ground of the riverbanks behind were also goats and chickens. We stopped for a break once at a floating shop, which had a doorway facing onto a little jetty. This store had two toilets attached to its side, from the outside looking like normal cubicles. Inside, we discovered the toilets consisted of a wooden floor over the river with a hole cut into it. Yellow-green water flowed underneath, even as naked children played in the surrounding river and fully clothed adults bathed. The reality of life in an environment like this began to sink in.

As could be expected from a world of floating villages, there were boats all around. Small wooden canoes were either paddled or driven by an engine, being used for fishing, transporting goods or as water taxis. Larger houseboats were common, with pretty curved straw or tin roofs built over the middle of the wide, shallow boats. They looked like the water-borne equivalent of gypsy caravans or travelling tinkers. One even pulled a procession of five boats strung together, as if these were the separate rooms of a mobile home.

In between the villages, the river was intensively fished. There were three main types of operation. The simplest consisted of woven bamboo baskets that were dropped in the water beside the bank, often within reeds or weeds. They were shaped into tubes or cones, with two small barb-like jaws across the entrance at one end, which allowed fish to swim in but kept them trapped inside.

The same entrapment principle was used for lines of orange or green nets that criss-crossed the river, secured with upright bamboo poles. These nets funnelled fish into ever smaller areas, finally ending in a series of arrow-head enclosures. We could see fish splashing within their confined space, jumping ineffectually out of the water in an effort to escape the nets. The most elaborate fishing system used a mechanical device to increase its efficiency. A net was suspended between a square of four bamboo poles, each perhaps fifteen feet long, making a giant scoop. To lift it in and out of the water, it was fixed to the end of two crane-like bamboo arms that were hinged about a fulcrum. Rocks or logs counterbalanced the opposite end, which could then be pulled easily to raise the net, hopefully catching unsuspecting fish at the same time. The whole affair was built on a raft of bamboo poles, often with a small house alongside. In some places along the river there were fishing machines every hundred metres or so, looking together like a squadron of predatory insects, poised ready to strike. How any fish remained alive in the river at all was a mystery.

After about four hours of travel, the floating villages ran out and so did the intensive fishing. Only left were the bamboo traps, now more numerous than ever, and a few men or couples in small wooden canoes who were checking on their catches. The river became narrow and bendy, contorting itself almost into knots as it meandered through a landscape of flat farmland. Houses were on the top of the banks here, although in any city they would be described as slums. They were ill-fitting patchwork quilts of metal, wood or plastic sheeting, often with gaping holes in between. Many were built on a raised platform, but others were just sorry huts on the ground, little more than rudimentary and ineffectual shelters. The worst we saw were single sheets of plastic draped over a low pole into A-frame tents, looking for all the world like scenes from an emergency refugee camp.

Sometimes chickens were running loose on the banks and now and again a white cow stood on its own. As rain started to fall, families stood or squatted under the best shelter they had. To see such poor conditions in what appeared to be a settled rural existence was disturbing. No wonder people move from the country to cities in search of better lives. There seemed precious little to leave behind here except open space and fresh air.

At last, as the rain cleared, we left the fields behind and began to approach the city. A road joined the river, and suddenly houses came thick and fast, now built out of brick, with fences and walls around them. From out of the houses and banana trees came children, running down the bank to wave at us and shout, 'Bye-bye!' as a greeting. They were full of joy, climbing trees, cartwheeling into the water, splashing and laughing. We smiled and laughed and waved back, infected by delight ourselves. And yet at the same time it was sad to see that they were sliding and slithering down what was often little more than a communal rubbish tip. At long last our boat pulled in to a metal staircase leading up a steep bank, beside a bridge – a real concrete bridge, with traffic going across it, the first and only bridge we had seen all day. We climbed up the steps and, as we should have expected, into the arms of waiting touts, who put us into a minibus and took us to the door of a hotel.

Chapter 41: Battambang and Phnom Penh

Given that Battambang was the second largest city in Cambodia, it was a small, undeveloped place, more like a provincial town, and a poor one at that. In its centre was a market square, where covered stalls were selling a range of basic clothes or shoes, and vegetables and fruit were laid out on the pavement around the outside. The pink maggot-like things we saw in baskets were edible silkworms. One or two hotels were close to the market, serving the tourist trade. A few shops were dotted around – one sporting a full-size portrait of David Beckham – and a large school building was not far away. There weren't a great many sights in town. Beside the river there was a row of houses built in a French colonial style, much like the Sino-Portuguese houses of Penang in Malaysia, with faded blue and yellow coats of paint that hinted at a former Parisian elegance. But most of the streets in Battambang had an uncared-for feel, looking plain and grey. At night, looking out over the city of mainly two-storey houses and palm trees dotted between, it was striking how few lights could be seen. After dusk the streets were virtually deserted.

Battambang was not a lively or colourful place, but its dullness was more than compensated for by its people. They were as delightful as any we had met or were to meet around the world. We were developing a real fondness for Cambodians. Everyone in town was gentle and friendly, with ready smiles. When we asked people if we could take their photographs, the response invariably was a shy giggle and then a smiling pose, as if they were flattered to be asked. Here we felt that we were visiting a country before it had been jaded and spoiled by too many tourists passing through – such as Vietnam would be, for example.

We were fortunate enough to stay in a hotel that had a fourth-floor café overlooking a side street and the market square. From this vantage position we could have an early morning breakfast while watching one of the most memorable dramas of our travels unfold. In the quietness before the town began to properly stir, Buddhist monks from the monasteries in town set out on their quest to find their daily food. They were dependent on alms for sustenance. We saw several townspeople giving generously every day, as a way to improve their own karma. In particular, just opposite our hotel, one lady set out dishes of rice and other food on chairs outside her door. Down the street would come a line of monks, all dressed in flowing orange, yellow or red robes. They always walked one behind the other in single file, and in total silence. Sometimes they came in little groups of three or four, at other times in long lines of twenty-six or thirty-three. They would form a semicircle facing the food, holding in front of them gold or silver bowls that had emerged from under the folds of their robes. Patiently, they stood and waited.

The lady would eventually appear and, taking up her pots of food, scooped a spoonful of rice and a dollop of stew into each bowl in turn. When all the monks had received their alms, the pots were returned to the chairs and the lady turned to face the silent line of silent monks. She bowed her head in a dignified prayer and then the monks began to lead off, one after the other. Down the road they gracefully went, to the next serving station. Throughout the city we could catch sight of these ordered lines of orange, weaving their way serenely through the streets. Several weeks later we would see a similar event on a much larger scale in Laos, but this daily alms-giving in Battambang was the most touching religious scene that we would see anywhere in the world.

Buddhism was more than a religion in Cambodia; it was interwoven with the fabric of life and culture of the country. Most men would become a monk at some point during their lives, often either as a young boy or as an old man when they didn't need to be at home supporting their families. The period of time was highly variable, from a matter of days to several years – but always in multiples of odd numbers. Apparently one day was common. One man we met had become a monk for three days after his father died, in order to help his father's soul through the next stage. It was very difficult, he said, as there were a great number of very strict rules that it was hard to adhere to, such as only eating in the mornings and always looking at the ground a fixed distance ahead. Perhaps this was why we had been a little surprised to see supposedly devout monks sneaking a cigarette on street corners, or staring impiously at us as we passed. Despite Buddhism being ubiquitous, it has not pushed out the traditional animist beliefs of the Cambodians, as described by Elizabeth Becker:

> Cambodians are not 'good' Buddhists in the formal sense. They have clung to superstitions that are not part of their faith and they worship primitive animist spirits as much as Lord Buddha. Many were never even schooled in the precepts of the Buddhist faith. It is impossible to say what is Buddhist and what is not Buddhist in the Cambodian culture…to be Cambodian is to be Buddhist.[9]

We came across a strange example of this in a newspaper article, concerning one Preah Meadda Keo. He was considered to be sacred, credited with miraculous powers, like curing chronic illnesses and providing good fortune. Any

---

[9] Becker, E, *When the War Was Over*, New York, Public Affairs, 1998, p.190

waters that he swam in were thought to have healing powers. These properties had been discovered after he had taken shelter under a sacred book inside a temple for two consecutive nights, during heavy rains. Preah Meadda Keo was a turtle. It was noticed that he had 'elephants, young girls and snakes within the intricately patterned shell – icons deeply symbolic within Buddhist theology'. 'He has a sacred mark on his left front claw, magic numbers in the patterns of his skin, and his shell is symbolic of the leaves of the banyan tree,' said his intermediary, a fifty-eight-year-old monk who believed that the turtle represented the Buddha.

One morning, we took a trip on the back of two motos to have a look around several villages just outside Battambang. Dirt roads took us past wood and bamboo mat houses on stilts. Tools and animals were being kept in the shelters underneath the houses. Usually there was a dirt yard in front that had been swept into a clean, hard floor, shaded by banana or palm trees. Wooden carts with large wooden cartwheels – hay wagons – sat idly beside golden stacks of hay that were piled up by the sides of the road. Often white cows lounged nearby. The scenes were picturesque in their domestic simplicity, looking something like Turner paintings. Apart from two small lorries, the only vehicles we saw were two-wheeled. Most families seemed to own a cow, a moto and a one-hectare plot of land. After the Khmer Rouge's communes had collapsed in the early 1990s, the land was divided out equally between villagers. Fields were divided up into segments about 50 m^2 in area, with each segment owned by a different family. The land was fertile, but nevertheless with just one hectare of land it must have been difficult to break out of a cycle of subsistence farming and poverty. In fact, 75 per cent of the population in Cambodia were still subsistence farmers.

We drove through villages which had diversified into local cottage industry specialities. One was famous for its ricepaper. White rice was turned into a pulp, from which a thick liquid that looked like paint was drained off, smeared over muslin cloth and dried in the sun. It turned into the wafer-thin wrappings for spring rolls, sold here in packs of one hundred for 50 cents. On a good day they might be able to make 2,000 pieces, we were told. In another village the traditional industry was making bamboo sticky rice: a rice, coconut and black bean mix that was stuffed into hollow bamboo tubes and roasted over a fire. We bought one from a wizened old lady, who had risen at 4 a.m. to prepare the rice. We asked her how long she had been doing this, and she said, 'Forever.'

The bamboo rice was far more appetising than the plate of fried grasshoppers that our guide munched through at one stop, even if they were dipped in a chilli relish. People ate fried spiders here too, but only the ones that live underground, not the ones in trees. So that was all right, then. And, in a weird reversal of the idea of vampires, people also drank the blood of flying foxes.

On our tour we passed a motorcyclist who was carrying a loudspeaker, which was blaring out information to the villagers. It was encouraging mothers to take their children to a local nutrition clinic, run by a charitable organisation. We were told that doctors didn't visit the villages and as the hospital in town charged for its services, traditional healers were still active, performing such services as midwifery. It seemed telling that the presence of NGOs was significant in town, from Land Rovers with logos of the UN, the World Food Programme, World Vision, Mine Action Group and the Cambodian Mine Action Centre, to offices for programmes focusing on water, HIV and education. The government was managing to provide free education to all children up to the age of fourteen years, but to accommodate everyone the school classes had forty children and the day had to be split into two shifts of four hours each. There are a lot of children in Cambodia; out of its total population of 13 million, 52 per cent are under eighteen years old.

Leaving Battambang, we took a bus to the capital city, Phnom Penh. On the way we stopped twice for a break. At the first stop we saw a group of Khmer ladies with their traditional chequered dishcloths around their heads, selling tasty snacks from their wicker baskets. On offer were the gourmet delights of steamed snails, fried grasshoppers and roasted black beetles. The second stop was more of a snack bar, where alongside the packets of biscuits and fizzy drinks were several racks of deep fried little frogs, skewered onto slivers of bamboo like long kebabs, with their legs all outstretched. A fellow passenger told us that the frogs were 'country food', not eaten by people who live in the city. That didn't make it much better – and although it was true that we didn't see fried frogs in Phnom Penh, we certainly came across more bowls of steaming snails and plates of black beetles.

Before we reached the capital, I saw out of the bus window another road sign, again with a picture of a machine gun broken in two. It was titled 'Say no to guns' and had written across it the slogan 'Society without guns is a society of peace, technology and development'. The longer we spent in Cambodia, the more we felt the haunting presence of the recent past, however much the people were trying to move on. After centuries during which the Kampuchean territories had been eaten away by the Siamese on one side and the Vietnamese on the other, Cambodia was overrun – along with Vietnam and Laos – by the French in the second half of the nineteenth century. Cambodia regained independence in 1954, ruled by a king who was largely content for his subjects to remain as farming peasantry. But in 1967 the Cambodian communists began to fight a guerrilla war against the king, who was deposed in 1970 and replaced by a coalition government.

By then, the war in neighbouring Vietnam had already spilled over the border, with US forces bombing Vietnamese troops inside Cambodia. The Cambodians turned on the Vietnamese as well, and this bombing and fighting continued until 1973. In 1975 the Khmer Rouge marched without resistance on Phnom Penh – just days before Saigon fell to the North Vietnamese. From this point until a ceasefire in 1991 and then elections in 1992, the country was plunged into a spiralling cycle of enforced migrations, labour camps, starvation, communist purges, invasion by the Vietnamese and multi-sided resistance fighting.

To give just one example of the nightmare that was the Khmer Rouge regime, between 1975–8 a total of 38,400 people were executed within just one of the thirty-three sectors that the country had been divided into, according to Elizabeth Becker. And this was not even one of the sectors affected by the extreme purges ordered by the Khmer Rouge leader, Pol Pot. Estimates of the total numbers of Cambodians killed by the Khmer Rouge vary between 1.7 and 3 million people. The lower figure was 21 per cent of the entire population. During the subsequent Vietnamese occupation, only 1 per cent of the population had access to safe drinking water. One in seven children died before their first birthday and one in five didn't survive to five years old. At the end of it all, Cambodia was a ruin.

When we reached Phnom Penh itself, we found that in stark contrast to Thailand's capital – let alone Malaysia's or Singapore – there were no concrete flyovers, no Skytrains and no gleaming tower blocks. There were no shopping squares and no multinational stores. We found only one local supermarket. We didn't see any banks and there were no international ATMs. This was a city without any gloss or glamour. But there was plenty of dust, dirt, sweat and fumes. Even quite close to the centre of town, the quieter side streets quickly become rubble-strewn dirt roads, blocked with grotty market stalls and piles of rubbish or building materials. The houses were often quite attractive and there was a fair bit of new development going on, but little stood out and generally the buildings blended together as a backdrop to the traffic-filled roads – which were actually the dominant feature of the city. The streets were filled with a hectic activity that appeared similar to columns of frantically busy ants, with individuals streaming here, there and everywhere in a mad rush, hurrying to get somewhere but always ending up in someone else's way. Motos dominated, followed by bicycles and then everything else from lorries to hand-drawn carts. Private cars were way back in terms of numbers.

Crossing the roads was a daunting adventure at first. Lanes didn't really exist; even in an apparently stationary queue of traffic there might well be something coming from the opposite direction; at junctions, traffic would just cut across anywhere, so we had to continually look in all directions. The trick was to choose a likely moment and then just walk straight across, not going too fast, as all the traffic weaved and whizzed past. We would become a part of the fluid entity, its individual parts moving aside to avoid us and everything else. We would hold our breath and cross our fingers, and reach the other side in safety.

The pavements were also thick with people, so crowded that it was hard to see beyond the throng. But behind were rows of small shops, all fairly repetitious. There were lots of eateries and food stalls, mechanics' workshops that sold petrol in plastic drinks bottles, a couple of simple furniture shops, a few electronic shops selling computers and DVD players, a handful of mobile phone shops – and that was about all.

The exception was beside the river, where a palace stood as an island of luxurious calm in the maelstrom. Here, wide roads with grassy park-like verges and ornate street lamps were almost eerily empty. The beautiful gold and orange pagoda-style rooftops of the palace shimmered and gleamed in the sunshine. It was separate and different from the rest of the city, somehow a world apart. And alongside the river bank for a little way were attractive buildings, making it almost like a relaxed seafront. Cafés, restaurants and hotels provided favoured hangouts for the wealthy and the foreigners. And they in turn attracted young children hawking books or newspapers, and disabled or deformed beggars.

Cambodia must be – it is – more than its history. It would be a travesty to conceive of the country solely in terms of its past tragedies. On the outskirts of Phnom Penh we passed a large group of young women on the road, some of the 270,000 workers – 85 per cent of whom were women – in the garment factories, which were an increasingly important part of Cambodia's economic growth. Along with tourism, this industry was one of Cambodia's success stories. And yet, particularly for tourists in Phnom Penh, the recent past was very much kept alive, within the context – we felt – that Cambodia had been a victim and the world outside was to blame for its suffering. There were daily showings of films that told stories from the war years; there was a torture museum in Phnom Penh; and there were frequent trips to the Killing Fields of the Choeung Ek Genocidal Centre.

Some way out from the city centre, down a dirt track and behind a building site, was the site of the Choeung Ek mass graves. Past the ticket booth, shop and waiting guides was a single glass tower – a Buddhist stupa – that was filled with many shelves of skulls, bones and items of clothing that had been found in the graves. To one side were display boards which passionately tried to convey in words the brutality that took place here and the motivation behind it. Behind was a grassy lawn which turned into a series of shallow pits: 129 mass graves. Some had signs beside them stating the number of bodies found in them: 'mass grave of 166 victims without head' or 'mass grave of 450 victims'. Disconcertingly, beside a couple of graves were small piles of broken bones, stacked against a tree or collected in a silver urn. Tatters of faded clothing lay half-buried on the path and in the sides of the pits. In total 8,895 human bodies had been found, although forty-three pits remained undisturbed. In the four years from 1975–9, the number of murders in killing fields like this one reached a total of 20,000. The average rate of killings here was one hundred per day. One particular tree had held a microphone that was used to drown out the noise of the killings. To save bullets, people were mainly butchered with knives, swords, hoes or picks.

Today, trees overhead gave a soft, dappled shade. It was quite green and pleasant, almost like a small park. About twenty children of all ages were playing beneath the trees, small girls chasing each other across the site. It was unexpectedly tranquil and serene, as if the horrors that had taken place here had exhausted all possible evil, leaving nothing except a calming peace.

Chapter 42: The Mekong Delta

It would have been easy to travel from Phnom Penh in Cambodia to Ho Chi Minh City in Vietnam by road, but we decided to cross the border by the waterways of the Mekong Delta, taking the opportunity to see more of Cambodian river life. Over the next weeks as we travelled north through Vietnam, Laos and China we would meet the Mekong River several times. It is the thirteenth longest river in the world, starting in Tibet some 2,800 miles away and ending up in the delta of southern Vietnam.

It took two hours driving from Phnom Penh before we reached the boat terminal, providing us with a fascinating study of Cambodian road transportation. The route was fairly busy with traffic, mainly consisting of white minibuses. These were literally stuffed full of bodies as if competing in a mobile game of 'sardines'. When no more passengers could fit inside, others sat on the roof – and stayed firmly put even during the process of changing a wheel. The same principle applied to the slightly smaller pickups and jeeps that also acted as public transport carriers. We drove behind one jeep for a while that had bench seats inside the back, but to make more room the rear trailer flap had been lowered and two more seats were welded onto it. I counted eighteen people squeezed in the back, with another nine sitting on the roof, together with their assorted belongings.

Next in size came the strange vehicles that could be described as 'boat-bikes'. These were motorcycles that pulled a trailer behind them, looking very much like a wooden rowing boat with a wheel on either side. Wooden planks were fitted across the boat for seats, perhaps six rows that would each normally fit two people sitting side by side. So of course some 'boat-bikes' had up to twenty-five passengers, some sitting uncomfortably around the edges or even on the ends of planks that extended outside the boat.

Then came wooden carts, usually pulled by a pair of oxen. Some carried loads of firewood or random collections of greenery, but the most interesting fitted my impression of a 'tinker cart' perfectly. These had solid walls and thatched roofs, making them look like caravans, and the outsides were strung with collections of orange-coloured pottery. They were virtually identical to some of the houseboats we had seen on the river, except that the 'house' was now placed on a wagon rather than a boat.

The most numerous vehicle on the road was, of course, the ubiquitous moto, which carried anything and everything. Families of four or even five people travelled on a single bike. Young children who looked as if they were barely toddlers would sit astride a bike in front of their parent, as if in Cambodia children learn to ride before they can walk. There were many pedal bicycles too, often with wicker baskets and a single mattock-like tool strapped to the back, so probably being ridden by manual labourers setting off to work during a kind of rush hour.

When we reached the Mekong we were transferred to a yellow barge, which was similar to the canal boats of the English Broads. The river was wide and sluggish; we lazed on the top of the boat as a world of green fields and wooden houses on stilts drifted slowly past. At the border we pulled into the bank and walked for several yards through a sequence of immigration checks before boarding another, smaller, boat in Vietnam. It had a young Vietnamese guide in it, who was to accompany us to Ho Chi Minh City. This was efficient, we thought, as we looked forward to being shepherded around for a couple of days rather than having to work out for ourselves where to go and what to do. Later we realised that the tourist industry in Vietnam was almost entirely packaged and managed like this, which had its pros but also its cons.

An early example of this came when Claudia had to visit the toilet at the border crossing. She headed towards it and a young child skipped after her, taking her hand in a companiable manner. As they returned, however, the child began to angrily demand a payment for having shown her the way. Such experiences can quickly make travellers wary of apparently innocent encounters, taking away the pleasure of spontaneous interactions with other people. Sometimes in Vietnam, and particularly later on in India, it sometimes took an effort for us to remain open to individuals we would meet, rather than becoming cynical about any stranger's approaches.

Soon after entering Vietnam the river narrowed, as it began to split into branching channels within the delta. We began to notice differences from Cambodian river life. We were still passing houses on stilts with their associated pigs and ducks underneath, delighted children waving and jumping into the river, the odd fisherman or fishing net, and even small herds of buffalo being brought to water, but gradually the houses were changing. They became more numerous, and from being wooden boxes they became corrugated metal ones. Soon these silver tin houses were packed side by side like a terraced row, their wooden stilt legs underneath as thick as a forest. Wooden ladders provided routes both down to the water and sideways to the top of the bank. The boats that plied between the houses were different to the Cambodian ones too, being rowed in a curious manner. Instead of the rower sitting backwards in the centre of the boat, he or she stood up facing forwards in the front of the boat, turning two long oars that still passed through one rowlock on either side of the boat. It was vigorous work, but seemed to be effective. The ladies we saw were all wearing the conical 'lampshade' hats that are the stereotypical image of the Vietnamese – and which were very photogenic. Claudia tried on one of the conical hats and found it to be a practical solution to the high temperatures; it gave plenty of shade and because of its shape only a small part was ever in contact with her head.

The metal box houses were sat on platforms in the middle of the river too, the Vietnamese version of floating houses, looking like a collection of industrial shipping containers. Many of these were small-scale fish farms. There were over 1,000 such farms on the Mekong, each one a self-contained operation. The floating farms had nets suspended beneath them, which trapped their stock. Twice a day the fish farmer had to drop into the water through a trapdoor in the floor and swim underneath in the inky blackness to clean out any dead fish. Our guide didn't have a very high opinion of this way of life. She seemed to think that the people had little regard for the cleanliness of either their lives or the river, despite their fish being vulnerable to pollution. She told us that the fish farmers use the river water for literally everything, even for drinking. Across Vietnam, only about 20 per cent of the rural population have access to water that is clean enough to drink safely.

There were floating markets on the river too, of a totally different scale to the ones we had seen outside Bangkok. Hundreds of barge-style boats were stocked with fruit and vegetables of all kinds, advertising their wares by a bamboo pole sticking up into the air with exhibits skewered onto its end. Carrots, onions, jackfruit, melons, potatoes, cabbages, pineapples – all were hoisted aloft to stand against the sky. It was a colourful sight, a confusing melee of barges and small rowing boats, decorated with conical hats and piles of fruit. No one took much notice of our little boat squeezing in amongst the rest, despite the rows of clicking camera lenses. Everyone was far too busy passing fruit out of hatches between boats to be distracted by tourists.

Rocking alongside the seller boats were buyers, loading up with produce to be taken to shops or markets elsewhere. These were wholesale business operations, where the minimum sale was 15 kg. It looked like an age-old process, very efficient and well-organised. Sellers were contracted by farmers to move their produce, while buyers called their contacts by mobile phone to check on suitable prices. One profitable operation, apparently, was to load up boats with fresh produce here, take them to the coast where saline water prevented good quality harvests, sell everything at a profit, then load up again with squid and fish and repeat the process in reverse.

One evening we had a rare chance to walk up a solitary hill. From the top we could look out over the delta landscape we were passing through. All the land around was flat, for miles and miles. Almost everything was covered in bright green rice fields; the Mekong Delta produces 20 million tonnes of rice every year. Vietnam as a whole grew 38 million tonnes in 2006, which makes it the second largest producer in the world after Thailand. Rice is a vital commodity; 80 per cent of the Vietnamese population depends on rice production.

As we walked up the hill, Claudia and I passed several small groups of Vietnamese people on their way down. We smiled at them and said 'hello', but I had the feeling that they just laughed at us. The girl running our grubby, mosquito-ridden hotel was friendly enough, though. Our little tour group sat together for an evening meal there, pleased to see a range of food on the menu cards. But we soon discovered that the kitchen had run out of chicken. And there were no eggs. Our first orders finished off their supply of rice, and before we were all finished the potatoes ran out, too.

As we travelled further into Vietnam, the nature of life began to change around us. Instead of rural houses with fields behind, the jumble of buildings became increasingly industrial. We passed warehouses, sheds, timber yards and building supplies. Floating barges even operated as mobile petrol stations, complete with standard gasoline pumps. The river was busy with long, narrow wooden canoes laden with goods or carrying lines of passengers, all wearing their conical hats.

We stopped off at a ricepaper factory, where the process was the same as the cottage industry we had seen in the village near Battambang, but the size of operation was different. This factory was a barn, large enough for four sets of workers. Interestingly, the waste rice husks were burned as fuel, the ash was then used as fertiliser, and any other waste was fed to the pigs which lived in pens surrounding the barn – nothing was wasted here. We saw a similar scale operation later on beside a road, which this time involved half a dozen workers sitting together in what could have been a large front room of a house, making incense sticks. Here, each worker made 5,000 sticks per day, which gave them wages of 35,000 dong, or US $2 per day. Average wages throughout the country were US $60–90 per month, but in one of the 1,000 textile plants in Vietnam, which employ over 2 million workers, workers could earn US $200 per month. Vietnam's economy is booming, with a growth rate in 2005 of 8.4 per cent, which in Asia was second only to India and China. Although a fifth of the population still live in poverty, the numbers have been falling rapidly.

Leaving the Mekong Delta behind, we drove towards the town of Can Tho. Along the roadside the differences between Vietnam and Cambodia continued to be evident. Houses lined up along the roadside were now made from metal rather than wood. There were also plenty of shops and businesses; we even passed small industrial sites and factories for brick and rice processing. Instead of a rural feel, as if everyone were farmers, everything was far more urbanised. Vietnam was appearing altogether more developed, more productive than Cambodia, and with a sense of being more cohesive and organised.

Differences between the countries were obvious in Can Tho, too. Here there were plenty of banks and higher-order shops selling fashionable clothing and shoes. Advertisements showed more pictures of David Beckham – there was no doubt that his was the most universal sporting image around the world. After a bit of searching, we even tracked down a couple of international ATMs in town. We had re-entered a modern, more affluent world. Restaurants placed frogs on the menu alongside chicken, beef or squid, and market stalls sold the new culinary treat of duck bills and feet.

Along the landscaped riverside was a well-kept little park being used by people to relax and socialise in, reminding us very much of Mexican or Chilean parks. Teenagers posed together in their jeans, denim jackets, T-shirts and baseball caps, a picture of globalised youth culture. Their mothers, on the other hand, typically wore what looked like flowery cotton pyjamas beneath their conical hats. Women would cycle along with their conical hats secured by wide cloth straps passing underneath their chins and triangular masks over their nose and mouths, making them look like highway bandits. But it was hard to be intimidated by them, as they were typically petite young girls in pyjamas, wobbling along on a bicycle. As night fell, the roads filled up with hundreds of families and couples promenading along the road, either on foot or on the back of a motorcycle. Obviously this was the thing to do in the evenings in Can Tho.

Beyond Can Tho the roadside houses changed and improved again, becoming quaint cottages, freshly painted in pastel shades, with orange terracotta roof tiles. Pretty houses actually turned out to be one of the characteristic features of Vietnam. A lot of building was going on, and many of the houses looked new and modern, but every single one had been carefully styled to look attractive. In towns the houses were often very thin, taking up little more floor area than a garage, but rising up three, four or even five storeys, colourfully painted in green, blue or yellow, and typically with large windows and balconies on each floor.

As we approached Ho Chi Minh City, we had a couple of views over it from arched bridges. Apart from a few shanty-style shacks squeezed into spaces on the outskirts, most of the houses were well-built two- or three-storey buildings. In the centre were only a small number of shining glassy tower blocks, most of which were modern hotels. Ho Chi Minh City turned out to be the most pleasant city that we would see in South East Asia.

Chapter 43: Ho Chi Minh City

Ho Chi Minh City – often abbreviated to HCMC – was a delightful place. Wide, clean, tiled pavements were easy to walk along, under the shade of plentiful trees that made streets appear like French boulevards. The roads were wide and buildings low, bringing a sense of space to the city. Buildings were painted pink, blue and yellow; well-maintained parks and ornamental gardens provided greenery, splashed with the colour of bright flower beds. Shops actually had windows that kept goods safely inside, rather than spilling them out all over the pavement. This was a novelty to us after Thailand and Cambodia, and here seemed arty and stylish. In the business centre of the city the high quality hotels and offices reminded us of Santiago, all very quiet, respectable and pleasantly up-market. Having said all this, the roads were totally manic, the worst of any in South East Asia, even more crowded and chaotic than in Phnom Penh. We were told that there are two things that Vietnamese are passionate about: karaoke and motos. There were estimated to be 26 million motos in Vietnam and 3 million of these were in HCMC.

There seemed to be one rule governing the traffic at crossroads and roundabouts: never, ever stop moving. At a junction, the traffic – mainly motos but also, more scarily, cars, lorries and buses – would flow in a dense stream in one direction. Any drivers who wanted to cross the flow would gradually edge their way in, slowing as they did so but never stopping, until as if by a miracle the passing stream would first bend around them and then, all at once, would shift direction and flow behind, so that the crossing vehicles could continue on their way. With this happening simultaneously at the five roads of the roundabout, and no obvious rules over which stream of traffic had priority, the result was a visual mess of intersecting, criss-crossing, free-flowing traffic – several times we just stood and watched in disbelief at the entrancing spectacle.

We visited the palace and the Notre Dame-like cathedral, but were more impressed with the café we stopped in on the way back. It could have been a chic coffee house of London or Paris, decked out with modernist orange and blue sofas, water features and potted plants, and stylishly framed black-and-white portraits on the walls; there must have been a stratum of the citizenry who were bourgeois enough to appreciate their cafés! During the Second Indo-China War, Saigon – as it was called then – received billions of dollars in US aid, which allowed its citizens to develop European lifestyles. Their relative affluence was a complete shock to the North Vietnamese soldiers who arrived from the poverty-stricken north, as described by Denise Chong:

Many would be wide-eyed, bewildered at the sight of televisions, refrigerators and ceiling fans. Few had known the luxury of television. All were startled to see that southerners were better fed and clothed than any northerner, and rich enough to own motor scooters and cars, unheard of among peasants of North Vietnam. Southerners even appeared well spoken and well bred, contrary to what northerners had been taught.[10]

The Vietnamese society had historically been centred in the north of the country, where it had always struggled to separate itself from Chinese rule. Only briefly in the eleventh century and then more decisively in the fifteenth century did the northern Le Dynasty achieve actual independence. It occupied ground all the way to Nha Trang, but fighting between northern Hanoi and southern Nha Trang created a divided country in 1620. In 1802, after more decades of warfare, the south gained victory over the north and established a capital in central Hue. Vietnam as we know it today was united for the first time in its history, but this only lasted for sixty years, as in 1862 the French arrived. By 1900 they had occupied all of Vietnam and divided it into three administrative regions.

In 1930 Ho Chi Minh began his leadership of the Indo-Chinese Communist Party, with the explicit aim of ending French occupation across the region. From 1935 onwards this became the fiercely nationalistic freedom-fighters League for Vietnamese Independence, otherwise known as the Viet Minh. China helped them to power in Hanoi, but the USA supported the non-Communist government in Saigon. The resulting conflict – the Second Indo-China War, which spread well beyond Vietnam alone – devastated much of Vietnam. Three times as many bombs were dropped in Vietnam as during all of World War II, damaging over half the villages and hamlets in southern Vietnam. 10 million refugees fled both the fighting and the Communist forces, including tens of thousands of 'boat people' in 1978. Ironically, many of these were Chinese, because the Vietnamese Communists had turned against their initial allies, accusing the Chinese of siding with Cambodia and plotting to invade Vietnam.

When the Communist forces gained control of Saigon, they renamed it after their inspirational leader, Ho Chi Minh, or 'Uncle Ho' as he was still called. We were in the country for the celebration of his 116th birthday, and for the occasion the secretary of the Party Committee in Hanoi gave a speech, saying that all citizens should live up to the title of 'children of Uncle Ho' and that 'each of us should regularly train ourselves, particularly in political and theoretical quality and revolutionary virtues'.

There were a few other telltale signs that this was a Communist country.

---

[10] Chong, D, *The Girl in the Picture*, London, Scribner, 1999, p.149

Posters showed bold hand-drawn images of people striving to improve themselves and their country, which in the West would be labelled as propaganda. There were many stark Communist statues, symbols of revolutionary strength, which sat on pedestals in pristinely maintained small parks, fenced in and with the gates locked. And each morning and evening, loudspeakers attached to lamp posts would blare out another form of propaganda for all to hear, regardless of whether anyone wanted to listen or not.

In Vietnam as in Cambodia, the attitude to the recent war years seemed to be one of putting any blame on the shoulders of the outside world, particularly the USA. Nevertheless, there was also a distinct degree of official pride in their victory, for example in the showcasing of features like the Cu Chi Tunnels just outside HCMC:

> The Tunnel Network represents the undaunted will, intelligence and pride of the Cu Chi people. It is also a symbol of the revolutionary heroism of the Vietnamese people. Due to this, Cu Chi has been bestowed the honorific title of 'The Steel Land and The Bronze Citadel'.

Above ground, Cu Chi was a village district, rich in fruit orchards and rubber plantations. Its population had been exposed to war in 1948, when they fought the French occupiers and began hiding in tunnels dug into hard clay. When Vietcong resistance against the South Vietnamese army and the US soldiers began, the tunnels were enlarged and extended. In all, 250 km of tunnels were dug. The system was built on three levels, the deepest of which was 10 m below ground. Water came from wells 25 m deep and fresh air through thin ventilation shafts maintained with hollow bamboo tubes. Eventually the tunnels became home to two or three generations of resistance fighters. Underground kitchens had covered chimneys and separate 'smoke rooms' to try to avoid detection by overhead bombers. The tunnel network even extended undetected right underneath a US army base that had been built specifically to fight the Vietcong soldiers. At the visitor's centre for the Cu Chi Tunnels, we, along with other tourists, including Americans, were shown a piece of archive film footage that celebrated the awarding of 'hero' status to a brave Vietcong fighter who had killed five US soldiers.

Although most of the tunnels have since collapsed, a couple of sections have been opened and reconstructed as a tourist attraction. We followed the dark, narrow passageways on hands and knees. It was a sweaty, claustrophobic experience that was too much for some of our tour group. It was difficult to imagine living in these tunnels, let alone fighting in them. Many of the tunnels had defensive traps, with tight bends, steps up and down, dead ends and hidden pits. Above ground, the Vietcong had devised many crude but effective booby traps, often based on the principle that the weight of a misplaced footstep could drive poisoned wooden spikes into a leg or torso. When the fighting eventually finished, the remaining traps and any mines had to be found by driving buffalo through the woods.

In an effort to flush out the Vietcong, the US Air Force took to dropping Agent Orange on Cu Chi. Apart from the immediate death and destruction that this inflicted, there was a legacy of deformities in the population which continued to fuel local anger. We visited one factory that described itself as selling 'handicapped handicrafts', where amputees produced exquisite paintings and collages, some made from crushed eggshell fragments put together like a microscopic mosaic. Despite the human legacy, Vietnam appeared to have healed its scars – particularly economic ones – more successfully than either Cambodia or Laos. There was also an explicit desire among the Vietnamese to move forward as a united country and to learn from countries like the USA how to create economic growth and development.

In Ho Chi Minh City there was a tourist backpacker quarter, composed of a few corners of small streets filled with travel agents, hostels, restaurants and art galleries. It wasn't on the same scale as Khao San Road, although it was certainly heading in that direction. Alongside Italian pizza and pasta places, the streets retained a real flavour of Vietnamese life, with everyday folk still using the street to sell vegetables and hawk their wares from their traditional baskets. Street stalls sold French baguettes in the mornings, sometimes calling them 'hamburgers'. Beside these were glass bottles full of rice wine, with the added twist of whole snakes and scorpions preserved in the clear liquor. These would have made interesting souvenirs, but we had enough doubts about the chances of them being allowed through customs to stop us from buying one.

We stayed in a lovely little hotel with a spotlessly clean and modern double room for the standard price of US $10 per night. It was possible to find rooms for a few dollars less, but with a significant drop in quality. In Ho Chi Minh City we also found excellent travel agencies: competent staff gave out maps, brochures, timetables and advice, and even offered free meals, Internet usage or T-shirts for people who went on their tours. They put together complete travel packages, which would take care of everything between HCMC and Hanoi. Company buses ran between cities, linking up with hostels and hotels and providing sightseeing excursions. They were cheaper than public transport and ran door-to-door services. It was all incredibly efficient – we didn't come across a tourist industry like this anywhere else in the world – and in one sense it made travel very easy, but we were to learn that such organisation had its disadvantages.

All the tourists that we met in Vietnam had all travelled exactly the same route through Vietnam, condensed into the ten-stop tourist trail between the Mekong Delta, HCMC, Mui Ne, Dalat, Nha Trang, Hoi An, Hue, Hanoi,

Halong Bay and Sapa. It made for quite a sociable time, with quite a few travellers in this corner of the world turning out to be on around-the-world journeys, or halfway-around at least. From some of these we began to hear stories about Vietnamese travel experiences. One unfortunate young man staying in HCMC had left his money in a locked room and returned to find 300 Euros missing. He confronted the owner, who insisted that it was impossible for the theft to have happened because – he claimed – there was only one key to the room. So he went to the police, but they were watching television and were not interested enough even to record the details of the robbery. In the end he left having achieved nothing but frustration. There was simply nothing he could do other than move hotel.

Chapter 44: Mui Ne

It was almost inevitable that after Ho Chi Minh City our next stop would be Mui Ne. This turned out to be a small coastal resort, which was something that we hadn't previously associated with Vietnam. With 2,000 miles of coastline, Vietnam actually has some superb and relatively undiscovered beaches – really beautiful beaches of white sand under waving palm trees – and is becoming increasingly popular with package tourists from places like Germany. There are plenty of well-built resorts, but alongside them Vietnam prides itself on retaining traditional ways of life.

We certainly found both in Mui Ne, a small fishing village that lay at one end of a strip of small beach-hut-style resorts, hotels and seafood restaurants. It was easy to relax on the endless beach during the heat of the day, taking an occasional dip in the choppy sea as windsurfers raced past, and then stroll out to select a likely restaurant from the wide selection on offer. Pulled up on the beach were often several hemispherical wicker boats, usually with a fisherman sitting nearby, mending his white nets in the sunshine. Sometimes out to sea were lines of these small boats bobbing in the waves, like beads on a string. But to see the fishing action close up, we had to be on the beach at dawn.

Even before the sun was colouring the sky a warm pink, the boats were coming in after their night's fishing. As they approached the shore the waves tossed them around, but they kept on coming, being rowed by the peculiar means of a single oar that was held at the leading edge of the boat and worked in a circular motion. When the boats reached the shore, there were crowds of people waiting to help haul in the long nets, everyone grabbing a corner and lending a hand. After all that effort, one catch that we saw seemed small. It was made up almost entirely of crabs, although we did spot a lobster, a squid and a seahorse too. The catch was piled into a heap on the sand and several women squatted beside it, sifting through and sorting it. As soon as that was finished, the women left the beach, taking their children with them. The fishermen settled down beside the boats and began to work through their nets. As they did, the surf filled up with local people coming out for an early-morning swim, which was a very popular activity along the Vietnamese coast. By the time the sun was yellow in the sky, it was all quiet again – the beach was too hot a place to be for most people during the day.

During our first few days in Vietnam we had begun to feel a niggling disquiet about the attitude of some of the Vietnamese we had encountered. There

Mui Ne

was something not quite right about the Vietnamese smiles that didn't stay, the disinterested half-conversations and impersonal interactions that were sometimes – not always – brusque to the point of deliberate rudeness. The people on buses, in restaurants and on tours seemed to have an insincerity about the way they provided services, as if they considered themselves superior and were only playing a role for foolish tourists in order to relieve us of our money.

Such had been the case with our guide for an excursion in Mui Ne, who was booked to drive us to nearby orange-and-white sand dunes for another sunrise experience. Unfortunately for us, he arrived late, then had to fill up with petrol twice, then realised that he had forgotten two other tourists and had to go back to collect them, so it turned into a very post-sunrise experience – not that our guide seemed to care in the slightest. From the wind-scalloped ridges of the dunes we looked out across a thin band of green treetops to the blue Pacific Ocean. We were facing east; it had been a long time since we were looking the other direction from the beaches of California. The dunes were a popular gathering place for Vietnamese tourists, young ladies hawking food from their bamboo baskets, and even younger boys waiting with sandboards to rent out. Also on the sand dunes that morning were a couple from Innsbruck; we overheard them repeating the same line that Claudia had used so often during our trip – 'No, not Australia, *Austria*!'

When we returned to our resort, we found the pleasant restaurant empty and so sat down to have breakfast, to do some writing and to play a little pool. At some point, several of our belongings were stolen from the chairs beside us, including – devastatingly – our camera and its memory card full of 200 photographs taken between Battambang and here! We could hardly believe it; we were normally so careful with our possessions. And there had been no one else about. So we informed the resort staff, making a nuisance of ourselves by asking everyone time and again if they had seen the camera. Perhaps, we suggested, someone had just tidied it away? But all to no avail. Apparently no one had seen our camera.

And so we took a trip to the local police station ourselves. We didn't expect much to be done about the camera itself, but we needed a police statement for insurance purposes. A friendly young man was on duty in the station. He met us wearing a casual white T-shirt but soon disappeared to change into a full dress uniform of smart green, with gold buttons and red flashes on his shoulders. He showed us his little notebook with English translations of useful police phrases, like 'You have been hurt. Go to hospital.' We gave him a couple more words for his collection. But when it came to our camera, there was nothing he could do. He had heard our story many times before and however sympathetic he was, he couldn't give us a report for our insurance company.

At first he claimed that this was because there was no official document on which to file an official report. That's OK, I told him, a statement on ordinary file paper would do, as long as it had a police stamp on it. My experience is that every official not only has a stamp to prove they are official, but also loves an opportunity to use it. However, in this case the policeman told us that he would need the authorisation of his senior officer, who just happened to be off duty. Seeing that I was prepared to visit his superior at home, he gave in a little. The real problem, it eventually transpired, was that he was not going to take the risk of putting his name to anything that could come back to give him trouble later on – for example, if an insurance company came asking questions. The resort, he feared, might then deny that anything had happened, leaving him in a difficult position.

We needed a statement and weren't showing any signs of leaving until we had one, but the only way that the policeman would sign anything was if the resort first accepted in writing that the camera had actually been taken. So the owner of the resort was called, not too happy about being dragged into the mess. He didn't want to sign anything either, in case there were repercussions against his resort. But we still needed a statement. In the end, it was a fudge over wording that broke the impasse. We would all write on a single piece of paper that the camera was 'lost' rather than 'stolen', which meant that it could have been our fault and could even have happened elsewhere. They were even happier when I wrote that the camera was lost from a restaurant with an incorrect name. After this blame-avoiding contrivance, they both duly signed and double-stamped the paper. We finally had our police report. It had only taken a whole day and three visits to the police station to achieve. It made us reflect on what it must be like to live in a country where even the police could refuse to accept that an incident has happened, for fear of official blame being attached to them. It is often said that when negotiating with the Vietnamese – and the Chinese, come to that – it is important not to create a situation when an individual would 'lose face' by appearing to be at fault. We found that the efforts people made to avoid accepting responsibility could become farcical.

One morning a couple of girls were due to move on from our Mui Ne resort and had booked themselves seats on the early tourist bus. Being sensible, experienced travellers, one had even gone back to the office in the evening just to check that all was well with the arrangements – it was. But in the early morning, when the bus came, the driver had no record of their booking and he refused to let them board. The bus drove off without them. When they found the manager of the resort, the girls asked what had happened. He immediately tried to shift the blame, saying 'It was your fault – you hadn't booked.' This didn't go down well with them, so he tried something else. 'You were late and missed the bus.' The girls were even less impressed with this suggestion. If the blame wasn't with them, then it must have been with the bus company – the manager then said that 'the bus didn't run today', despite the fact that the girls had talked to the driver. Apparently, that particular bus 'was from another company', despite it having the same logo on its side as that above the resort office! In desperation, the manager eventually said that 'the company had changed the schedules for that day' and he had 'only just been told about it'.

Nothing the girls could say would induce him to concede that his office had made the simple mistake of forgetting to book them onto the bus in the first place. The girls gave up and settled down to wait for the next bus, with a free drink from the restaurant to make up for the inconvenience – which, the manager took the trouble to make clear, wasn't an admission of responsibility, but was merely a gesture of goodwill.

Chapter 45: Nha Trang and Hoi An

Despite the annoyances of some of the people involved in the tourist industry, Vietnam continued to pleasantly surprise us with its diverse and very attractive landscape. Indeed, the physical scenery was, for me, the highlight of our southern Vietnam travels. We had plenty of time to look at it, too, as driving between towns took a long time: 500 kilometres took 12½ hours on one leg of the 'tourist trail'; another 130 km took six hours; 220 km elsewhere took seven hours. Leaving Mui Ne, we passed through green fields of rice and vegetables. White cottages with graceful arches and pillars reminded us of Tuscan villas, complete with a clear blue sky and attractive palm trees. Soon afterwards came dry and dusty coastal plains, where drab fields were being ploughed by hand, toiling men pushing a wheeled implement through the soil. Then came vineyards, fruit orchards, maize fields and more pretty rice paddies. We saw women tending the rice, their legs totally straight but their backs bent nearly double, as if they were trying to touch their toes. Where their heads – at knee height – faced towards us, their conical hats totally obscured their bodies, leaving only a pair of ankles poking out from underneath. Spread across one flat landscape of fields we could see several workers, each one a dark figure absorbed in his own individual task: one was struggling behind a buffalo, another digging with a mattock, another clearing a drainage ditch.

One moment the land was flat and fertile, and the next we were going over hills of white rock and sparse vegetation, and then down into sweeping bays of white sandy beaches and rocky headlands, with green islands out to sea and boats rocking gently on the waves. We passed a salt factory, the surface gleaming in its crystalline whiteness. Everything was a jumble of new scenes, almost all quixotic in some way, fascinating and engaging. As we approached Nha Trang after a night's journey, the roads were busy in the early morning with people carrying goods to or from a market on their motos or bicycles. Along the sides of the roads women walked along, always carrying their obligatory pair of bamboo baskets slung from a pole across one shoulder. They had a hip-wiggling gait that seemed to reduce oscillations in the pole, and they shifted the pole from one shoulder to another as they walked in a dexterous manner that didn't cause them to break their stride at all.

In Nha Trang itself the streets were typically busy with noisy motos. No one seemed to be walking except us – perhaps because it was almost impossible to do so, as every pavement was clogged with bicycle repair outfits, stalls selling petrol in small bottles, or piles of building material. Nha Trang came across as a developed town, despite informal lines of sewing machines on the pavement down one street and lines of barbers down another. These barbers had pinned little mirrors to walls or tree trunks, set chairs out underneath them, and were waiting for passers-by to ask for a haircut. Many people did just that. Incidentally, here in Nha Trang we saw our one and only Vietnamese Buddhist monk, which was a significant contrast to the numbers we had encountered in Cambodia and would do in Laos.

The centre of Nha Trang was almost glitzy, with big hotels and brash neon signs. There were ATMs and banks, expensive restaurants and beach-side parks. Perhaps it was the Vietnamese version of Blackpool. The beach was better here, though. It was stunning: a six-mile long strip of sand, with palm trees waving, blue sky above, blue ocean below and picturesque islands offshore. And it was very hot, at around 40°C. That was the upside. The downside was that almost no one was friendly. In fact, it was the reverse.

On the beach women were huddled around little baskets of fruit or seafood, looking as miserable as their giant lobsters, crayfish and crabs. Men squatted beside their motos playing cards and ignoring the rest of the world. Children hawked postcards, their selling approach being to stand in our way and demand, 'You buy!' followed almost immediately by a rude, 'Why not?' As we walked along the dusty, polluted roads – and we walked a fair way – we made a point of catching people's eyes and smiling, as we had done everywhere else. Here the only responses were blank stares, either expressionless or almost hostile. There was no reciprocal friendliness as there had been in countries further west. It began to depress us, too.

A similar story was repeated in Hoi An, the next stop northwards. This small town was actually built on a piece of land with water on three sides, a bending river having being trapped behind a sand bar along the coast. Boats travelled backwards and forwards across the river, usually being small canoes paddled by ladies, always carrying their baskets. There were also motorised ferry barges that filled every available inch of space on board with bodies or bicycles. Hoi An was famous for its old centre on the riverbank, which consisted of several blocks of French colonial houses. There were lots of yellow paintwork, white trim ornamental decorations, balconies, graceful arches, columns and red tiled roofs. Narrow alleyways and small streets lined with art galleries made it very reminiscent of Paraty in Brazil.

Indeed, Hoi An was also a World Heritage Site, as an example of a trading port from the fifteenth to the nineteenth century. It so clearly had the potential to be very attractive, if only it could be better preserved. The streets had piles of sand and litter on them and the walls of the houses were blackened with mould. It seemed like no one really cared to make the place tidy, which was a real shame. Yet behind this old town were newer building sites where slender houses and hotels were springing up, always looking graceful and pretty.

One of the few people who took an interest in us was a lady who seemed to spend her days cycling through the streets specifically in order to accost us and request that we visit 'her' shop. Eventually we gave in to her, largely out of curiosity, and she showed us to a warehouse which had been partitioned into many separate areas, each little more than a row of shelves stacked with rolls of material, a desk strewn with clothing catalogues from companies such as Next, and a couple of elderly sewing machinists waiting nearby. We were told that anything from the catalogues could be made to order within a day, although even this didn't induce us to actually purchase anything. Hoi An was famous for its tailors, reputedly able to manufacture high-quality garments at cheap prices. More mainstream shops nearby were full of tailored clothing, from three-piece suits to ballroom dresses. Once our cycling lady had escorted us to the shop, she left without another word, no doubt to patrol the streets in search of more potential customers.

Hoi An friendliness rarely seemed to be genuine. Once we were having lunch in a restaurant when the waitress asked us if we wanted to see her home, which was next door. It was a strange request, but one which was hard to decline without being rude, and besides, we were vaguely curious to see inside someone's home. Once inside the front door, however, we were sat down and shown a basket of jewellery that she said her son sold at weekends to fund his education. Did we want to support him? Once we had duly done so, it was time to leave; we never did see much of the house.

Getting up early had become routine for us, as it was for the locals, because by 11 a.m. it was simply too hot to be out and about outside. We wandered into town one day and had a coffee beside the river in the company of a group of men playing cards, before making our way to the fish market. It was 6 a.m. which we hoped was a good time to see the market in full swing. On the way a young man on a bicycle stopped beside us for a chat, initially about nothing in particular and so quite pleasant. He told us that the market wouldn't be open yet, which surprised us – until he asked whether we wanted to go on a tour with him instead. We declined, and he soon left us to continue on our way.

On the roads outside the fish market sat lines of women, chatting to each other behind their piles of fruit and vegetables that had been laid out. It was an eye-catching scene, full of bamboo baskets, colourful produce, flowery cotton dresses and conical hats. Inside the market, beyond the tables of fruit, freshly caught fish was being sold. Silvery scales and red bloody liquid covered the floor. Buckets, pots and plates full of fish had been deposited everywhere, leaving little room for saleswomen to squat, let alone for buyers to walk. The displays were incredible: we came across a shark 2½ feet long, about to be chopped into steaks; a baby hammerhead shark laid out on a plate; several tuna fish easily four feet in length; huge eel-like creatures coiled in buckets; squid of all sizes; and a small but cute swordfish.

Looking across the market, which was not too difficult, as the women were generally very small, I saw nothing but a dense crowd of straw-brown conical hats. Most people avoided looking at us; only one or two people returned our smiles. When we asked if we could take photographs, a common response was to ask for money in return. Perhaps as tourists just passing through we deserved this treatment, for it would be easy to perceive tourists as caring for little unless there was a photograph in it, rarely bothering to learn even basic courtesies in the local language, and being both very rich and very stingy. A comment that we heard a few times in Vietnam went along the lines of 'It's only ten dollars, that's nothing to you', or, 'You are lucky – we work hard and can't afford to travel'.

We couldn't help but pick up a sense of bitterness and resentment in Vietnam that was not apparent to the same extent anywhere else. Packing everyone into the same limited tourist trail could hardly have helped matters. Sometimes I felt that we were being herded along like cattle, allowed to stop at certain places simply in order to relieve us of our wealth, which was the only thing that justified a toleration of our irritating presence.

One particular impression from the fish market became a distinctive image of Vietnam for us. It was the faces of the numerous old ladies who were still toiling with baskets of greenery or fish. Their frail bodies were often stooped and hunched, their intensely wrinkled, wizened faces shaded by conical hats. Their expressions were a thoroughly sad mixture of tiredness and sourness, as if conveying a lifetime of harsh experiences. Their mouths were horrible to see, being toothless and coloured a frightful red from something they were chewing. Many also held fat cigarettes, and were puffing away furiously. In many ways, these old ladies' faces were shocking to behold.

And yet there was another face of Vietnam that we also saw in Hoi An, typified by the receptionists in our hotel. These were young, courteous, well-spoken girls, very polite and often genuinely friendly. They were also pretty, being slim and perfectly shaped for their elegant traditional costume of white flowing trousers under a tighter top that reached right down to the knee, with a long split in its side beneath the waist. They were as attractive as anyone we saw anywhere. Sometimes Vietnam was just a schizophrenic enigma.

We were curious as to whether our unsavoury impressions of the Vietnamese were purely personal, or whether they reflected a broader opinion. In Hoi An we shared a meal with the couple of girls who had missed their bus in Mui Ne. We asked them what their experience of the Vietnamese had been. 'Deceitful', 'two-faced', 'rude', and 'superior' were four terms they quickly used, which seemed to sum up the feelings of one of them at least. Several weeks later, when we were in China, we met another girl who had travelled through Vietnam and we asked her what she thought. Her immediate response was, 'Dishonest.' She didn't like the way that she had learned to treat everyone with suspicion; it was an unpleasant way to travel. To illustrate her point, she told us how she had taken an overnight bus journey with one of the tour companies. She put her bag underneath the bus and found in the morning that items had been stolen from it during the night. She reported this to the company and they refused to accept that anything had happened. Indeed, they even began to accuse her of lying for her own benefit. She went to the police, but they refused to give her a report of the incident. As before, there was absolutely nothing she could do.

When we arrived in Hue, we checked into a hotel that had several travellers' letters displayed in its lobby. One of these seemed to us to capture exactly the experience of Vietnamese travel:

> *Maybe it is due to the different culture and social life of Vietnamese people, that sometimes made me feel quite lost and subject to being cheated… I lost smiling in your country a bit.*

And yet, in the next city of Hue, Vietnam changed its character all over again. It was almost a complete reversal of what we had found in Nha Trang and Hoi An. There was nothing but the friendly face of Vietnam, courteous and going out of the way to be helpful. Early one morning we walked to yet another market and suddenly ladies on the streets were making eye contact with us and returning our smiles plentifully.

Hue was the largest town in central Vietnam; it had been the capital city from 1802 to 1945. Its Citadel was famous for the quality and preservation of its buildings. The central city was quite cosmopolitan, although we didn't find many attractions here. We did, however, manage our first main meal without rice since the pizza in Bangkok. Two rice-less meals in 2½ months and five countries was not bad going! Hue was holding its annual festival when we were there, which appeared to be something like a cross between the artiness of Edinburgh Festival and the open air theatre of the South Bank in London.

We spent most of our time looking around camera shops, hoping to come across a decent replacement digital camera. After exhausting the options on both sides of the river, we had determined that most photography still used film. The few digital cameras on sale were very small and not suitable for our purposes. We were told that the only places to get more expensive cameras were HCMC or Hanoi. And, we thought, surely Vientiane, the capital of Laos. After Hue we were leaving Vietnam with a positive experience in our minds. We had decided not to press on northwards any further, foregoing the pleasures of Hanoi, Halong Bay and the Sapa hill country. This was partly due to the continued mixed reports of travellers coming south, partly due to our own contradictory experiences in Vietnam, and partly due to our uncertainty over the condition of the northern borders between Vietnam and Laos. We never did get a clear picture of whether the crossings were opening up to allow more travel between the countries or closing down due to the rainy season; whether transport was straightforward or a nightmare lottery; or whether they were only open to locals or to foreigners as well.

So we decided to cut our losses and strike west again, crossing into central Laos and from there travelling through Laos all the way to the Chinese border. Everyone who had been to Laos had told us that it was lovely – and that it would not stay that way long under the onslaught of mass tourism. We were looking forward to finding out what it was like for ourselves.

Chapter 46: Savannakhet and Vientiane

We bought a bus ticket in Hue that was supposed to give us a direct 'luxury' coach journey to Savannakhet. We were used to transport arrangements not always living up to their descriptions, but were still a little surprised to be picked up by a minibus so crammed full that people were bending double over each others' knees to fit in. We were told that this minibus would only take us to the next town, where we would join our transport to Laos, so we handed over our tickets and squeezed in. We were duly transferred but only to another minibus, and now without our tickets. The second minibus was mercifully less crowded and did indeed take us to the border – but no further. We placated ourselves with the knowledge that other passengers had paid double the fare that we did for the same journey, and hoped that in Laos there would be transport whose drivers would believe that we had already paid for a through ticket. Incredibly enough, the system worked out in the end, as was invariably the way. And as it turned out, this was a good introduction to Laotian travel.

As we crossed the border, two sets of uniformed and officious Vietnamese policemen made their presence felt by officiously checking our passports. We left Vietnam under a grand archway that seemed to proclaim the superiority of the country. In contrast, when we ducked underneath the wooden bar that marked our entry into Laos, we were merely watched by a couple of men who were reclining comfortably in chairs under the shade of a nearby tree. We strolled over a bridge, through the official immigration post, and past a couple of wooden houses on the riverbank, with chickens and pigs running around beneath them. A group of ragged children shyly waved at us and then hid behind one another as Claudia took their picture. When she tried to show them the image, as was our habit, all but one ran off. Curiosity was too strong for this brave girl and she looked into the camera, shouting with pleasure at what she saw and calling the others back for a look too. For us, the surprise was to come across children who didn't seem to know about digital cameras, in contrast to everywhere else we had been.

We wandered on into a small village, where we found our rickety onward bus. As we sat and waited for it to leave, a family of black pigs walked past us down the dusty main street. They were followed by a string of brown cows, slowly but determinedly progressing the length of the village, apparently totally of their own accord. Also watching the animals pass were a small group of women sitting on the edge of the pavement, having a friendly chat. Everything seemed a notch slower and more relaxed than the bustle of Vietnamese life – several notches, actually. This was laid-back Laos.

Once we were on the move, I noticed that there was almost no traffic on the road, another contrast to Vietnam. Gone were the crowds of motos; there were only a couple of them and a few trucks. We were driving through rounded, forested hills that contained wooden houses clustered together within clearings in the forest. The houses were still raised above the ground on stilts – sometimes a strikingly high ten feet off the ground – but they were considerably larger than Vietnamese buildings, looking like sizeable wooden barns on legs, with wooden ladders running up to the house doors. The clearings were often full of tree stumps that were charred from burning. Pigs and goats wandered around beside naked and semi-naked children. All in all it was a very primitive scene, one that reminded me strongly of the reconstructions of Borneo forest houses we had seen in a Malaysian museum. A fellow passenger on our bus confirmed that these Laotian villages did indeed look exactly the same as lowland villages in Papua New Guinea, where he had lived for some months. But even here there were occasional satellite dishes poking up from roofs.

As we progressed towards Savannakhet, the green ridges flattened out to a broad plain, which extended all the way to the town. Savannakhet itself was a sleepy place, formed by several roads running parallel to a broad river – the Mekong again. 'Sleepy' is perhaps an understatement to describe Savannakhet, although it was the second largest city in Laos. Nothing very much seemed to be happening in the quiet streets, which were almost entirely empty. There was, however, a pleasant mix of houses for us to look at as we wandered around. Some were large wooden barns on stilts, similar to the ones we had seen in the forest clearings near the border, but now with whitewashed stone walls forming a ground floor beneath the wooden house. There were also two-storey houses in a French colonial style, often in pastel colours of blue and yellow, their paintwork fading with age. Some of the town had the feeling of decay, almost like a ghost town, partly because the streets were virtually deserted. Some large compounds that looked as if they could once have been schools or hospitals were closed and overgrown with weeds. There were a couple of restaurants, presumably catering to a high season tourist trade, but these were typically empty and their owners seemed surprised that they had any custom at all when we made our appearance. Outside almost every one was a birdcage, with a sadly trapped songbird inside.

As we walked around, those people we did see would look at us out of the corner of their eyes, quickly followed up with a sweet smile. The young girls passing on motos waved and called out a friendly '*sabaidee*'. Small children were encouraged by their parents to say 'hello' to us in English, as if training them to be welcoming to foreign visitors. Immediately there was a personal rapport that had been missing almost entirely from Vietnam.

Young women on bicycles typically held brightly coloured umbrellas aloft to shield them from the sun; they were a distinctive sight along the main road in town. Inside houses other women and girls lay on sofas watching karaoke on television. Men and children seemed to spend their time playing games: pool, tennis, table tennis, foot-volleyball and, most popular of all, *petang*. Small crowds would often gather to watch a group of men throwing their silver balls down the length of a sandpit beside the road.

The brightest places in town were the highly ornate Buddhist wats, colourfully painted in white, reds and yellows. We liked seeing the orange robes of the monks stretched out to dry on clothes lines between trees in the grounds of the wats; images which merged monastic religiosity with mundane domesticity. Unfortunately, we were realising that we were reaching our saturation point of wat sightseeing. There were only so many buildings with pointy red-tiled roofs, painted walls and gold-filled interiors that we could take in a relatively short space of time, however beautiful each individual wat was.

One evening we came across a strange sight. We passed a riverbank temple that had a gold statue of a national leader in front of it. Unusually, the temple was full of people. On the pavement were stalls selling a typical religious offering that looked like origami banana leaves folded into the shape of a small pointed hat. Motos and bicycles were parked all along the roadside. The steps up to the temple were full of people, most of whom carried fistfuls of incense sticks that were glowing orange inside great wafts of grey smoke. Everything and everyone was shrouded in smoke and even the road was thick with it for quite some distance. The sight appeared like an ancient ritual, worshippers brandishing small fires in their hands and reverently bowing before an altar in an unnatural half-light, but everyone was dressed in modern blue jeans and white T-shirts. We never did identify the reason behind the ceremony.

It was easy to continue from Savannakhet to the capital city of Laos. Vientiane was made the capital of the local kingdom of Lan Xang – which means 'Land of a Million Elephants' – in 1563, but a bid by the king to create an independent state in 1826 was literally smashed by the Siamese, who claimed the allegiance of the Laotians. When the French arrived, they re-established Vientiane as the capital of the small area they now called 'Laos' – effectively a buffer zone that protected their more precious colonies from British influence. During the First Indo-China War, the country was split between Communist Pathet Lao forces and American-backed Royal Lao forces. French withdrawal didn't create stability, and during the Second Indo-China War Laos gained the unfortunate title of the most bombed country in the world as the US Air Force attempted to disrupt North Vietnamese forces using the Laotian section of the Ho Chi Minh Trail. Once the Americans pulled out of Indo-China in 1975, the Pathet Lao forces gained control, the monarchy was abolished and the Laos People's Democratic Republic was formed.

We caught sight of a poster in a Vientiane tourist office window, referring to the bombing during the Second Indo-China War:

> More than 2 million tonnes of ordnance were dropped on Laos over nine years – more bombs than were dropped on Europe during the Second World War – equalling 10 tonnes per kilometre, or 1 plane load of bombs every eight minutes, 24 hours a day for nine years.

One of the most powerful comments relating to these events that we heard came from a Laotian businessman. His perception was that Laos' development had been put back decades compared to other South East Asian countries, and it was only just beginning to emerge from the wreckage. We then asked him whether people were still resentful of the actions of the USA and he said no, partly because Americans had subsequently helped to clear the unexploded ordnance and to set up development projects. The apparent willingness of ordinary people right across South East Asia to leave the past behind and pragmatically move on with their lives was a humbling lesson. For most, the priority seemed to be economic progress.

Vientiane was far more clearly a city than Savannakhet had been. It had wide roads that were busy with traffic. There was even a palace and a distinctive concrete arch straddling a wide pathway, reminiscent of the Champs-Élysées and the Arc de Triomphe in Paris. Public education signs, all written in English, were similar to those in Malaysia and Singapore: 'Good people don't ruin their country and have manners not to litter thoughtlessly' and 'The love of cleanliness is shown in the manners of civilised people'. Businesses were doing their best to look modern and professional beside the dusty roads. Just as in Savannakhet, the colonial French buildings looked charming, even if they were visibly decaying, but here they were overshadowed by large new hotels and banks. There was a buzz of activity, of industry and commerce about the city. Within and despite all the activity and the growing, boomtown feel of the place, however, the pervasive atmosphere was of a slow, relaxed Laotian pace of life. Vientiane had a good-natured feeling about it that seemed to encourage having a drink of beer in the afternoon heat beside the sweeping curve of the wide, brown river – the Mekong again – while looking across the muddy waters to Thailand on the far side.

We had hoped that Vientiane would be a likely place to find a decent digital camera. We set out on fruitless shopping trips on a couple of occasions. The couple of small photography shops with big 'Kodak' advertising boards around their windows told us that we should try looking in the Morning Market instead of their shops. This was good advice, for the Morning Market turned out to be Vientiane's department store. It had plenty of cookers, fridges, mobile phones, televisions and just about every other item of good, electronic or otherwise. Except our digital camera, which was 'too expensive' for the capital city of Laos. We should try Vietnam, we were told.

This seemed one indication of the country's state of development. Another was that there were no international ATMs in Laos at all, although some banks did offer cash advances from a Visa card, which in practice amounted to much the same thing. We discovered that most tourist services and upmarket products quoted prices in the hard currency of US dollars. In the Morning Market and more local shops, the usual denomination was Thai baht, which didn't depreciate in value as quickly as the Laos kip. The kip was really only used for small change in cafés and street stalls.

There was at times a European atmosphere in Vientiane, and not just because of the many roadside stalls that sold French baguettes. We had lunch one day in a small café that had spread its plastic chairs and tables – covered in red-and-white checked tablecloths – out over the pavement. We sat under the shade of green and yellow parasols, with a portable electric fan blowing directly at us, but we still dripped with sweat. There we had potato soup and a tuna-and-cheese baguette, washed down with ice tea and a pineapple shake. From the billboard that advertised the menu in English we could have chosen anything from egg and baguette for breakfast to curries or fried noodles for dinner, perhaps served with the local speciality of papaya salad.

The signs further down the street included a 'budget laundry', an 'Internet and travel centre' and then 'motorbikes for rent'. They were all written in English, as was the copy of the *Bangkok Post* – not officially allowed to be sold in Communist Laos – that we were reading. Beside us on the pavement was a gleaming red Toyota Tundra jeep; the adjacent building was a Mexican restaurant. We had thought that we were travelling to see different places and people, but sometimes we found ourselves merely in a home from home. Until, that is, a little girl of perhaps seven years old came along the pavement. She was dressed in grubby clothes and was leading a grown man – probably her father – behind her by means of a stick held between them. He was holding out a pink plastic bowl, pathetically begging for some loose change. The unbridgeable gulf between our world and theirs was suddenly all too clear.

As if to ram this point home, when we travelled from Vientiane to Vang Vieng we found ourselves joining a complete bus-load of foreign tourists making exactly the same journey. It gave us an idea of the number of tourists travelling this route – often in a loop from Bangkok to Chiang Mai, through northern Laos to Vientiane and then back to Bangkok again – but the tourist bus also kept us well separated from any local people. This time, we had traded the experience of authentic travelling the way locals did for the comfort and security of tourist services. This was what people had referred to when they had said that the experience of travelling through Laos would soon be ruined by mass tourism. It was ironic that the 'unspoilt' attractions of Laos, its 'untouched' appeal, were the very things that had brought commercialised tourist services. In Vang Vieng we would see how quickly the tourist industry could remove virtually any connection or interaction between tourists and the local people or culture.

Chapter 47: Vang Vieng

Vang Vieng used to be just a small riverside village, situated opposite an imposing eruption of limestone cliffs and ridge-like hills. This was a welcome return to the dramatic landscape of karst scenery. Partly due to the physical geography and partly because Vang Vieng was a convenient staging post between Vientiane and Luang Prabang, these hills had become an 'adventure sport' playground for tourists. The original village houses still remained at the riverside, where old ladies sat outside trying to sell handfuls of sorry vegetables as children played nearby in the dirt street. Men and boys were fishing and splashing in the river, or crossing it on spidery bridges of bamboo poles. But even here, right beside the river, some plots were being redeveloped as modern hotels, where their bedrooms could have uninterrupted views of the majestic green wall of hills.

Further back from the river, parallel to the remnants of the older village, was a new tourist road, conveniently close to an old airstrip that tourist coaches were using as a bus park. This tourist road was comprised of two solid rows of four-storey hotel blocks, restaurants and tour offices. Just about the only people we saw were tourists, most of them wearing sandals, varying styles of baggy trousers bought in Thailand, and, often, skimpy European tops. Less than a hundred yards would take them from the door of their newly built hotels to restaurants with comfy chairs that faced television sets endlessly showing *Friends* videos. Everything was written in English – we even saw a menu board that advertised a full English roast dinner, complete with roast beef and Yorkshire puddings. An alternative offered 'Wiener Schnitzel with chicken/beef/pork, served with chip'. But it was pizzas and pancakes that seemed to rule supreme. At night, the open air bars and hotels stayed open until 3 a.m., long enough for everyone to watch World Cup football. We were there in time to see one of England's matches on a big screen, which competed with music from a loud karaoke stereo system behind it. There must have been 50–60 travellers in the open-air bar at 1 a.m., mostly English by the sound of them and therefore very happy to watch England win the match.

When tourists felt inclined to burn off the calories they had ingested, the hotels and tourist offices could arrange numerous activities provided on a plate, including kayaking, caving, tubing, cycling, climbing and trekking. From the descriptions, most of these included a substantial portion of time at riverside bars, offering a popular combination of beer and swimming. It was interesting to draw comparisons with the settlement that Dervla Murphy had found in 1998 and to note the trend of subsequent development:

> During the American era it grew in a haphazard way to become, by Laotian standards, a biggish town with one winding mile-long 'street' (rough and dusty), many shophouses, a small market, a mix of traditional dwellings and mini-bungalows...the atmosphere even now is of a settlement created by outsiders. Since the door opened to tourists Vang Vieng has become a popular stopover for backpackers. Of the three simple guesthouses I chose the least modernised... only a few weeks previously this region had been electrified.[11]

We walked down the town's strip one evening, hoping to get a picture of the sunset as it coloured the sky pink and orange behind the hills. We stopped at a local Buddhist wat on the edge of town, where four young monks were hanging around the outside of the building. One talked to us a little, asking hesitantly where we were from. We were happy to pass the time with him until he summoned up the courage to say, 'Please, you give me money,' which seemed to us a sad reflection of the relationship between tourists and locals.

To explore the local scenery, we hired bikes – the tourist services had their advantages – and set off on our own. Getting across the river was the most challenging part. After we had found the right bridge, we had to push our way past children who tried to demand 2,000 kip from us to cross. Once we had passed, we discovered that the bridge was being rebuilt and so abruptly stopped halfway across the river. We had to wade across the rest, pushing our bikes beside us. But once across, we were away from Vang Vieng and in a different world. Small villages and intensely green paddy fields nestled beside the road, hemmed in by sheer limestone cliffs that met the flat fields at right angles. The cliffs ran upwards until their tops rounded out to be covered in green forest, with clouds swirling beneath their peaks. It was incredibly picturesque and was our very own Laotian 'Dervla Murphy' experience. The limestone cliffs of Vang Vieng were riddled with caves, now tourist attractions even though they were not very easy to access. These were often enormous caverns, lined and studded with long stalagmites and thick limestone pillars. I for one would have liked to have explored them further, but we hadn't thought to bring a torch with us.

Along the roads we passed local villagers going about their daily business, invariably giving us a friendly *'sabaidee'* as we passed. A young boy of perhaps five years old was minding two buffalo that were wallowing in a muddy pond. A group of women all wearing conical hats were coming back from the fields, so we took what we thought was a sly picture until they all crowded around

---

[11] Murphy, D, *One Foot in Laos*, London, Flamingo, 2000, p.43

the camera, wanting to see the photograph. Another group of young children, perhaps a dozen of them, were struggling up a small hill with various plastic containers filled with water. Each time we passed a river or a water pipe we saw children and women washing either themselves or their clothes.

Now and again the Laotian version of a tractor would chug past: a green engine that sat over a pair of wheels. On roads the wheels had tyres and the engine was stabilised by a wooden trailer behind it. In the fields, the tyres were replaced by paddles that ploughed through the mud, held from behind by the farmer. On the roads, the trailers were often full of people – the tractor engines also formed the local public transport. One trailer we saw was covered with a plastic canopy like a wagon, under the shade of which a man was sleeping in a gently swaying hammock.

After Vang Vieng we drove on to Luang Prabang, which was by common consensus the most attractive town in Laos and a major regional tourist destination. Our journey there was supposed to have been four hours long. By now, we had already developed a rule of thumb for Laotian public transport: nothing would leave until it was an hour late, and then the journey would take at least another hour longer than it was scheduled to. This one was true to form, taking from 9 a.m. until 3.30 p.m. At least there were stops along the way for passengers to buy cucumbers from road-side stalls – which they proceeded to carve up using machetes that were produced from within their belongings – or for the driver to answer a call of nature. When this happened, he would pull up, turn around and shout out 'toilet'. Half the bus would then file off to stand or squat on the verge and in the bushes. In its own way, this was quite an efficient process, and Claudia certainly appreciated the frequent nature of these stops.

The highland scenery along the journey to Luang Prabang was the most impressive that we saw in Laos, reminiscent of one made many months before through the Peruvian Andes. Here in Laos we wound our way through sweeping valleys, passing one small village after another. The road became one of the most sinuous I have ever been on, as the only way to cross the valleys – which were too steep for switch-back turns – was to traverse virtually the entire length of one side, always gradually climbing, until eventually reaching the ridge top, then turning around and going all the way down the length of the next side. The vegetation on the hillsides was typically divided into three bands: at the very bottom, where there was enough flat land beside rivers, there would be a huddle of rice paddies; higher up was thin forest, with patches of rough fields cleared within it, fringed by banana trees and with maize or jungle rice growing; and above the limit of this 'swidden agriculture' the untouched jungle grew in a thick, dense mass of large trees strung with vines.

The houses lower down the slopes seemed to be better off, with more wooden plank houses and sheet-metal roofs. The hamlets that perched on ridge tops were basic and sometimes fairly squalid affairs, often comprising bamboo mat houses that had thatched roofs reaching right down to ground level, completely enclosing the house. And everywhere it seemed that a satellite dish was bought before a metal roof or wooden plank was invested in. Horses tethered beside the roads on these cloudy ridges would indicate that a village was one of the Hmong tribe, who excelled at animal husbandry. There was no sign of other industry or agriculture. Perhaps not surprisingly, the government was trying to encourage people to move down from the hillsides to the flatter land below, where wet rice farming was more productive and people would be closer to services.

From out of our open jeep, we saw the same pictures of rural Laos repeated over and over again. The rudimentary houses we passed were dark, but a pair of legs sticking into the light of the open doorway would reveal that someone inside was having a rest. Naked toddlers played in the mud outside, wearing just bead necklaces that looked like charms designed to ward off bad spirits. As numerous as children in the villages were black pigs, which wandered about everywhere. Scrappy chickens joined them to peck at the verges. Older children would walk in twos and threes along the roadsides, often barefoot and sometimes carrying bundles of wood.

There were usually a couple of water pipes or rivers in every village, and at every one people were washing. This was a national pastime in Laos: it happened all the time, everywhere. Beside the taps, in full view of everyone, women would wash themselves with a sarong wrapped around them, which they would exchange for a dry one when they had finished. Men usually stood beside the road in their underpants, their bodies all lathered with soap. Children didn't bother with clothes – having fun splashing under the tap was their priority.

Rather oddly, in most of the larger villages we would also see a pool hall, often just one or two old tables underneath a shelter. Right the way through Laos and into China pool tables were a fairly ubiquitous roadside feature. Otherwise, the roadside villages seemed extremely primitive. Across Laos, eighty per cent of the population were still subsistence farmers. In 2005 the GDP per capita was US $2,120 – even less than in Cambodia. When we reached Luang Nam Tha we had the opportunity to stay in remote villages like these, where the reality of their lifestyles was frankly shocking.

Eventually we arrived at Luang Prabang, which had been the capital of the kingdom since the fourteenth century and was a centre of Buddhism. According to UNESCO, which had given it World Heritage Site status, Luang Prabang was the best preserved colonial town in all of South East Asia. While this may have been true, it was not what made the town so attractive for us. In Luang Prabang we were to find a place that seemed to have achieved the Holy Grail of tourism: developing as a thriving tourist centre whilst managing to maintain its own friendly atmosphere and distinctively Laotian identity.

Chapter 48: Luang Prabang

Luang Prabang's physical location was similar to that of the English cathedral city of Durham. It was built on a neck of land bounded on three sides by water – on one side by the Mekong and the other two more by a tributary river that curved around a hill. This hill wasn't topped by a cathedral, but it had perhaps the Buddhist equivalent of a peaceful stupa. Beneath the hill was the preserved colonial town. Complete streets were composed purely of wooden French-Laotian buildings, decorated with delicate balconies and window shutters. And here they had fresh coats of paint or varnish. Along the central main road the charm of these buildings had been somewhat reduced due to their colonisation by restaurants, Internet cafés and tourist offices, producing something like a line of high street shops. Further back, an old silversmith's quarter seemed to be undergoing a complete renovation, as its houses metamorphosed into modern guest houses. So it was along the banks of the Mekong that the prettiest buildings could still be found, in a quiet residential setting, under the shade of waterside palm trees.

During the day there was very little traffic in town; barely a couple of motorbikes and just a few three-wheeled tuk-tuks parked beside the offices or hotels. Mainly the roads contained tourists wandering through, monks coming and going, or street sellers offering fruit and baguettes. The people of the town were welcoming, keeping up a fairly constant mantra of '*sabaidee*' in a cheerful and open manner. When we said hello to people they were quick to respond with a bright smile. Little girls on bikes would give a wave and a smile as they went past, just for the sake of it. As in Malaysia, people here seemed to have decided to embrace tourism warmly.

At night, the main street changed into an open air market, the road suddenly full of rows of handicraft stalls selling a relatively limited variety of touristy goods. Colourful woven cloths, monochrome patch-work quilts, ricepaper lanterns and stylised paintings were spread all down the road, similar to the street markets of Chiang Mai. The women and young girls behind the stalls were dressed up in pretty traditional costumes as a ploy to attract attention.

One night thunder began to roll around the hills and there was a sudden panic amongst the stallholders. Everyone began to pack away, scooping their goods into rolls of plastic. Then down the road they ran, literally, with bundles stuffed under their arms. Within just a few minutes the road was empty, where previously there had been a thriving market. The thrill of anticipation and excited energy was tangible. We ran too, back towards our little hostel, but before we got there the heavens opened. Lightning flashed repeatedly across the dark skies, a squally wind tugged at the tops of the palm trees and rain lashed the town. Safely in our room, we looked out at what seemed like a mini-hurricane – but it was just the normal Laotian rainy season.

Luang Prabang had long been an important religious centre, and the old town contained many Buddhist wats. These were very distinctive buildings, each notable for a slightly different style of multi-tiered curving roofs of orange tiles, gilded doors, fantastic columns and walls, and gold statues. Inside all the wats and on the streets nearby were dozens of orange-robed, yellow-sashed monks, typically youths or young boys. As such they were easy prey for tourists with cameras, which they took in good spirit, stoically putting up with the attention. Around Luang Prabang we had seen several posters that said, 'Please help us respect the alms giving ceremony.' Although we had seen early-morning alms giving in Battambang we were ignorant of what the 'ceremony' was.

Curious to see what it would be like, one morning we arose at 5.30 a.m. and walked into town through the grey morning light. Soon we passed women with baskets that contained packets of food wrapped in banana leaves and little pots of sticky rice. They tried to tempt us to buy their offerings, saying to us, 'You like monks? Sit here, monks come here. You give food to monks.'

We thought we liked monks, but we weren't Buddhists, and so we carried on. A little further we came across two ladies unrolling a mat on the pavement. They set out a line of perhaps fifteen plastic stools and placed a pot of rice in front of each one. A minibus pulled up beside the row of stools and a dozen Asian tourists hopped out. They sat on the stools and waited. Looking further down the road, we could see a group of monks in their orange and yellow robes, just standing around on a corner. They were waiting, too – our sense of anticipation grew. Several more Western tourists appeared in the road, and then more ladies, hawking more packets of food.

Then, outside the gates of a large wat some distance away, we saw a blur of orange appear. It grew steadily as its front end came towards us while the back end stayed where it was, as if the line was being stretched and stretched. As the front came closer, we could see that it was a line of monks in orange robes, walking in single file. On it came, always getting longer. Elderly monks were leading groups of young boys, each of whom had a closely shaven head and carried a metal bowl at waist height. They were all totally silent: only the pitter-patter of hundreds of bare feet padding along the pavement could be heard. The leading monks reached the group of tourists sitting on their stools, but there was still no end in sight to the unbroken orange line that stretched all the way down the road. As the monks filed slowly past, one by one, they bent slightly, allowing the alms givers to place pinches of food in their bowls.

The monks didn't pause, didn't look around, didn't say a word. It was all very rhythmical and dignified. Beyond the kneeling row of alms-givers were four or five young children, also lined up but holding out tatty plastic bags in the hope that the monks would share some of their daily meal with them. Once the monks had passed us all, they turned down a side road and were suddenly gone. We continued to be entranced by the monks who were still filing past. It took many minutes for the entire line to come and go – my estimate was that there had been between 350 and 400 monks in the line.

It had been an orderly and respectful process, unfortunately much spoiled by the behaviour of a couple of pairs of English girls who had, like us, come to watch. Around the world, time and again, we were appalled firstly by the rudeness of every single group of Israelis we met, who without exception treated everyone else with a loud, arrogant disdain; and secondly, by young English girls who could be second to none in their capacity to behave like ignorant bimbos. This morning was no exception. The only noise came from the girls' chatter. They stepped across the line of monks, pointing cameras right in their faces, even using flashbulbs in the half-light.

Their behaviour had so ruined the atmosphere for us, let alone everyone else who took a more active part in the ceremony, that we returned the next morning to see if we could have a different experience. Thankfully, on the second occasion there were only Asian tourists watching the procession and so only a cockerel crowing broke the silence as the monks passed down the road. We saw more local people sitting outside the doors of their houses this time, waiting for smaller groups of monks to come past in search of alms. The sight of hundreds of orange-robed monks forming their single file procession was one of the most striking images we saw anywhere around the world. It was just a little spoiled by learning that some monks had been unhappy at the quality of the cheap food they were being given by tourists, but town authorities had told them to continue with their 'ceremony' or risk being replaced by actors, in order to continue the tourist attraction.

In order to see more Laotian scenery, we decided to travel by boat from Luang Prabang to Nong Kiaw, which was reputed to be a superb journey. The eight-hour trip gave us a different viewpoint, but the sights didn't compare to the landscape around Vang Vieng or the river life in Cambodia. Mostly, all we looked at were forested hillsides at varying distances from the river, usually scarred with patches of brown earth and charred tree stumps that marked fields of jungle rice. The river wasn't being intensively used. Women and children could occasionally be seen close to the banks, bathing in the water. A couple of herds of buffalo were also cooling off, lolling half-submerged like hippos with horns. We passed a few fishermen, often standing thigh-deep in the river and throwing their nets into pools or holding a spear and waiting to jab a fish, like human herons. Plastic bottles bobbing in a line on the water looked like floating rubbish, but they were actually buoyant markers for a fishing net that stretched beneath the water. Children were often playing too, diving off rocks and, unexpectedly, swimming with plastic snorkelling masks. The odd wooden canoe passed us, paddled by naked boys who looked as if they had emerged from the depths of the Amazon rainforest. Usually, however, there was little to see but rocks, water and bright green stands of bamboo, which sprouted like giant ferns, their long, thin fronds easily reaching 15 m in height, at least to the tops of the surrounding trees.

All day only two bridges crossed our river. The second of these was at Nong Kiaw. It was an impressive bridge, spanning a chasm between hills on either side of the river gorge. The scenery here was at last dramatic, particularly in the late afternoon when white clouds rolled over the green hilltops and a stark rainbow curved across the sky. Nong Kiaw had been built on both sides of the river, linked by the bridge. There wasn't much to see in the small village, especially as it was raining and muddy when we arrived. The collections of shack-like buildings made Nong Kiaw look like a very rudimentary affair – small, basic and remote. However, it had become something of a staging post on the tourist circuit; therefore, tucked into the banks of the rivers was a selection of tourist resorts, each with several cottages and a restaurant. They even had televisions, but the staff were using these to watch pop music rather than the World Cup football that we were interested in.

We ate our dinner and watched the river go by as the sun set, turning the sky a rich wash of purple. The menus were more ambitious than the resources of the kitchens, so we resorted to our staple of rice and vegetables, or rice and curry. In Laos a meal like this would typically set us back between one and two US dollars. Our little house on the riverbank, complete with clouds of pretty butterflies in flower beds outside our door and loud geckos that called in our ears at night, cost a bargain US $2 for the night. We used to judge the relative cost of different locations by the prices of the large bottles of Beerlaos, which was always a good complement to our meals. These bottles varied in price from 80 cents to US $1; not an insignificant difference in Laos! Beerlaos was very much part of Laotian culture and was generally reckoned to be the best beer in SE Asia. Production had begun in the early 1970s with the help of a French investor, but was now owned jointly by the government and Carlsberg Asia, who claimed to have a 99 per cent share of the market in Laos. We heard that it was the country's most successful foreign aid project!

Various other foreign tourists had found their way to Nong Kiaw. A French couple were waiting for a boat to take them to Luang Prabang, but for a couple of days they had been the only people wanting to make that journey. A pair from Canada was about to head east, intending to cross into North Vietnam. Like us, they were very unsure if the border would be open. They had tried phoning various embassies in Laos, some of whom had never heard of Nong Kiaw. None knew about the state of the border, including the Vietnamese Embassy. It was a little bewildering to be in a country where reliable information, even from supposed authorities, was scarce. But the couple set off anyway. In the little bus park – really just a small, muddy square – we enquired about transport to Luang Nam Tha from the small wooden booth that claimed to be the ticket office. We were told to be there at 9 a.m., but when we turned up the next morning, the standard response to any enquiry was that anything was possible and everything left at 11 a.m., even if the time was by then 11.30 a.m.

Several blue vans and an assorted collection of foreign and local travellers were waiting with us. It transpired that the van drivers were waiting to see if there were enough customers to make it worth their while to run a service. Any hopeful passengers – like us – had to wait for their decision. Meanwhile, we haggled with the guy in the office over the price of the journey, which fluctuated with the number of people on board. Laotian transport was the most disorganised that we encountered anywhere. It made me reflect on the relevance of the typical shared phrase when parting company: 'Good luck to you!'

In a country where systems were neither organised nor reliable, concepts of fairness and justice lost some of their significance. Life became a more variable product, dependent on one's own ingenuity and the hand dealt by fate – and luck did indeed play a large part in how our days turned out. As it was, we did finally leave Nong Kiaw, but it would take us two days to reach Luang Nam Tha, a distance that would have only taken a few hours in Europe.

Chapter 49: Luang Nam Tha

Luang Nam Tha had the feel of a frontier town, perhaps because it was very close to the border with China. As well as catering to Chinese businessmen, Luang Nam Tha was a central marketplace for no less than fifty surrounding villages, and therefore also had become a base for tourists looking to venture out on treks to the villages. There are thirty-nine ethnic minorities in Luang Nam Tha province, the highest of anywhere in Laos, and twenty-three of these tribes live in the vicinity of the town itself. The large market itself was tucked away at one end of town, where it was busy in the mornings with women coming to buy and sell their produce. They laid out their wares on rows of wooden tables in a giant hall, creating the overall impression of an enormous harvest festival.

Down the road was a succession of hotels that catered to Chinese traders, new and grand but decidedly unsavoury. Along the main road to the border were a handful of tourist guesthouses and restaurants. All the indications were that Luang Nam Tha was developing at a rapid pace as people cashed in on the opportunities provided by the tourist industry. Meanwhile, surrounding farmers in their traditional villages carried on life much as ever, resulting in a fairly diverse range of cultures and lifestyles. Two ladies from one of the nearby minority tribes spent all day every day walking up and down the main street, hawking bead necklaces and cloth bags. Vans and tractor engines drove through town, alongside a handful of motorbikes and bicycles, but really there wasn't much going on. It was a quiet and friendly place.

As in South America, we were getting tired again from the continuous travelling that we were doing. Luang Nam Tha was a good place for us to stop for a few days and rest a little. For US $1.50 per day, we hired decent mountain bikes that had been imported from Thailand and used them to go exploring. Just out of town a road passed through one of the most picturesque scenes of our world trip. On either side was a wide, flat expanse of rice paddies, rimmed in the distance by soft blue hills. It reminded me of the wide vistas across the Bolivian altiplano near La Paz. Scattered across the green, brown and silvery fields were small square huts on stilts and tiny black silhouettes of men and women bent double, working to plant out their rice seedlings. The colours were bright and intense under an early morning sun. We loved cycling along the road, in the midst of such beauty. Everyone we passed would turn to look at us, with '*sabaidee*' constantly ringing back and forth. 'Where are you going?'

some would call out in English, and then, 'Good luck to you!'

It was a busy time for the farmers; whole families would join in the work for an intense few days at this time of year, and then again at harvest time. The thin green rice seedlings had been growing in nursery beds, where they formed a thick carpet. Now the seedlings had to be pulled out one by one, gathered into little bundles, and carried to other fields where they were planted out again in neat rows, all spread out. We could see all stages happening at once; people were even still ploughing muddy fields in preparation for the seedlings to arrive, which they did on wooden carts that were pushed by hand down the road. It was all labour-intensive and back-breaking work. Where the planting had been finished, we could see people lying in the little huts, as if waiting for the rice to grow beneath them. The more we travelled in this corner of the world, the more I marvelled that every single rice plant had been planted, thinned and then harvested by hand, individually, a single stalk at a time. Especially considering that Asia produces 90 per cent of the world's rice, which feeds 40 per cent of the world's population.

Turning off the road along dirt tracks, we cycled through various 'minority villages' that each consisted of four or five large wooden houses on stilts. Their balconies were bedecked with all sorts of clutter: wicker baskets, metal pots, clothes lines, maize heads, even the ball-like nests of weaver birds. We saw clusters of these graceful nests hanging in trees beside the roads, balls of stick and straw dangling at the end of long woven funnels – each one a masterpiece of construction. Walking along one track were three ladies from the Akha tribe, who are ethnically related to Tibetans. These ladies were a sight to behold. They carried wicker baskets on their backs, suspended from a broad, flat wooden yoke that was fitted on their shoulders around their neck. Black-and-white headbands studded with silver coins had fresh leaves stuck into them as a form of decoration. They carried cloth bags slung around their bodies, presumably full of green foodstuffs. Most striking of all, however, were their horrible mouths. These were foul, pitch-black and dribbling with revolting red saliva. The ladies had been chewing betel nuts, which turn teeth black. This was, incredibly, considered to be a sign of beauty!

Here in northern Laos the ethnic minority groups were as distinctive as those of Guatemala. Indeed, the colourful handicrafts of Luang Prabang and some of their indigenous clothing had reminded us strongly of Central America. But there was a difference in the atmosphere between the two places, perhaps due to the size and nature of their tourist industries. Here people were outgoing in their warmth and friendliness, making us feel really welcomed. Locals ran the tourist services and we seemed closer to the everyday life that was going on in towns and villages. The brief encounters we were able to have with people were delightful; we really enjoyed these interactions. Travelling through Laos had been a very different experience to Thailand or Vietnam for us. It didn't have world-class beaches or luxuriant palaces, modern cities or well-developed infrastructures. But in its own rustic way, at its own slow pace, it provided a more down-to-earth and wholesome experience.

Laos had seen its neighbour, Thailand, develop a booming tourist industry that brought in vast amounts of wealth to the country. But it also had an opportunity to learn from some of the mistakes that Thailand had made in not controlling the industry before it had damaged – in places – both its environment and its people. Just as Chiang Mai in northern Thailand was a centre for trekking to visit hill tribes, so Luang Nam Tha was building up its own trekking industry. The first treks began in 2000, started by an American with funding and consultancy help from New Zealand. With the benefit of a later start, this and the three other centres in Laos were established specifically as 'ecotourism' operations.

It took a full year to get the treks off the ground, because at first the local villagers simply weren't interested in receiving visitors or learning about sustainable lifestyles. Repeated visits explained to them the potential of tourism and provided some education. They were taught to speak Lao, trained to be guides and told about principles of conservation for forest wildlife – such as gibbons – instead of merely hunting them to extinction. Villagers were even taken on rides around the local area simply to see more developed areas and the possibility of progress that money from tourism could bring. When we saw the isolated remoteness of the villages for ourselves, we began to understand the necessity of this process. Now the not-for-profit government-supported organisation has 500 trekkers per year on several routes through the local area and nearby Nam Ha National Biodiversity Conservation Area, which is home to rare tigers, leopards and elephants. Indeed, according to UNESCO, it was 'thought to be botanically unique and diverse, although no thorough surveys have been conducted'.

We booked a two-day trek just before two girls we met in town told us that they had recently given up on the same trek after a couple of hours due to the difficulty of the path and the plagues of leeches. It was too late for us to have second thoughts, but we began to wonder what we would find. On the drive to the Khmu village where the trek started, we passed through a narrow valley, which provided a characteristic scene of Laotian rural life. Its hillsides were littered with blackened tree stumps, between which bright green shoots of jungle rice were growing. On flat land in the valley bottom there were several wet and muddy rice paddies. In the only green field, a row of fourteen women were squatting in a line, pulling the rice seedlings out. In an adjacent field two men struggled to plough the wet mud, slipping behind a straining buffalo. At the edge of the fields were a couple of wooden houses on stilts, with clothes strewn outside, a blackened cooking pot beside the door and a fire alight on the floor inside.

Our guide, who was a local farmer who had been trained by the eco-tourism operation, and his apprentice from one of the minority villages we would be visiting, led us up a narrow, muddy path that ran alongside the Khmu village. We could tell when the village stopped because we passed under a simple wooden archway. Immediately afterwards, to the right of the path, was a small bamboo arch, about five feet high. It was decorated with fresh leaves and had built been very recently. It was a spirit gate, put there to appease the spirits. Our guide told us that it had been built because two people had been hit by lightning during recent storms. Only 22 per cent of the people of the Luang Nam Tha province were Buddhist; the rest still practised a mixture of spirit and ancestor worship. This little spirit gate on the edge of the forest was a glimpse of that world.

We climbed up a hillside to its ridge top and then down the other side to a river that had a string of minority villages along its length. The route took us through bamboo thickets and into old forest dominated by giant mango trees, which had vast branchless trunks that seemed to climb upwards forever. There were a few leeches, but more pretty butterflies, flies, beetles that hummed past us, and large ants foraging for food. Once we nearly stepped onto a bright orange crab, which surprised us. Apparently they live in the forest too.

By late afternoon we had reached the river. We were walking to the most remote pair of villages, the first of which belonged to the Khmu tribe. We realised that we were approaching it when we passed a wooden platform that had been erected inside a small fenced area. This was a kind of altar, where animal offerings were made before planting rice or harvesting it. Khmu animals are used for sacrifices as often as for food. The people often survive on rice and other crops at a subsistence level and actual money can be scarce in their villages. We passed underneath another archway and were in the village. As part of the ecotourism arrangement, we stayed in a purpose-built lodge that had been built beside the river at the edge of the village. The local women took it in turns to cook for any trekkers in an adjacent cooking hut, ensuring that the income from trekking was evenly distributed throughout the households.

The village was sited on a gently sloping river bank. There were thirty-eight houses clustered together, all on stilts. Mostly the houses had bamboo mat walls and thatched roofs, much like those we had seen in northern Thailand, although a few used wooden boards or metal sheets. Under one house three old ladies sat together on a bench, contemplatively smoking pipes. Beside others, ladies pounded rice with giant wooden pestle and mortars, energetic work that required them to strip to their bras. There didn't seem to be any pattern to the layout of the village and there weren't specific pathways between the houses. In the middle of the village was a single open area, where later on older youths started an athletic game of foot-volleyball, the boys playing while the girls stood and watched. The ground underneath and between the houses was all bare earth – or rather, mud. In this mud, barefoot children squatted to play a version of marbles.

Scattered in the mud throughout the village were scraps of litter. Animal waste was pretty much everywhere, courtesy of the numerous black pigs, chickens and dogs that roamed anywhere at will. Once I counted how many pigs I could see from a single point. It was thirty-eight – and there were just as many chickens in sight. Underneath some houses there were feeding troughs for the animals, but we also saw food scraps being thrown from out of the doors of houses onto the mud below for the animals to clean up. Everything seemed to be mired in filth and, as in Cambodia, we wondered if this was what it might have been like in Europe in the Middle Ages. Later in the evening a herd of cows came through the middle of the village, followed by several buffalo that walked right past our lodge to have a bath in the river.

One thing we didn't see in the village, except one behind our tourist hut, were toilets. We asked our guide about this and he told us that there were none. This partly explained the poster on the schoolhouse that used cartoon pictures to teach children that if they went to the toilet in the vegetable patch and then didn't wash their hands and the food before they ate it, they might get worms. A teacher walked over the ridge a few times a week to give basic literacy lessons.

As daylight faded, people retreated to their houses and sat just inside their doorways. One boy lifted his baby brother up their ladder, pausing at the top to shoo a couple of chickens out of the house. White smoke drifted out from the roofs, literally, as cooking started. It was also washing time at the several water taps in the village, some of which drained onto the bare mud and flowed between the houses. Most water taps had simple bamboo stake fences around them, but there was no privacy. We had taken due note of the 'Sensible Trekking Guidelines' that advised staying decently covered up, making for pretty ineffectual attempts at washing ourselves under a running tap. Common sense prevailed for the villagers: women only kept on a sarong around their waist, while washing and the old ladies of the village walked to and from the taps topless, although still smoking their pipes. Men stripped to their underpants to wash and children discarded all of their clothes.

The water taps also provided drinking water for the villagers, which came straight from the hillsides. Boiling the water was not common. We asked about food and were told that every meal – even breakfast – every day, was rice. It was usually accompanied by a vegetable soup or chilli sauce, which was cooked once and then eaten over several consecutive meals. Fish soup was quite common, but it was rare to eat meat. We did, however, once meet a young girl walking into the village from the river, who was carrying something precious in each hand. We had a closer look and saw a pair of grotesquely bloated frogs, destined for the dinner pot.

The impression we had was of a very self-contained village, isolated, changing very little, and content to be that way. The young people however apparently did now prefer to get an education in Luang Nam Tha, although the adults still farm their crops of rice from fields beside the river and forage in the forest for bark and plants to sell at the market. The standard of living was very low, shockingly so to us. It came as a further surprise to learn that adjacent villages along the river were peopled by different tribes, who had different customs and even different languages. Neighbouring villages hadn't even been able to communicate with each other six years ago when the trekking operation started. The Khmu villagers couldn't speak Lao then either. They had been literally cut off from the outside world – and the next village we saw was even more remote.

We continued walking the following day until we reached the last settlement that had been built along the riverside. This was home to people from one of the Lanten tribes that originated from China. Outside the village in a rice paddy we saw a woman leading a buffalo across a ploughed field and then three girls carrying baskets full of maize on their backs. They were all dressed in traditional Lanten clothing. This consisted of simple black long-sleeved gowns that were decorated around the edges with pink and blue bands. Sometimes black trousers were worn underneath these gowns. A length of brown string or a pink sash was tied around the waist. Some women wore another string cord above their knees and I wondered at their purpose, thinking that they might have had some kind of spiritual significance, but they turned out to be a practical way of keeping trousers up out of the mud. The women also wore large, solid silver hoop necklaces. Their black hair was always done up into buns on the tops of their heads and they had no eyebrows, having completely shaved them off.

The houses of the Lanten tribe were of a different style from the Khmu dwellings. Instead of being on stilts, the Lanten houses were set on the ground, even sunk a little into the earth. Inside, a single room had a raised bamboo platform along one side which formed a sleeping area. The other side was just bare earth with a stone fireplace in one corner. That was all there was. Around the outside of houses were bamboo fences and more grassy paths, but otherwise the village was much the same picture of pigs and chickens as the previous Khmu village. A pair of naked toddlers were playing at harvesting by carrying small wicker baskets and filling them with leaves or an empty glass bottle that they picked up from the path. People in the Lanten village were friendly, greeting us with smiles. A group of women came forward to welcome us, proffering trays full of small handmade cloth bags that were coloured in exactly the same way as their clothing. Handmade cloth bags – and cans of Coke!

After lunch we hiked back over the ridge, away from the river. As we entered a patch of bamboo forest, where huge stands of old bamboo splayed sideways to form a dense archway over our heads, we came across the leeches. We could see them wriggling on the leaf litter underfoot, waving their outstretched heads in the air at us. At times at least three were visible within the length of each single stride. Whenever we stopped they raced towards us from all directions, like a miniature army closing in with almost comical bravado. Each of us was surrounded by six or seven tiny brown worm-like bodies, never more than 5 cm long. To ward the leeches off, we mixed soap powder with a little water into a paste and spread that on our shoes, which kept them at bay effectively enough.

Soon we left the bamboo and the leeches behind, as we climbed up through lush, mature forest that had towering trees of 400 to 500 years old. It was fun to walk under the thin creepers and beside mossy stones, at times having to follow a tumbling stream bed. We found it hard to believe, though, that this slippery little trail was the main route for the Lanten villagers to the road, until sure enough we met a little group at the top about to descend, wearing only flip-flops on their feet. Apparently villagers undertook a few trips into town per week, mainly going to and from the market. It had taken us two hours of climbing to reach the top and it would be another hour of descent until we reached the nearest road, where we then had to wait for a lift into town.

And so ended our little trek, and our time in Laos. We were already looking forward to China, having talked to enthusiastic travellers in Luang Nam Tha who had just come from there. They told us that it was far more developed than Laos; a place where transport ran on time, for example. We even heard that in the tourist centres we wouldn't have any problem with not speaking Mandarin or, later, Cantonese. We were beginning to build up the impression that we would find travelling in China manageable, after all. This seemed a far cry from the challenges we had imagined when we first considered going there a year before.

Nothing at all prepared us for the country we would find, however. It stamped its presence on us even before we reached the border, where the Laotian roads gave way to a wide, perfectly smooth tarmac Chinese-built highway. As we left Laos, we were given a final reminder of the state of its development when the border officials copied passport details out by hand into a huge book, wordlessly accepting the 10 kip 'fee' that everyone was giving them to be allowed through. One kilometre further on was the Chinese border control, where at first I thought that we had driven into Disneyland…

Part Seven
China

Chapter 50: Jinghong

In the middle of the new tarmac road was a flower bed, fenced in by small red and white curved metal railings. Wide pink tiled pavements were completely clear of any obstructions. A row of neat trees provided greenery and shade. Behind those were immaculately maintained two-storey houses, newly painted in clashing colours of orange, blue and yellow. A modernist sculpture spun gaudy red, blue and white plastic balls around a metal pole. Down side alleys were pool tables, being played by young men wearing white gloves. Everything was manicured, too perfect, slightly surreal, like a fictional world. Such was our first sight of China. The fairy-tale facade didn't last too long.

In the immigration office – which not only had a proper waiting room but also a chilled water dispenser that worked – Claudia had to convince the blue-uniformed officer firstly that Austria actually existed, then that her passport was genuine, and finally that her visa was correct, despite the final digit of her passport number having been omitted on the visa. Once that was done, we stepped into the road to be met by a money-changer, brandishing a ream of notes. These people always posed a dilemma for us: they provided a useful, sometimes vital, service, yet we always knew that somehow they succeeded in ripping us off – it seemed an unwritten rule of border crossings. Having been caught out by the exchange rate when entering Laos, here we were clear about what we should expect. We duly haggled and insisted and finally settled on a rate we were content with. The lady handed over her yuan and we handed over our dollars. We both counted – and there was a telltale pause during which the lady waited for us to confirm all was well. We thought so, until some while later when we entered a shop and tried to use one of our 5 yuan notes – it was a 5 fēn note, a hundredth of the value!

With money in our pockets, we set off into rural Yunnan province towards Jinghong. Yunnan is the most ethnically diverse province in China, with twenty-five different ethnic groups. It is also one of the poorest. In 2004 each person in Yunnan earned on average just US $650. Our small, windy road followed a river valley that was broadly similar to the agricultural landscapes we had come from in Laos, but had slightly different details. Gone were the houses on stilts made of bamboo mats, now replaced by solid wooden or mud brick walled houses that sat firmly on the ground, covered with distinctive dark grey roof tiles. The rice paddies were nearly all planted out, being finished off by teams of workers who worked across the fields in regimented lines, now wearing straw bowler hats instead of conical ones. In the hillside forest there were no clearings for rice; just forest and, where cultivation was possible, terraces that were full of a wide variety of plants. We saw tea bushes, rubber trees, fruit orchards, and tobacco, which was one of Yunnan's main industries. This was one of the remoter corners of China, but that, along with everything else in the country, was changing rapidly.

The wide new road that we had entered China on was part of a highway that was being built through southern Yunnan, aiming eventually to connect China with Laos and Thailand. More new roads were being built in Yunnan than in any other province; there were plans to connect every main town by a highway by 2010. For at least five hours of driving along the old country road, we would see different sections of the highway being built alongside us, all at virtually the same stage of construction along its entire length, courtesy of teams of workers camping in plastic tents by the sides of the road. The new highway seemed to make no concession to anything, least of all the landscape.

While our old road had followed the natural course of rivers and valley sides, winding in and out and up and down, the new highway had been designed to take the most direct route that could possibly be engineered. Raised embankments ran for hundreds of metres in perfectly straight lines across what used to be fields; hundreds of enormous great bridges looked like identikit viaducts, their legs always made out of the same uniform grey concrete. Wherever a hill threatened to force the highway to bend, it was simply cut through. One incredible section of the highway had to traverse a tight series of sharp river bends that had eroded deep into the rock. The highway simply bridged the channels and sliced straight through the necks of land in between. Seeing this highway absolutely dominating the landscape brought to mind imperial Roman constructions in Europe. Perhaps Roman roads and bridges had created a similar sense of wonder 2,000 years ago.

We often came across road-building projects in Yunnan, and it seemed indicative of the country as a whole that this incredible drive for development was frequently being completed by primitive manual labour. Men and women would move mounds of soil and rubble by hand, using picks and shovels for digging and wicker baskets for carrying. Horses and carts would still clip-clop their way through traffic, hauling rubble or bricks. A twenty-first-century transport system was being built with first-century labour.

The passengers on our bus made us wonder too, for an altogether different reason. The driver kept up almost continual conversations with various people, who were only too pleased to break into animated discussions. We hadn't heard such raised voices for months. To our ears, the loud exchanges sounded like heated arguments, but that wasn't the case at all; this volume was normal for China. It made us realise how calm and peaceful conversations had been since arriving in South East Asia, and told us that the Chinese culture was different.

The men – only the men – chain-smoked throughout the journey, offering each other cigarettes in a most companionable manner. They were surprised when I declined, but didn't even consider Claudia. The women may not have been included in this activity, but they could hold their own in another Chinese habit that we never did get used to: spitting. Not just any kind of spitting. If there were world championships for the most prolonged, loud, disgusting spitting possible, the Chinese would win hands down. It would merely be a competition amongst themselves, for they were surely in a different league to anyone else. The protracted, throaty noise of gathering phlegm had to be heard to be believed. And the resulting great puddles of saliva would end up anywhere that was convenient for the spitter. Usually this was out of a window or door, but if that wasn't possible, as on buses and trains, then often the floor would do. During the 2003 SARS outbreak, the government had tried to curb the practice of spitting with fines, and in Beijing there were increased efforts in the run-up to the 2008 Olympics, but here in the backwater of Yunnan province there was nothing holding the Chinese back.

The public toilets took a fair bit of getting used to, too, especially for Claudia. These consisted of a room with an exposed trench running along the back of it. That was all, literally, at times. One person's waste flowed from one end of the trench to the other, right beneath anyone else who happened to be squatting over it at the time. Sometimes low walls partially divided the trench into cubicle-sized lengths, but as there were no doors and the walls were barely three feet high, they didn't really provide much privacy. These were very definitely communal toilets. And they were often pretty filthy affairs, as smelly and dirty as might be imagined.

Jinghong turned out to be a busy town built on the banks of – yet again – the Mekong River. We were dropped off at the side of a wide road that had four lanes of traffic and a cycle path along each side. We hadn't seen anything this metropolitan for a while. Directly opposite was a bright red shopping mall fringed by palm trees, which for some reason surprised me. We were stumped as to where we were, let alone which direction to walk to find a place to sleep, but it wasn't long before a man stopped and offered to give us directions, despite his having no English at all. In fact, for the first time since Brazil we were in a place where the only possibility for communication was to use the local language, in this case Mandarin, or resort to hand gestures, scribbled pictures and written numbers. Just as elsewhere in South East Asia, our attempts at speaking were hampered by our lack of pronunciation – or, more correctly, intonation – skills, for Mandarin was also a tonal language.

We initially had fun in restaurants copying out the script for various dishes from their menus. Some characters have twenty-three separate strokes within them, making reading them difficult and writing them an art form. In fact, reproducing the characters was a surprisingly therapeutic pastime. Not that we really made use of all our efforts, for rather than ordering from menus it was far more common to describe the ingredients that we wanted to eat – or, in our case, point to them – and then wait for the cook to produce the standardised dishes. We didn't know this at the beginning, of course: it was quite a novel experience on our first evening to be led into the kitchen and face an array of vegetables, with several cooks all waiting expectantly for their instructions. In the end, ordering drinks proved more challenging to us that evening. We tried asking for a beer and were given a glass of water; we pointed to a bottle on an adjacent table and were given tea instead. So we drew a bottle of beer on paper and that achieved the desired result. It wasn't quite as good as Beerlaos, though.

Jinghong reminded us of a Chilean town, partly because of its level of affluence and perhaps also because arriving from Laos into China was a similar experience to entering Chile from Bolivia. Many of the buildings in Jinghong were four- or five-storey apartment blocks, painted white and with lots of blue tinted glass windows. Everywhere a screen of palm trees tastefully lined the pavements. Much of the town had a manicured feel about it, with polished statues and neatly trimmed bushes. There were litter bins everywhere and an army of cleaners with brushes and handcarts was in constant operation, which was just as well as shopkeepers tended to throw their rubbish out into the streets. People from surrounding villages came into town each day to make a living by peddling cycle-rickshaws, or pulling wooden carts, or hawking baskets of fruit on the pavements, or by shining shoes. In the centre of town one morning we sat in an open air café and treated ourselves to a Vienna coffee, which came in a china cup and saucer. It was all very civilised. A Carlsberg sign protruded from above the door of the café; a poster of David Beckham filled up one window; next door was an Adidas sports shop; music from the Bangles was coming out of a nearby doorway. So this was what China was like!

In the evenings, the public squares filled up with people who were socialising or taking part in recreational activities. Mothers and children jumped on bouncy castles in one corner; old men played a version of croquet in another; individuals stood in their own spaces performing t'ai chi routines; and several large groups of adults were taking part in mass open air folk dancing. Their sliding steps with raised hand-claps made them look as if they were practising some form of slow-motion synchronised aerobics. By 10 p.m. the square was empty again, although the streets were still busy and all the shops were still open. This was a time for relaxing in the cool air after the sweaty heat of the day; elderly ladies were playing badminton on the pavements outside their homes.

We quickly noticed that despite a high proportion of young mothers on the streets who were pushing their baby or toddler around in a buggy, virtually none had more than one child. It was strange to see in reality the effects of the widely known policy of Deng Xiaoping to supervise the number of births in China, often imposing fiscal penalties on families who had more than one child. This policy, combined with the natural effects of economic growth, had reduced China's fertility rate from 5.9 in 1970 to under two in 2005. Nevertheless, the population was still estimated to be just over 1.3 billion people in 2006, and it was still growing by 12 to 13 million people each year. A staggering one out of every five people in the world live in China.

One young man we talked to in southern China opened our eyes to some of the side effects of one-child families. A generation would grow up who had no brothers and sisters, and so their offspring would have no aunts, uncles or cousins. This seemed rather sad. Furthermore, the single child could be faced with having to care for two parents and four grandparents. When we spoke to people about families, there was a common agreement that single children were being spoilt by their parents; we certainly often observed that children were well provided for and frequently fussed over.

Jinghong was a relatively small provincial town, a pleasant mix of urban and rural influences. Our next stop would be quite different. This was the capital of Yunnan, Kunming, which was booming as the Chinese government was developing it into a regional centre – regional in the international sense, that is, as befitting Chinese ambitions. We took a sleeper bus there from Jinghong. We had heard about these buses from travellers in Laos, but we weren't really sure what to expect. They turned out to be an example of Chinese inventiveness and practicality. From the outside they looked just like an ordinary coach, but inside there were no seats. Instead, the buses were filled with three rows of thin, small metal double-decker bunk beds, each with their own thin mattress, pillow and blanket. Everyone took their shoes off inside the bus, depositing them into handy orange plastic bags, and then almost immediately went to sleep – but not without the usual competition for the longest, loudest hoicking spit, of course, out of the door or windows, into a bag, or onto the floor. We left Jinghong punctually and every three hours stopped at a roadside service area for a break, in case anyone should want to stretch their legs or brave the toilets. It was all most efficient.

We arrived into Kunming bus station and were immediately lost between rows of hundreds of parked buses. The city was big, too, with nearly 4 million inhabitants. It was the fourteenth most prosperous city in China and a significant step upwards from Jinghong. Busy, developed and commercial, there were many large banks, hotels and up-market shops. Immaculately marked multi-lane roads streaming with modern cars passed beneath glossy high-rise office buildings. Gone were all but a few motorbikes and bicycles, despite the wide cycle lanes. Everyone wore proper shoes or trainers instead of flip-flops. Everyone had a mobile phone, too.

We were surprised to learn how texting works, having seen that the phone screens were displaying Mandarin characters. These characters were created by spelling out the pinyin version of the word. 'Pinyin' is a phonetic writing system, based on Mandarin words but using roman characters. Its use was being encouraged by the government, who even told shops that they had to write their names in both Mandarin and pinyin. The most – and from what we could tell, the only – common usage of pinyin, however, was for texting.

For the first time since Bangkok we needed to take a taxi to get across town to a hotel, where a room and breakfast cost us an extortionate 100 yuan (US $13). Our room had the advantage of a television, so we watched England go out to Portugal on penalties in the World Cup at 3 a.m.

We had fun looking around Kunming, trying unsuccessfully to find either a bank to change our left-over Laotian kip or a new digital camera. The city was as easy to get around as any modern, efficient urban centre in Europe. Multiple pedestrian bridges spanned its wide crossroads, with spidery arrays of steps descending to every pavement. When it rained, as it often did – it was still rainy season, of course – the pavements were instantaneously transformed into a multicoloured display of umbrellas and plastic capes, commonly a combination of shocking pink and bright yellow. It made for quite a dramatic picture at traffic lights and pedestrian crossings. People quite often turned around to watch us as we walked around; here, it seemed, we were a curiosity to the Chinese, who were all quite friendly.

Kunming was a kind of crossroads for us. To the east lay Hong Kong, where we had a flight booked to Beijing. To the north-west were several tourist destinations that we wanted to visit, particularly the Tiger Leaping Gorge. We hadn't been sure of our plans – no change there either – but we had found that travel in China was far more straightforward than we had imagined it might be. Therefore we decided to head for the gorge, via the historical towns of Dali and Lijiang, which were famous within China for having escaped the destruction that had come with Mao's Cultural Revolution. And so we set off on the Chinese tourist trail.

Chapter 51: Dali

To leave Kunming, we booked a ride in the hotel minibus to the bus station. It turned out to be full; there were three more passengers than seats. It says something about China that rather than squash the remainder in somehow, as would have been done everywhere else since Malaysia, an additional taxi was provided. Once outside the city, the traffic suddenly vanished and we re-entered rural China, a different world from the urban centres. We were driving along yet another newly built highway, but virtually nothing else was using it. In the green paddy fields and hillside terraces, workers in the fields hoed their crops and cleared ditches. Women in traditional clothing walked along muddy paths with loads on their backs; a donkey pulled a cart up a hill; small herds of buffalo threatened to cause a traffic accident. Every so often small villages contoured around the hillsides, mostly made from orange-brown mud bricks. The barn-like buildings were often arranged so that they formed three sides of a square, with a wall completing an enclosure around a central yard. These traditional compounds were a far cry from the offices of Kunming not many miles away.

I was quite surprised to see a white-domed mosque from the road; this wasn't a place I had associated with Islam. Actually, Yunnan has a Muslim population of about half a million. Their origins go back to the grandson of Genghis Khan, called Kublai Khan, who had been governor of the southern territories of the Mongol Empire in the thirteenth century. He became emperor in 1271, established Beijing as his capital, and then set about expanding his territory, which did not yet cover all of China – Genghis Khan's empire had 'only' reached from the Sea of Japan to the Caspian Sea in a long but relatively thin east-west swathe of land. Kublai Khan managed to bring all of China under the Mongol Empire by destroying the remnants of the Chinese Song Dynasty, overrunning Yunnan in the process and destroying the historical city of Dali. He sent a Muslim governor to Yunnan province, who established twelve mosques in Kunming. There are now over 700 mosques in Yunnan.

Through a range of hills we came to the old city of Dali, sitting a little way back from a large lake. It quickly became the most pleasant town in China that we found, with a mix of ancient charms and modern conveniences. Although Dali was an ancient capital city, dating back to the eighth century AD, the present city had been built from the late seventeenth century. It was a small place, surrounded by an 8 m-high stone wall that had several large and ornamental gateways around its 3.5 km length. Between the one or two main arteries crossing the old city there was a network of narrow lanes squeezed between the stone walls of more square domestic compounds. The walls were often unplastered and fitted with misshapen wooden doors and windows.

Larger central buildings had wooden second storeys, supported by red columns and often decorated with hanging red paper balloons. From a distance, the grey tiled roofs of these higher buildings were a picture of grace and symmetry, the edges of their tiered layers all gently curving upwards into ridges and pinched corners, making many of them look more like temples than houses. Modern buildings that retained the original style of architecture were exquisite, with beautifully carved wooden panels between pillars draped in cloths painted with Chinese characters. Some walls were even more attractive, having been whitewashed and painted with black patterns around their edges, some of which framed larger black line paintings of willow trees, rivers, bridges and mountains: classic Chinese artwork, all produced with a beautiful economy of brush-strokes.

It was all very pretty – and irresistible for the hundreds, even thousands, of Chinese tourists that flocked to the main streets. My preconceptions of the Chinese didn't include imagining them as tourists, but they travelled in their millions to see the sights of their own country. China was proving itself to be a country of surprises. In 2002 there were 780 million domestic tourists in China. In addition to these, 120 million tourists from overseas travelled into China in 2005. It was estimated by the World Tourism Organisation that by 2020 China will be the world's premier tourist destination, and furthermore that Chinese tourists will be the fourth most numerous by nationality in the world.

Dali was a major attraction for the Chinese, all wearing jeans and T-shirts, smart trousers and shirts, or elegant flowery dresses, and all carrying sunglasses, umbrellas and cameras. These tourists were being shepherded past the souvenir shops, batik stalls, tourist offices and banks of Dali by young girls who wore traditional costumes and spoke into hands-free mobile phone headsets. All the women and girls involved in the tourist industry made a point of wearing traditional costumes: that was part of the appeal of Dali. The main feature of their dress was a colourful tight waistcoat of bright blue, green, pink or yellow. This was worn over a white blouse and accompanied by black trousers and a small black apron, which was tied in front with a bright sash around the waist. Perched on the top of their heads were large white and coloured headbands, looking something like a cross between a tiara and an elaborate feathered headdress. The overall effect of these clothes was a combination of petite stylishness and comely practicality. Young ladies tended to the former, of course, while the older women exhibited more of the latter.

We did see a couple of people in even more elaborate costumes, based on the same waistcoat, trousers and apron design, but in red and green material that had been very heavily embroidered. This was the most colourful, elaborate costume that we had seen being worn since Lake Atitlan in Guatemala. As for the men, only a handful wore any sort of a costume. These few were ageing men, walking in pairs or standing around in a group reading papers. They had on distinctive thick cotton jackets of a faded blue colour, with large black buttons up the front. Nearly all also wore dark blue or black trousers, plain black leather shoes, and blue cloth caps. They were the archetypal image of the Communist era, dressed in the Maoist uniform that had been compulsory throughout China under Chairman Mao. Today, however, it was European-style shirts and nondescript trousers that were ubiquitous.

The pedestrianised lanes were usually full of all sorts of people wandering up and down; it was a very cosmopolitan place, despite the old town setting. Once or twice we were stopped in the street by a parent who encouraged their child to ask us our names and where we came from in English, which they did quite boldly, to the proud parent's obvious satisfaction. Impressed by such self-confidence, we were only too pleased to answer. Hostels and restaurants cluttered the side streets near the main thoroughfare, catering to international tourists as well as groups of Chinese. We came across a wholemeal bread café, a nightclub and plenty in between. One of the features of Dali for us were the Chinese restaurants. Often with no more than three or four tables inside, these little places would attract customers with their displays of food in plastic tubs and bowls that cascaded down their front steps and onto the street. The live fish, seafood, and colourful arrays of vegetables all constituted the daily ingredients on offer.

Ordering food was often done whilst standing and looking at the food. We were familiar with this process by now and also the standard results. Pretty much every dish would arrive swimming in oily fat, having been treated to a more or less effective attempt at a stir-fry. We had found that it was best to avoid ordering green vegetables, as these invariably arrived in a giant pile in the middle of a plate, looking like a dripping wet mound of garden weeds. Aubergines were similarly presented like purple sponges fresh from a vat of liquid fat. We preferred to choose tomatoes and eggs, which were always combined into a form of scrambled eggs, and potatoes, which came grated and stir-fried with green peppers. Any variation to the theme of plain white rice was welcome, such as additions of stir-fried pineapple, sweetcorn and peppers. When we first arrived in China we were pleased to find that food was served in large, generally tasty portions. The more time that passed, however, the less impressed we became with the same dishes repeating themselves time and time again – complete with generous helpings of MSG – despite our best efforts to mix things up a bit. Nevertheless, one of the best things about Dali was the cost of eating out: we could have three dishes, plus more rice that we could eat, and a large bottle of beer, all for 20 yuan (US $2.60).

Another thing that we enjoyed in Dali was the interaction with stallholders – or indeed, just about anyone from the town. It was an incredibly friendly place, full of broad smiles and laughter. We had gotten into the swing of shopping by now, having developed something of a 'good cop/bad cop' routine. Claudia would show a keenness to buy something – shopkeepers tended to target her anyway – but I would feign disinterest and walk away if the price was not right. It was a very successful strategy, but usually depended on having a feel for prices beforehand and a predetermined price that we considered to be fair. If we spotted an item we liked the look of, we would check out similar items on nearby stalls first – where the cost always fell dramatically when we left without buying. We once had a lady chase us around a corner, leaving her stall behind her to offer us a succession of ever lower 'final prices'.

The stallholders in Dali appeared to enjoy the process of haggling just as much we did, which made it all the more fun. On one occasion Claudia spotted a batik cloth hanging on the wall of a side alleyway that she wanted. The bargaining with the cheerful lady in charge of the stall began, swapping unrealistic figures at either end of the price spectrum via a small notepad. This was as much about demonstrating that you weren't a sucker as anything else. More numbers were written down, crossed out and replaced, original ones encircled vigorously, both jousters laughing at each others' obstinacy.

Down the alleyway came an elderly gentleman, carrying a wicker basket on his back. He stopped to peer over Claudia's shoulder, watching the tug of war over prices. Soon they were joined by another lady in traditional dress, making a small huddled group. The new lady decided to play and took over the bargaining for a while. When all was done and the price was settled, everyone seemed just as satisfied with the fact that Claudia had, by general agreement, obtained a respectably good price. It really was as if good sportsmanship was as important as winning the game.

We often passed a man who lurked at one of the busy crossroads. Several times he sidled up alongside us and began to take a close interest in my shoes. Stopping and bending down to inspect them, he would triumphantly point out where the seams had begun to split – and promptly offer to glue them back together again. Slightly bemused at our breaking into laughter at his audacity, he would return a cheerful grin, but he never did get the job. Neither did the men offering pony-and-trap rides from just outside the city walls, their wagons colourfully painted bright oranges and reds. They didn't seem to mind either;

they were happy just to be friendly, waving us on our way with no grudges.

How different this was to other places around the world – notably Vietnam and, later, India. Everyone was cheerful in Dali, it seemed. We found it a really pleasant place to stay. There were also plenty of quiet excursions possible outside the city, once the people-watching had lost some of its interest. The ponies and traps had been waiting to take people towards one of the famous sights of this part of China, the Three Pagodas. It didn't take long for us to walk there, past an army of workers who were – no surprise now – upgrading the road into a three-lane highway. It seemed to be largely being built by women working with picks and wicker baskets. The contradiction between the vision and scale of these large infrastructure projects and the means of completing them was jarring, but one couldn't help but admire the determination to progress that they embodied.

The Three Pagodas were what they sound like: three very tall white and gold pagodas that stood almost side by side within a walled park. The towers were ringed with multiple small apron-like roofs, layered one on top of the other between the base and the top, separated by windows. The tallest pagoda was 70 m high and had been built in the ninth century AD, which made it one of the oldest standing structures in China. Behind the pagodas a green range of hills rose up, usually topped with grey clouds. Actually, the highest of the fourteen peaks of this range was over 4,000 m high, so really they were mountains. The pagodas were striking, and the view of them reflected in a small lake was one of the most famous sights from Yunnan province, but we were dismayed to find that the entrance charge to foreigners was a whopping 121 yuan (US $16) per person. This seemed to us exorbitant, so we walked around the outside instead. In the ancient side streets we found elderly Chinese men sitting on a wall, smoking their long pipes, and equally elderly ladies carrying baskets on their bent-over backs. As ever, it only took a short distance to get off the tourist trail and into another world.

In the villages beyond Dali, it was interesting to see that the traditional clothing was virtually ubiquitous and was worn as a part of normal, everyday life. The styles of trousers varied, but all the women were wearing a jacket and an apron, mainly in shades of blue. It was easy to spot the women, as they were the ones working in the fields. I only saw two men weeding in the rice paddies. Middle-aged and old, sometimes very old, women were bent double, either ankle-deep in water or struggling along the road under the weight of a wicker basket. Often the basket was carried by means of a single broad strap across the head, but a modern adaptation used two shoulder straps, more like the design of a modern rucksack. There were even a few plastic versions, which nevertheless maintained the traditional angular shape. As we drove away from Dali, up over another range of hills where it began to rain, men and women were wearing Mongolian style fur capes and wide-brimmed fur-lined hats. Perhaps this was their wet-weather gear. The surroundings looked more like the remote rural China that we had imagined, but it did not last very long. We descended again to Lijiang, the only Chinese town that had been recognised by UNESCO as a World Cultural Heritage Site. It was even more touristy than Dali.

Chapter 52: Lijiang and the Tiger Leaping Gorge

The bus stations in Lijiang were in the modern part of town, which ringed the old city. This modern area was bright and commercial, the roads were busy with traffic, and multi-storey buildings sported an array of shops and banks. The shopping street could have come from anywhere in the developed world, with its cinema complex, glassy high-rise office blocks and KFC restaurant. Perhaps the only difference – apart from the language – was that some local restaurants had set their food out on the pavement, in spherical silver bowls that were stacked one on top of the other.

Across the street, underneath a hill that dropped abruptly down a rocky cliff to a river, was the Ancient City, which had once been a staging post on an old Horse and Tea Trail. The river split up into several small channels, around and between which the old city was built. Many grey stone bridges linked intertwining paths that ran alongside the waterways. With plenty of willow trees gracefully lining the wider paved streets, much of the old town was charmingly quaint. The old wooden houses – some of which were 800 years old, although many had been restored following earthquakes – were the main attraction of the city. At night, windows and doors of the buildings were closed up with solid rows of carved wooden panels, as if being barricaded in. It was at this time that the quiet streets were at their most atmospheric, with green pot plants set outside on steps, red paper balloons hanging down from balconies, delicate window shutters above them, and everything topped off with curving grey roof tiles.

Our first night we stayed in a traditional Naxi house, built around a central open courtyard as we had seen before. Our hosts did not seem used to having foreign guests, but they were perfectly friendly and hospitable, despite being totally confused when we asked for a towel. We went through several possibilities such as being taken for a walk and being offered an umbrella before Claudia's miming achieved the desired result. Many traditional houses in Lijiang had been converted to make rooms for visitors, or turned completely into upmarket hotels. During the day, the buildings along the main streets opened up to reveal an array of tourist shops, selling all sorts of artefacts and handicrafts to the Chinese tourists who came in their thousands, filling the streets with heaving crowds. No wonder that in 2000 the number of tourists who visited Lijiang was 2.8 million.

In the old market square we saw daily performances of traditional dances by the local Naxi women – in costume – put on for the benefit of the tourists who had come to see this kind of thing. Other women walked through to the local market in just the same clothing. The distinctive new element of their dress was a thick blanket worn down their back, tied by two bold white straps that were crossed over the chest. The blanket had originally been designed as padding for the back-baskets, but was now part of the ethnic costume. It was worn behind a tight waistcoat, a blue blouse, dark trousers and a large plain apron. Younger girls had brightly coloured waistcoats; the older generation were more austere. The old ladies often wore a blue peaked cap, too, reminiscent of the Maoist uniform.

The Naxi culture originated in Tibet and has historically been a matriarchal society, with the women firmly in charge of domestic affairs. It is also noteworthy for retaining the only hieroglyphic language in use in the world, with examples of the colourful hieroglyphs printed within square boxes proudly on display in a small cultural museum.

We saw one other distinctive minority costume in Lijiang and again later in more numbers at the Tiger Leaping Gorge. The couple in Lijiang were strolling down a cobbled street, arm in arm. The man was dressed in a smart but ordinary brown Western business suit, but the young lady beside him wore a severe black dress that billowed out at the bottom, ringed with bands of bright colours all over it. On her head was a huge black hat that looked like a cross between an oversized mortar board, a raised umbrella and a flowing cape. It was very odd, probably the most unusual piece of costume that we saw on all our travels.

Along with all the shops and Naxi culture were other touristy attractions. Men dressed up in furs – imitating the Mongols, I supposed – were offering horseback rides to children or young women, who could pose for photographs holding fearsome weapons. Another enterprise was being run by several girls along the riverbanks. They would sell goldfish that were kept in quaint wooden buckets, the idea being that returning the fish to the waters of the river would bring good luck to the customer. In the river waters there were indeed several shoals of goldfish. I could just imagine the girls dipping their nets into the rivers early each morning, collecting the same fish ready for another day's work. Not a bad little earner. As we walked the lanes we also came across men playing mah-jong on little tables set up outside their houses. The men rarely seemed to be very busy, it has to be said.

There wasn't much cheap accommodation in Lijiang – or, rather, it wasn't easy to locate in the maze of back streets. We did look at a few more obvious international hotels, but these were all well out of our budget. We once walked into the entrance of one, but were totally ignored by the two girls behind a desk, so eventually we turned around and walked out again. Only when we passed the entrance again later did we realise that we had been standing in the entrance of a rather grand public toilet!

We did finally manage to track down a Lijiang institution that was being talked about by almost every tourist on the trail between Dali and the Tiger Leaping Gorge. One poor guy we met had heard about it and had spent four hours walking around Lijiang in search of it, but had to give up in the end. We had a business card that we showed to locals when we tried to find it, but we still had to backtrack several times and even when we were facing the front door we were unsure if it was the right place.

Mama Naxi's guest house needed no advertising. Its courtyard was full of backpackers and every bed was taken. Luckily for us, Mama Naxi had expanded into a relative's house around the corner. As we were shown in, a young girl instructed us to come back for dinner at 6 p.m. As ever we didn't really understand what this was about, and so arrived an hour late to find that a meal had already been served to the guests seated in the courtyard, who were sheltering under plastic sheets with rain drumming down and pouring off the edges. We weren't the only ones who hadn't eaten and so were able to join other latecomers, comprising Japanese, Korean and New Zealand tourists besides ourselves.

More food was produced and set down in the middle of our table, dish after dish after dish. We helped ourselves as politely as we could by stretching across the table with chopsticks. It was a banquet – and the final bill came to a grand total of 8 yuan (US $1.05). A beer cost 3 yuan (US $0.39). And, returning for breakfast in the morning, a plate of banana pancakes and tea was 2 yuan (US $0.26). Little surprise that Mama Naxi's was popular! But there was more to come; Mama Naxi herself was interested in our plans after we asked for directions to the bus station. She declined to tell us how to get there, but told us not to worry and turned to her mobile phone. We had no idea what she was doing, but a couple of minutes later we followed her through nearby streets to a waiting minibus. This turned out to be nothing other than a free lift across town to the bus station – all done apparently out of the goodness of Mama Naxi's heart. For travel-weary tourists, such kindness makes a big impression.

One of our less pleasant moments in Lijiang had been discovering that our remaining camera's memory card had become corrupted whilst taking the very last picture on it. Nearly two hundred photographs, everything since Luang Nam Tha, right through Jinghong, Kunming and Dali, were liable to be lost. *Not again, please not again*, we thought. Inside a local camera shop several very friendly young staff did their best to help, running various recovery programs but in the end succeeding only in wiping all information from the card. So that was that. We had a cream cake in a coffee shop to recover from the trauma and consoled ourselves with the thought that as we had to buy another memory card – these were thankfully widely available in touristy Lijiang – we could be fairly sure that any images of the renowned Tiger Leaping Gorge would be safe. This gorge, one of the deepest in the world and often described as having the best scenery in China, was where we headed to next.

In the Lijiang bus station there was an information counter that could give us the departure time and cost of our bus. At the ticket desk, where a lady sat with an abacus to hand, the price of the ticket had inexplicably risen slightly, as it did each time we were there. Several stern, uniformed ladies guarded the doors from the waiting room, periodically barking out the name of a bus and allowing only the correct passengers through. As we couldn't understand what they actually said, each time they shouted out across the hall we got up and asked whether it was our turn yet. They never smiled and never moved from their position – I had the distinct impression that they would not bat an eyelid if we sat right in front of them and then missed our bus – but finally they let us through and we were on our way.

The road towards the Tiger Leaping Gorge took us very close to the county that used to be called Zhongdian. In September 1997 it was officially renamed as 'Shangri-la', after a team of experts concluded that the fabled location of James Hilton's 1933 novel, *Lost Horizon*, was indeed located there. The evidence put forward included the convincing detail that the local Zhongdian dialect of Tibetan has a unique name for a part of the county: 'Shangai-la'. However, there are several other contenders across the Himalayas, from Pakistan through Tibet to Bhutan. As it was, we felt strongly the call of the wildness and beauty of Zhongdian, and indeed of the Tibetan plateau, to which we were tantalisingly close. So close, but so far. We simply didn't have the time to travel further west if we wanted to make it to Hong Kong and then Beijing. Instead, we told ourselves that should we ever have the resources for another trip, this would be the corner of the world to where we would come first.

We gazed out of the bus windows at the various deep valleys meeting the wide, flat, grey Yangtze River. The Yangtze happens to be the longest river in China, the longest in Asia, and the third longest in the world. It is 6,211 km long. It drops off the eastern edge of the Tibetan plateau, parallel to the Mekong and the Salween Rivers because they all flow through deep gorges that follow lines of geological weakness – stress lines – around the edge of the Himalayan mountain chain that were created as the landmass of India collided with Asia, and finally reaches the sea near Shanghai.

As we sat on the bus with time passing, we wondered which valley contained the famous gorge and whether we had gone too far. We had absolutely no idea where to get off! We did try asking other passengers, but their noncommittal replies could have meant anything from 'not yet' to 'I have no idea what you are saying'. We needn't have worried as the driver pulled to the side of the road opposite a hotel building and told us in broken English that this was our stop.

Following his instructions, we found ourselves in a little car park. There was a handy young man loitering around – somehow there always was – who showed us the next part of the way, past an official ticket office. The man offered to drive us the couple of hundred yards, which would cost us a taxi fare but save on entrance tickets, he said, as the people in the office were his 'friends'. By doing this, we would save money and he would earn money – it was a perfect win-win deal. He just didn't seem to understand why we declined it, and so several times tried to spell it out to us, as if explaining self-evident logic to young children. Ethics didn't seem to enter his equation.

After the ticket office, we came across the first of a couple of hostels at the start of the trail. Out of its front door came an Australian proprietress, who shouted loudly after us. She wanted us to stop, to turn around and to stay in her hostel. It hadn't taken many words from her to determine that staying there was the last thing we would do. When we continued on she angrily harangued us from behind, increasingly rude and aggressive, until almost shouting insults in her rage at having been ignored. 'The locals on the trail are not to be trusted!' she yelled. 'Don't believe any of them!'

This display of unpleasant, uncivilised behaviour surprised and shocked us. On further enquiry we learned that there was considerable tension between the various guest-house owners in the Tiger Leaping Gorge, who were a mixture of locals and foreigners. It was a shame to see how tourism could drive wedges between neighbours as well as bringing prosperity. At the far end of the gorge we also heard rumours about local men who set up impromptu 'toll gates' on the pathways. One had supposedly even erected a simple door frame around the path to make his point. Tourists were then charged to pass – a modern version of highway robbery. I asked what would happen if people refused to pay, but apparently the result was normally violent, with several people having had their precious cameras thrown into the raging river.

Thankfully we encountered none of this, and after our first unsavoury experience we had nothing but an uninterrupted sequence of extremely pleasant stays at local guesthouses, whose families had opened up their traditional Naxi homes to tourists. The homes all had four buildings set around a central yard. We passed several farmhouses that were using one side as a barn and another for pig pens, but the guest houses had typically converted these farm buildings into little bedrooms. Decorated with flowers and hung with strings of drying maize heads, these homes were attractive and cosy places to stay, run by friendly and hospitable families.

One owner showed us photographs of his house taken just a few years ago: then the yard had had a dirt floor and only one side of the square had been a habitable building. Now, while the family still lived in their old house, there was concrete across the yard, a separate kitchen block on one side, and a pair of new two-storey guest wings being finished. Bright red hollyhocks and fuchsias were in flower beds and a white satellite dish sat in the courtyard. This illustrated the positive impact of the tourist industry. I suspected that the traditional farmhouses had hardly changed for generations – many were still mud brick buildings and some had roofs made from wooden tiles weighted down with stones – but within just a few years these guest houses had been transformed.

The Tiger Leaping Gorge was a V-shaped valley, fairly narrow but with its proportions distorted by the height of its sides, which for most of the time were lost in clouds. The river roared its way through a gully far below us as we hiked along a high path: we estimated that there was a near vertical drop of 400 metres immediately on either side of the river, above which rose the steep dark green faces of the mountains, streaked with the grey scars of cliffs and landslides. From their summits to the river – both of which were occasionally visible at the same time – was a drop of some 4,000 metres.

The gorge was 16 kilometres long, and so for two days we had views of nothing but this impressive Andean-style scenery. We walked through stands of pine trees, rhododendron bushes, bamboo forest and maize fields, the paths brightened by blue flowers and brown butterflies. Loud cicadas whirred past our faces, red-and-yellow birds darted out of sight. Men on horseback using the same path as us stopped to offer us a lift, one unexpectedly pulling out a mobile phone as we passed. Other people we saw were gathering herbs from the steep hillsides; there were plenty of villagers just going about their simple daily business, such as weeding the fields. The walking was fairly easy, the views impressive, and the days gentle and pleasant.

Below us – at times vertically below – was a 'low road' which was now suitable for tourist buses to ply their way to the end and back again. We eventually dropped down to this road and hitched a lift back on what transpired to be the first minibus of the day. We hadn't realised it, but the night before there had been a large landslide that had blocked the road. This was apparently a common hazard. The views from the bus ride along the bottom of the gorge were, if anything, more spectacular than those from the higher path. There was much more of a sense of being enclosed between two rock walls which rose to dizzying heights far above. The gorge was called Tiger Leaping Gorge, incidentally, after the story of a hunted tiger which had escaped by bounding across the river. We could tell the spot where it was said to have happened because this was where coaches containing hundreds of Chinese tourists were stopping and turning around.

Lijiang and the Tiger Leaping Gorge

We followed them out of the gorge and back to the main road, where we waved down a public bus that would take us back to Lijiang. From there we retraced our steps to Dali and Kunming, taking replacement photographs as we did so, before heading east out of Yunnan and into Guanxi province. From the Guanxi regional capital of Nanning it was just a short journey northwards to Guilin and possibly the most famous landscape in all China. The karst scenery around Guilin had even been printed on Chinese banknotes, so every Chinese person knew how special it was.

Chapter 53: Nanning and Guilin

We had our first experience of Chinese trains on a 'hard sleeper' between Kunming and Nanning. This railway line passed through a tunnel or over a bridge for no less than one third of its 827 km-long journey. There were various degrees of privacy and comfort available on Chinese trains, with both sleeper carriages and seating compartments being divided up into 'hard' and 'soft' categories. Having 'hard sleeper' meant that we were in a little berth that had three narrow beds one above the other against each wall. When we bought the tickets we had requested that we be given bunks in the same berth. The seller obliged by giving us tickets which did indeed have adjacent row numbers – but unfortunately on opposite sides of a wall. At later stations we found that this was not unusual. We gained the impression that ticket sellers preferred being disingenuous to making the extra effort of providing what was actually asked for, as long as they weren't actually caught out in the process.

Anyway, in this first instance a kind lady was happy to exchange bunks with us. Most of the passengers seemed to be fairly well-to-do business people who were invariably pleasant and helpful towards us. One of the features of Chinese trains, just like in the buses, was that because each passenger was given so little room, huge numbers of people were fitted into the carriages. Seats had been provided in the narrow corridors for the people who inevitably burst out of the tiny berths, but this only meant that the corridor as well as the berths became crammed with bodies, knees and feet. Trains were definitely not places for personal space or privacy. But they were perfectly clean and orderly; we were always quite comfortable and felt safe – which was more than could be said for our later experience of Indian trains.

One of the features of Chinese trains was that they all had a little room with a tap dispensing hot water. This was invariably next to the toilets and was the favoured hang-out for loitering smokers. The tap itself was perhaps the most visited place in the train. There were two items that almost every passenger carried with them. The first was a tub of the Chinese version of pot noodles, which here were large round cartons complete with various plastic sachets and even a fork inside. The sachets provided the spices – but were far too hot for us to use. Come dinner time, people would clamber out of their bunks and negotiate all the legs in the corridors to reach the queue for the tap. There they would add hot water to their instant noodles and make their way back to their bunks, gingerly trying to avoid spilling any of the scalding liquid they were carrying. The second item that elderly Chinese men in particular carried was a glass jam jar. The modern version favoured by younger ladies was a plastic beaker with a screw-on lid. In these jars was a dose of green tea leaves, so with the addition of the hot water from the tap, everyone could have a popular drink. The tea jars were not just carried on trains, though; we saw people clutching them in their hands like security blankets wherever we went in south-west China.

We didn't stay long enough in Nanning to be absolutely certain that there wasn't really anything to hang around for, but we had tried to find things of interest as we wandered around the streets and never came across anything. The city had a drab, monotonous and slightly depressed feeling to it, reminding me of a grey Russian town. So did the concrete pedestrian subways underneath road junctions, home to dingy stalls selling cheap jewellery and clothes. The only time these subways came alive was when it rained. Then they were suddenly crammed with people taking shelter and buying yet another blue or yellow umbrella for 10 yuan (US $1.30).

We failed to find a local eatery on our first tour of the city and were forced to eat chips from a very busy McDonald's in one of the modern shopping centres that had large department stores inside. Our only alternative restaurant was a KFC across the road. As we watched the world go past our window, two little boys sat down on the pavement. They were ragged and dirty, and each carried a little plastic pot in their tiny fists. One extracted a small coin from his pot. They were taking a rest from begging for small change. As ever, the pane of glass between us suddenly seemed to represent an impenetrable barrier between two painfully remote worlds.

The next day we went looking for something more pleasant, which required wandering the quieter back streets. In one we eventually found two local restaurants, side by side. We tried the better-looking of the two, which had the merit of red-and-white chequered cloths on its tables. We hadn't brought our phrase-book with us, which we realised was a mistake immediately that we were presented with three Chinese menus. Not having any idea where to start, we used our limited Mandarin to tell the young waitress that we didn't eat meat, only vegetables. She seemed to get this idea, but that was where our vocabulary stopped. She was a schoolgirl and game enough to try the few English words that she knew, but they didn't progress us much further. We persuaded her to choose three dishes for us, which she reluctantly did. The first was a plate of meat slices. The next was better, being tofu-and-greens. Then came a plate of greasy spinach, quickly followed by a bowl of sweet-and-sour vegetables. Enough, we thought – we'd never be able to finish all of that. Then she put two portions of rice on our table, but not the usual teacup-sized version. There was enough rice to feed six hungry people. To our consternation, the rice was followed by a similarly vast quantity of battered sweetcorn kernels. There was no room on the table for any more food.

We decided that to make a noble attempt on all this grease would require a beer. We knew this word well enough, and the waitress beamed enthusiastically at our prowess. She offered a choice of three words and I selected the last – resulting in us being brought a little bottle of 35 per cent proof spirits with two glass tumblers. Eventually we managed to get the beer as well. We had become something of a spectacle in the restaurant, objects of benevolent interest and curiosity. Our friendly little waitress was enjoying being at the centre of attention too, proud at having been able to serve two hapless foreigners. In the end, as we exchanged addresses and photographs, it was all the smiles and laughter that made the evening so pleasant and memorable. The bottle of spirits we took back to our hotel room – for strictly medicinal purposes, of course.

Our hotel staff also seemed to take pride in being able to speak basic English. In turn they each had a go at practising a few phrases on us when we passed through the lobby. There was a leaflet in our room that had been translated into English, too. Having seen several examples of 'Chinglish' already – wholly commendable efforts at translating Chinese into English, often with comical results – we were tickled by some of the lines in the leaflet: 'If you are in an emergency, you'd better obey with the attendant, and evacuate the exit.' Or, 'Forbid to bring the combustibles, squib, poisonous substance and radioactivity into the hotel.' One of my favourite examples of Chinglish I saw over a little shop in Nanning, which read, 'Envelops, impressions and first day covers.' It took a little thought to realise that it was a post office selling envelopes and stamps. Another sign in a petrol station would have had us stumped were it not for the picture of a matchbox beside it. 'No kinding', it said, which was, I assume, supposed to have been 'No kindling', meaning 'No fire-lighting'.

For the train ride from Nanning to Guilin we chose to take 'soft seats'. They were not soft. They were thin and hard. The double-decker train carriage was as usual designed with a single aim in mind – fitting the maximum number of people in as possible. No concession had been made to comfort and unfortunately the train was packed full. The best that anyone could do was shut one's eyes and try to sleep, which everyone around us promptly did. I had been hoping for five hours of good views out of the windows, but the curtains were drawn tight by our sleeping neighbours. We started a game of chess, but as our seats, supposed to be next to one other, were across an aisle, we were continually interrupted by passengers walking through the carriages with their noodles or tea jars. We gave up, resigning ourselves to discomfort and boredom. Only from out of the doors could I catch glimpses of people in conical hats pushing bicycles down little lanes between fields of maize, or of double-storey red-brick rows of terraced housing next to Dickensian-looking cement and brick works with tall chimney stacks.

We stopped in Guilin in the hope that we would be able to extend our China visa here. On arrival at the railway station in Guilin, we asked a taxi driver to take us into the centre of town for a quick look around one of the most exclusive tourist locations in China. We were followed into our taxi by a tout who seemed certain that we would eventually agree to buy a tour from him. He was to be disappointed. We were dropped beside the river that flowed through the centre of town, alongside a row of high-class restaurants.

This was where our taxi driver had assumed we would want to go, and with good reason. Parked beside the road were coachloads of Chinese tourists stopping for lunch in the restaurants, which were selling food at five times the prices in Yunnan. The restaurants served up the food that rich Chinese wanted as holiday treats, the ingredients of which we could see displayed outside on the street. Glass tanks and large plastic tubs held live fish, eels, crabs, crayfish, lobsters and snails. In wire cages little bigger than shoeboxes were scraggy chickens, ducks and pheasant. One cage held a writhing mass of intertwined snakes. The food display began to look more like a ghastly animal market. In another plastic bucket were tortoises. A wooden box on the floor contained two furry animals with stumpy legs and fat bodies – bamboo rats. And worst of all we even saw a pair of armadillo-like pangolins, which are an endangered species. All these creatures were on some kind of death row, just waiting for someone to put them out of their misery by ordering them for dinner.

Guilin was famous for its karst scenery, although really it served as a base from which to visit the most impressive locations that were best seen outside town from the Li River. A couple of limestone towers were visible in town, part rounded hills and part craggy cliffs, but these were just a foretaste of the landscape we were to see a little later. Before that, we had to ask another taxi driver to take us to the Public Service Bureau. He did, but it turned out to be the police station rather than the foreign immigration department. We explained to a kindly policewoman what we were looking for and she wrote directions down on a piece of paper to show to the next taxi driver. This one took us over the river to a small office, where it didn't take long for us to be told by a curt official that we couldn't extend our visa, and that the only way to enter Beijing after Hong Kong would be to buy a completely new visa. But we couldn't do that here – only in Hong Kong.

We were out of the door again before our taxi driver had turned her car around, so she took us back to the bus station. We left Guilin for Yangshuo, which was where many tourists, both Chinese and foreign, hung out. From the bus we began to get a sense of the landscape we were in. On both sides of the road we could see line upon line of karst hills, poking up from a plain in regular formation. The thousands of peaks were mostly shaped a bit like broad tombstones, of remarkably uniform height and dimension. They were covered in green vegetation, with patches of white limestone gleaming through. In the distance the hills faded into hazy blue-grey lumps, right to the horizon and beyond, in all directions. The sheer number of these most unusual features, the scale of the topography, was incredible. It was one of the few truly extraordinary landscapes that we had seen around the world, and highly attractive. We were in for a special treat over the next few days.

Chapter 54: Yangshuo

Situated in the middle of the karst 'forest' landscape, wedged in the gaps between limestone hills and towers, was the small tourist town of Yangshuo. It was made of two discreet halves, one on either side of the bus station. The first was centred on a concrete-lined main road, with several side streets parallel to it all full of identikit concrete hotels. This was the Chinese quarter, catering to the Chinese version of package tourism. We tried it out for our first couple of nights and found the hotels to be perfectly clean and functional, if a bit devoid of much in the way of character. On the other side of the bus station was the second side of Yangshuo, the foreigners' quarter. It was appropriately called 'West Street', although that might also have referred to the Wild West atmosphere it generated. This was where the Chinese tourists or indeed groups of Chinese schoolchildren were taken to goggle at the Westernised tourist industry in full swing.

West Street was something of a phenomenon, the up-market Chinese version of Bangkok's Khao San Road. There were banks and souvenir shops at the beginning of the main road, which progressively narrowed and became increasingly dominated by loud, brash western-style pub-restaurants. Outside every building hung painted signs and globalised brand logos, advertising such things as chocolate cake and Carlsberg respectively. Red neon lights provided an element of kitsch. During the day uniformed waitresses hovered next to their English menu boards, hoping to entice passers-by to sample the relatively expensive international cuisine. In the evening, live music blared out from the bars, their different bands competing with each other all down the road. Everywhere was packed with people: it was an intense, unrestrained onslaught of tourism and was initially too much for our tender senses.

More to our taste were the Chinese open air eateries that were set up in the town's central car park during the evenings. Several competing places sprang up next to one another, each a carbon copy of the ones either side. A table at the front would have all available ingredients laid out; behind were cooks slaving over steaming woks on gas cookers; and further back came rows of tables under a simple tent-like shelter. Everything was greasy, but despite always being overcharged it was still far cheaper than in West Street. One night we sat next to a Chinese pair who were eating their way through a huge plate of snails, discarding the waste broken bits of shell onto the ground as they went. These ended up being scattered all around the table legs in a disgusting slimy mess. It was yet another Chinese conundrum for us to see how people could be so self-contained, clean and tidy when stuffed together in a train compartment, but also be capable of the disgusting – to us – habits of spitting or spewing snail shells all over the floor.

It was the school holidays in China, and Yangshuo had a significant number of schoolchildren visiting there for an educational trip. Apparently there was an ever-increasing trend for summer holidays to be used as an opportunity for children to be sent on educational camps, where they could be topped up in sports, computing or – as in this case – English. These children were from the privileged strata of Chinese society, such as the nouveau riche of Shanghai. Six weeks of summer schooling cost 15,000 yuan (US $1,963); in Shanghai the average amount spent by a family on additional tuition was 5,000 yuan (US $654) per year. While we were in China, news programmes were reporting on the issue of children as young as two years old being sat in front of televisions or playing computer games in order that they could progress intellectually, even if it meant damaging their eyesight.

The children we encountered in Yangshuo were wearing bright yellow T-shirts emblazoned with the motto 'Success in English: Success in Life'. One of their tasks was to interview foreign tourists, which they did with an admirable precision of articulation. A couple of English schoolteachers working in China told us that in the countryside many students say that they study hard because it is 'good for their family and their country'. This was a very Confucianist attitude, which was apparently undergoing something of a renaissance in modern China.

There was plenty to do around Yangshuo, making it an easy place to while away several days. Our first excursion was a combined cycle tour and raft trip down the river, which we booked over a beer with our hotel manager. We had been surprised at how expensive the tours were initially, but discovered that minimal resistance brought the price down to almost half of the original quote. Whenever prices fell quickly we could be pretty sure that there was plenty of room yet for further reductions, and so it proved here. In fact, Yangshuo was the worst place in China for shopkeepers brazenly attempting to rip off tourists, so much so that we soon felt aggrieved that a fair game – which could be good sport – had been abused by the gross distortion of prices. A bit of haggling could actually produce a price that was just 25 per cent – or even less – of the original quote. There must be enough vulnerable and gullible tourists to make it worth the shopkeepers' while asking high prices, unfortunately. In the beginning we felt a bit cheeky asking for amounts that were just a fraction of the figure asked by storekeepers, such as suggesting a 'much too low' offer of 30 yuan (US $3.90) instead of one shopkeeper's opening price of 165 yuan (US $21.60). It was justified in this case when the item– a Chinese painting – was sold willingly enough for 50 yuan (US $6.50).

Not that we felt that we had got a good deal when we set off on our bicycle tour the next morning. We were picked up from our hotel before sunrise by a guy on a motorbike. We initially assumed that he was simply taking us to a rendezvous point to meet our cycle guide, but we didn't get a chance to ask him as he was twenty yards in front, his engine harsh and loud. We got on our bicycles and followed him into the misty gloom. Soon we realised that there wasn't going to be anyone else. We were still sleepy, our promised breakfast hadn't materialised, everything was misty so we couldn't see anything, and we were following a motorbike that shattered the peace of dawn. It was not the best start to our day. Our guide's efforts at being helpful consisted of waiting for us to catch him up, pointing to a rice paddy and saying, 'Rice', then revving his engine and driving off again.

Actually, the sight of rice crops being harvested was interesting for us because we had seen the other end of the planting cycle previously in Laos. The stalks here were turning yellow and brown and were beginning to flatten in the fields, so they were being cut with long-handled scythes and collected into pretty little bundles that stood upright in the fields, like two-foot high corn dollies.

The cycle ride took us to a river, where a collection of bamboo rafts were tied up together by the bank. They were similar to the rafts we had been on in Chiang Mai, in that they were essentially several long bamboo poles lashed together, but these were larger and had a pair of chairs tied down in the centre, like a regal dais. A younger man emerged out of the mist to meet us; he was our punter. By now the sun should have risen, but we could still see nothing except greyness, so I suggested that we wait a while to see if the mist would burn off. The men weren't averse to this, as it gave them an opportunity for a chat and an early morning smoke, which cheered their spirits a bit. After half an hour of waiting the mist was thinner, but hadn't broken yet. Our bored motorcycle guide had an idea: we could get on the raft and he would push us around the river for a while, so that the real punter could go home and get his breakfast.

As soon as we began, the surly bloke turned into a giggling kid – he barely knew what he was doing, so we crashed into bushes and bounced off the riverbank, as he tried to avoid toppling right into the water. We had a go at conversation, too: he would say a team from the recent World Cup and we would try to guess what nationality it was that he had just tried to pronounce. It was like a verbal game of 'snap' and sometimes just as random. After that icebreaker, we started on teams from the English Premiership.

While we were having fun, the mists parted and we found ourselves facing the beautiful sight of a row of karst towers, their edges softened by the pale dawn light, fluffy white clouds still lingering halfway up their sides, and graceful bamboo stalks bending in the foreground. Everything was perfectly still and quiet; there was a crystal clear reflection in the water. We grabbed our camera. This had been well worth waiting for. It was an exquisite picture.

Our punter returned and in a few minutes we were gliding serenely downstream, past giant bamboo fronds and various smaller trees, with only an odd kingfisher or moorhen as company. On either side of the river were karst towers, forming a silent guard of honour, at times with reflections of breathtaking symmetry. It was idyllic, exquisitely pretty, like being inside a piece of refined Chinese artwork. These were magical, enchanting moments, the most purely beautiful of all the experiences on our world voyage.

All too soon, however, the river widened and we began to pass more and more flotillas of moored rafts. Our tranquil isolation was over. Other tourists in bright orange life jackets were clambering onto their rafts, which were now bedecked with large parasols shading the thrones underneath. As the river filled up and buildings started to line the banks, we saw several cormorant fishermen. These men would stand or sit in their wooden canoes as their black birds did the work of fishing in the water. Apparently the birds are prevented from swallowing fish by a ring around their necks, so they learn to give their catch to the fisherman for the eventual reward of being tied to a perch, having their necks freed and being fed some of their own fish. We could see the birds bobbing in the water, or perching in a line on the side of the boats, holding their wings outstretched in a distinctive 'M' shape to dry their feathers. At the very end of our rafting experience we came across the eccentric sight of a complete musical orchestra floating on a vast bamboo raft in the river, playing a musical accompaniment to breakfasting guests in a riverside hotel. All the time, the karst hills loomed in the background, making the scene even more unusual.

Our now friendly motorcycling guide was waiting for us on the bank and we persuaded him to give us breakfast. He chose what must have been the cheapest option available, a roadside noodle stall. The white rice noodles and dried beans were delicious and afterwards we felt prepared for the ride back to town through country lanes. The only other traffic we passed was a lady pulling a wooden cart with her child sitting in it, and a woman walking behind a buffalo. In the small rice fields all around us the rice harvest was in full swing. Several people would be working together in a single field, the women threshing using small wooden mechanical contraptions and the men lugging huge sacks back towards their houses. The buildings were very rudimentary, all built from mud bricks, their plain simplicity reminding me of Scottish crofters' cottages. They had a soft tan colour that perfectly complemented the ripening crops of rice, making very attractive images of medieval farming. But the real visual treat was the karst scenery that surrounded us. Each individual tower was so distinctive in its pillar shape that just one or two would have been a pretty sight, but the hundreds of them receding into the distance in all directions must be one of the natural wonders of the world.

The most famous location of all – the one on the 20 yuan banknote – could only be seen from the River Li south of Yangshuo. Taking a cruise from Guilin to this spot was an activity that had reached almost fabled proportions and had a price tag to match, but the advice from travellers we met beforehand was that it wasn't worth the money, partly because it was unnecessary. A ninety-minute boat trip from the village of Xinping formed the budget version, which ran right past that famous location. It was easy to know when we had reached it, because the handful of Chinese tourists in our boat ran to the front and held up their notes, posing for a photograph. We smiled at them – and then did exactly the same. On this stretch of river, it sometimes seemed as if we were in a canyon with limestone towers and cliffs on either side that merged into one another to form undulating walls, their knobbly tops looking like protruding knuckles and fingers. It was impressive, but this river trip lacked both the exquisite beauty of our raft trip and the incredible vistas of the cycle ride.

We were often touched and impressed by the considerate courtesy and innate honesty of the people we met on our travels through southern China. On local buses around Yangshuo, for example, people would often help each other with their baggage, always in a friendly and respectful manner. The expression that summed up their behaviour seemed to me to be 'neighbourly'. And we were included in this neighbourliness, often being helped along our way by passing strangers who saw us in need. We found ourselves having a great deal of respect for ordinary Chinese people as we watched numerous small but significant kindly, humane interactions, which too often seem to have been lost amid the hurly-burly of the Western world.

During our last days in Yangshuo it began to rain and didn't stop for three consecutive days and nights… it was still the rainy season. Water was pouring off every roof, flowing down the streets, soaking everything. All the Chinese in town wore thin plastic capes as they hurried from building to building. In the fields the villagers carried on working, bent over in their plastic capes and wearing wide-brimmed hats that acted like umbrellas. We took a bus back to Guilin, and then stood in the rain arguing with touts over the price of buses to Longsheng. Eventually we followed a lady around a corner away from the bus station, where we stood beside the road, dripping wet, as one bus after another passed us. Eventually a minibus stopped and we boarded with relief. Sometimes it was just not worth saving that extra 10 yuan.

Chapter 55: Pingan

Longsheng was a small town close to a series of villages collectively called Longji. They are famous for their 'Dragon's Backbone' rice terrace architecture. We stayed one night in Longsheng, wandering out of the bus station and over a river to the small but bright town centre. No one we asked could point us in the direction of a hotel, so we were left to explore for ourselves. The first one we came across looked too much like a brothel for our taste, with a row of skimpily dressed young girls sitting on a bench in the foyer. We eventually found another that was in the process of being refurbished, meaning that various workmen were blocking the stairways with ladders and the lifts didn't work. Never mind, it was a place to stay out of the rain.

Longsheng was the ugliest of the Chinese towns that we had seen, but we suspected that it was far more typical of China than either Dali or Lijiang had been. The buildings were dominated by rows of angular concrete constructions, put up with no aesthetic feeling whatsoever. The only decoration they had were white tiles that covered their outside walls, serving only to emphasise the coldness of the regimented square windows. We had seen exactly the same buildings in rows on the outskirts of Yangshuo, too, looking distinctly unattractive. Once we had settled into our Longsheng hotel, we went searching for dinner in the rain. We assumed that we would find cheap eateries around the bus station, but the road was filled with small stores selling everyday items like tools and hardware, basic foodstuffs and so on. There were several mechanics workshops, an electrician and a bakery. It was all very down-to-earth and practical, without glamour or prettiness. Longsheng was a plain, functional kind of place.

Just as we were about to give up on dinner, we came across a tiny little café, made of a couple of tables in a small room and a stove next to the pavement. As ever, the family who owned it seemed genuinely pleased that we were there. Claudia was pleased too to have an opportunity to practise her recently-acquired Mandarin phrases, carefully learned from a friendly university student met on a recent bus journey. '*Wo shai yau mi fan,*' she said. The mother laughed – we had no idea why, but we certainly didn't seem any closer to getting a meal. Claudia tried again and more laughter followed. So we opened our picture-dictionary and used that instead. The plates of grated potatoes, fried sweetcorn and rice were very welcome this evening.

We spent a while deliberating on our itinerary, toying with numerous variations of timing in order to reach Hong Kong with enough days to get another visa. The upshot of it was that we planned to get the earliest bus next morning out of Longsheng, get to Pingan quickly, see the terraces and return the same day. In the morning it was still raining, so we stayed in bed. When we pitched up at the bus station with our bags at 9.10 a.m., in good time for the 9.20 departure, our bus was there with a friendly young ticket collector on board, but no driver. By 9.30 we were wondering why this was the only bus in China so far that hadn't left punctually. The reason turned out to be that there had been a landslide on the road and we were actually sitting on the first bus of the day – the one we had initially planned to get – which had become the 9.20 a.m. and was now being changed again into the 11 a.m. departure; hopefully we would leave then. So much for plans. As the sister of the ticket collector worked in a noodle bar just opposite, we went there for a tasty breakfast. Claudia tried out her Mandarin again, asking for soup without meat, and to her delight was understood first time.

On eventually reaching Pingan, we had a short but steep walk from the bus park along a paved footpath to the village. We passed a crowd of waiting porters who wanted to carry our bags for us. Even ladies from the bus who had their own loads offered to put our rucksacks inside their wicker back-baskets and carry them uphill for a charge. We later saw whole convoys of porters with suitcases and rucksacks balanced on their heads, making their way up the stone stepped paths to various hotels in the village. Several portable carriages that looked like sedan chairs were also sitting beside the path, each with two men waiting beside them, offering people the chance to be carried up the hill rather than having to walk up. Most tourists were Chinese here, and they had no qualms about offloading their baggage or being carried themselves as if they were royalty. After all, they were on holiday.

All the houses of Pingan were nestled closely together on the hillside. Well-built stone paths twisted their way between the buildings, invariably passing right in front of windows and doorways. At first this seemed like an invasion of privacy, but these paths were the public footpaths – there was no other way through. What had once been traditional wooden family homes had without exception been extended, refurbished and converted into family-run hostels and hotels, their gleaming new tan-coloured wooden planks almost touching the next-door buildings.

They were rather like traditional Alpine farmhouses, their ground floors often painted white and the upper storeys – three, four or five of them – always wooden, with twee balconies outside the windows. In fact, the village in general was not too far removed from an Alpine ski resort, come to think of it, only without any cars or ski lifts. There were plenty of homely cafés, restaurants and little touristy shops. Stalls were laid out on the paths selling various souvenir trinkets and postcards; old ladies sat under their houses knitting socks and offering them to passers-by.

We found a very pleasant couple to stay with – or rather, they found us, as the husband chased after us up a path in the rain, to inform us only that he couldn't speak much English but his wife did. We investigated and ended up staying in their best room, with a superb view over the famous rice terraces. Just about the only downside of the place was the shower, which was positioned directly over the squat toilet. Within a few hours we had torn up all our plans of the previous night. Trusting to good fortune in Hong Kong, we ended up staying longer in this one place than we did anywhere between Australia and home. During the days we wandered around the hillsides, and in the evenings we helped the husband with his English. In return he tried to teach us a little Mandarin, and together we shared the process of knocking back his home-made and quite potent rice wine.

Just half an hour's walk away from Pingan, along narrow little pathways that traversed the valley side, was the next village. Here there were only two guest houses on the outskirts. The rest of the houses were made of dark, old wood and grey stone. The houses were still packed closely together, with hardly any room for the dividing pathways that seemed to run almost underneath the houses. Chickens and piglets were wandering around, but it was a clean and tidy place and had clearly been built to last through the ages. It was a world away from the metamorphosing tourist centre of Pingan. The next village in the other direction was two hours away and was presumably similarly traditional.

Tourism, however, had changed Pingan dramatically, our landlady told us. Less than a generation ago, the village used to be like any other. Those were times when people had to work hard in the fields to eke out a meagre living. There was no school, no new clothes and not enough food. Each month the village used to hold a kind of festival, which was the only reliable opportunity to dress up and get a decent meal. That didn't happen any more. Now tourists bring in money and the families running hostels often hire workers to farm their terraces. They hope tourism will be a sustained boom, for the building has all been done on credit from banks. Other villagers work in the tourist trade, cleaning and cooking, or acting as tour guides and porters.

Some had set up small businesses on the hillsides, fully equipped with digital cameras, desktop computers and printers, selling photographs of tourists who posed in front of the views, perhaps next to a pair of peacocks or girls dressed in traditional costumes. The costumes of these girls were beautifully elaborate, it has to be said, making the girls look extremely pretty – far more attractive than the women who walked into Pingan every day from a nearby village. Those women had a reputation for the length of their hair –

their village had even been awarded 'The Prize of Longest Hair of Group Female' although I have no idea who by. They chased down tourists on the various paths around Pingan, virtually begging to have a photograph taken for a few yuan: 'Hello, hello… long hair, long hair… photo, OK? Photo, long hair, boootiful, photo, photo, OK? OK?' Only, they were ugly, not 'boootiful', and their hair was artificially extended.

The focus of traditional life, and the reason that Pingan had been turned into a tourist resort village, was rice farming. The villages were perched three-quarters of the way up the side of a large valley. In order to farm the hillsides, the steep slope had been landscaped into terraces. These were not just ordinary terraces, though – this was agricultural engineering on an astonishing scale. The terraced area extended laterally right along the length of the valley, only broken in a few places by wooded river gullies. From top to bottom the terraces stretched no less than 800 vertical metres. We counted over 300 stepped layers, one above the other. The terraces had taken several hundred years to build, being completed in about the seventeenth century. The China International Travel Service poetically described the result as 'shining terraces lacing the mountain slopes like silver ripples… the fields have combined magnificence and elegance, and form some of the finest scenery in China'.

In previous places throughout Asia the terraces we had seen had been wider than the height of their supporting walls, but here the terraces themselves were often barely two or three feet wide, while their walls were often four or five feet high. Usually these thin strips contoured their way continuously around the hillsides, making the landscape look as if it was composed of hundreds of thinly sliced layers, but where the space was tight the individual terraces could be just a few square feet in area. Where the valley side contained small ridges and hillocks, which was the case near Pingan, the terraces formed concentric circles around the topography, getting smaller as they climbed up, until on the very top would be a final green topknot. Not a patch of land was left uncultivated. It was a marvel of landscaping, one of the man-made wonders of the world, heightening by knowing that it was still very much a living landscape.

Most of the work going on in the rice terraces was weeding or fertilising. Men carried two wooden buckets full of slopping slurry, slung from a bamboo pole on their shoulder, and trod it into the rice paddies, either wearing brown plastic boots or simply in bare feet. We did see some more modern versions of fertilisers – portable plastic pump-action spraying machines – but only one or two. As was often the case, it was the women who appeared to do the more back-breaking work. They were usually weeding the fields, filling their back-baskets with greens that we joked – only half in jest – would reappear as dinner.

The weight of the baskets bent these women double as they stooped under their loads. All the elderly women had perpetually crippled backs. They would hobble along with their heads below their waist, one arm outstretched in front of them holding on to a stick for support, and their necks craned upwards to see where they were going. It was the same posture as we had seen in Bolivia – the same sad way to end up in old age after a lifetime of hard labour. We would watch these women still making their way along the tops of the rice terraces, their bent shapes clearly silhouetted against the skyline, creating a defining image of the landscape.

We soaked up the picturesque countryside and enjoyed the hospitality of our hosts until the rains abated. The weather we were experiencing had been caused by Tropical Storm Bilis. Closer to the east coast, it caused the deaths of 164 people, affecting some 20 million people at a cost of US $1.5 billion. We had avoided travelling right into the danger area more by luck than judgement, not for the first time on our trip. Eventually, however, we had to travel east ourselves all the way to Hong Kong in time to get our new visas. To get there from Pingan we took six buses over three days, culminating in an overnight sleeper bus. It was a surprisingly straightforward journey.

This, it has to be said, was largely due to the spontaneous assistance of a range of local people. They showed us where the bus stations were, purchased tickets for us and generally kept us moving in the right direction. We could almost rely on being helped out by someone brave enough to try their English, which was tremendously reassuring. Without the friendliness and generosity of ordinary people, life would have been so much more difficult for us. From having been uncertain and apprehensive of what we would find in China, Yunnan and Guanxi provinces had been full of people and places that gave us some of the most enjoyable and memorable experiences of anywhere around the world.

Leaving the mainland city of Guangzhou on the mainland of China towards the 'New Territories' of Hong Kong, we drove for two hours past a continuous concrete forest. Endless series of grey and orange tower blocks and factories stood side by side. Where a hole appeared between them, it was a building site. There was nothing else. This in itself was a dramatic landscape, in a nightmarish kind of way, and couldn't have been more of a contrast from the green terraces of Pingan. This industrial forest was an indication of the way that places on the prosperous east coast of China were developing. It was the kind of place that was driving China's economic miracle. China had consistently been the world's most successful economy since 1978 in growth terms, expanding its economy by almost 8 per cent per year, on a per capita basis. In 2005 China grew by 10 per cent and had a trade surplus of US $200 billion. Nevertheless, there were still 800 million rural Chinese earning on average 20,000 yuan (US $2,618) per year.

China's economy looked set to face some increasingly serious environmental issues. 12 per cent of the land was drought-ridden, as rainfall in the past seven years had averaged only 70 per cent of its usual amount, and the water table in northern China was falling. Weather had caused 60 per cent of the natural disasters in China, through hurricanes, floods and sandstorms. In a newspaper, I read that natural disasters in China over the past five years alone had cost US $113.8 billion, which it claimed averaged out at an astounding US $73.3 million per day. It was estimated that these factors reduced China's GDP by 3–6 per cent – and it was predicted that this would only get worse as global warming caused even more climate change.

Interestingly, China is investing in billions of dollars into developing state-of-the-art environmentally sustainable cities. It needs to, for over the next fifty years it is estimated that 600 million people will migrate into Chinese cities – enough to give any centralised bureaucracy a serious headache. Chinese television had an English-language channel, which featured enough programmes covering environmental issues to portray the government as being at the very least well aware of the issues facing it, and at best trying to find real solutions to them. We had the feeling, however, that economic development would always come first, environmentally sustainable or not – and large-scale, imperialistic development at that. Our overriding impression of China was of a powerful presence that was coming of age in the modern world, confident of its expanding capabilities and without limits to its ambitions. It was fascinating, captivating, beautiful – and not to be underestimated.

Chapter 56: Hong Kong

Hundreds of people were crossing to and from Hong Kong, which is now a Special Administrative Region within China. Fleets of coaches had pulled up on one side of the vast border post, where passengers were all given coded stickers on their arms and directed into the passport control halls. I had never seen so many people queuing to get through immigration at one time, and it seemed notable that only three of us that I could see were Caucasian. On the other side of the border, everyone was processed again into coaches according to their armbands. It took another drive to reach the city of Hong Kong, along superb roads which gave coastal views of showcase bridges that had been built to connect the various islands of the Region.

Hong Kong sits partly on the mainland and partly offshore on an island, with Victoria Harbour in between. The mainland is called Kowloon; the island is Hong Kong itself. Hong Kong was ceded to Britain in 1842 after the First Opium War with China, when the British Navy forced China to allow the trade of opium from India to China, partly to offset the cost of importing tea to Europe from China. China had previously insisted on being paid for its tea in silver bars, as it claimed to have no use for European goods – a policy which was not surprisingly unpopular with European countries. Hong Kong was used as a British base during the war, and afterwards became the main port for British traders. However, China continued to be reluctant to embrace trade, and in particular it refused to allow foreign embassies in Beijing. This led to an English and French army actually capturing Beijing itself in 1860, after which the opium trade was legalised in China, foreigners were allowed to travel freely within the country, and trade was expanded. After 400 years of relative isolation, China was being forced to open itself to foreigners – in particular Europeans.

The island of Hong Kong and the peninsula adjacent to it were permanently given to Britain, and in 1898 the 'New Territories' on which Hong Kong depended were granted on a 99-year lease. When this lease expired in 1997, all of Hong Kong was given back to China. In the view of the last British Governor, this act at the very end of the twentieth century was 'where the story of Empire really ended'.

We got off the bus in Kowloon, in the middle of a crowded, confusing urban mess. We were surrounded by numerous fairly grotty apartment blocks, some ten to twenty storeys high. The narrow roads were congested with cars and buses, and were full of hustle and bustle, making Kowloon feel very claustrophobic. Colourful signs hung over the pavements in riotous disorder. We were overwhelmed by the noise, the brashness, the ugly tattiness, the fumes and the people everywhere. We even had to take refuge in a coffee bar to gather our wits, after which we found our way to one of the massive apartment blocks – called 'mansions' – near the waterfront. These blocks had been colonised by private enterprises, so that the ground floor of our block was full of clothing and souvenirs stalls, the second floor was dominated by Chinese and Indian restaurants, and above were a mix of private flats and small businesses. Touts lounged in the ground-floor entrance, waiting to intercept any passing tourists on the street and try to convince them to eat or sleep within the depths of the block.

On the top floors were several budget hostels, converted from apartments into dormitories and tiny bedrooms. It was all pretty dingy and seedy, with the strange exception of the smartly uniformed bellboys operating the lifts. Not really the 'deluxe hotel' that large, aged letters on the outside of the building proclaimed. To our surprise, however, our hostel matron offered to arrange Chinese visas for us, with a prompt service and a good price. We were in luck, and immediately took advantage of her offer before setting out to explore Hong Kong.

The adjacent shops along Nathan Road were gaudy and bright. They sold the latest electronic goods and jewellery, flaunting signs such as Rolex, Nikon and Sony. As if the pink or blue neon writing in the windows were not enough to attract attention, more touts stood in shop doorways, offering the latest deal: 'Watch, sir? Rolex, very cheap.' Or, 'Smart suit, sir? Dress, madam?'

The people on Nathan Road were the most culturally diverse of any we saw in the world, with only the streets of New York coming close. Here there was an intense mix of widely different nationalities and religions, often proudly wearing distinctively ethnic clothing. Indian and Pakistani men were predominant – which may have accounted for the restaurants in our tower block – but there were many others besides: African, Middle Eastern, Chinese and European; Hindu, Muslim, Jew and Buddhist.

English was not the first language for most people, but it was the most widely used – and all writing was in English. Everywhere were colourful signs, strung on wires across the road like a bridge, perhaps three signs wide, five high, and as deep as the road was long. Within twenty yards they offered everything from massage and reflexology to cafés, canteens, a tea house, an inn, Indian cuisine, visas, locks, medicine, haircuts and a tailor. Around the corner was a five-star hotel, a row of shops selling goldfish, and numerous expensive restaurants. Double-decker buses drove alongside red taxi cabs in the busy streets but, unusually for Asia, there were no bicycles. Further away the roads turned into street markets full of cheap clothes and leather goods. Kowloon was a chaotic, schizophrenic place that changed character at every turn. At night the streets lit up with advertising and the traffic quietened down, but it was still a heady experience.

Central Hong Kong – on the island – was home to a much photographed harbourside skyline. As we crossed Victoria Harbour on the famous Star Ferry, all we could see were blurred, misty grey shadows. It was a very foggy day – or was that smoggy? – so we decided not to climb up the 'Peak' for the view. Instead, we explored the city, giving ourselves headaches from the fumes and smog. The city spread sideways along the shoreline, occupying the only available flat ground between the hillsides and the water. A fair proportion of the city was actually built on reclaimed land. The modern, wealthy commercial centre was only a small part, and was surprisingly compact. The tower blocks here rose up as fairly uniformly square columns of blue-tinted reflective glass, all shiny and silver. At pavement level there were businessmen and women in suits and ties, striding importantly through the oppressive humidity and 32°C temperatures.

Central Hong Kong actually had a fairly open feel about it, with green spaces and pseudo-historic buildings that had been 'preserved' between the overlooking office blocks. Numerous double-decker buses came and went, as if in central London. We boarded a dark green slim-line double-decker tram that took us away from the centre, parallel to the coast. After a few streets the clean, sharp and stylish centre gave way to decrepit and dirty apartment blocks, always very tall and thin. Some were fifty storeys high, but barely a house width wide. Out of the windows hung either washing lines or dripping air-conditioning units. This was one of the most densely populated areas on the planet. The island as a whole averaged something over 6,000 people per square kilometre, but it is estimated that in the urban core there may be 28,000 people per square kilometre. By contrast, the centre of London has a maximum population density of 15,000 people per square kilometre, just over half of that of Central Hong Kong.

Between the mouldering walls were hundreds of red-and-white advertisement boards, this time a sea of Chinese characters suspended above the roads. Shops and stalls sold all sorts of goods; stretches of food markets displayed cuttings of red meat above bowls of flapping fish, chicken feet, toads or crabs with their pincers tied shut. Butchers hosed down the pavements under people's feet. Packed into even smaller alleyways were market stalls with more clothing, leather goods or fake Rolex watches, always cheap and tacky. We did, however, find the camera that we wanted at last, in a small backstreet which surprisingly housed several camera shops, all small outfits that nevertheless offered the latest goods at relatively cheap prices. There was nothing too glossy about any of the shops or streets; it was a far cry from our expectations of ultra-modern, glamorous shopping malls and international brands.

Despite the image portrayed abroad, Hong Kong was still essentially a Chinese city, which just happened to have a phenomenally dynamic Westernised quarter within it – in 2006, its GDP per capita was US $37,000. For me, Hong Kong was summed up by a single street corner. On one side was a street that had Chinese red lanterns and signs hanging over it, with grim apartment blocks rising up on either side. Over the road, across the junction, there were shiny modern office blocks, with a McDonald's sign being the only visible advertising above the wide street that flowed with cars. It was as if the city contained two different forces that were counterpoints to each other. Modern, globalised influences were gradually usurping the widespread, established but ultimately degenerating Chinese culture, it seemed to us. On the news while we were there was a story about the traditional street-restaurants of Hong Kong, which were no longer to have their licenses renewed and therefore represented another aspect of traditional culture that would inevitably pass into history.

Hong Kong City was, however, only one part of the Region. Under 25 per cent of the territory had been developed; the island itself was almost a wilderness, with steep forested slopes that rose up to sharp peaks and fell down to rocky beaches and coves, not dissimilar to the lush coastal landscapes of Brazil and New Zealand. It was very scenic and was calling out to be explored at leisure – which unfortunately was not possible for us as we had a flight scheduled to Beijing. Driving past some trendy new coastal developments that had opted for 45-storey apartment blocks rather than suburban houses, we did manage to make an outing to a hilltop Buddhist monastery. Here were signs that read, 'Keep clean, no alcoholic drinks and vegetarian food only'. Worshippers waved fistfuls of incense sticks and bowed before the largest outdoor seated Buddha in Asia. Nearby was a modern sculpture of one of the most profound Buddhist texts. The text was called the Heart Sutra, which:

> ...subsumes the essence of the Wisdom of the Buddha ... The Heart Sutra articulates the doctrine of 'emptiness' ... When one acquires this Wisdom of 'emptiness' one will realise that all physical and mental things are in a constant process of change ... Understanding the relativity of all standpoints will also prevent one from becoming irrationally attached to things. In this way one will come to be free from all mental obstructions and attain to perfect harmony and bliss.

The peacefulness of the sculpture kept us there for a while, looking out over the ocean. It was a far cry from Kowloon; Hong Kong was extremely diverse, but each part had its own riches. We left having discovered that it deserved more than a few days' stopover. As it turned out, we nearly had more time there than we had intended, for at the airport the friendly airline staff informed us that our flight tickets had all expired and all onward flights were no longer valid. The only way we could convince them that they were mistaken was by providing proof of the date of our first flight from London to New York. This could have been tricky, for we did not have the flight coupons from ten months ago exactly to hand, but Claudia's lateral thinking came up with the idea of showing her New York immigration stamp, which as it was the only one in her passport had to correspond to the date of our flight.

The check-in staff had the grace to accept this, but then queried our visa, which we had obtained on the cheap courtesy of our 'deluxe' mansion hostel. The reason it had been cheap was that it had been obtained at an immigration office at the Chinese land border, which was not the place we were leaving from. The airline couldn't allow us to board without correct immigration documentation – but we couldn't let the plane leave without us, or all our onward flights would be cancelled and we would be stranded. After a tense hour during which our passports were checked and double-checked, all was well. We were on our way to Beijing, home of the Forbidden City and close to the Great Wall of China.

Chapter 57: Beijing

The first things that caught my eye on arrival in Beijing were the signs for Starbucks and KFC in the airport's arrival hall – China was continuing to confound preconceptions. Walking around the remains of the old Beijing city wall several hours later, I couldn't help but think that the city strongly resembled Moscow. This was partly because Beijing was grey, with a misty gloom so thick that visibility was reduced to a couple of blocks. It was like being trapped inside one of those November days when the fog refuses to clear and the sun never gets through. That was what it was like all day long in Beijing. We saw the sun just once, through the haze: a golden disc that looked like a full moon, only not so bright, just weakly visible through the greyness. The fog was as much to do with the weather as it was smog, although the air was quite rancid.

Another similarity with Moscow, it seemed to me, was the dense mix of varied traffic filling the broad roads: numerous red or green-and-brown taxis; black or metallic grey private cars; ordinary buses; trolleybuses using overhead electric cables; bendy buses made of several segments; and an incongruous handful of bicycles and wooden carts. Everything careered around corners using all lanes at will, and raced across pedestrian crossings without a thought of giving way. The roads were often quite wide and well maintained, but somehow that didn't help the overall system much. There was a sense of danger about the urban road traffic that we hadn't felt for a while. And then there were the monotonous, dreary apartment blocks, for some reason often painted pink. They made large parts of Beijing look like it was comprised of multi-storey council-housing estates.

A welcome contrast to the dull, grey city was a strip of park beside the ruined city wall. It had fresh green grass, ornate trees and colourful flower beds, like a little oasis. A noticeboard had no less than twelve pictures of prohibited activities, including walking dogs and lighting fires. The old city wall itself was just a wall, 11 m high, with sloping sides. Its construction had begun in 1419 and it had survived until the 1950s when, along with so much of China's heritage, most of it was demolished. In this case, it was to make room for the above apartment blocks. Today, small sections of the wall had been restored, making it was impossible to tell what was really old and what wasn't.

In search of something more interesting, we took the efficient bilingual metro to Tiananmen Square, where we emerged to see a large McDonald's in front of us, occupying a drab white-tiled building just like the ones we had seen in Guanxi province. We crossed the road to find our way blocked by a low white railing, behind which a crowd of people obscured any view, although from the empty skyline we could tell that there was a large space ahead. To access Tiananmen Square we had to walk along its side until we were beside one of the two large entrance 'gates' – one a complete reconstruction – that straddled the periphery road. These large gates were a cross between an archway and a defensive tower. A sign proclaimed them to be 'part of Beijing's precious cultural heritage'; China had come a long way since the Cultural Revolution.

Adjacent to the gates of Tiananmen Square was a large, low building that would have looked just like a town hall or public library if it were not for the pair of imposing Communist-era statues and the presence of uniformed guards in front of it. It squatted across almost the entire width of one end of Tiananmen Square, as if having to go one better than Lenin's Tomb. For this was the Chairman Mao Memorial Hall, a mausoleum containing the Communist leader's body, which was still partially visible inside. In theory it would have been possible for us to have had a look, but the queue of Chinese waiting their turn to do so was enormous. It stretched not just out of the door but along one side of the building, down the entire length of the next side, and even along the back of the hall too. There must have been more than 1,000 people in that line. So instead we asked a couple of university students in the square what they thought of Mao. Their opinion was that old Chinese people still considered Mao to be a hero, but for them he was merely 'OK'. Certainly better than George W. Bush, they added. People we met were quick to refer to Mao as being '70 per cent right, 30 per cent wrong' – which was the official line on his legacy.

Chairman Mao Tse-tung had been, if nothing else, extreme. As Paul Theroux notes, a Chinese proverb exists which advises not going beyond sensible limits in order to correct a wrong. Mao, however, said, 'To right a wrong it is necessary to exceed proper limits.' He explicitly believed in the virtue of going too far. Two of his casually inhuman policies brought tragedy to China. Between 1958 and 1961 he introduced the Great Leap Forward, designed to communise agriculture, abolish private property and initiate worthless steel production on a mass scale. Millions starved as a result – estimates range from 30 to 60 million people. It may have been the largest famine in human history.

The Cultural Revolution that began in 1966 was conceived by Mao as the perfect way to shock the Chinese people. It has since shocked the world. Almost everything about China was turned on its head. Academics were sent to work on farms, Muslims were forced to raise pigs, children humiliated and beat their teachers, the Red Guards – often children and students – destroyed at will much of the cultural heritage across the country. Anything and anyone that could be branded as capitalist or feudal was a target for persecution. Further millions died during the cultural madness.

Imposing state buildings flanked the sides of Tiananmen Square. One of these was the National Museum, outside which was a large sign with the logo for the Beijing 2008 Olympic Games on it. It displayed an electronic countdown that could be seen from across the square. There were 740 days to go. Around China we had seen buses, walls and T-shirts emblazoned with the Olympic rings. It was as if the whole country was gearing up in anticipation of this event, however premature it seemed to us. In Beijing itself, the idea of the Games never failed to conjure up an image of athletes gasping for fresh air as they tried to compete. Cleaning up the city would surely be a monumental task, even for China's government.

Dotted across Tiananmen Square were several hawkers trying to sell watches containing a portrait of Mao. Others strolled around clutching a handful of small kites that were tugging at their strings. Kite flying was a big thing in the square, particularly for the children who had come with one or both of their parents for a wander. The grey, flat, featureless space was filled with the colour and life of hundreds of people just pottering around, as if in a green and grassy city park. Some even sat around in groups on the hard floor having a picnic. The square was at the very heart of Beijing and it was notable that it was an open, public space being well used by everyday people, even if many of them were tourists and there was plenty enough space for everyone, all minding their own self-contained business. Tiananmen Square is the world's largest public square, 880 metres long and 500 metres wide.

We did ask if the square had been used for any protests recently, but the answer was that no one would dare to start anything here. Not only was there a significant police and army presence – the only vehicles driving across the square were police vans – but there was a fear of plain-clothes secret policemen who permanently lurked within the crowd, on the lookout for any trouble. However open China might have seemed to us travelling casually through it, the authoritarian hand of the government always lurked behind the scenes.

In China we found that we couldn't open one of our online email websites, presumably because it had been blocked by the government. Hundreds of online forums were shut down annually by the Ministry of Information, which used multiple search engines to find illegal or undesirable content. In Beijing alone there were reportedly 40,000 watchdogs checking Internet cafés and monitoring emails and websites. Amnesty International has been campaigning for journalists and students who have been imprisoned for years for posting 'subversive' or 'sensitive' pieces on the Internet. Reporters Without Borders count China as the world's leading jailer of journalists, with thirty-two in custody, alongside some fifty Internet campaigners.

As we moved towards the underpass at the far end of Tiananmen Square that led to the Forbidden City – so called because ordinary people hadn't been allowed in without the Emperor's permission, although its name seemed ironic today – we began to be part of a swelling crowd. By the time we emerged on the other side of the road, we were small bodies within a mass of people that was surging forward. We crossed over a stone bridge and past soldiers who stood stiffly to attention under parasols, like toy figures. Straight in front of us was a long red wall – actually called a gate – perhaps forty feet high and ten times that in length, with eight red flags flying overhead. A similarly enormous building on top of the wall was covered with a two-tiered orange roof, supported by red columns. Hanging on the face of the wall was the famous huge portrait of Mao, directly over the several small black tunnels that everyone was heading for. So many people were passing through that it was a testament to the Chinese sense of conduct that no one was squashed and injured. Nevertheless we were jostled and pushed by the crowds, at risk of having our eyes gouged out by hundreds of small umbrellas.

After the tunnel we emerged into another large open space, a bit like a vast courtyard. A tree-lined avenue ran down its centre to another huge red wall some distance off. There were people milling about everywhere, just as outside. We headed for the second wall and the ticket queues, then passed through another tunnel. On the other side was a second courtyard, smaller than before but still perfectly large enough for a football pitch or two. Around the edge ran red buildings that in another setting could have been stable blocks or sheds, but here were fabulously painted with gold, blue, red and green designs, fronted by pillars and containing a series of latticework doorways.

These buildings had all been restored and repainted, using a bright, glossy paint that made the structures look like gaudy modern plastic. All sense of ageing had literally been brushed over, which seemed a shame to us, particularly as deeper within the city we reached places that the restorers hadn't and there we found much more of a sense of history. Across this second courtyard ran a river, with small marble bridges gracefully arching over it. And on the far side was a third giant gateway, this one covered in scaffold poles and green netting, although a replica picture of the gateway – full-size – had been draped over its front like an enormous curtain.

Beyond the third gate was yet another central space, but this one was filled with ceremonial halls that had been built on the top of a large raised platform. These had been given wonderful names, such as the 'Hall of Supreme Harmony'. In fact, one was originally called 'Hall of Scrupulous Behaviour', which had been changed to 'Palace of Proper Places and Cultivation of Things', followed by 'Palace of Peace and Tranquillity' and, in 1562, 'Hall of the

People's Sovereign', before in 1645 being given its current name of 'Hall of Preserved Harmony'. It alone was 1,240 m^2 in area. Beyond these three halls was yet another raised platform and more buildings, this time including the 'Palace of Heavenly Purity'.

Meanwhile, spreading out to the sides of the entire complex was a network of smaller roofless passageways that led through gateways into smaller courtyards. Most of these had the same basic design of walls or buildings in a square around a central building that was isolated from the rest. These buildings had once been used for such things as ladies' quarters, but now they often housed collections of museum artefacts. All of the walls throughout the Forbidden City were painted red, all the roofs were tiled orange, and everywhere there were gold gilded edges and carved decorations. It was almost garish, like some kind of lurid modernist paintwork run amok – but somehow it worked and was even attractive. The internal gateways in particular were each separate works of art, six feet wide and twelve feet high, set within red walls twice as high, with gold and green tiles and decoration all around the doorways.

The Forbidden City did feel at times like mini streets leading to small houses, but really it was a vast, opulent palatial complex – the largest in the world, in fact. The number of buildings and the scale of the site took a fair while to comprehend. There were 800 buildings within the Forbidden City, which is a World Heritage Site recognised by UNESCO as having the largest collection of preserved ancient wooden structures in the world. It took us the best part of a day just to walk through its length to the juniper garden at the end and back again. As we explored the parts of the City that tourists were allowed into, we couldn't help but feel that this was the closest we would get to seeing what the stone corridors and temples of places like Angkor Wat might have been like before they decayed into ruins. This imperial residence for China's dynasty of emperors was a modern equivalent of the ancient grand cities, perhaps the last surviving example of their type.

The Forbidden City was built from 1406 onwards by Emperor Yongle, who had relocated the capital of China to Beijing as a defensive move to stop the Mongols from re-conquering the country. It took fourteen years to build and subsequently was the home of twenty-four emperors over 500 years, right up until the last emperor abdicated in 1912. As Gavin Menzies has described, when the Forbidden City was inaugurated in 1421, there were 26,000 guests in attendance, including twenty-eight heads of state from all around Asia and north-eastern Africa – but none from Europe.

In the early years of the fifteenth century, China was the most civilised, technological and sophisticated nation in the world, at a time when western Europe was still medieval. China had well-established trade links with the Indonesian Spice Islands, Malaysia, India, the Arabian peninsula and even the coast of East Africa. Vast ocean-going expeditions – which may have reached Australia and the Americas, according to Menzies – used the largest sailing boats ever built in human history. China had invented the compass, whisky, umbrellas, kites, cast iron, steel, the crossbow and gunpowder. Paper had been in use since the third century BC, the first printed book was produced in AD 868, and printing presses had been invented by the eleventh century. Unfortunately, from 1434 onwards China abandoned its global ambitions and began to retreat inwards, a condition that persevered until the Opium Wars with Britain and France.

Emperor Yongle also began to rebuild the Great Wall of China, which had been first constructed in the third century BC. He extended it to over 6,400 kilometres in length, running inland from the Pacific Ocean. It was built as a hilltop line of earth ramparts, faced with stone and studded with watchtowers. We made our way to a section of the Wall via a couple of public minibuses early one morning. It was a four-hour drive along a good, fast road that was at times a dual carriageway. The landscape could have been European: flat, large fields of lush fruit and vegetable crops were separated by rows of tall poplar trees, while the roadside was dotted with residential suburbs and modern business parks. What was not so European was the driver's apparent death wish. The close shaves with oncoming traffic as we swerved around slower vehicles were heart-stopping – it was better not to look! Although China contained only 2 per cent of the world's cars, these were responsible for 15 per cent of road fatalities worldwide. An estimated six hundred people were killed every single day on China's roads.

We survived the journey to reach a small, nondescript car park. A tarmac path led away through thick green woodland, which we followed. We steadily climbed up a slope for a while, becoming steeper until it turned into zigzag steps, which suddenly stopped at the base of the Great Wall of China. It was much higher than we expected; the top ramparts were some twenty feet above us. It was also extremely well constructed and in good condition, having been partially restored. We walked inside the wall itself through a little archway and climbed the stone steps within it to the ramparts, where we emerged in the middle of what looked like a solid paved road about six to ten feet wide and perhaps a dozen feet off the ground. Flanking each side of us were thick stone walls over six feet high, with slits and embrasures in them for firing arrows from, just like in British castles.

This fortified roadway had been built on the top of the low ridge that we had just walked up, so the ground fell steeply away either side of it and gave us the impression of being even higher than we were. We looked out over the dark green treetops to an endless series of bumpy hills, without another human feature in sight. All along the ridge top, linking this hill with the next and the next, never straying from the highest possible route, ran the stone ribbon of the Wall. It flexed up and down and bent from side to side, doggedly following every contour of the topography. It made me think of a spine: the solid backbone of the undulating landscape. And it didn't stop. It just kept on going, over the hills and far away, until we lost sight of it between the hills and in the grey mistiness of the morning.

Every so often, square watchtowers had been built into and above the Wall, like fifteen-foot-high castle keeps. From their windows were the best views of the Wall. As it receded into the distance, the watchtowers were the last things that could be seen, like a line of stone beacons on the hilltops. Around us, the mists swirled around, with just the stone Wall and the green trees in sight, creating a palpable atmosphere. The stage seemed perfectly set for Mongol warriors to emerge out of the mist and attempt to storm the battlements, as if it was part of an extravagant Hollywood film set. Only, everything remained quiet and still, there was no one else around, and the Wall was – almost unbelievably – very real.

We had chosen to visit a section where we could walk along the wall for a few hours. We quickly found that the steep undulations between hills turned our pleasant stroll into a stiff hike, particularly after the restored section was left behind and we had to pick our way across rubble and broken steps. In places the watchtowers and battlements were somewhat tumbledown and even overgrown with plants. But it was magnificent to see how the Wall had been built without compromise: where the land went up, so did the Wall, turning the paved road into a flight of steep steps. In a way, it reminded me of the new highway being built in Yunnan province – as if the same visionary, determined mentality had been behind both projects.

As we walked, we came across various other people on the Wall. Tourists were picking their way along; cleaners in orange bibs walked with plastic rubbish bags; and hawkers were selling a variety of food, drink and souvenirs. Some set up shop in the shelter of the watchtowers, where they waited like spiders in a lair to trap passers-by into buying their goods. We were overtaken by one guy who was triumphant at having purchased a T-shirt from a lady, proud of having bargained her down from 100 yuan to 80 yuan. We kept quiet about the fact that just before, as we had walked past the very same seller, she had offered it to us for 20 yuan. Other hawkers had a different sales tactic, which became quite irritating. The ladies – they were all ladies – would fall into step alongside us, trying to be part guide and part friend. They patiently built up a cheerful rapport for perhaps half an hour or so, before coming around to their inevitable sales pitch, digging books and postcards out of their plastic bags. When pleading and wheedling didn't work, they would come up with their trump line: 'Yes, please, I'm a poor farmer, thank you, so I can go home.'

At the end of our hike we came to another reconstructed section and found the Wall interrupted by a river gorge. It didn't bridge the river, but plunged down the cliffs on each side right to the water line. A modern swing bridge allowed us to cross the river, with a toll gate at the far end for having done so, which seemed a bit of a cheek considering that we had already paid to walk the section and had no choice other than to use the bridge. On the far side was one of the steepest sections of the Wall: a long climb of stone slab steps up a hillside into the clouds. Its sheer solid presence, remote and isolated yet believed to extend for nearly 4,500 miles – the longest man-made structure in the world – had a real impact on us. The sight of it winding away into the far distance was like looking at a fairy-tale creation that had come to life. It was wondrous. Among all the human constructions that we saw around the world, only Machu Picchu in Peru made a bigger impression on us than the Great Wall of China.

The final steep section was close to a road and therefore was popular with tour groups, including a girls' school trip from Sheffield. What a place to come for a history lesson! It was touching to hear one teenage girl saying to her friend, 'When I get home, I won't care so much about being so dressed up or having perfect fashions any more.'

I had been fifteen years old when I first visited India, an experience that significantly affected my own outlook on life. If one's mind is receptive, there is nothing like travelling to gain new perspectives about the world, its people and indeed one's own place within it. The worst culture shock, I always found, was returning home, where it is hard for anyone else to understand what has been seen and learned. Even worse, it can seem that no one particularly cares about these profound but intensely personal experiences, or the questions they may pose about our comfortable lifestyles.

However, if I had to select one country in the world which was profoundly challenging to the Western traveller, it would not be China. We had expected China to be difficult to travel through, to be very different to our European culture and strange to us. It had turned out to be easy, friendly and fascinating. It was far more developed, globalised and open than we had expected. More than anything, China was an endless series of surprising juxtapositions which changed their form and character at every turn.

We had been travelling around the world for some eleven months now, through Central and South America, South East Asia and finally China. We assumed that we were fairly travel-worn and experienced. We knew that our next country, India, wouldn't be an easy ride – I had been there twice before, had travelled all around the subcontinent, and had been warning Claudia for some time about its challenges – but we were still unprepared for the sights, sounds and smells that assaulted our senses and minds when we arrived into Delhi. India would be like nothing we had previously encountered.

Part Eight
India and Nepal

Chapter 58: Delhi

Our flight into Delhi landed in the early morning, at about 2 a.m., which is never a good time to arrive in a strange city. Previous experiences and the advice in our guidebook all warned against taking our chances with a taxi at night. There was an official taxi booth at the airport, which was open and could offer us taxis to a selection of hotels, but unfortunately not the hotels that we actually wanted. So we found a couple of plastic chairs and dozed for a while, along with a handful of other assorted passengers. As morning dawned, Claudia went in search of a coffee from one of the several stands in the arrivals hall. The first declined to serve her coffee, but tried to force tomato soup on her instead. The second stand did sell coffee, for a price that was clearly displayed. That didn't stop her being overcharged, which all the loitering men standing around smilingly insisted was absolutely correct. This, then, was India, where even buying a coffee could be a difficult and frustrating experience. Eventually we returned to the taxi booth, where it was now no problem to go to the hotels of our choice, once we had declined all the others again.

Our taxi was characteristic for Delhi: an old, battered black London taxi cab driven by a gaunt, unshaven man wearing a thin, dirty shirt. Our first views of Delhi reminded me of Nairobi: patches of waste ground beside the road, dirt paths criss-crossing the scrubby grass, houses lurking behind lines of dusty trees in the background. In places we saw shacks built from corrugated metal beside the road. Along the sides of the road men were sweeping with hand-held brooms, clearing the verges of soil and litter. They would push their small piles of rubbish out into the road, from where it was inevitable that they would be blown all over the verges again. The odd bony cow stood motionless in the centre of the road, doing nothing, as if hypnotised. We swerved around the cows and narrowly avoided colliding with the sweeping men or bicycles that wobbled alongside.

As we entered the planned roads of New Delhi, where tall green trees flanked the roads, the traffic began to increase. Motorbikes, three-wheeled tuk-tuks, bruised cars and battered buses would squeeze closer as each junction, edging forward in an attempt to be the first to get ahead as soon as space opened up in front. We passed into Old Delhi, where the roads suddenly shrank, turning into what looked like the back lanes of a miserable township. Our speed slowed as the narrowing road became blocked by street stalls, tuk-

tuks, rickshaws, bicycles, cows and pedestrians. It was rough and dirty, and there was litter everywhere. A small herd of thin brown cows was eating from fodder strewn across the middle of the road. Along with the rest of the traffic, we just negotiated our way slowly around them. Buildings crowded in from either side, grotty signs sticking out from their decaying walls.

The whole scene was one of congested, impoverished urban squalor. It was hard to take in; we were initially overwhelmed by it all, being driven right into the heart of the mayhem. We eventually ground to a halt, not able to progress any further through the crowds. This wasn't some tucked away corner of Delhi; this was the Main Bazaar, the main backpacker hang-out, where the buildings and shops were indeed touristy hostels, eateries, souvenir shops and Internet cafés. In the following days we would adjust to the environment, coming to accept the dirt and the smell and the crowds. But stepping out of our dingy hotel room never failed to shock us. This was the heart of the capital city of India, after all.

We found a place to stay, down a tiny alleyway. Standing outside our door when we arrived was a black cow, its horns pointing right at us. On the corner of the alleyway was a row of three dirty white enamel urinals, open to the street. Men stood and used them as everyone and everything streamed past. The acrid stench of stale urine was painful from yards away. Incidentally, despite seeing a number of these urinals beside pavements, there were never any public toilets for women. Walking down the Bazaar, we had to step carefully to avoid the muddy puddles, the litter and the cow dung underfoot. There was a constant background smell of traffic fumes, rotting rubbish, unwashed bodies, and urine. It was astonishing to see slender young ladies dressed in colourful saris – bright apparitions of blue, orange, and yellow, their wrists and ankles dangling with silver or gold jewellery and their faces made up – daintily picking their way over the muck of the road.

Flip-flops, high heels and smart shoes were all mixed up together. Hindu holy men – sadhus – walked from shop to shop, asking for sustenance. They were wrapped in orange robes that jarred with their white hair and the streaks of white and red paint on their foreheads. The only other things they carried were a bead necklace, a wooden staff and a silver cup tied to a string around their waist. Skinny men walking past often wore faded European trousers and shirts. The careering cycle-rickshaw-wallahs sometimes had little on but a blue-green miniskirt, a grimy cotton vest with holes in, and a dishcloth over their shoulder that they used to wipe sweat from their faces. They wouldn't stop for anyone or anything as they struggled down the street; a shout in our ear would cause us to jump immediately to one side, before a wheel coming from behind bumped into our ankle. The only other thing that the crowds parted for were the holy urban cows, mournfully wending their way through the city.

Shopkeepers sometimes brushed their front steps clean, sweeping the litter and dust with a flourish into the road again, regardless of whether pedestrian legs were passing or not. The shopkeepers would often stand in their doorways, as if trying to spot potential customers. As we passed they tried to attract our attention, but they always managed to turn an otherwise polite 'Hello!' into a rude, almost aggressive demand that we stop, followed by an indignant, aggrieved, 'Excuse me!' Any eye contact elicited a shout at us, so we learned to avoid looking at anyone. There were no smiles, no pleasant exchanges, no conversations. It was like running a gauntlet of unpleasantness.

At one end of the Bazaar was a huddle of wooden carts with piles of colourful fruit stacked up. It was a mini-market, blocking the entrances to small alleyways that contained food stalls, which only the seriously foolhardy would brave. The only way we could progress was to push our way through the crowding traffic. Crossing the main road beyond meant stepping into a slowly moving mass of black metal and cycle-rickshaw wheels, trying to find spaces for our feet between bumpers before being hit by something else pushing forwards. Overhead, a huge billboard advertised the latest computer hardware, as if mocking the poverty on the street below. Kites circled in the skies above, like vultures searching for the dead and dying.

We saw a man crawling on the ground through the crowds, with a gaping wound open on his swollen leg. Amputees and cripples begged at the roadside. On the dusty pavements we stepped over men and women sitting or lying outstretched on the floor, apparently without the strength or will to move further. One man had not a stitch of clothing on him. They were listless, almost lifeless bodies, disconnected from the world, oblivious to everything around them. And then, every so often, a rich, fat Indian lady rode past, sitting side-saddle on the back of a motorbike, a colourful sari wrapped around her body and draped over her coiffured head, exposing rolls of blubber that bounced around her midriff like a statement of her wealth and social status.

Sometimes we would see slum-like shelters by the sides of the roads, tucked underneath trees. Plastic sheets, sacking material, and even newspapers would cover a makeshift framework of wooden poles. Litter might be strewn around bamboo baskets that sat outside these hovels, or a cycle-rickshaw might be parked beside a doorway, giving clues as to how the inhabitants survived. These were utterly depressing sights. *Chai* sellers frequently set up outdoor canteens on rickety wooden tables beside the street, where silver teapots brewed the sweet milky tea for passers-by to drink from dirty glasses.

Paint was peeling from the walls of the houses. Tangles of black cables mixed with faded shop signs that looked as if they were about to fall from their loose hangings. Everything was rusty, dirty, grotty, battered, decrepit and poor. Above all, poor. Walking through the streets of Delhi was tiring. There was no rest, not from the moving people and dense traffic, not from the smells, the colours, the noise and the arresting sights of urban poverty. Everything was in our face, a constant barrage on our senses. At first it was shocking and daunting, mentally exhausting. Then we began to accept it, as we had to, and it was just tiring.

There were refuges of a kind. Connaught Place was an upmarket centre, comprising three large concentric rings of roads. Sheltering underneath colonnaded archways were high-class shops with globalised brand names. Inside, the restaurants and cafés were air-conditioned and clean, the service by uniformed waiters – always men, never women – was excellent. This was where rich Delhi-ites came to impress their girlfriends and to do business deals over expensive coffees. But even here everything needed a good dust and a new paint job. There was still rubbish on the floor, there were newspaper stalls and displays of books spread out on the pavements, and the taxis and tuk-tuks were still crowding and hustling.

We had our lunch and read the paper, coming across details of official inefficiency and ineptitude, corruption, murders and slum clearances in the capital. The impression we gained was one of little or no progress, where conditions approaching anarchy sucked the life out of any good intentions or aspirations for development. There had been a political drive to enforce the law on overloaded vehicles entering Delhi, which destroyed the roads and polluted the city. But nothing had changed, because the checkpoints weren't working – and so still 90 per cent of the lorries entering Delhi were overloaded.

A story on TV reported an investigation into the repairing of Mumbai's potholes, of which there were countless thousands. The council had paid a contractor to complete the work, who was insisting that all the potholes had been repaired – even though it was visibly evident to everyone in the city that nothing at all had changed. The contractor blamed the weather, saying that rains must have washed away the infill, and promised to have another go. The only reason this story was in the news at all was that there had been a legal investigation into the affair – that level of concern was the unusual thing.

There were tourist sights in Delhi too, of course. The vast Red Fort with its imposing walls was the most impressive, after which came smaller features of Mogul tombs and maharaja palaces. Many of these looked slightly musty, as if they were gathering dust as they aged. Often they stood partially hidden behind wispy trees or inside dusty parks, even in the centre of roundabouts – relics of previous eras that had been left standing as the city moved on around them. Much of the slightly confusing character of Delhi is a legacy of its convoluted history. William Dalrymple captures well some of its patchwork-quilt flavour:

> However hard the planners tried to create new colonies of gleaming concrete, crumbling tomb towers, old mosques or ancient Islamic colleges – medreses –

would intrude, appearing suddenly on roundabouts or in municipal gardens, curving the road network and obscuring the fairways of the golf course. New Delhi was not new at all. Its broad avenues encompass a groaning metropolis, a graveyard of dynasties. Some said there were seven dead cities of Delhi, and that the current one was the eighth; others counted fifteen or twenty-one. All agreed that the crumbling ruins of these towns were without number.[12]

Like outdoor exhibits in a living museum, these lingering buildings hinted at the richness of India's colourful history. It was a story of regional powers, feuding and allying with one another, their fortunes waxing and waning through the ages. Civilisation in the form of cities had existed on the Indian subcontinent since 2,500 BC. But it was also a story of conquest and domination by a succession of outsiders, forging ever greater empires that gradually, in fits and starts, with much breaking up and rebuilding, created the unified country of India. Most recently it had been divided in 1947 into India and Pakistan, with Bangladesh breaking away in 1971. Storybook figures like Alexander the Great, the Buddhist ruler Ashoka, the Turkish Sultan Ala-ud-din, and the tolerant Mogul emperor, Akbar, came and went with a host of smaller players – sultans, Rajputs, princes and warlords. The north was always the main battleground, with the far south remaining the Hindu stronghold that it still is today.

In the twelfth century AD the rule of the Muslim sultans began, fighting off Mogul incursions until the sixteenth century. It was to be the Mongols who brought India largely under the control of a single power for the first time. Britain was given or gained its own coastal toeholds in the seventeenth century, with the East India Company becoming involved in regional power struggles between northern and central India. At the beginning of the nineteenth century, the Company itself was the dominant force, supplanting Moguls and Indians alike, until in 1858 Queen Victoria claimed for the Crown all the rights of the Company. This made her the new Queen of the British colony of India. As historian John Keay points out, it was a measure of the fractious nature of Indian politics that a ceremony in her honour in 1877 was attended by nearly all of India's sixty-three ruling princes.

One place that I was eager to see in Delhi was the Nehru Museum, sited in what used to be his official residence. Nehru was the first Prime Minister of India once it had gained independence from Britain, and the museum records this more recent piece of history. However, the museum is also a tribute to Mahatma Gandhi, the self-disciplined leader of what aspired to be a non-violent independence movement. He achieved independence for India

---

[12] Dalrymple, W, *City of Djinns*, London, Flamingo, 1994, p.8. Reprinted by permission of HarperCollins Publishers Ltd © Dalrymple, 1994.

through perhaps the most remarkable story of political and national leadership of the twentieth century. Unfortunately, he couldn't prevent religion from dividing the country, and following independence tens of millions of Hindus and Muslims migrated east or west, into India or Pakistan respectively, in what was probably the biggest exodus in human history. Blood flowed wantonly as the migrants passed each other and at least 500,000 people lost their lives. India and Pakistan have yet to resolve the dispute over where their border lies within the province of Kashmir.

Delhi was too much for us; Claudia in particular was not enjoying being there and was beginning to fear the weeks ahead. I gave Claudia the benefit of my previous experiences: it takes at least two weeks to adjust to India but after that it becomes more enjoyable. This would prove to be true enough, and ultimately India would become the country that left the most profound impressions on our minds, her images so stark and so exotic. Another quote that summed up India nicely for me was that when you are in India all you want to do is leave, but once you have left all you want to do is go back. For now, it was the first part of that quip that was relevant, and we decided to travel north to the relative sanity of Nepal. But to get there, we had to travel east, across the Ganges plain to Varanasi, the holiest place on Earth for Hindus.

When we went to the train station in Delhi, we were sternly warned to pay no attention to the people who would intercept us and say that the ticket office was shut, or temporarily closed, or anything else to get us to follow them to their shop. The trouble was, just as this did indeed happen – causing us to rudely ignore the equally rude shouts of 'Excuse me!' – so other people waved us in the right direction, trying to be genuinely helpful. One of the horrible things about travelling in India was that it was impossible to know who to trust or what to believe. At first it was irritating and annoying to be faced with blatant untruths; then it became a depressing background to almost every interaction. A few days in Varanasi would be a crash course for learning this particular lesson. Indeed, in Varanasi we would experience India at perhaps her most extreme.

Chapter 59: Varanasi

One of the requisite items for travel in India was a good quality chain and padlock. On the sleeper train to Varanasi there were signs telling passengers to chain their luggage to the metal bedposts. We felt a bit silly doing this, especially in front of the young Indian couple who were sharing our berth, but feeling stupid for a while was better than waking up in the morning to find things missing. There was no doubt that the risk was real enough: we had heard stories of thieves moving through train carriages looking for cameras to snatch. In China we heard a second-hand traveller's tale of two guys on an Indian train who had carefully chained their packs to the bedposts, only to have the chains cut through and the packs taken anyway. Sometimes there was only so much that one could do. A friend of mine who had been in India a few years back had lined his rucksack with wire mesh, to prevent any knives from slashing it open. This measure would no doubt have worked very well, but he didn't get the chance to test it as his entire pack was stolen at a railway station.

However, nothing disturbed us in the night. There was something about the rattle and hum of trains that usually induced a good night's sleep. The only difficulty came in knowing where – or when – to get off the train. I had asked a conductor before we went to sleep and he told me that we would arrive in Varanasi at 8.30 a.m. So at 7.30 I checked this with a different conductor, who said that we had three more hours to go. For some reason, being told that there was plenty of time made me even more nervous about complacently sailing past our desired station. As was usually the case, it was the couple in our compartment who were the most helpful, telling us when to get off, which happened to be at 9.30 a.m.

Getting from the railway station to the hotel was an example of how something that would have been straightforward anywhere else became a tiring hassle in India. I knew that the best way to reach the hostel of our choice was to take a rickshaw to the riverside and walk, following the maps in our guidebook. So we found a tuk-tuk driver, who insisted on taking us to a little booth where some guy with a pad of paper 'officially' charged us the prepaid price of 55 rupees (US $1.35). The reverse journey, of course, could be done for 30 rupees, but never mind. Then our tuk-tuk driver gained a companion, no doubt part of the deal. As soon as we left the station, the driver stopped the tuk-tuk and asked us which hotel we wanted to go to. Just the riverside, I said, not wanting to get into a discussion about why our chosen hotel wasn't

373

suitable and why another one was much more preferable. But the driver persisted. 'I take you to hotels, you look, see, choose which one you want.'

I remembered arriving in Delhi a few years ago and having a similar discussion with a taxi driver then. I had insisted on going to a specific hotel, which resulted in the taxi driver taking us along a road that he claimed was the correct one and telling me to call out when I saw it, which of course I didn't, leaving me with the choice of getting out into a dark, unknown part of Delhi, or accepting the offer of an alternative hotel of the driver's choice. So now, in Varanasi, I just wanted to be driven to the riverside, as had been originally agreed. But we were going nowhere, literally.

Claudia gave in first, feeling that we were being rude, and so told the driver the name of one hotel we knew of. But no, we didn't want to try any others. Really, no. So finally we were off – not the riverside now, of course, but to somewhere unknown that was 'close to the hotel'. From here the driver said that he would show us the way on foot, and the reason for the companion became clear: he would watch the tuk-tuk while the driver escorted us to the hotel, which had been their intention all along.

There was little we could do as we had no idea where we were, so off we went, following our driver/guide. He led us down a narrow alleyway, which twisted and turned, with other similarly small passageways meeting it at every corner. It was like being led through a maze; we knew within a few minutes that we would have no idea of the way back. Later on, we met a couple who had tried to find their own way through but had taken a wrong turn and were lost for two hours.

Little doorways faced onto the alleyways, sometimes revealing shops the size of a broom cupboard, perhaps with a few shelves of goods, or the stove and silverware of a chai-wallah. These shops were all dark and grimy inside. The pathway was dirty, too, with patches of mud, cow dung, straw and litter. Overhead ran tangled messes of black cables, reminding us of the Brazilian *favelas*. Small shrines – often statues carved in relief into a stone wall – were stained red with dye. Beautiful temple spires were obscured and overshadowed by the flat concrete walls that pressed in on them.

The people we passed just stood to one side and silently watched us go by. Now and again a cow blocked our way – the claustrophobic alley was just about as wide as a cow – and we had to jump aside into doorways, giving way to the animals as they stalked past us without deigning to even turn their heads. We were hot and sweaty, getting tired from our walk and worried about where we were being led. But then, around a few more corners, down a couple of steps, following the directions of words and arrows painted on walls, we came to the very hotel that Claudia had requested. When the owner saw the three of us, he had a brief word with our guide, who told us that the hotel was full. I've never forgotten the experience I had once in a Cairo hostel, where my taxi driver followed me into the reception. That hostel was full too, until I had sent the driver away and returned, to be sternly told that they would not tip taxi drivers for bringing custom to them.

Anyway, now we really were at the mercy of our guide. Having set out with the intention of finding a decent place to stay after the last few nights in Delhi and on the train, now all we wanted was anywhere as long as we weren't wandering around this freakish maze any longer. Not to worry, our guide knew a place close by. Only, that place was truly awful and we weren't about to sleep there, however much commission he would be paid. It was the same for the next place on his list. The fourth was reasonable enough, however, and there we remained. It was a long way from where we had originally intended to get to, when we were back at the railway station. All we had wanted was to find a hotel!

Varanasi was the holy city of Shiva, and it was on a bank of the holy River Ganges. Beneath the riot of pink, orange and brown temples and other buildings that crowded the riverside, were a succession of what are called ghats – flights of stone and concrete steps that ran right down into the water. These were not just thin staircases, though: they were long and wide, spreading over a couple of kilometres along the Ganges. When the river was low, it was easy to walk along the series of ghats right from one end of town to the other. But we were there when the river was high, although the water's edge had still not covered the tops of the biggest ghats. These were public spaces, a bit like small marketplaces, busy, lively and colourful – the exotic face of India as often seen on postcards and calendars. Their main function was to give Hindus access to the water of the Ganges.

The thick, brown, muddy, filthy river was incredibly polluted – reputedly even cholera could not survive within it – but Hindus believed that its holiness kept them safe. Even our hotel landlord recommended sampling the waters to us. Alongside the locals who did their washing in the river, laying out their clothes to dry in the sun on the steps of the ghats, and the small herds of cattle half-submerged beside the ghats, Hindus came to bathe in the waters. Men stripped to their underwear, ducking their heads underneath to get fully 'cleansed'. Women more modestly stepped into the water in bright saris, changing afterwards into fresh, dry robes.

Many people – including tourists – just sat and watched the multicoloured scenes in front of them. Families picnicked on the concrete floor, men sitting in one circle and women and children in another. Hawkers offered food, postcards, trinkets and on-the-spot massages. Sadhus chanced their luck by asking for alms, or just squatted pathetically in a line next to the infirm and the disabled, silently begging. Small children roamed with coloured paints, looking for a chance to daub someone's hand and then charge for it. Cows wandered aimlessly through the crowds, stray dogs ran backwards and forwards, there was even an odd goat and a flock of white ducks. Monkeys clambered over the rooftops. Offshore, a boat fought the dangerously strong current and choppy waters, perhaps showing a group of Indian tourists the riverbank sights from a different angle – a very popular activity when the river was low. More likely, it was rowing a family out so that they could cast the remains of a bereaved relative into the water.

To have one's ashes mixing with the water of the Ganges was considered to be the most holy of final resting places for Hindus, and could prevent reincarnation by transporting the deceased straight into nirvana. Many families would bring their dead to Varanasi to be cremated, if they could afford it. We often saw small groups of shaven-headed men, shoe-less and dressed in white robes, hurrying through the streets to one of the two 'burning ghats'. They carried a stretcher at shoulder level, a dead body clearly visible underneath the white sheet that was draped over it. Along the main roads and down the alleyways, these small processions had to push their way through the crowds and traffic just like everyone else. There was little dignity or reverence; no one else paid them any attention. It was, after all, just another cremation.

Down to the 'burning ghat' they went, into an area that looked more like a lumber yard than anything else, complete with sets of large green scales to measure out the wood for funeral pyres. On an elevated platform the dead bodies were placed onto their pyres, which burned throughout the day. Orange flames and plumes of grey smoke constantly rose up, the air around thick with it, making our eyes water. It took three hours for a single pyre to burn out, during which time the white or orange cloth quickly burnt away, leaving the body fully exposed for all to see, its flesh blackening and holes burning through. It was a pretty ghastly sight, but here it was a routine part of everyday life. Ashes and any unburned body parts would be collected together and taken out onto the Ganges, where men wearing orange shorts, headbands and T-shirts – with a picture of Shiva printed on their chests like a corporate logo – would ceremonially deposit the remains into the water. At the day's end, workers would go through the cinders again, sifting for jewellery and gold teeth, anything that they could collect and sell.

There were five groups of 'non-burnable' dead: animals, children under fourteen years old, pregnant women, holy men and lepers. In addition to these groups were all the people who couldn't afford to be cremated. These groups could still be laid to rest in the Ganges, however. They would be taken out over the water, their bodies weighed down with stones, and dropped overboard. Which was why it was perfectly possible to see the bloated bodies of cows and even people floating down the river in Varanasi.

As we walked around the ghats we were frequently accosted by apparently friendly men and children. They tried out their English on us, starting little conversations. The banter didn't last long: the boys wanted to show us the way in exchange for a tip; the men wanted to take us to their silk shops. In fact, everyone wanted something. From leaving Delhi until the very end of our time in Rajasthan there were many, many times that a local started up a conversation with us, but there were literally only two occasions when there was no ulterior motive. This created a perpetual dilemma for us.

Making a point of smiling and being friendly to people, as we had tried to do for a whole year, would here only end up with our having to refuse to be taken somewhere that we didn't want to go and which we definitely didn't want to pay for. Furthermore, it was impossible to be friendly to everyone who approached us, which sometimes happened as often as every couple of minutes. We had to resort to stony-faced rebuttals and unsmiling disinterest in order to process all the hassle as quickly as possible. We couldn't blame people for trying their luck – poverty was in our face the whole time – but it was tiring having to continually fend off false pretensions of amicable familiarity.

At the 'burning ghat' it was commonplace for men to come out with a particular story, as one did to us. 'Welcome to Varanasi, is this your first time in Varanasi? I can see you are interested in the burning ghats. They are very special, the most holy place in India. I live nearby, I tell you some information about the ghats if you interested. This would not be more money, no tips, no baksheesh. I come here every day to tell tourists about our ghats for no charge. Do you know why? Have you heard of karma? By helping people here I get good karma. It is for that reason that I tell you some interesting things. Would you like to see the funeral pyres? Don't go that way – that is not allowed. Come this way, I will show you, I can take you to a special place because I live here.'

And so it went on, patter patter. I had been here before, so I knew what was coming – although I didn't expect it to be quite so blatant. Claudia was still trying to find someone who was just nice and genuine, so she followed the man and listened.

'There are lots of old women here, they come because they want to be cremated, but they are so poor that they cannot afford to buy the wood for the funeral pyre.'

On cue, there was an old lady in a corner, dressed in rags, doing nothing but sitting listlessly. 'These old women are helped by everyone here, we take pity on them and want to help them, because it is good for our karma too. If you want to, you can give her some money to help her. She will die soon, but doesn't have enough money for a cremation. It will be good for your karma too.'

And on, and on. It was hard to walk past, just as it was always hard to pass the heart-rending, awful scenes of poverty that we witnessed time and again on the streets. But in India there are times when one has to walk on, and there are times when one should walk on, because it is all a con trick. So it was here. The whole set-up, the friendly local and the frail old lady, was a scam. The local wasn't doing it for karma, the lady didn't keep the money. It was all a hypocritical deceit.

A deceit made worse by the truth that lay behind it. There was indeed a home in Varanasi for women who were as poor and needy as any in India. It was a house of widows. When a husband dies, his wife can be seen as redundant and an economic burden on the remaining family. One of the stories in the national newspapers we read reported an incidence of sati – a woman burning herself alive on her husband's funeral pyre. The women in the village concerned were quoted as having said, 'What future does a woman have after her husband is gone?' They added that the woman 'would have been at the mercy of her sons', even giving the opinion that, compared to the alternative, sati was 'more dignified'. Widows were – in some parts of India – effectively used property to be cast out from the household and left to wander in poverty, usually unable to marry again. Many of these women make their way to Varanasi and the house of widows, where they do indeed exist on charity until they die. It was this sad state of affairs and the compassion evoked by it that was being exploited by the con artists at the burning ghat. We never understood why nobody, neither the tourist policeman who was sitting at another ghat nor the locals who were at the burning ghat all day, ever stopped the tricksters. Across India, it seemed to us that the general public would stand by and watch virtually anything going on.

Away from the ghats, the streets of Varanasi were as extreme as everything else about the city. Underneath the peeling paint and tattered signs that hung at every conceivable angle except straight, the roads were filled by a maelstrom of cycle-rickshaws. Wheels and metal were everywhere, with barely an inch of room between them. The rickshaws often bumped and collided as they wove contorted routes through the chaos, the drivers using their bare feet to push one another off. There were no mirrors and no one looked behind; each driver was only concerned with avoiding hitting the vehicle in front. We saw traffic policemen in their khaki uniforms standing by, but they didn't seem to be doing anything other than watching the vehicles stream either side of them without any regard to rules or sense. In Varanasi, where collective order was so clearly lacking, it was as if the authorities were simply overwhelmed by the madness, and there was nothing they could do but stand futilely by as individualist anarchy reigned and cows walked the streets. Which perhaps was just an extreme version of the rest of the country.

Varanasi

Walking beside the roads was a struggle, as we constantly stepped in and out of the road to avoid bumping into the shopkeepers and sadhus and funeral processions and everyone else, whilst all the time being irritated by the inevitable cycle-rickshaw-wallah cycling slowly alongside, calling out 'Rickshaw? Rickshaw?' to us over and over again, oblivious to the chaos that was being caused behind them. In fact, travelling by cycle-rickshaw was actually the best way of getting around, as we were then in the very midst of the seething mass, but relatively comfortable and with a good view from the carriage.

There were other sights in and around Varanasi – such as the 'Monkey Temple', painted red and surrounded by the most picturesque ladies in their best clothes, rubbing shoulders with the very poorest beggars and rickshaw-wallahs – but for us the city was defined by the utterly manic roads and the weird life of the ghats. Varanasi was a crazy place.

Chapter 60: Pokhara

We queued in the waiting room of the Varanasi railway station for an hour, only to be told that we couldn't reserve any tickets for the train that we had wanted to take northwards. So we took an overnight bus to the Nepali border instead. The bus was crowded with people standing squashed in the aisle, but everyone seemed friendly enough. The lazy ticket collector didn't shift from his seat, expecting people to pass their money from hand to hand down the bus, and he returned their tickets in the same way. The landscape north of Varanasi reminded me of Cambodia: flat brown and green fields with many trees in between and nothing else for miles except a few red-brick cube houses dotted here and there. Where rice was growing, ladies were working in the fields, their brilliant red, orange, yellow and blue saris splashing colour into the green paddies, creating a highly picturesque sight. The roads were quite straight and generally good, with just an odd large pothole or two for our bus to violently swerve around. More of a hazard were pedestrians, cyclists and cows – the cows especially, because they would stand literally in the middle of the road, chewing their cud, minding their own business and certainly paying no heed to the trucks and buses that sped toward them. Several mashed bovine carcasses – a giant form of roadkill – vividly illustrated the danger.

We were supposed to arrive at the Nepali border at 5.30 a.m., which seemed a half-respectable time. It was a bit of a surprise therefore when the bus pulled up into what look liked an area of waste ground at 2.30 a.m. It wouldn't have mattered too much, but we were kicked off the bus along with everyone else, because the bus driver and the conductor wanted to settle comfortably into the empty chairs for a sleep. We didn't know where to go or what to do, stranded with our luggage in the middle of the night. All the Indian passengers evaporated swiftly into the darkness, leaving only us and a small group of young Nepali men and women, who had even more bags than we did. They didn't seem too concerned about the situation, and invited us to settle down on the ground with them until daylight – a simple gesture that was significant to us, as we couldn't imagine that having happened in Delhi or Varanasi. The group didn't sleep, but instead passed the time laughing and joking with one another – a lightheartedness that we had also missed since arriving in Delhi. When a cycle-rickshaw driver appeared out of nowhere, the young Nepali men took turns gleefully cycling around the car park, like a scene out of *Butch Cassidy and the Sundance Kid*.

So we were in good spirits when the group decided to head for the border at 4 a.m. and we followed along behind. They simply crossed the border without formalities, but we had to get our passports stamped. We woke up the Indian official who was asleep on a table outside his office, partially hidden by the folds of a white mosquito net. He turned on the lights and fished a stamp from a desk drawer. Obligingly, he gave us the stamp, and then began to tell us that the office was usually closed during the night – presumably he had woken up enough to start fishing for a little baksheesh. We then carried on to Indian customs, where a man sitting on a chair waved a torch at us and told us to duck underneath the barrier. At Nepali immigration the office was officially open, but the men were asleep again, so we woke them up too.

The street was clean and tidy; the people we could see were smartly dressed; things looked superficially better than India already. We bought a bus ticket from a pair of cheerful and efficient young men in a nearby office, who made us a cup of sweet tea while we waited. One of them took the trouble to ensure that our bags were loaded on the roof of the bus properly and showed us to our seats in the front of the bus – the best we had been given for ages. We could get used to this treatment! I was reminded of my first visit to Kathmandu, where I was offered a cup of tea by a man sitting on the steps outside his shop. I declined, not wishing to get involved in a sales pitch, to which he said, 'This is not like India, you know!'

Once we were on our way, our bus filled up with people as the team of workers enthusiastically chased potential passengers down the streets and encouraged them to board. Once they did so, the touts would clamber like monkeys onto the roof to pack their luggage, while the bus moved off again. Some people understandably didn't want to be packed in like sardines, so we were asked with a smile whether we wanted to give up our seats and join the group of young men who preferred the roof – for an eight-hour journey! We declined that particular offer.

The journey to Pokhara was superb, full of magnificent scenery and interesting people. It was one of the few really great drives of our trip, like those of Peru and Laos. We passed quickly into a succession of long, wide, deep valleys. In the flat bottoms were expanses of fields, which became impressive series of terraces up the hillsides until they petered out amid the forest trees. Houses were wedged into tiny spaces between the road and the hillside, ranging from huts made of woven sticks with mud plastered on for walls, to stone huts painted orange and yellow with thatched roofs, and the worldwide two-storey brick house with corrugated metal sheets for roofs.

At one point our bus stopped and the passengers peered over the edge of the road, down a nearly sheer drop into the huge U-bend of a river far below. The road stretched away in front and behind, no more than a thin ribbon winding its way halfway up the valley side. We strained to see what everyone was staring at. About a third of the way down the dizzying slope was an overturned truck which had rolled off the road... not a pleasant thought.

We often passed Nepali women wearing red saris, typically sporting a gold nose ring or stud and plenty of plastic bangles on their wrists. One such lady was smoking a fat cigarette as she squatted by the side of the road. Many carried woven cloth bags or cone-shaped bamboo back-baskets from a wide band around their foreheads. We saw four young lads standing in a line by the side of the road, each with either a back-basket or a great bundle of sticks balanced on the top of their heads. Lots of young boys and girls were collecting wood, with and without their mothers.

Nepali men had plenty of style and character here, too. The most distinctive feature about them was their hats, which can only be described as looking like patterned tea cosies. Their clothes would be smart, almost formal; usually plain European shirts and trousers, often accompanied by an elegant black waistcoat. Their faces were quite long, with sharp, distinguished profiles. Many wore a pair of spectacles and they often carried a rolled-up black or grey umbrella over their shoulder. All in all, they had a dignified, stately, almost intellectual air about them.

We finally arrived in Pokhara, where we collapsed into a pleasant hotel run by several ever so friendly young Nepali men. We were travel-tired again and I had a cold, so for a few days we rested, doing little but wandering along the Lakeside strip of tourist hotels, trekking companies, restaurants, banks and cafés. If transport provides a good indicator of a country's state of development, then the lack of motorcycles and bicycles, let alone cars, on the pitted and potholed roads of Pokhara – Nepal's second largest tourist destination – did not bode well for Nepal. Almost everyone seemed to be walking along the roadside. Beside the roads were water taps, which were always occupied by a cluster of metal water-jars or plastic containers set on the ground, waiting their turn to be filled up. Seeing the local women coming and going from these taps was a reminder of the world beyond Lakeside.

Every office seemed to provide just about every service, from exchanging money to arranging international flights or providing Internet access. We sampled the Nepali staple menu – dhal baht – and filled up on tasty international cuisine, once to the slightly surreal accompaniment of 'Jingle Bells' played on Nepali traditional instruments. Incidentally, the mosquitoes in Pokhara were the biggest we ever saw. They were huge nasty-looking insects, more like small whirring helicopters lining up for a kill. It was their attacks that usually forced us to retreat to our hotel room in the evenings.

During the days, we were harassed by cheerful Tibetan ladies, who relentlessly asked us to have a look at their handmade, real silver jewellery. 'Have a look now?' they tried. 'Just looking? OK, when? After eating – when finished? I will wait here. Later on? When you come back? Tomorrow you look?'

We met them so often, and they were so persistent, that eventually we did take a look and inevitably bought a couple of necklaces. Strangely, after we had done so not a single lady asked us again. They kept smiling and greeting us, though – and that was nice. The local shopkeepers were friendly, too, calling out 'Namaste' to us as we walked past, but in a cheerful way that we could almost believe was sincere.

Chapter 61: Annapurna Trek

Yet again we had arrived during rainy season, which meant that although the mornings were clear, the afternoon weather could generally be relied on to be cloudy, grey and wet. On the plus side, this meant that it wasn't high season, which suited us very well. In one of the many travel agent/bank/Internet café/trekking shops in Pokhara we arranged an eight-day trek that would take us up to Annapurna Base Camp. We had been offered the choice of paying for a guide – who would speak good English but not carry any bags – or a porter – who would carry our bag and look after us but would not be able to communicate as well – or both. Always tending to prefer peace and quiet over chatter, we opted for a porter and ended up with a typically respectful and attentive man called Bir. At least, part of his name included 'Bir', and he didn't seem to worry about the rest. The following eight days contained surely among the best trekking that the world has to offer, full of majestic scenery, natural splendour and glimpses of traditional culture.

To reach Annapurna Base Camp, we walked along pathways that wound between isolated houses and small hillside villages. The paths were often extremely well made; indeed, it was common for them to be completely paved with stones. Every so often we would pass a square mound beside the path, about four feet high and five feet long, with a stone ledge running around its edge. These were resting places for porters who manually hauled goods up and down the mountain paths. Their loads were always carried from their heads, with thick cloth bands passing across the top of their heads. We passed men carrying wire cages on their backs stuffed full of white chickens, or massive beams of wood that could only be carried twenty yards at a time, and even a man carrying his wife down the hill in a modified back-basket, taking her to the nearest doctor. Porters' loads were usually about 30–35 kg, and it seemed to us that mostly they comprised tins of tomatoes, gas canisters, beer bottles and other provisions for the numerous 'tea houses' that offered food and lodging to trekkers.

The paths were not gentle going, however well built they were. In places the valley sides were precipitously steep, so the paths had to climb up and over the ridge behind, to be almost inevitably followed by a descent all the way back down to the bottom to where an incised river gorge could be bridged safely. We would walk down stone steps, dropping 450 metres in altitude, only to cross a bridge and spend the next hour toiling straight back up the other side. One day we ascended a total of 2,000 metres but only finished up a net 250 metres higher than when we had begun.

Nepali farmhouses were as quaint and pretty as any we had seen, being solid two-storey stone buildings, painted all in white, with double-layered grey slate-slab roofs. From the ceilings of kitchens and balconies were hung hundreds of yellow maize cobs – the harvest safely in and drying. Outside the blue-green wooden front doors were paved areas, like stone patios, that ran to the edge of the steep valley sides. Small flower beds blazed red and pink with geraniums, roses, nasturtiums and gladioli. Lines of white-blue-yellow-green-and-red Tibetan prayer flags hung from roofs or flagpoles, their sun-bleached triangular pieces of cloth fluttering in the wind. Small sheds near the houses turned out to be dirty, dark barns for goats and buffalo that were tethered in their stalls. Above and below the houses, filling the valley sides, were terraces that were sometimes just as extensive and dramatic as the Longji terraces of China. Here they were planted with bright green rice shoots and tall brown stalks of maize. The few terraces nearest the houses had often been turned into vegetable allotments, full of pumpkins, cabbages, beans and potatoes.

Women would be washing their plates and pots at water taps beside their houses, at the edge of the paths. Some were washing their clothes or their hair under the taps. Young girls picked greens from the terraces, stuffing the plants into their bamboo back-baskets. Women were bent double in the rice paddies, photogenically working at whatever it was that rice-growers had to do. We saw a man weaving thin strips of bamboo into a new back-basket. His wife worked beside him, splitting the canes with an evil-looking machete. Slightly gangly men walked up and down the hillsides in black knee-length shorts, waistcoats, tea-cosy hats and sandals – and usually an umbrella. The women were more colourful, wearing bold green and orange print sarongs wrapped around their waists, cotton T-shirts and more cloth wrapped around their heads. They also wore armloads of red plastic bangles, and some had several gold rings hanging from their ears or nose.

Landslide scars and waterfalls added a sense of drama to the landscape, where huge chunks of stone as large as apartment blocks had come to rest halfway down a terraced hillside. Landslides were a real danger here. We walked down past one that had happened only a month before, spewing its ugly muddy, boulder-strewn mess in a vicious streak down the hillside. Houses at its edge had been ripped in half, pieces of their timber still poking out from the mud, which had set like concrete. Twenty-six villagers had been killed by this landslide, we were told by a quiet gentleman in rainbow-coloured plastic wellington boots. He had spent hours digging through the mud, but all in vain, he said sadly: many bodies were still buried within the mud.

As we gradually made our way up one valley after another, towards the high mountains, we left the houses and terraces behind. We entered mature rhododendron forest, the familiar ornamental bushes having grown into proper trees, their dark boughs dripping with moss and bright green plants sprouting from their branches. At times the forest was spooky in its dank stillness, where nothing moved except the leeches that periodically plagued us. In one place we almost ran along the path, because slowing or stopping would only invite more leeches which appeared from nowhere to hitch a ride. Along a 100-metre stretch I collected on average one leech every five metres. And still our guide would say, 'When it is wet, then there are many leeches!'

At other times the forest was delightful. Bamboo, ferns and balsam would carpet the floor, the latter adding touches of yellow, white or purple colour. Bright yellow sorrel flowers would suddenly appear in clearings. Butterflies and birdsong would lift the atmosphere. Two or three times we spotted white monkeys fleeing through the treetops, their black faces peering curiously at us for an instant before they went. Early one morning we watched a whole troop resting in the branches nearby, their tails – twice as long as their bodies – dangling beneath them.

Bir, our porter, spoke little English, but he did know how to say that in March, April and May the rhododendron forests were ablaze with the reds and pinks of their blossom. It must indeed be a fantastic sight. One morning Claudia tried to make conversation with him, based on one of his favourite phrases:

'So, in March, April, May, all red?'

'Yes! March, April, May, all red!'

And that was the end of that dialogue.

Even higher, the trees dropped away and we walked into an area of meadow and bushes. The plants beside our path began to look like an English hedgerow. I spotted cow parsley, dogwood, dandelion, forget-me-not, nettle, thistle, dock, pink campion, wild strawberries, redcurrants and raspberries, purple daisies, tall stalks with white bell-like flowers, and so many more small wild flowers.

Above us on either side now rose forbidding rock cliffs, their metallic walls glistening with wetness, broken only by equally oppressive dark green vegetation. Somewhere above and behind these walls were the high mountains. We knew, because every so often during our trek we had seen glimpses of their peaks, sometimes as starkly bright snow against clear blue skies, sometimes as shadowy silhouettes under a starry sky. Here Bir was in his element: 'There Annapurna I, there Annapurna South, there Machhapuchhare…' He always lost me by about the fourth peak.

As on every day, the morning brightness had given way to an enveloping grey mistiness, adding to the imposing atmosphere around us. We turned a corner and the narrow valley flattened out as it split in several directions. This was the location for Machhapuchhare Base Camp, at an altitude of 3,703 m. Machhapuchhare was a particularly beautiful mountain with a strikingly fluted peak, looking something like a fishtail. Hence its Nepali name – although it was just as commonly referred to as 'Fishtail'. It was considered holy and therefore shouldn't be climbed, but that didn't stop it having a Base Camp. We had lunch here, cooked by a guy who hadn't left the hut at all for five months. As we ate, the grey mistiness thickened around us and rain began to fall. We continued on, through gloomy drizzle, sploshing through puddles and mud that soaked our feet. The broad grassy valley was strewn with large grey boulders, but its steep sides disappeared into cloud and mist just above our heads, so we couldn't see what was above. We huddled inside our ponchos – the ones we had bought months before in Cuzco – or, in Bir's case, under a clear plastic sheet that he held over his head, and plodded on.

Our pace was being slowed by the altitude. My head began to feel as if the inside was pressing against my skull, giving me a headache. Each breath wasn't going as far as it used to, so our footsteps were made in laboured slow motion. It wasn't really discomforting, but it hinted at the possibilities of altitude sickness. In the gloom we reached the clustered huts of Annapurna Base Camp, at 4,130 m. Everything was damp and chilly, including ourselves. We had been told that we could get a shower here, so we asked the hut owner if we could have one. He told us to sit down and wait, and after twenty minutes he brought forth a bucket of hot water and showed us to the shower room. We tried to heat ourselves up, but this wasn't easy when standing on a cold concrete floor and with open windows all around us. Soon we returned to the common room and wrapped ourselves in blankets to keep warm instead. A small group of Nepali porters huddled there too, playing cards. They were wearing good quality weatherproof jackets and woolly hats, but had taken their flip-flops off and so were barefooted.

On the wall of the hut was a tribute to the mountaineer Anatoli Boukreev, who was killed in 1997 on Christmas Day while trying to climb the dangerous Annapurna I. For mountaineers, he had already become a legend before he died, famous for climbing alone and without oxygen – but very fast. He reached 8,000 metre summits twenty-one times, including Everest four times. His words remain at Annapurna Base Camp, which seemed to me to capture something of the ideal spirit of mountaineers:

> The mountains are not stadiums where I satisfy my ambitions to achieve. They are my cathedrals, the houses of my religion. Their presence is grand and pure. I go to them as all humans go to worship. In their presence I attempt to understand my life, to purify myself of earthly vanity, greed and fear. On their altar I strive to perfect myself physically and spiritually. From their vantage

point, I view my past, dream of the future and with unusual acuteness I experience the present. My ascents renew my strength and clear my vision. They are the way I practise my religion. In the mountains I celebrate creation, on each journey I am reborn.

We couldn't help but celebrate creation too the following day when we were standing before dawn in the centre of a vast amphitheatre of snowy mountains. They curved all around us like a giant wall, perfectly clear under a cloudless sky. The ridge-like line of peaks on top were a full 4,000 m above us, the highest peak – Annapurna I itself – being at 8,091 m. A silver full moon shone brightly just above the mountains. The stage was all set: we shivered and waited. Then a faint yellow patch appeared at the top of the ridge – the very first rays of sunlight at dawn. The yellow grew and turned into an orange glow, spreading across the mountain faces. Ice crystals sparkled and the snow gleamed. It took half an hour for all the entire wall to be bathed in light, transformed into an intense bright whiteness that was starkly beautiful. Even the Nepali porters had come out to gaze at the spectacle. To have seen this mountain sunrise, witnessing Nature in all her glory, was a true privilege. When we finally turned away, to get a hot breakfast and to melt our frozen feet, there on the opposite side of the valley was the magnificent Machhapuchhare, lit up by bright sunlight. These were sights that made us gasp, literally breathtaking, moments too perfect to hold all at once.

On the way down the valley, past Machhapuchhare Base Camp again, we were recognised by locals, who were happy to share a little conversation with us. A couple of days later, in another valley, the pathways became more touristy. Several large groups of Europeans almost formed queues as they sweated their way up to what was considered to be one of the best viewpoints for a panoramic vista of Himalayan peaks, called Poon Hill. Just below it was a Pingan-like tourist resort called Ghorepani, full of new, large lodges. The lodges were well managed, with a centralised committee standardising all menus – including pizza and pancakes alongside dhal baht – and prices to ensure equality. What it would be like if there was a free-for-all doesn't bear thinking about. Our landlord told us that in high season there were 300 tourists staying here every day, but that didn't include their entourages of guides and porters. In 2004, over 42,000 foreign trekkers visited the Annapurna Conservation Area. The use of firewood for cooking in the lodges and teahouses had caused significant deforestation on the hillsides, leading to soil erosion and land degradation. Gas cookers were being encouraged and we saw several solar panels for water heating, but they were by no means ubiquitous yet. Nepal's tourist industry was hoped to provide economic development for the country, but there were real concerns that mass tourism was simply unsustainable in fragile environments like this.

We were glad to have a hostel virtually to ourselves, with an owner who was typically pleased to stop for a friendly talk with us over a game of chess during the last two evenings of our trek. Everywhere we went in Nepal the welcome and the friendliness was warm and genuine – and the conversations would usually turn to politics, with people hoping that their country was at last free from violence. In Kathmandu we would find out that this wasn't quite the case, not yet.

We stayed two nights in Ghorepani to give us a second chance at seeing the view from Poon Hill, which the first morning had been shrouded in cloud. On the second morning the skies were clear and we sat with Bir at the top of the hill for an hour or more, content to feast our eyes on such mountains as Dhaulugiri, 8,167 m high, before reluctantly turning our steps downhill towards Pokhara again. It was a suitable end to a fabulous week of trekking.

From Pokhara, we quickly took a bus to Kathmandu, leaving from a grassy field that had a view of snow-capped Himalayan peaks in the background. While we were waiting to depart, a couple of buffalo wandered across the field in front of the buses and passengers. No one batted an eyelid except us and a stray dog. The bus journey took us through more stunning scenery, along one of only three highways that led into the capital city. Road travel was dangerous: there were frequent newspaper reports of traffic accidents and we regularly passed vehicles that were either stranded or broken down. The trucks on these minor winding roads – the main highways of Nepal – were very solid-looking, with thick metal sides. I liked them: they were usually painted blue or orange, but the brightest had gaudily painted patterns and decorations all over their bodywork and cab, giving them a jaunty, extrovert character. Their artwork almost as fantastic as their macho names, like 'Road Pirate' or 'Speed Devil'. A heart-stopping game of chicken was continually played out by them, and they frequently pushed our bus off the tarmac onto the verge as they passed, with neither vehicle slowing down for an instant.

All the way to Kathmandu the roadside was littered with the carnage of wrecked trucks. We saw a succession of broken axles, burst tyres, and smashed or crumpled bonnets. Our bus driver was more careful than most, but that didn't stop him overtaking uphill on blind hairpin bends of the mountain roads. The only things that humbled all the lorries and buses, bringing them patiently to a halt, were cows nonchalantly chewing cud in the middle of the road.

Some of the houses that we passed appeared like old country cottages, the kind that would be preserved as museums in England. They were small and had stone walls, only some of which were plastered or painted in orange and yellow. The roofs were made of stone tiles, like thick grey slates. The cottages had only a single dark wooden door and a couple of tiny windows with wooden shutters. The smallest houses only had two rooms. A porch extending out from the doorway would shelter an outdoor kitchen, with a mud brick oven emerging seamlessly from the mud floor. A couple of benches might be placed alongside. Water can from an outdoor standpipe. Leaning against the side of the house might be a small, dirty stable, with a lonely buffalo or goat tied up. A back-basket might have been left against the wall of the house. Maize cobs would hang from the roof; through a window might be seen tables covered with potatoes. Along an outside wall might be a string of dried plants, looking like a forgotten Christmas decoration. And that would be all.

Chapter 62: Kathmandu

Kathmandu hit us with noise, congestion, grime and dirt. Its streets were hemmed in between three- and four-storey brick buildings, all crowded together. The evidently poor hustle and bustle of street life reminded us immediately of La Paz, only with more cars. On a road wide enough for perhaps four cars side by side, there were six abreast, all jostling and jockeying with each other. Motorbikes somehow squeezed their way between the densely packed cars, doing their best to progress through the jam of traffic but generally just getting in each other's – and everyone else's – way. Just when I thought there was literally no more space between vehicles, pedestrians calmly stepped into gaps between wheels and bumpers. And there, in the middle of it all, was a traffic policeman, doing absolutely nothing.

There was a heavy army presence on the streets. Groups of green-uniformed men with heavy guns slung over their shoulders stood on pavements, at junctions and corners. We even saw some lurking, half-hidden on rooftops. It was like a scene from an imaginary Colombian town – not what we had expected in Nepal. We didn't know whether to be reassured by the soldiers or disturbed by them. I had told Claudia that Nepal was one of the best countries in the world to visit, like a sanitised version of India, and that Kathmandu was one of my favourite cities. These first sights weren't quite what she had expected, and she wasn't too impressed.

Serendipity took us to a small hotel that was run by the brother of a man on our bus. The tourist area of the city was called Thamel, a rabbit warren of bright and breezy streets lined with buildings that invariably had shops or offices in the ground floor and hostels and restaurants above. Mountaineering equipment stores could be found beside souvenir trinket shops and bakeries. It was a relaxed and safe atmosphere; a tourist colony. In the shops and the streets we met helpful local people whose smiles didn't drop and interest didn't fade. Nepali people were genuinely nice, which was a large part of why being in Nepal was so enjoyable. And here they knew about Austria, which scored brownie points with Claudia; there was no problem naming the Alps or Vienna, for example. One Nepali mountain guide we met described the Alps a little patronisingly as 'mini-mountains' – which is how, back at home, Claudia now always has to think of them.

Kathmandu was a city that had collected together an unusually eclectic mix of people and buildings, often seeming far more like a living museum than a modern city. The central historic Durbar Square had been largely built between the twelfth and eighteenth centuries. It was a public space, broadly forming an 'L' shape around the outside of the old palace buildings. The King of Nepal used to live there until the early twentieth century, when he moved to a new palace elsewhere in Kathmandu. One of the most distinctive attractions of the old palace and indeed the old city were the intricately carved window frames and doorways of the old buildings, sometimes the frames being broader and more of a feature than the windows they surrounded. One of the buildings was a beautifully ornate palace, where a seven-year-old goddess lived. She made a Juliet-like appearance at a balcony window twice a day.

Within Durbar Square itself was a slightly confusing jumble of pyramidal towers. These were often formed from flights of brick steps topped by ornate wooden temples up to nine layers high: pagodas on small pyramid bases. The pagoda design was actually believed to have originated here in the Kathmandu valley – these were among the first such buildings. Durbar Square was cluttered with their red-brick walls, dark woodwork and orange-brown roofs. They made the square unusual and quirky.

For the most part, however, Durbar Square was a kind of central park for Kathmandu. People came and went across the square: men bent double under the weight of boxes or bundles; demure women wearing green and pink saris; cycle-rickshaw drivers sitting and waiting for custom. Beside and above them on the temple steps were many people simply passing the time, chatting and watching life go by. Men seemed particularly good at this, often smoking a cigarette as they relaxed. Small shops and stalls were tucked into corners between the temples; in one area was a tourist market laid out with souvenir bric-a-brac, each stall selling a virtually identical collection of odd artefacts. In another corner was a giant stone relief of a ghoulish Shiva, which seemed to be the most popular shrine in the Square. We watched innocent schoolgirls stooping beneath its fearsome face to daub some red paint on their foreheads. Fake sadhus loitered in strategic corners, all bearded faces and outlandish robes, ready to pose for photographs – but hiding behind newspapers to avoid being caught by sly snaps. Durbar Square was a busy, colourful, weird and noisy place, fascinating and tiring at the same time. It took repeated trips there for us to make sense of it all.

The roads leading to and from Durbar Square were one of the features of Kathmandu. These narrow bazaar-like streets were squeezed between old houses that showcased ancient wooden carved architecture. Hundreds of pedestrians – mainly women out shopping – pressed shoulder to shoulder formed good-natured crowds. Small roadside doorways, perhaps only half my height, led into tiny shops which were stuffed with goods. The nature of these shops varied according to their location. Some areas were full of fabric, with multi-coloured rolls of cloths draping the buildings up to two storeys high on either side of the road. Elsewhere the shops were like an Aladdin's cave, stuffed with gold, silver and brass pots and pans that overflowed into the street. Occasionally we heard a great crashing as the crowd was pushed into the displays. On other corners were fruit stalls, where salespeople stood behind wooden carts or squatted on the pavements. It was sad to see so many people who had simply laid out a sheet of newspaper or a cardboard box on the pavement, setting trinkets, grilled corn or glasses of tea on them – the best they could do to make a living.

Scattered throughout the streets were several Hindu shrines and temples, some extravagant and some simple, but always slightly weird. The only haven amid the bustle was a side square that contained a white hemispherical Buddhist stupa. This had a peaceful dignity that we found missing from Hindu temples. It offered a little open space for people to stroll around or sit quietly in, a bit like a small city park, complete with plenty of feral pigeons flying between the streaming prayer flags. The difference between the Hindu and Buddhist religious buildings was exemplified to us by a day's excursion, walking first to the holiest Hindu temple in Nepal and then to one of the largest Buddhist stupas in the world.

Pashupatinath Temple was easy to spot from a distance, because a curling column of grey smoke was rising up from the burning ghats that were sited at one end of the complex, similar to those at Varanasi but on a smaller scale. Indeed, the river that flowed through Pashupatinath was holy because it flowed directly into the Ganges. The river was lined on both sides by pagoda-style temple buildings, and there were a couple of bridges crossing between them. The main temple was reserved for Hindus, so from the opposite bank we watched men, women and children going up the high flight of steps and into the main entrance, all in their best clothes. We sat down on the bank to rest and absorb the riverside sight.

Many women came down to the river, kneeling to wash in the water. In the early morning light, their saris seemed to radiate colour like an iridescent waterfall, cascading down the concrete steps of the temple and collecting at the riverside. Without any privacy, it seemed as if the only dignity was contained in the faces and poise of the individuals as they knelt by the water. Flower petals and ashes mixed together as they floated slowly downstream. Other ladies were washing their clothes in the same water, their saris revealed as long strips of bright reds, blues and yellows. To one side a bunch of naked children jumped into the water and afterwards stretched their bodies out along the steps to dry in the sun. A little way off was a woman sitting cross-legged on a stone pillar in the still pose of meditation, her palms turned upwards to the sky. The whole scene appeared busy and disordered to the point of being chaotic: a melee of colourful individuals focused on their own form of worship, or their daily ablutions, side by side. A herd of cows walked across the bridge. Monkeys clambered around the steps, mothers clutching their babies to their chests. Fake sadhus with painted faces posed amongst the stone buildings for groups of tourists, while their genuine counterparts hid away in small caves dug into the riverbank at the end of the temple complex. It was all typically Hindu.

After finding a *chai* stall to refresh ourselves at the top of the small hill behind the temple, we could see across the city to the enormous white dome of Bodnath Stupa, with prayer flags fluttering on many of the surrounding rooftops. The stupa wasn't nearly so visible from ground level, as it was hidden behind a row of houses with only a small alleyway for an entrance. However, once we reached it we suddenly found ourselves standing at the edge of a large compound which was almost totally filled with its gigantic presence. It was perhaps 40 m in diameter and 15 m high, sitting on three tiers of a white platform that was something like 80 m across. This colossus had been built in the fourteenth century, but there was thought to have been a stupa here since the seventh century AD. On the top of the dome was a square golden tower with a pair of Buddha eyes painted onto each side, looking out across the rooftops. Above that was a golden spire, a bit like a conical hat. The shapes of the stupa represented earth, air, fire and water. Multicoloured prayer flags radiated from the very top of the spire to the edges of the platform, as if it was a giant maypole. Flocks of pigeons wheeled around and settled on the high ledges and the prayer flags.

Around the compound and sometimes spiralling up the stupa itself walked – perambulated – numerous men and women. They always walked clockwise, usually brushing their hands along the lines of bronze prayer wheels that were set into the stupa base. Some thumbed through strings of prayer beads, others were rhythmically swinging little hand-held drums back and forth. These people were usually round-faced, comely Tibetans, dressed simply but smartly with a waistcoat and an apron over plain clothes. White hats or umbrellas provided some relief from the hot sun, and I was surprised to see that white modern trainers were popular footwear, even for the oldest ladies, as if this daily routine was a fitness programme. The men and women often perambulated in small groups, chatting quietly to each other as they walked. They were sometimes joined by Buddhist monks, wearing dark red or orange robes. Even uniformed schoolchildren came and went. The stupa had the feel of being a central meeting point for the community, both sociable and pleasant.

The Tibetan community in Kathmandu was a population in exile, as had been the Tibetans we met in Pokhara. Over 100,000 Tibetans fled their country after it was occupied in 1950 by China; probably 1.2 million Tibetans died as a direct result of the Chinese invasion, out of a total population of 6 million. All but five of the 6,000 Buddhist monasteries and nunneries in Tibet were systematically emptied of all their contents and literally torn down, piece by piece. When Paul Theroux visited Tibet in the late 1980s he said:

> The most serious development in recent years is the Chinese discovery that Tibet is a tourist attraction ... China has said it would like to have 100,000 [tourists] a year. In that event, the destruction of Lhasa might be assured ... It is the one great place in China that the railway has not reached. The Kun Lun Range is a guarantee that the railway will never get to Lhasa. That is probably a good thing.[13]

These thoughts were echoed by the Dalai Lama in 1990:

> Sadly, to many visitors, Tibet is probably little more than an exotic destination, another stamp in the passport. They see enough monasteries to satisfy their curiosity and enough colourfully dressed pilgrims visiting them to allay any suspicions they may have...
> ...The Chinese tour guides inevitably only show those monasteries and buildings which have been or are being rebuilt. They do not show the thousands still in ruins ... Furthermore, contact with Tibetans [is] minimal, since the great majority of accommodation available [is] Chinese owned and run. The few Tibetans working in these establishments [are] in menial jobs as servants and cleaners...
> My countrymen and women are today in grave danger of becoming nothing more than a tourist attraction in their own country.[14]

Defying Theroux's predictions, while we were in China the new railway connecting Beijing directly to Lhasa was opened with great fanfare. It was truly an engineering and technological triumph: apparently Swiss consultants had advised that a railway couldn't be built across the permafrost, so the Chinese designed their own system and went ahead anyway. The railway ticket offices were overwhelmed with the numbers of Chinese wanting to be among the first to travel to Lhasa. The Chinese were avid travellers in their own country, as we had experienced first-hand in places like Dali and Lijiang, and there was no doubt that Lhasa was the latest must-see curiosity destination.

Meanwhile, the Dalai Lama has called for Tibet to be turned into 'a state of ahimsa', free of all weapons and dedicated to promoting peace and environmental protection. Until such time as they feel able to return to their homeland, Tibetans around the world continue to live in exile.

---

[13] Theroux, P, *Riding the Iron Rooster*, London, Penguin Books, 1989, p.486 © 1997 by Paul Theroux, permission of The Wylie Agency.
[14] Gyatso, T, *Freedom in Exile*, London, Abacus, 1998, pp. 262, 268–269

Back at Bodnath, we found a roof-top café to escape the glare of the sun, have a cold drink and a plate of chips, and chat to yet another friendly waiter about Nepali politics and the impact of the Maoists. We weren't to know then that in just a day or two we would taste their particular brand of civil unrest for ourselves.

We were doing a little shopping when it began, buying souvenirs and presents that we could carry home to Europe. Incidentally, here the salesman explained to us his system of flexible pricing. If the buyer was American, the price would automatically go up to the highest level. Elderly shoppers were also charged more, followed by anyone who looked smartly dressed. We fitted none of those categories, but that hadn't stopped him trying it on with us anyway.

While we were in the shop there was a commotion on the street outside and our salesman ran out of the door, hurriedly taking in the racks of clothing he had on display outside. He didn't stop there; metal shutters were pulled down over the windows, as if he was closing up shop. He wasn't the only one – every shopkeeper was doing exactly the same, the street resounding to clattering and clunking as the buildings were secured.

As this was going on, a small group of young men, some with bandit-like scarves covering their mouths and sticks in their hands, swaggered jauntily past. We could feel apprehension in the air, a nervous, tense excitement tinged with genuine fear. The men were parading the streets, calling for a general strike in response to the government's snap decision to raise oil prices by 30 per cent. The standard reaction to unfavourable government action in Kathmandu, we were later told, was to get out onto the streets.

The salesman said that although he didn't like the government policy much, he still needed to keep his shop open for trade. But he feared violent reprisals from the demonstrators, such as broken windows or ransacked goods, if he did. Everyone else clearly thought the same, for the shutters stayed down all that day and the next. The strike didn't just involve shops. The protesters wanted to bring the city to a halt, with no traffic moving around. They did this very effectively – by attacking drivers who defied their strike.

A couple of Spanish tourist whom we met later related to us their experiences during that first day of protests. They had been out of Kathmandu, sightseeing elsewhere in the valley. On the way back, their taxi stopped 9 km outside the city centre and the driver refused to go any closer. They had no choice but to get out and walk. As they did, they passed fires burning on the roads, tyres set alight. They saw cars being pelted with stones, windows cracked and lights smashed in. Motorcyclists were being dragged off their bikes and beaten.

Unfortunately for us, the strikes and street violence just happened to occur on the days that we needed to go to the airport, six kilometres from our hotel. On the second day of the protests we had booked an early morning taxi from our hotel. This was cancelled the day before, as the driver could no longer be sure of getting to the airport safely. We managed to arrange another one, for a very high price, but in the morning this too failed to materialise. A few taxis were around, braving the streets because, as the driver who did take us to the airport explained, it was too early in the morning for the protesters to be up and about. By the time we returned to the city, however, the protesters were making their presence felt again. In fact, it became was our turn to walk home.

In the airport car park were stranded vehicles, their owners not willing to risk driving them into the city. Several of their windows had been smashed anyway. We walked past an impromptu roadblock, formed by a straggly line of young men and boys. The few cars and motorbikes that were on the road simply turned around in their tracks well before reaching the crowd. No one bothered us; we weren't the only ones walking along the strangely traffic-free roads. As we passed the palace gates, we came across a solid wall of policemen in full riot gear: padded clothes, helmets, plastic shields and batons. Their armoured trucks were parked alongside. They had formed a human barrier, blocking the way of a few dozen lively protesters who were shouting anti-monarchy slogans and waving red flags.

The young men didn't really seem to know what to do with themselves. They clustered into a group for security, putting on displays of bravado by running towards the police and then backing off again. A few picked up stones in the background, but none were brave enough to start anything more serious than a show of bluster and noise. In the end they all turned and walked down another street, shutters clanging down ahead of them. As before, the threat of violence hung in the air, and the people of Kathmandu were afraid of 'the Maoists'. Even though it neither affected or threatened us directly, this undercurrent of fear made us shiver. To live in such a state, always frightened by the sinister presence of violence, must be a terrible thing to endure.

What a blessing for us that we lived in a peaceful society, open and democratic, accountable and fair. It was something that was so easily taken for granted, assumed to be normal. Viewed through the prism of history, however, it can be seen to be very much the exception, a remarkably recent development. And around the world today it is still the exception. Tasting the alternative was one way of learning to appreciate the value of our very rare society.

Nepal had been blighted by ten years of near civil war, as Maoist rebels fought for a share of political power. Their campaigns had often been violent and over 13,000 people had been killed. We were told that it had been easier for drive-by killings to occur in the anonymity of Kathmandu, but even in rural villages people had often been led away into the woods, never to return. Extortion had been commonplace, with roadblocks set up to collect 'tolls' and businesses having to give 'donations'. Everyone from the lodges on our trek to businesses in Kathmandu had had to provide funds. In Kathmandu some factories had closed rather than hand over all their profits, creating even more unemployment at a time when thousands were migrating to the city, fleeing violence in the countryside.

While we were in South East Asia, we had been unsure whether it would be safe enough for us to visit Nepal at all, for this was the year that riots in Kathmandu had forced the King to hand back power to the government after fifteen months of unilateral rule. He lost control over the army, had to pay tax, was no longer needed to authorise legislation and couldn't open or close parliament – it seemed a direct parallel of the history of Charles I and his conflicts with Parliament! When we arrived in Kathmandu there had been three months of ceasefire, a seven-party alliance including the Maoists had been in government for one hundred days, and there was much talk of a referendum on whether to abolish the monarchy altogether.

The protests we experienced had included Maoist and anti-monarchy elements, but they only lasted a few days. The government retracted its increase in oil prices and things returned to normal. The national oil company presumably went back to making monthly losses of 800 million rupees (US $12 million). Nepal is one of the poorest countries in the world. We were told that in Kathmandu a typical wage is 300 rupees (US $4.63) per day. The challenges that Nepal faces to development are tremendous. 90 per cent of its population live by subsistence agriculture, farming on steep hillsides. There are few mineral resources. Its only significant trade routes are overland to India. Some economists even argue that it is not worth trying to bring about development, as the environmental damage inevitably caused would outweigh any benefits. Currently, one of the main sources of income and development for the country is foreign aid. Even its tourist industry is limited to a bare handful of centres, despite the wealth of attractions in the country. Perhaps with a ceasefire in operation and a democratic government, that at least might change in the coming years.

Chapter 63: Everest

Our last activity in Nepal was a treat that we bought for ourselves as we neared the end of our travels. From Kathmandu Airport it was only half an hour's flight to the top of the world, Mount Everest, 8,848 m above sea level. Several companies offer daily tourist flights around the peak in small sixteen-seater planes. The experience turned out to be a bit of a farce that dragged on over three days, just happening to be the days of the protests and strikes in Kathmandu. To begin with, we were told to check in at 5 a.m., which was before the domestic terminal of the airport actually opened. We stood by the shut entrance with an assortment of other passengers and their piles of cardboard boxes until 5.30 a.m. We were checked in by the complex process of ticking our names off on a sheet of paper and given boarding cards, which we were told were for the 6.30 a.m. flight, as we had been promised. This was apparently the best of the four morning flights, each an hour apart, as the chances of clear weather were higher earlier in the morning.

When 6.30 a.m. came, one planeload of passengers was called forward by a lady wandering through the departure lounge shouting their flight number. As this was unintelligible to the foreign tourists, many of them clustered expectantly at the gate, only for most – including us – to be told to sit down again. It all seemed a bit shambolic. The officials calmly informed us that one plane was just going up to check on the weather conditions: not to worry, everyone was still on the 6.30 a.m. flight. But time passed and we were told eventually that the first plane had reported that there was no visibility, and therefore there would be no more flights today. We could either claim our money back or try again tomorrow.

We tried again the next morning, with the routine slightly more familiar this time. It was the same story: everyone was on the 6.30 a.m. flight – all the four flights were the 6.30 a.m. flight – except that today it was 7.40 before we were told that the 'test flight' had come back and no more would leave today. Throughout, the officials insisted that even the passengers still waiting at 7.30 a.m. would have been on the 6.30 a.m. flight. This was a true charade. The manager of our hotel explained to us why there was so much confusion. Every passenger wanted to be on the earliest flight, so the airline managed to sell seats on the later flights by describing them all as being the first.

The third day we – and several other passengers who had by now become familiar faces to us – barged into the airline office as soon as we were able to, insisting that we did not want to sit waiting yet again while another 'test flight' left without us. This method worked and we were called forward first, much to the chagrin of two newcomers. We squeezed into the two lines of seats on the plane, each with its own blurry porthole-like window. The plane climbed up into cloud; it was frustrating to sit there, seeing nothing out of the windows but the blanket of cloud, and wondering if we would turn around at any minute. But all of a sudden we popped out above the cloud layer and could see two distant white peaks poking their noses up out of the whiteness. One of these was the holy mountain Gauri Shankar, which has never been climbed. Then the front passengers were called forward into the cockpit and it became evident that they were looking at nothing less than Everest itself. When it was my turn to go forward, I saw a blanket of whiteness spread out below us and in front, a fair way off, a blue-grey triangular mountain peak, with a dark flat ridge beside it. This was my first view of Everest and Lhotse! There was little time to get my head around the fact that I was looking at the highest point on Earth, let alone to get a really good look at it, before I had to give way to the next person. It was hard to know what to make of it all.

Back in my seat, I began to see more mountains below as the cloud thinned, and then all at once I was looking down at an expanse of Himalayan ridges and valleys. As we progressed, it dawned on me that one of these mountains was Everest itself, rapidly approaching. I stood up to let Claudia have a look, just at the moment that the plane banked sharply, pushing my face up into the ceiling of the plane. As the window angled towards the North Face of Everest, all I had was a close-up of the interior decor of the plane. We straightened out with Everest on the other side of the plane and then I did indeed get a fantastic close-up view of the awesome mountains. Between us and Everest was the white peak of Ama Dablan, a particularly impressive sight, all sharp ridges and steep drops. And then it was all behind us and we were headed home, far too soon – but with the precious photographs as mementos. Everyone was happy in the plane, almost euphoric, partly out of relief that our flight had finally been successful. It had been a unique experience, a close encounter with majestic mountains, although ultimately too fleeting to fully absorb and appreciate that we had just seen Mount Everest.

That was our final adventure in Nepal. The next day we flew back to Delhi for the last leg of our journey around the world. There we wanted to fulfil two final ambitions: to see the Taj Mahal and to visit the desert city of Jaisalmer.

Chapter 64: Agra

Delhi was less of a shock the second time around, although it was just as crazy. We didn't have time to hang around long, as Jaisalmer was in the far west of Rajasthan, near the Pakistan border. To get there we had the choice of fighting our way through the bus and train systems again, or hiring a car and a driver to take us on a tour of the main sights. After nearly a year of travelling independently, the idea of being escorted around was a strange one to us, but we realised that it was a luxury which might ensure our trip would end on a positive note. As usual in India, it wasn't very hard to organise a car and driver: we simply mentioned the idea to the owner of our poky backstreet hotel, who promptly said that he could arrange it for us. My experience in India is that where business is concerned, not a trick is missed by wheeling and dealing entrepreneurs – in fact, the hard part is avoiding handing over cash for something that isn't really wanted.

In this case, it wasn't long before a very gentlemanly Sikh arrived to discuss our tour, assuring us that he had lived and worked in England and therefore could be totally trusted and knew exactly what English people wanted. Only at the very end of the discussions did it transpire that he wasn't actually going to be our driver – that would turn out to be another elegantly turbaned gentleman called Mr Singh, who spoke far less English. He was also hard of hearing, but he more than compensated for this by his careful, skilful driving – an unusual combination on Indian roads – and his exceptionally courteous behaviour towards 'Sir' and 'Madam'.

Before leaving Delhi we heard that the area around Jaisalmer had received more rain in two days than was usual in four years, causing the worst flash flooding for forty-five years. The floods killed an estimated 300 people and 4,500 animals. More positively, the rains also refilled underground reservoirs and created surface lakes in the desert, somewhat relieving the perennial problem of water shortages in the area. We had intended our trip to culminate at the Taj Mahal, but these floods caused us to change our route and visit Agra first.

Agra had for a long time been the capital city of India, not that it was really evident today. It was a city that managed to contain both the best and the worst of India. The best was the Taj Mahal, one of the world's most iconic and beautiful buildings. The worst was the condition of the city and its population. The nature of Agra itself was one reason why the hordes of tourists who flock there stay on average for only half a day. We stayed longer, but didn't particularly enjoy it. A local newspaper was decrying the state of the city's facilities: no decent public transport, traffic chaos, litter in the streets, a lack of clean water supplies. A large proportion of the residents still relied on hand pumps or rivers to get their water. On the street outside our hotel, we were soon put off by the nauseating piles of rotting garbage that lined the road. Pigs, goats and cows were all nosing through it – we could hardly believe the sight in front of our eyes. Cyclists, motorcycles and cycle-rickshaws careered past us, making walking a hazard. But worst were the unpleasant stares and clearly rude comments that groups of men gave Claudia as we passed them, for no apparent reason other than she was a Western woman. This was the one and only place in our travels that this had been the case, to such a degree at least.

We went to the Taj Mahal in the late afternoon, so that we could see it at sunset. The entry fees were possibly the most disproportionate of any tourist site in India – it was the extreme example of a common phenomenon. Foreign tourists were charged 250 rupees, plus a further 500 rupees in tax, making the entrance charge a total of 750 rupees (US $18.50). Indian tourists, on the other hand, were charged just 20 rupees (US $0.50).

After passing through a security check – in place after a recent bomb threat – we entered a large square courtyard that was ringed by red sandstone walls. Each wall was broken in its midpoint by a great archway, immaculately decorated with white geometric patterns created from lines of inlaid stone. This distinctive red and white architecture was very typical of the grand Mogul monuments – usually tombs – of northern India. It was extremely graceful, despite the large scale of the buildings.

Looking through one of the arched gateways we had our first sight of the Taj Mahal, looking squat and smaller than expected from this distance. Its white marble gleamed in the sunlight, perfectly framed against the black curving archway around us. As we stepped forward out of the gateway, we saw below us in expanse of green grass lawns, enclosed by a perimeter wall. Directly in front of us, running straight towards the Taj Mahal, was a long, narrow strip of water, elegantly lined by trees. It always drew our eyes back to the white centrepiece, which was perfectly reflected in the water. From here, the shape of the Taj Mahal was at its most attractive, its features most clearly proportioned.

Sitting on a raised square base was a bulbous central dome, outsized compared to the rest of the building. Around it were four smaller domes and beyond them four tall thin minaret towers, one at each corner. It was sited on the bank of a river, so there was nothing behind it except sky, which accentuated its features. Everything was aligned, symmetrical, proportioned. It was unusually graceful and easy on the eye. The more I looked at it, the more I thought it had the same visual appeal as a beautiful baby, with perfect features and an outsized head – it was almost cute!

Tourists and sightseers were everywhere, Westerners and Indians alike. The locals seemed to be having a day out, taking time to sit peacefully on the lawns. They were invariably dressed in their best colourful saris and had new henna paintings on their hands. It was like being at an Indian version of a Buckingham Palace garden party. The same could not be said for the Westerners, whose clothing was all too often inappropriate, especially when set against the obvious efforts of the Indians. Slowly, everyone moved through the gardens, along the edge of the water, towards the Taj Mahal. As we walked it became clear that it was only the jewel in the crown of an entire complex. On either side of it were a large mosque and its counterpart, one a mirror image of the other. Each was a magnificent construction in its own right, made from red sandstone and richly decorated with white patterns.

The Taj Mahal was also covered in decorations, which could be appreciated from closer up. These ranged from geometric designs to giant inscriptions from the Koran around its doorway arches. There was barely a surface that had not been ornamented in some way, either with inlaid patterns or sculpted with graceful archways. Most of the inlaid decorations were made from black marble. Everything was flawlessly constructed and everything was identically repeated on each side of the building to keep it all symmetrical. The sizes of the marble blocks and inlaid lettering even changed in size as they rose higher, so that from below they all appeared perfectly uniform, undistorted by perspective. It was this attention to detail and precision that made the Taj Mahal so special. I have not seen its match anywhere. This was my third visit, and each time I had been more impressed by the artistry on display.

The richness reached even greater heights in the very heart of the building, under its dome. Inside this mausoleum – for that is what it was – the white marble walls were adorned with hundreds of exquisitely intricate flower patterns, each one made from inlaid black marble or gemstones. Black stems curved gracefully into green leaves and red or blue petals perhaps no more than 3 cm across, each one perfect. The tombs themselves were then enclosed by delicate lattice screens, each one carved from a single piece of white marble.

It had taken 20,000 craftsmen to build the Taj Mahal, between 1631–1653. Architects had been brought from Persia and Europe. The gemstones used – up to forty-three different types – had been imported from China, Russia and across Central Asia. A macabre story that captures something about the perfection of the Taj Mahal is that after it was completed, some of the workers had their hands or fingers amputated to prevent them from ever replicating its beauty. The building had been created by a Mogul emperor, Shah Jehan, as a mausoleum for his wife, but after he died his body was also laid inside to one side of his wife – thus becoming the only component of the entire complex that defied its symmetry.

We lingered in the grounds long enough to see the setting sun change the complexion and atmosphere of the Taj Mahal. From an almost harsh bright white it turned a softer, mellow, romantic pink and then finally seemed to glow orange, as if being coloured from within. It was a pretty farewell, as we were shooed out by the guards.

Shah Jehan had not only built the Taj Mahal, but had also founded New Delhi and built the Red Fort there. He was possibly the most extravagant of the Mogul emperors. His 'Peacock Throne' alone contained jewels that had a value of 10 million rupees. As we would see on our journeys through Rajasthan, the opulence of Mogul rulers was stunning – part of their legacy forms some of India's most precious heritage – but there had been a darker side to their rule too. William Dalrymple tried to understand this:

> In all of Delhi's history, at no period was that thin dress of civilisation more beautiful – or more deceptively woven – than during the first half of the seventeenth century, during the Golden Age of Shah Jehan. In public the actions of the Emperor and his court were governed by a rigid code of courtliness, as subtle and elaborate as the interlaced borders the Mughal artists painted around their miniatures. But for all this fine façade, in private the ambitions of the Mughal Emperors know no moral limitations: without scruple they would murder their brothers, poison their sisters or starve their fathers. The courtly ceremonial acted as a veil around the naked reality of Mughal politics; it was a mask which deliberately disguised the brutality and coarseness that lay hidden underneath.[15]

The rulers of India throughout its history seem to have combined decadent extravagance with widespread poverty, leaving a sad legacy for the present day. According to John Keay, during the sixteenth century rule of Akbar – whose grandiose tomb lies just outside Agra – the nobles consumed 82 per cent of the empire's entire budget. Farmers had to give multiple tributes, leaving them barely enough food for their own survival. Subsequent Maharajas continued to live in luxury: 'the eye-catching profusion of solid gold and chased silver, precious silks and brocades, massive jewels, priceless carpets and inlaid marbles was probably without parallel in history.' The British didn't do much better, with a quarter of India's revenue having been paid directly into English hands.

As Jeffrey Sachs notes, between 1600 and 1870 India experienced no per capita growth at all; from 1870 to independence in 1947 the per capita growth was a mere 0.2%; even from 1950 to 1970 the figure was only 1.9%. At the

---

[15] Dalrymple, W, *City of Djinns*, London, Flamingo, 1994, p.190. Reprinted by permission of HarperCollins Publishers Ltd © Dalrymple 1994

time of independence in 1947, Indians had an average life expectancy of 32.5 years and only 17 per cent were literate. Now, life expectancy is 63 years, adult literacy is 61 per cent, and the per capita GDP is US $1,720. It is difficult to comprehend both the depth and the breadth of Indian poverty. The UN estimated in 2006 that 30 per cent of the population was malnourished. Nearly 300 million people live in extreme poverty. There are 600 million Indians living without basic sanitation. One child in eleven dies before they reach five years old; every year 1.5 million Indian children under five years old die of diarrhoea. Stories we read in newspapers told of cotton farmers who were committing suicide after being refused bank loans. In the ten years prior to 2003, the number of farmers who had done so was 100,000.

Chapter 65: Palaces and Forts – Jaipur, Jodhpur and Udaipur

The 'Golden Triangle' of Indian tourism encompasses the relatively accessible cities of Delhi, Agra and Jaipur: these are the first places that the majority of tourists will see, and in many cases the only ones. Jaipur was the capital city of Rajasthan, land of the Maharajas and Rajputs. While it contained the same Indian madness as the other cities, it did so with far more character and style. It had been built as a planned city in the 1720s by a maharaja who obviously considered it a priority to be able to hold magnificent processions along wide streets, safely within its city walls. These main thoroughfares still maintained an air of grandeur, of extravagant pomp and ceremony, although the outer city walls themselves were now in poor repair.

We entered the Old City through large orange sandstone gateways that were prettily decorated with white and blue patterns. That didn't stop men from openly urinating against them. Beyond the gates, the broad ceremonial avenues were not wide enough to contain the Indian traffic, which was every bit as chaotic and noisy as it had been in Agra and Delhi. The roads were full of cars, motorcycles, bicycles and rickshaws; gaunt cows and streetwise dogs; camels pulling wooden carts; sheep in the road; and monkeys scampering along the walls. The buildings that lined the streets formed a blocky row of shopping emporiums, two to four storeys high. They were all a uniform sickly orange colour, courtesy of an 1856 decision to paint the entire city in honour of a visit by Prince Albert. This resulted in Jaipur being given the slightly erroneous nickname of 'The Pink City' and started an enduring tradition.

Many of the buildings were finely carved, which gave a sense of elegance and charm to the city, but this didn't hold central Jaipur back from being intensely commercial. The wide pavements that ran underneath a colonnaded walkway were lined with small shops selling everything from dried foods and spices to clothes and fabrics, jewellery, precious metals or shoes. Side streets and alleyways quickly turned into crowded bazaars, stuffed with individual stalls. Along the sides of the main roads, even on the inside of roundabouts, people had laid out their wares on the ground.

Shopkeepers were desperate for us to 'just step inside' and 'just have a look', where prices were 'only ten rupees' – although we never tested their claims. Some shopkeepers would even brazenly block the pavement and grab hold of our arms, as if they could physically manhandle us into parting with our money. However, people were noticeably more friendly here, willing to make eye contact and smile. With a deep breath and a sense of humour, it was all good fun. For an Indian shopping experience, these streets and bazaars were the best we encountered.

The architectural highlight of Jaipur was a facade that had been built so that women of the royal harem could watch the Maharaja's parades from behind screens, safely invisible from impure eyes. It was five storeys high, sticking up above the adjacent buildings, and was composed of many sandstone windows that were each shaped like a small sail billowing outwards in the wind. It was indeed designed to be aired by the breeze and was called 'Palace of the Winds'. The facade formed an outer part of the City Palace, which didn't have much of an impact on us, despite its opulence.

At its ticket office I was short-changed by 50 rupees, which the cashier had set to one side in case I happened to notice the deliberate mistake; he handed the note over without a single word when I did. It seemed a shame that these incidents occurred, even in such touristy places, but such was the way of this country. There were plenty of official men inside the City Palace, posing in their red turbans and white robes, hoping to get some small change by posing for photographs despite the signs saying 'No tips'. One such photo opportunity was in front of the world's largest pieces of silverware, which had been built in 1902 by a maharaja to carry water from the Ganges during a voyage to England.

Again, the extravagance of the Maharaja lifestyles – reflected in the forts and palaces they had built – was staggering. Outside Jaipur we saw a palace that had been built at the edge of an artificial lake so that it could be gently cooled by the waters in the heat of summer. This was on the way to Amer Fort, a grandiose fortified palace for the local maharaja family, occupied from the late sixteenth century onwards – but only until the family felt safe enough to relocate out of a mere fort down to their entirely new city!

The approach view to Amer Fort – or Amber Fort, as it was more commonly called – is one of the most magnificent sights in Rajasthan. Right on the top of the hillside perched battlements that looked across to the plain of Jaipur. Leading away from this small fortress along the ridges of the landscape ran stone walls, reminiscent of the Great Wall of China but on a far smaller scale. The chunky cream-coloured buildings of Amer Fort itself sat imposingly on the side of the hill. Below them zigzagged a paved stone pathway, passing underneath several stone gateways. The whole thing looked like something from a film set – complete with colourfully painted elephants that were slowly carrying tourists to and from the fort. Unfortunately, the inside of the fort didn't really match the grandeur of the exterior. It was being refurbished – it needed to be – and so we saw loads of rubble being moved across courtyards by donkeys and by women, who carried the debris in metal plates that they balanced gracefully on their heads.

After seeing the sights of Jaipur, we continued on our way to Rajasthan's second city – Jodhpur. Claudia was feeling under the weather when we arrived there and so instead of sightseeing she opted to rest in our family-run guesthouse, which happened to contain both a snooker table and a stuffed tiger. As a consequence, she missed out on one of the most splendid sights in Rajasthan. This was one of the very few times that illness had been a problem for either of us, right around the world. It is common for travellers to India to warn of 'Delhi-belly' but it wasn't until further into Rajasthan that Claudia was properly brought down by the effects of Indian food and hygiene. A night of wretched vomiting followed by a day of weakness could have been worse, and as ever a complete day without further intake of food seemed to cure the problem.

In many ways the city of Jodhpur resembled Jaipur: the same busy roads of three-wheeled black and yellow tuk-tuks, colourful rickshaws, motorbikes, wandering cows and lonely sadhus; similar old city streets lined with shops leading to a street market; all the concentrated richness, diversity, chaos, colours, dirt, and smell of urban India. On the top of a hill in the middle of the city was a fort, its imposing walls looking totally dominant over the houses below. From its battlements were views across the city, over the square, flat, blocky rooftops of the houses. Jodhpur was famous for being 'The Blue City' because many of its houses were painted with indigo, which was indeed a bright pastel blue colour. This apparently had the dual effects of being cooling and being an insect repellent. Pigeons were huddling together on window ledges, no doubt hiding from the kites that were soaring around the walls of the fort. At one point I counted fourteen kites visible in the air at the same time.

Jodhpur Fort had never been captured by attacking armies, despite the best efforts of forces from Jaipur. It was easy to see why: there were seven huge gates towering over the entrance roadway, one after the other, with the walls of the fort climbing high above. Some of the gates had been designed specifically to foil charges by elephants, with a right-angle bend immediately before the gate and enormous wooden doors that had huge spikes protruding from them, ten feet up – at elephant head height. Jodhpur Fort was the best of all those that we visited in Rajasthan, combining exterior strength with an interior beauty. As with all the forts and palaces, the design inside was based on a series of courtyards that had rooms and passageways around their outside. Here the guards specialised in wearing green and yellow striped turbans and sporting great bushy, bristling, curling moustaches that were quite fearsome to behold.

The highlight was a room that had been built for entertainment, which was described as the 'ultimate in oriental opulence... all the exotic beauty of India condensed into this one exquisitely breathtaking room'. It was a fairly accurate description, as the walls and ceilings were totally covered in gold, combined with rich decorations of majestic red, shining silver and general rich extravagance. Unlike so much elsewhere, it was all perfectly preserved, a glimmering wonder.

From the best fort, we were taken by Mr Singh to the best palace, which was located in the lakeside city of Udaipur. The Lake Palace had been home to the greatest of all the maharajas and was the largest in the state, having been built by no less than twenty kings from 1559 onwards. It is now part museum and part hotel. Its finest courtyards and rooms were to be found on the upper floors, joined by a series of balconies with elegantly sculpted windows that looked out over the city. One of the courtyards was more a marble-walled garden, with no roof and green trees and bushes planted within it. Around its edges was a cloister-like colonnaded walkway, with carved pillars and gracefully crenulated archways. To one side was a room that reminded me of a Roman bathhouse, full of marble columns and with a decorative fountain at its centre. Its outer wall was a marble latticework that was filled with bright red and yellow stained glass. Further on, there were more and more rooms set around open courtyards, each with a richer decoration than the last. One was covered in white and blue painted tiles, while another had pictures of flowers made from inlaid marble that were far more detailed than those of the Taj Mahal. There were wall-to-ceiling mosaics made from shards of silver mirrors, and still others using coloured glass. Three-dimensional silver, green and blue peacock mosaics emerged from the walls. The richest of all covered a balcony overlooking a plain yard. This mosaic was built in 1874, but had recently been restored to incredible splendour.

Udaipur itself had a mix of historical sights, tourist shops and old-world streets and houses. Possibly the most visually distinctive palace of all sat just offshore on an island, a gleaming white building in splendid isolation that looked as if it rose from the water itself. Beside an entrance to the Lake Palace were twisting alleys that had been partially colonised by hostels, German bakeries and souvenir and curio shops that looked like antique dens. Leading to a lakeside ghat was a gateway that deserved to be preserved as a museum piece for its carved marble pillars, crenulated arches and blue tiled decorations.

As the sun set, we watched boys splashing in the water and a lady washing her clothes. A small group of tourists sat quietly watching the view and a couple of local men chatted as they leant against their motorbikes. Several youths sidled up to us with their stock questions: 'Where are you from?' and

'What is your name?' before always asking us if we wanted to see their art gallery. After at least eight different people had tried this on us, it began to get a little tiresome. But it didn't detract too much from the chilled atmosphere.

Slightly further away from the lake, the old houses of the city were unlike any others in India. Their small doorways were often graced with crenulated arches, some even with matching thick wooden doors, carved for a perfect fit. On creamy walls there were numerous incredibly detailed paintings of black elephants and brown horses in their finest costume. Beside metal drainpipes and doorways, these pieces of artwork were a kind of high-class urban graffiti. They gave something special to the streets, making it look as if people had taken pride and care in the appearance of their city. But that must have been some while ago. The paint was fading, the pictures scratched, some were covered in black mould and others were disintegrating as the plaster underneath fell into the filthy gutters below.

I had previously told Claudia that Udaipur was the prettiest Indian city I had seen during earlier travels. As we looked around together – at the piles of litter, a cow eating a discarded newspaper, donkeys being used as beasts of burden, girls collecting water from a street handpump – we wondered how this could be the best there was. Yet, beyond the scenes of dirt and poverty, which visitors to India have to get used to, it was indeed possible to relax here and to begin to appreciate the eccentric, exotic, but also pretty charms of the country. Perhaps this was easiest in Udaipur because it lacked the crowded hassle of other cities, whilst still being a showcase of ageing Rajasthani flair and decadence. Slowly but surely, as we travelled through Rajasthan, we found that the balance of our perceptions of India was shifting.

Chapter 66: Rajasthan Journeys

The sole 'modern' road of our Rajasthan journey was a new three-lane motorway devoid of traffic. it was part of the new Indian 'Quadrilateral Highway' that connected Delhi, Mumbai and Calcutta. The only reasons for breaking our smooth ride on this highway were avoiding ladies who walked across the road with bundles of wood balanced on their heads, or donkeys standing in the outside lane, or cows on the central reservation, or sheep and goats using the verge for pasture. As ever, there was no sense that these animals should not be there. Their existence was simply part of Indian life, and Mr Singh just calmly drove around them. Some other vehicles on the motorway were driving in the wrong direction, including a truck coming towards us in our outside lane. I had the distinct impression that the concept of a functioning motorway had some way to go before it would be established in India.

When parallels were made between India and China, both described as the emerging giants of Asia, I thought of the difference between the road networks of the two countries, or between the relative conditions of Delhi and Beijing. China impressed its development on the visitor; India only conveyed disorganisation and a lack of development. Nevertheless, the southern cities of India were undergoing an economic boom, exploiting high-tech services that didn't need good roads. Between 1990 and 2001 the poverty rate in India declined from 42 per cent of the entire population to 35 per cent. As Jeffrey Sachs has written, 'India has not yet matched China in the depth and breadth of economic modernisation, but it is easy to underestimate what has already been accomplished.' Nevertheless, the growth rates of 8 per cent per year that India can boast of were concentrated in urban areas. Rural area growth rates were estimated to be only 2 per cent per year.

Virtually all the other roads we drove on, some of which were thick with heavy traffic, would have been classed as minor country roads in England. The colourful orange lorries had signs saying 'Blow Horn' or 'Horn Please' painted above their rear number plates, asking any overtaking vehicles to make the driver aware of their presence so that he would hopefully refrain from swerving sideways into them. The horns created a lot of noise on the roads and made the brand name of the main car manufacturer in India highly apt: 'TATA'. We had experienced varying degrees of heart-stopping road journeys before, but the Indian roads easily matched them for white-knuckle, hair-raising close shaves. At times we seemed to have entered a surreal cross between the wacky races and a high-speed game of chicken. Most of the other vehicles were lorries or overcrowded buses, neither of which seemed at all inclined to reduce their speed at all. In between them motorcycles darted in and out, everyone bent on getting ahead of everyone else, weaving across the road, overtaking and undertaking. As two lorries steamed side by side along a two-lane road, the loser was the one that lost his nerve and swerved onto the verge just in time to avert a head-on collision with oncoming traffic.

Too many times I gasped as we rounded a corner to be faced with two cabs bearing down on us, forcing the experienced Mr Singh to stamp on the brake and miraculously find a gap between them. These near-death experiences were literally only inches away from being the real thing. It was a measure of the margins of safety that many cars drove with their wing mirrors tucked in, obviously judging that a mirror was more of a hazard than a help. Within India, it is estimated that 270 people die every day on the roads – and we could see why.

On quieter one-lane roads, a kind of jungle law determined who had right of way: it was always the largest vehicle. This allowed buses to tear along, lurching horribly as they bumped over the edges of potholed roads, always assuming that it was the responsibility of all other traffic to get out of their way in time. We experienced the vehicular equivalent of diving for cover time and again as our driver wrenched his steering wheel in a panic, sending our little car nearly ploughing into the hedges. The larger vehicle never slowed its speed when passing us, which was terrifying when the consequences of a collision were contemplated. This kamikaze system became even more dangerous when two oncoming vehicles both decided that they had priority. Several times we witnessed a pair of jeeps forcing each other aside at the very last moment. This was reckless driving taken to the most ludicrous extremes, but it was a normal, everyday occurrence in India.

Just when things couldn't get any worse, a dog would dart across the road between the wheels of cars, or a herd of buffalo would stand grazing at the roadside, or a cow would cause a sudden traffic jam, as if we were inside a surreal computer game that was giving us periodic hazards to test our reactions. Yet this was no game: carcasses of animals bloodied the roads, and every so often we passed stationary lorries with smashed-up cabs, trailers skewed across the road, on their sides, or even – once – upside down in a small lake.

We drove for hours with our noses pressed to the windows, silently absorbing the sights. The journeys were fascinating, an endless succession of exotic images and impressions. We saw white storks and blue-green peacocks in the fields and bushes. Weaver bird nests hung from branches. A man held a black bear by a chain through its nose; other men had monkeys that were trained to perform somersaults. We passed a camel farm, and saw goatherds with their shepherds sitting under nearby trees. A class of schoolchildren was sitting out in the open on the ground, in front of their teacher who sat on a chair. Much of the countryside we passed through in Rajasthan was fairly flat. The land was thick with green fields of alfalfa, grass and maize. Sometimes men chopped at fields of dry mud with mattocks. Many people were carrying bundles of long green stalks, either balanced on their heads, slung across bicycles, or piled in the back of wooden carts that were being pulled by hump-back cows with painted horns, horses, tractors or even camels. Standing outside houses were hand-powered grinding machines that would turn the plants into an animal-feed mash.

Everyone we saw seemed concerned with one of two things: collecting food for their animals or collecting water for themselves. Standpipes were always crowded by a group of people washing themselves or filling water jars. These distinctive jars were almost spherical pots made of brown ceramic or silver metal ware. Women often walked gracefully along the roadside balancing water jars on their heads, often steadied with a hand but sometimes not. Once or twice we saw ladies carrying several jars stacked one on top of the other, each jar slightly smaller than the one below. These were striking pictures of feminine elegance and strength. Indeed, the women continued to be virtually the only bright spots in the landscape, vivid splashes of iridescent colours that looked as if they had been drawn with a set of highlighter pens.

Otherwise, the surroundings were quite drab. Houses were usually squat, cuboid brick affairs with flat roofs, fairly dull and nondescript. We passed some that were in states of partial collapse, looking as if they had been hit by an earthquake, their walls broken and their roofs collapsed, half tumbledown and overgrown. Elsewhere were mud brick houses with thatched roofs that had been built next to mud brick stables and barns. It was impossible to distinguish which was for people and which was for animals. We saw only four new, modern buildings, which stuck out from the rest of the countryside as if they had been transplanted in from an alien world. One was a Pizza Hut, two were McDonald's and the last was a gleaming white marble Hindu temple.

It was always possible to tell when we were approaching a small town. The verges became strewn with litter, trodden into the mud. It was foul and disgusting, every single time, with only one exception which happened to be a strongly Muslim town in the west of Rajasthan. Otherwise, putrid black puddles could be seen right outside the crumbling front doorways of run-down, squalid, hovel-like houses. Everything was dirty, crowded and poor. The overwhelming impression was of rotting filth. Men tended to be squatting or standing around *chai* stalls, although sometimes we saw them sitting on benches reading a newspaper. Women were typically doing more physical work, filling up their water jars and making their way home through the dirt. Dogs slunk here and there, chasing each other. Cows stood beside the roads or lay in the mud beside houses.

It was almost impossible to imagine living amid these conditions, and yet they were the repetitive, normal scenes of life in India. I couldn't help but form the impression that few people in India took responsibility for their environment or indeed for very much else: in many ways I felt that the sights of the country exemplified an individualistic attitude to life, at the expense of collective endeavours. From the touts in the cities to the cows in the roads and the filth in the towns, it was as if no individual was taking any action to improve conditions around them.

As we drove further west the green fields began to give way to drier scrub and the roadside scenes became more and more biblical in nature. Men watched over their cattle by the roadside, balancing on one leg and a wooden stick, their other leg crooked so that its foot rested on the knee of the first. They increasingly wore the white salwar kameez – long shirts that came down to the knee, with baggy trousers underneath – and turbans that were coloured lurid orange, fluorescent green, bright yellow or even multicoloured. Mr Singh informed us that such turbans were reserved for elder men. We passed one character on a motorbike who was hunched over his handlebars in an old-fashioned racing position, complete with plastic eye goggles between his bushy moustache and coloured turban. He looked like a villain from an Indiana Jones film, but was fairly typical here.

The women became ever more striking as we drove further. They wore silver anklets, large gold earrings and nose rings, and white bangles on their arms that in some cases ran from their shoulders to their wrists. Sometimes coloured beads were studded in their lower lips. Their saris were the very picture of finery, laced with delicate gold patterns. Often women's heads were almost totally covered, using a thin length of cloth that was draped over the back of their heads, down the front of their faces, wrapped under their chin and then thrown back over a shoulder.

And we saw increasing numbers of camels, their long thin legs stepping briskly forwards and their bendy necks outstretched in front, ending in long flattened heads with thick lips and mournful eyes shaded with feminine black lashes. The crowds were usually pulling wooden carts with large rubber lorry tyres that were often loaded with logs. Sometimes they came in lines, up to eight camels plodding along nose to tail.

One day we also passed hundreds of pedestrians who were making a pilgrimage to a renowned local temple. They were spread out for perhaps 40 km on either side of the temple, and I estimated that we passed over 1,000 people. They walked singly, in family groups or in processions led by white-robed and white-turbaned sadhus. Many carried colourful flags, and most were walking barefoot, which was part of the pilgrimage experience. Hundreds of sandals and flip-flops were strewn beside the road, surely making it impossible for anyone to retrieve their own at the end – we wondered if they would simply claim any likely looking pair when they returned. Buses too were full of pilgrims choosing a softer option. Although many countries around the world had overcrowded buses, India once again proved itself to be more extreme than anywhere else: people swarmed all over the outside of the bus like bees in a hive, clinging on precariously with barely a hand- or toe-hold. The roofs of the buses were full, too, until that it seemed that someone would have to be pushed over the edge. Even more crowded, if that is possible, were the large three-wheeled tuk-tuks, which elsewhere would have been full if they had five or six passengers. In India we frequently saw them with eighteen passengers, plus luggage on the roof.

Chapter 67: Temples – Pushkar, Ranakpur and Bikaneer

Pushkar was a small town sited around a lake that is considered by Hindus to be holy, thus transforming Pushkar into a religious centre that was second only to Varanasi. It had 450 temples, including the only Indian temple dedicated to Brahma, who was said to have dropped a lotus flower where the lake now sits. There were fifty-two stepped ghats around the lake, approached via any number of small alleyways leading from the main street or through the temples to the lakeside.

Outside the ghats, the streets of Pushkar were a dense mix of pilgrims and tourists. There were no cycle-rickshaws or cars coming down the street; just a few intimidating cows and the odd motorcycle. The shops were touristy, but here people were friendly and not pushy. Either we were getting used to India, or this was a far pleasanter place than Varanasi. It was all quite manageable really, and the presence of 'hippie' Western tourists confirmed it as a place where people hung around for a while. Men all wore multicoloured turbans above their fabulous moustaches; women looked stunning in their saris, mostly half- or fully draped over their heads, hiding their surprisingly sharp-looking faces. Sadhus wandered along with their sticks and begging bowls. We saw a lady cooking chapattis on a fire that was burning dried cowpats. Children approached us with outstretched hands asking for food.

The lake itself appeared more like a square reservoir than a natural lake. It was edged with concrete steps and pretty white archways. The main sight, however, gathered beside small bathing pools that were built into the water's edge. Flat platforms between the steps and the water were crowded with men, women and children who had all come to wash in the holy waters. Wherever there was space, they would strip to the waist, leaving their clothes in a heap behind them. Shoulder to shoulder with the next pilgrim, they knelt at the water's edge, splashed water over their bodies, and doused their hair. Everywhere was dotted with colour and bodies. It seemed so typically Hindu for everyone to be absorbed into their own private ritual simultaneously with hundreds of strangers. And all the while cows made their way down the steps, scattering timid young girls; monkeys watched from ringside seats on walls and shrines; and flocks of pigeons strutted on the ground, periodically erupting into a mass of blurred, whirring wings.

The scene was more concentrated, more focused and somehow purer than the messy spectacles of Varanasi, and it was also larger and more crowded than the ghats in Kathmandu. Indeed, full as it was of the kaleidoscope of colourful pilgrims in the foreground, set against shining waters and white temples in the background, this was one of the most distinctive and memorable of human sights that we witnessed anywhere in the world. It was all so engaging, so eye-catching, that all we wanted to do was sit and quietly watch the spectacle. We didn't stay for long, though, in part because it was so busy and in part because everywhere was too dirty to sit down. This was a place where shoes had to be taken off within forty metres of the water's edge, but cows and pigeons and monkeys were allowed to cover everything with their mess.

There was another reason that we didn't hang around. Passing men would stop beside us and reach into their breast pockets, pulling out a pinch of flower petals. They offered these to us, saying that we could throw them into the water as a prayer. We must have been approached in the same way a dozen times. We always declined the offer, much to the righteous indignation of the men, who would appear offended and even angry. Some even tried to tell us that if we didn't accept their flowers then we shouldn't be there at all. Indeed, this was about the only place in the world that succeeded in breaking Claudia's usually cool and agreeable temperament. 'I don't want your stupid flowers' was actually the most effective repost of the day, producing a childishly petulant retort of, 'They're not stupid!' before the man stomped off.

Everything about the flower-bearing touts was designed to pressurise hassled, confused, gullible and polite visitors into agreeing to throw the petals into the water. Immediately they had done so, however, there would follow even more aggressive demands for payment, even though not a hint of this had been mentioned before when being invited to participate in a 'religious' ceremony. Pushkar was defaced by con artists just as much as anywhere else. Mr Singh told us that these men would charge between US $100–200 for a handful of petals and a prayer, which seemed ludicrous beyond belief to us, until we heard of a British lady of Indian origin who had visited Pushkar and parted with US $800 here, ostensibly as a donation to a temple.

From the beautiful chaos of Pushkar we travelled to the serene peacefulness of one of the largest Jain temples in India, at Ranakpur. This was one of the cleanest and most attractive places that we saw in the country – and it was also the location of the first genuinely pleasant, non-service-related interaction that we had in India. One of the temple supervisors stopped for a quiet chat with us in the temple grounds, and then politely left us alone. We could hardly believe it had happened!

Inside the temple were 1,444 pillars made from white marble, all uniquely carved. They supported twenty-four domes, also intricately carved. It was a light, airy building despite the density of the pillars. The temple had been built in the fifteenth century; inside it was a tree that was 550 years old, we were told by a priest. We were curious about the Jain religion and so had agreed to be shown around the temple by a mild-mannered priest, in return for a donation. He explained that Jainism was very similar to Hinduism, except that Jains believed in prophets too. Their main rule was of non-violence, so the strict devotees will not even pull up root vegetables for fear of harming organisms in the soil.

We saw Jains in another temple who had their mouths covered, for fear of inhaling and unintentionally killing insects. Jains also didn't have a caste system like Hindus, as they were all businessmen. The god of wealth, Lakshmi, was therefore one of their most important gods. In Jaisalmer we would visit more Jain temples, smaller in scale and darker inside. These were far more eerie places, with small half-lit corridors that were lined with idols and gargoyle-like statues. They gave the strong impression of being the spooky centres of occult ceremonies. It was almost reassuring when the Jain priests approached us asking for donations, despite our having already paid entrance fees and the signs inside which read, 'Don't give money to the holy men'.

If the Jain temples were spooky, then the rat temple of Bikaneer was freaky. Before we reached the temple, Mr Singh took us on a tour of the town. As we were driving around, I counted cows in the mad streets. Over a couple of stretches that were about 1 km in length, there was on average a cow every 20 metres along the roads. Looking in any direction, it would only take a few seconds to spot one. A roundabout had ten cows standing in various locations, such as in the middle of the exits. A T-junction had eight cows on and around it. These holy animals, like all the feral cattle in India, were thin, bony, depressing creatures, which seemed to survive by eating rubbish from the streets. We couldn't help feeling that it might be more respectful for someone to put them in fields and give them a bit of care – but of course, they were no one's responsibility.

We parked outside the gates of the rat temple, not knowing what to expect. People were coming and going through a large white marble gateway that was beautifully carved. Stepping inside, we entered a courtyard that had a floor made of black and white tiles, like a giant chequerboard. We looked around for signs of rats. One scurried along a back wall. Glancing down, I saw a group of three or four huddled in a corner beside my feet. But then, to our right, behind an area fenced off with iron railings, we saw that the floor was seething with rats. There were hundreds, climbing up ropes, squeezed between the railings, tumbling over one another on the ground. It was a rat infestation, conjuring up images of the Plague. Somewhere within the building was a white rat, which was considered to be the holy rat, a sighting of which would bring good fortune. So Indians of all denominations would wait in the temple for hours at a time, hoping for their piece of luck. It was the only place that Mr Singh entered with us, rather than patiently waiting outside beside the car. He said he had visited the temple many times, but had never caught sight of the white rat.

Ahead of us sat a couple of ticket collectors, calm behind their table even as rats crawled between their legs. The sheer number and density of rats was unbelievable. They were sitting on steps, inside doorways, on the tops of lockers and cupboards. In places there were holes in the walls and rats were pouring out of these like a stream under pressure, tumbling over one another in their hurry as if fleeing in terror from something inside. There were thousands of them. People crossed the courtyard in orderly lines, as rats ran between them, and entered an inner temple, where the numbers of rats just seemed to increase. It was unnatural to see so many animals sitting in the open, just inches from people's feet… bare feet, of course; shoes were not allowed to be worn here! We were taking care to avoid stepping on the rats, but we couldn't avoid the layer of dirt on the floor. There was a putrid smell of stale droppings hanging in the air. Claudia could hardly believe what she was seeing, and then that she was remaining standing there in the middle of it all. Even I felt that it was pretty disgusting. We had to wonder at a religion which has up to 333 million different images of gods, allows holy cows to wander the streets in states of misery, and contains a rat temple like this.

Chapter 68: Jaisalmer

Jaisalmer was a romantic city at the edge of the Thar Desert that I had long wanted to visit. It would also be the end point of our journey around the world. What we saw of the desert was fairly non-descript, just a flat landscape of small thorn bushes and dirt, within which a few goats scavenged and the odd herd of camels stood gracefully. As we passed isolated huts amid the scrub, we saw women hauling water up from wells. Just about the only other visible life were dung beetles pushing their black marble-like balls across the road. The desert houses were quite different to those we had seen further east. Many were made from stone panels placed in a circular ring to form the wall of a house or wider compound. Roofs were just brushwood. Other buildings were made from sand and cow dung, still circular huts but now with smooth walls that could be painted white or orange. Each walled compound would contain perhaps four or five huts, their conical roofs visible over the outer walls. Small herds of goats might be kept in adjacent compounds, or even fenced in by piles of brushwood. The impression was of a primitive, tribal way of life.

In fact, people in the remote villages lived on their animals and millet, from which they made chapattis. Until the recent rains, there had been a five-year drought, so the millet had not grown and people had had to walk 60–70 km just to find water. There were no doctors or schools in the desert; to get medical treatment would involve taking a camel cart to Jaisalmer. The only road beyond Jaisalmer was ten years old, built for the army who have a base here, close to the Pakistani border. Only six years ago had electricity reached at least some of the villages around Jaisalmer. Elsewhere, dried cowpat cakes were still being used as the fuel for fires.

The city of Jaisalmer had a calmer feel than other Indian cities. There was not so much traffic, for a start. It was cleaner and more airy. At dawn and sunset – always the best times of day in India – it was even peaceful. The centre of town was the Old City. This had been built within the 5.5 km-long perimeter walls of a twelfth-century fort that sat astride the dominant hilltop. It reminded me a bit of Edinburgh, with its castle over the craggy cliffs and the old houses strung out behind, sheltering in its shadow. Only, here the colours were not black and grey; they were soft sandy browns. This was the 'Golden City', and indeed every wall was made of tan-coloured sandstone. The alleyways and lanes of the old city were as jumbled and maze-like as those of any city we had seen, squeezed as they were between palace walls. Little old buildings had been turned into guest houses, alongside newer residences and grandiose royal mansions. In some places it was a shambles, with the rubble of mud brick walls still remaining in heaps after an earthquake nine years ago. The rains of ten days earlier had caused two walls to crumble down. Black wires ran everywhere, overhead and underfoot. Cows still pushed past, causing people to jump out of their way. And yet, it was all light, clean and sometimes exquisitely pretty. Many of the grander houses, ancient and modern, showed their wealth by decorating the outside of their walls and window frames with traditional stone carvings and latticework. These were the richest and most delicate that we had seen anywhere. In its finery, the old city was beyond comparison with any other Indian city. It was a jewel, and if only it could be properly preserved and cared for, it would be truly beautiful.

The walled city used to be the preserve of Brahmins and businessmen. Members of the untouchable caste would live outside, down on the plains of the desert. Times have changed, of course. The city's population had grown from 5,000 to 50,000 and now sprawled well beyond the fort. Tourism was the industry driving this growth, for in high season there were so many tourists that all the accommodation, from high-class hotels to budget hostels, would be full and people would even end up camping in the desert. All this from nothing in just fifteen years. Most of the tourists, we were told, came for just two nights – the city was, after all, a very small place. We were shown around by a guide, who told us that his uncle ran a shop that gave its profits to help the untouchables of the desert. We just happened to pass the door of the shop a minute or two later later, and were trapped for a while.

We politely sat and watched the sellers display item after item to us, saying that there was 'no charge for looking' despite our protestations that we didn't want to buy anything. The salesmen displayed an adroit skill, patiently pulling on our heartstrings of guilt and compassion while mercilessly exploiting our politeness that – for a time – prevented us from standing up and walking out. Their efforts were such that I was convinced many tourists would end up buying something that they had never wanted, costing 'only thirty/fifty/seventy dollars, nothing to you', just to extricate themselves from the pressurised situation. The pill was supposedly sweetened, of course, by the hope that some of the money would go to a good cause – only, our guide let slip that had we been wealthier tourists, he would have taken us to a more expensive shop, no doubt owned by the same charitable uncle! There appeared to be no moral or ethical boundaries in the efforts to extract money from visitors; even outright deceit was an accepted, normal strategy in India.

We drove out from the city of Jaisalmer to a desert village. All the traditional family compounds there had been turned into small guest houses and resorts. We were told by the owner of our guest house that the village would keep its traditional character despite being turned into a tourist centre – but the evidence of our eyes belied this, as we could see new brick three-storey hotels being built in modern architectural styles. It seemed sadly naive to think that this village would be able to withstand the tourism bulldozer. For now, however, we stayed in the traditional compound of a very sociable family, who made us feel immediately comfortable and at ease. We had the choice of sleeping in one of the round huts or on the flat roof of a square house. We chose the roof, going to sleep under the brilliant display of a universe of stars, while the family set their own camp beds out in the middle of the compound below. In the early morning we watched women and girls making their way through the surrounding scrubby bushes, walking with water jars in their hands or balanced on their heads, starting their day with the chore of collecting water from local wells.

Not too far away was a ridge of sand overlooking the village. The thing to do at sunset was to hire camels and ride them to the top of the dune. It was our first camel ride, and was great fun. We were surprised at how comfortable the ride was, especially when the camels broke into their lolloping run, which seemed to smooth the bumps and jerks. Our camel drivers were two very friendly elderly gentlemen, each wearing a white robe and bright orange turban. They pointed out to us the peacocks and deer, even finding a young fawn hiding under a bush that remained motionless as we approached. We were loving this experience. At the top of the dune we sat down on the sand crest and waited. More camels arrived – forty more, in fact – each bringing an Indian tourist. Some stopped to chat to us, often telling us about the times they had been to England or the USA. Here, at the edge of the desert, as the orange sun sank into the clouds we experienced a genuine friendliness and hospitality which we suddenly realised had been so deficient everywhere else during our travels in amoral, anarchic, individualistic India. At the very end of our journey around the world, we had another timeless moment of beauty and happiness.

Bibliography

Australian Government, Department of the Environment and Water Resources

Bakewell, P, *A History of Latin America*, Oxford, Blackwell Publishers Ltd., 1997

Becker, E, *When the War Was Over*, New York, Public Affairs, 1998

Central America Handbook: Footprint Handbooks Ltd

Chong, D, *The Girl in the Picture*, London, Scribner, 1999

Clayton, L, & Conniff, M, *A History of Modern Latin America*, Orlando, Harcourt Brace & Company, 1999

Dalrymple, W, *City of Djinns*, London, Flamingo, 1994

Dunford, M, *The Rough Guide to New York City*, London, Rough Guides, 2004

Gyatso, T, *Freedom in Exile*, London, Abacus, 1998

Harding, P, & Richmond, S, *South East Asia on a Shoestring*, Victoria, Lonely Planet Publications Pty Ltd., 2001

Harper, D, *China*, Victoria, Lonely Planet Publications Pty Ltd., 2005

Jensen, J, *Road Trip USA: California and the Southwest*, Emeryville, Avalon Travel Publishing Inc., 2000

Johnson, P, *A History of the American People*, London, Pheonix Press, 2000

Keay, J, *India: A History*, London, HarperCollins Publishers, 2000

King, C, [ed.] *Let's Go India & Nepal*, London, Macmillan Publishers Ltd, 2000

Menzies, G, *1421*, London, Bantam Press, 2000

Murphy, A, *Peru Handbook*, Bath, Footprint Handbooks Ltd., 1997

Murphy, D, *One Foot in Laos*, London, Flamingo, 2000

Newsome, C, *The Green Tree Snake*, Stanthorpe, Colour Productions, 1981

Patten, C, *East and West*, London, Macmillan, 1998

Prescott, W, *History of the Conquest of Mexico*, London, George Allen & Unwin Ltd., 1925

Reader's Digest: Australia's Dangerous Creatures – Understand, Avoid, Survive, Sydney, Readers Digest Services Pty Ltd, 1987

Rooney, D, *Angkor*, New York, Odyssey Publications Ltd., 1994

Sachs, J, *The End of Poverty*, London, Penguin, 2005

Theroux, P, *Riding the Iron Rooster*, London, Penguin Books, 1989

US Department of the Interior, National Park Service, *The Bears are Not to Blame...*, 1999

Williams, S, *A Ghost Called Thunderbolt*, Woden, Popinjay Publications, 1987

Index

Abel Tasman, 166, 172
Aboriginal culture, 197, 199
Agra, 401–5, 406
Aguas Calientes, 116, 118
Akha tribe, 308
Albert Namatjira, 197
Alcatraz, 42, 43
Alice Springs, 196–98
Amer Fort, 407
Anatoli Boukreev, 387
Angkor, 251–59
Angkor Wat, 96, 254–57, 361
Annapurna, 384–90
Annapurna Conservation Area, 388
Antigua, 87–93
Antofagasta, 133
Aoraki, 184
Asian values, 207–8
Atacama Desert, 132–33
Auckland, 171–74
Aztec, 64–66
Bangkok, 227, 231–39, 240, 273
Battambang, 259, 264–67, 303
Bayon, 257–58
Beijing, 319, 323, 357–64
Belize City, 98–100
Big Sur, 40
Bikaneer, 418–19
Blue Mountains, 33, 188–92
Bodnath Stupa, 394
Bondi Beach, 186
Boston, 22, 23–27, 37
Boston Tea Party, 26, 32
Brisbane, 194
Buddhism, 242, 265

Cameron Highlands, 214, 215–18
Can Tho, 275
Cape Cod, 27–30
Captain Cook, 166, 182, 186
Cay Caulker, 100–103
Central Hong Kong, 354
Central Park, 20, 21
Chairman Mao Tse-tung, 358, 360
Chiang Mai, 240–47, 309, 343
Chinatown, Bangkok, 238
Chinatown, Kuala Lumpur, 211–12
Choeung Ek Genocidal Centre, 269
Christ the Redeemer, 150
Christchurch, 183
Conway, 30–33
Copacabana, 147, 148, 149, 186
Cronulla, 186
Cu Chi Tunnels, 278–79
Cuzco, 108–14, 116, 118
Dali, 322, 323–28
Damnoen Saduak Floating Market, 236–37
Death Valley National Park, 46–47, 133
Delhi, 367–72, 401, 404, 406, 411
Dunedin, 182
Durbar Square, 392
Easter Island, 155, 156–62
Echo Point, 188, 189, 192
Emperor Yongle, 361, 362
Forbidden City, 360–61
Francisco Pizarro, 108, 110, 114
Georgetown, 213, 214

Index

Golden Gate Bridge, 42
Grand Canyon National Park, 50–53, 120, 190
Grand Palace, 237
Great Wall of China, 255, 362, 364
Grose Valley, 189
Guanxi, 335, 350, 358
Guilin, 335, 338–40
Haast River/Pass, 179–80
Harvard University, 24
Hat Yai, 219, 223
Hernan Cortes, 64–66
Hiram Bingham, 117–18
Ho Chi Minh City, 275, 276–80
Hoi An, 279, 286–90
Hong Kong, 205, 227, 352–56
Hue, 277, 279, 289
Ilha Grande, 152–54
Inca, 110, 114–19, 122, 123, 144
Jainism, 418
Jaipur, 406–8
Jaisalmer, 400, 401, 418, 420–22
Jinghong, 317–22
Jodhpur, 408–9
Jodhpur Fort, 408
Julia Pfeiffer Burns State Park, 41
Karen hill tribe, 242–44
Kata Beach, 227, 228
Kathmandu, 127, 381, 389, 391–98, 399
Khao San Road, 233–35, 279, 341
Khmer Rouge, 254, 266, 268
Khmu tribe, 310–11
King of Thailand, 237, 244
Kings Cross, 187
Ko Phuket, 226, 227, 229
Ko Samui, 229, 234
Kowloon, 352–54, 355
Krabi, 225
Kuala Lumpur, 208, 209–13
Kublai Khan, 323

Kunming, 321–22, 323
La Paz, 125–27, 137, 307
La Serena, 134
Lake Atitlan, 81–85, 95
Lake Palace, 409
Lake Titicaca, 121–24
Lake Wanaka, 180
Lanten tribe, 312
Las Vegas, 53–54
Lijiang, 322, 328, 329–32
Lima, 107–8, 126, 133
Longji, 346, 385
Longsheng, 346–47
Los Angeles, 35–37
Luang Nam Tha, 300, 307–13
Luang Prabang, 300, 302–6, 308
Machhapuchhare, 386–88
Machu Picchu, 114–20
Mana Island, 166–70
Mandarin, 313, 319, 322, 337, 346
Manhattan, 19, 20, 22
Maori, 172, 173, 178, 180
Mayan, 66, 68, 93, 95, 103, 258
Mekong Delta, 271–74, 279
Mexico City, 59–64
Milford Sound, 181–82
Mitre Peak, 182
Moai, 155–58, 162
Mount Cook, 173, 184
Mount Everest, 399–400
Mount Washington, 27, 32, 33, 48
Mui Ne, 279, 281–84
Murchison, 178–79
Nanning, 335, 336–38
Naxi, 329–31, 333
New England, 193–95
New York, 19–22, 59, 254
Nha Trang, 277, 279, 285–86, 289
Nong Kiaw, 305–6
Oaxaca, 69–71
Pacaya, 90, 91

Palace of the Winds, 407
Panajachel, 80–85
Paraty, 153–55
Pashupatinath Temple, 393
Penang, 213–14, 227, 264
Petronas Twin Towers, 210
Phnom Penh, 267–70, 276
Phuket, 226, 227
Pingan, 347–51
Pokhara, 380–83
Princess Bay, 177
Puerto Natales, 140, 141, 143
Puno, 121–22, 130
Punta Arenas, 139–41
Pushkar, 416–17
Quechua, 114, 118, 122, 173
Queenstown, 181
Quetzaltenango, 76
Ranakpur, 417
Rapa Nui, 156, 158–59
Rio de Janeiro, 145–51
River Ganges, 375–77
River Li, 345
Rocinha, 149–50
Rotorua, 174–75
Route 1, California, 32, 36, 39–43
Salar d'Uyuni, 128
San Cristobal de las Casas, 71–74
San Diego, 36–37
San Francisco, 42–43
San Pedro de Atacama, 132
Santa Barbara, 36, 37, 39
Santiago, 137–39, 159, 160
Santiago Atitlan, 84–86
Savannakhet, 292–94
Second Indo-China War, 276, 277, 293, 294
Shah Jehan, 403, 404
Siam Square, 231–32
Siem Reap, 253–54

Singapore, 205–8
Sisophon, 252
Songkhla, 219, 220–23
Southern Alps, 179, 183, 184
Statue of Liberty, 21–22, 53
Sydney, 146, 185–87, 196, 197
Sydney Harbour Bridge, 42, 185
Taj Mahal, 255, 401–4, 409
Taquile, 123–24
Tenochtitlan, 64–66
Teotihuacan, 66–68, 96
Three Pagodas, 327
Tiananmen Square, 357–59
Tibet, 271, 330, 332, 395
Tiger Leaping Gorge, 332–34
Tikal, 94–97
Tonle Sap, 260–61
Torres del Paines, 139, 142–44
Trang, 222–24
Twin Towers, 19
Udaipur, 409–10
Uluru, 196–201
Uros, 122, 243
Uyuni, 128
Valparaiso, 135, 149
Vang Vieng, 296, 297–301, 304
Varanasi, 372, 373–79, 393, 416, 417
Vientiane, 289, 293–95, 297
Vietcong, 278–79
Waiheke Island, 171–72
Wellington, 42, 171, 176, 177
Whakanewha Regional Park, 171
Xela, 78–80
Yangshuo, 339, 341–45, 346
Yosemite National Park, 44–46
Yunnan, 317–19, 321, 323, 327, 335, 339, 350, 363
Zion National Park, 47–49

Printed in the United Kingdom
by Lightning Source UK Ltd.
132271UK00001B/235/P